LATINBANKS.
STUDY ON THE LEGAL AND SOCIAL IMPLICATIONS OF CREATING BANKS OF BIOLOGICAL MATERIAL FOR BIOMEDICAL RESEARCH

3

WORKING GROUP
**Law, Science,
Technology and Innovation**
Editor: Carlos María Romeo Casabona

LatinBanks. Study on the Legal and Social Implications of Creating Banks of Biological Material for Biomedical Research

Co-Editors

CARLOS MARÍA ROMEO CASABONA

JÜRGEN W. SIMON

Coordinators

PILAR NICOLÁS JIMÉNEZ

EMILIO JOSÉ ARMAZA ARMAZA

BRUYLANT
BRUXELLES
2011

Pour toute information sur notre fonds et les nouveautés dans votre domaine de spécialisation, consultez notre site web : www.bruylant.be

© Groupe De Boeck s.a., 2011
Éditions Bruylant
Rue des Minimes, 39 • B-1000 Bruxelles

Tous droits réservés pour tous pays.
Il est interdit, sauf accord préalable et écrit de l'éditeur, de reproduire (notamment par photocopie) partiellement ou totalement le présent ouvrage, de le stocker dans une banque de données ou de le communiquer au public, sous quelque forme et de quelque manière que ce soit.

Imprimé en Belgique

Dépôt légal 2011/0023/018   ISBN 978-2-8027-3439-0

PREFACE

Latinbanks is a two year research project supported by the European Commission and the partners involved (Alfa Program) (1). Latinbanks is the first milestone in MEDNET, which is a cooperation tool between European and Latin American experts in the field of biomedicine, biotechnology, law and ethics. MEDNET is the first network with this thematic and geographical scope.

The general objective of Latinbanks was to study the legal, ethical and social issues raised by the use of biological samples in biomedical research and biobanks.

Toward this goal, we started by researching the current situation in each country, the final result of which is this monograph containing a series of reports and other useful information, from a comparative perspective.

Specifically this monograph includes national reports, a list of national biobanks, references to legislation and bibliography, links to national institutions, a guide for drafting a standard consent form, a list of frequently asked questions answered regarding each country involved and finally, the UNESCO International Declaration on Human Genetic Data.

The collaboration among the partners was settled on four meetings (Bilbao, Mexico City, Buenos Aires and Hannover). All of them were extremely fruitful not only for the discussions and sharing of knowledge but also for dissemination purposes.

We would also like to mention our Website that includes relevant information and will be updated and maintained in the future (2). As a matter of fact, our network is open to the future, and at this time the next steps are under discussion.

Going back to Latinbanks, as mentioned before, the research undertaken by the Latinbanks Project began with a review of the current situation in each country, specifically, making contact with researchers and biobanks.

---

(1) Contract No. AML/19.0901/06/18414/II-0520.
(2) See http://www.latinbanks.catedraderechoygenomahumano.es/.

In fact, one of the differences between Europe and Latin America is that in Latin America there are no specific laws, although data protection and patients' rights regulations are applicable. In addition, it was found that there is a lack of specialised bibliography in Latin America, which could indicate a lack of interest in this subject in academia. This project seeks to produce a change in this situation.

Specific legislation could benefit research because it would help to stimulate its progress, creates confidence among those taking part in it, provide legal clarity both for the researchers and the research subjects, and it would facilitate the consolidation of a research community for this specific area. Regulation should include systems for authorising, monitoring and controlling the quality of the teams of experts, and also the procedures, in terms of seeking transparency and safeguarding the rights and guarantees of the research subject. In particular, it would be advisable to create a biobank registry. This would make it possible to track their activities and facilitate the incorporation of researchers into research communities in other countries with more developed legislation.

Throughout the sampling process, both in countries with specific laws and in those with other types of applicable regulations, providing information for, and obtaining consent from the subjects, are the key factors to enable samples to be used. As a matter of fact, there were no difficulties for a consensus in the informed consent form that is included in this monograph.

But, while in Latin America legislative development is still presenting a challenge, in Europe the majority of the issues in this field are solved through the specific requirement of individual consent.

Another important difference to the European approach is that the research carried out in communities is very relevant in Latin American countries. In some of these countries there are specific regulatory provisions to protect ethnic groups. For this reason future legislation should contain very clear regulations regarding obtaining informed consent from individuals in ethnic communities, with the aim of ensuring that guarantees regarding them are respected. It should not be possible for biobanks to obtain and use samples in such way that represents a loss of control by the corresponding individual and community. Informed consent in communities differs from individual consent, and furthermore, cultural differences between the researcher and the research subject require special techniques for conveying information. The corresponding ethics committee shall ensure that consent is obtained using the appropriate procedure in these cases.

The question of the ownership of the samples has not been resolved, nor discussed in the majority of countries. Even if it is thought that the ownership of the samples had been transferred to the biobank, the personality rights of the donor/patient remain and must be protected. Therefore, biobanks may not use the samples in an uncontrolled manner. In particular, the rights over personal data limit those derived from ownership (or the faculty to use) of the samples. Largely unrestricted access to the samples is usually only possible if the samples have been absolutely or at least *de facto* anonymised.

The principle of free donation of samples is widespread. Furthermore, the subjects should not have financial rights in regards to the results of the research. However, it would be useful to establish mechanisms for sharing the benefits of the research with the populations that provided the samples, whether the research is conducted there or whether the samples are imported. Agreements regarding these issues should be arranged.

In summary, there is an urgent need to establish guidelines regarding the use of samples and biobanks in biomedical research in Latin America, and for existing international principles to be implemented. There is also an opportunity to draft these guidelines in a homogeneous way in Latin America, and which could be very positive for this continent.

Lastly, we must note that the team working on this project has undertaken a major effort to provide a «diagnostic» of the factual and legal situation in each country involved in our team, which is reflected in this publication. We hope this will be a step toward filling a gap in the academic field, and to generate an interest that leads to more ambitious legislative goals.

The countries represented in this Project have been: Argentina (Salvador Darío Bergel), Brazil (Fátima Freire de Sá), Chile (Lorena Donoso), Colombia (Emilssen González de Cancino, assisted by Carolina Figueredo Carrillo), Costa Rica (Carlos Valerio), France (Myriam Blumberg-Mokri), Germany (Jürgen Simon, assisted by Rainer Paslak and Jürgen Robienski), Mexico (Ingrid Brena), Portugal (Elena Moniz assisted by Sónia Fidalgo) and Spain (Carlos María Romeo Casabona, Manuel Lobato and Pedro Yanes, assisted by Emilio Armaza, Iñigo de Miguel and Pilar Nicolás, that have been in charge of the academic management).

Our deepest thanks must be addressed at this moment to experts and local authorities from which we have received a very relevant information for some parts of our work, as well as to the European Commission, for its funding and support along all the steps of this work.

Finally we are especially proud of the links created between institutions from two continents, and the team in charge of the project. We hope this team will continue to work and expand with new partners in the future.

Bilbao – Lüneburg, May 2010

Professor CARLOS M. ROMEO CASABONA
Professor JÜRGEN W. SIMON
Editors

PART I.

BIOBANKING:
A CHANCE FOR SCIENTIFIC RESEARCH
AND A CHALLENGE FOR INTELLECTUAL
PROPERTY RIGHTS AND PRIVACY

BY

Carlos María ROMEO CASABONA

AND

Jürgen W. SIMON

Co-Editors

1. – Introduction

All over the world, we find thousands of biobanks established in the last century until now. So, why is this subject so much trouble now?

It is known that genetic research often requires the use of biological samples, taken from research subjects of from other persons unconnected with the experiments. Regardless of the source of the materials, the results of genetic and other tests can prove very useful for advances in research in certain areas (pharmacogenetics, genomics, etc.).

Recourse to samples which have been stored in human biological material banks –biobanks- (cells, tissues, surgical waste, umbilical cords, etc) for reasons other than for research is becoming increasingly appropriate and common. Similarly, the creation of biobanks for specific biological materials linked to certain pathologies whose characteristics or evolution is of research interest (for example, cancerous tumours) or which are linked to a given population or population group (Iceland, Estonia, United Kingdom) is becoming more and more common also.

The creation of such biobanks and genetic databases can give rise to a range of problems, which are not generally covered by regulations on research and experimentation on humans or by personal data protection legislation. For example, in case of human biological specimens questions may arise as to the ownership of the material – however insignificant it may be – because of the potential economical relevance in the form of a patentable product or other research results.

After this general view first we should cast an eye on the traditional biobanks. Typically, one or more researchers or physicians collect a more or less great number of tissues and use them for their research. In the case of medical treatments, the tissues should only be used for this purpose and after a certain time be destroyed. In Germany for example, the storage time period for these purposes is not quite clear defined, and it varies very much as a current report in one of the German states documented. If the tissue was not collected for treatment, but for research, the tissue must be destroyed after the special research. In a lot of cases, I think in most of these cases, this principle has not been followed. Therefore, we find thousands of these biobanks in the traditional sense which partly are very old. Or in other words: Human tissue banks have existed at least since the medical community began using tissues and cadavers for research and training purposes. And small scale biobanks for specific genetic diseases, that is repositories that store information in digital format, have existed for decades.

2. – Large-scale Biobanks

Nowadays, the situation has changed fundamentally. Big biobanks are on the rise, especially in the western world, in Island, Estonia, the U.K., the USA, Canada Australia and Japan, and big international biobanking research projects as HapMap oder Genographic have been established all over the world.

What is the difference compared with the old biobanks? The goal of these large-scale biobanks is to collect lots of samples and data so that researchers could be able to analyse the relations between these and phenotype variations of the human population. The result should contribute to a better understanding of the genetic basis of the human health resp. illness. On this basis it is possible to develop exactly working screening systems and in the following better fitting drugs. Biobanking in this context is determined as the collection of genetic material in a wide sense (cells, tissues, organs). Collected are also health information and data in connection with human health. The purpose of the collection is to gain information for the development of personalised drugs. Altogether inherited risks could be identified. And in the macro dimension (health systems) the genome could be better understood as well as the influence of the environment in populations.

Researchers can compare the DNA sequence of affected individuals with the DNA of the general population. In the simplest cases affected individuals share a polymorphism, a variation in the sequence of their DNA not found in the larger population.

As we know, there are not so many genetic conditions which base on a single gene. The interaction of several genes is much more important. Therefore, and because the relations between individuals and the (social) environment research needs large-scale biobanks.

3. – Concerns on Biobanks

Regardless of their intended use, establishing and using biobanks raise a number of concerns. Commonly, these concerns focus on the potential use of information derived from biobanks whose access should be limited with regard to health care, insurance or employment. We also have to focus on the problem of impairment of privacy and confidentiality. One aspect of the «invasion» of privacy is that the collected material in biobanks can be used not only for the one but for several purposes which are not known in the moment of the collection and for an undefined number of researchers as well.

Biobanks enable research that cannot be wholly anticipated at the time the bank is created. Any defense of the benefits of biobanks must, therefore, be based to a large degree on the belief in the value of subsequent research.

The list of anticipated benefits derived from biobanks generally include:

i. *new knowledge of*:
– disease aetiology, and natural history;
– genomic contributors to health;
– pathogenic and environmental contributors to disease; and

– the genomic-organism-environment interaction;

ii. *new treatments in the areas of:*

– pharmacology; and
– genetic therapies;

iii. *new tests to:*

– reduce harm from pharmacological treatments with genetic risks;
– detect pathologies earlier;
– personalize risk assessment and preventive strategies; and
– support population-based risk assessment and preventive strategies;

iv. *new preventive strategies to:*

– personalize risk assessments and dietary/environmental advice;
– identify high risk populations most likely to benefit from closer follow-up;
– develop medications or other treatments to supplement missing genetic functions associated with increased risk; and
– stronger arguments for environmental policies.

It should be noted that biobanks do not constitute the research that might produce these benefits; biobanks are an intermediate step in a process that produces a collection of data and materials that facilitate further research. But it is also not excluded that biobanks do the research on their own collections.

4. – From identified to anonymised Biobanks samples

The legal aspects probably of greatest interest at present concern the protection of information relating to the source individuals, particularly in view of the potentially predictive or pre-symptomatic capacity of the information that could be obtained from genetic tests made on these materials. There is concern that such information can be abused and that the right to have control over one's own genetic information, the right to privacy and private life, and the prohibition of discrimination and stigmatisation will not sufficiently respected. Crucial to this concern is the fact that the biological sample is considered a medium carrying personal information and the genetic information should be granted at least the same protection in law as information relating to a person's health.

The majority of biobanking initiatives reflect emerging, not established standards of practice. Biobanks samples may be identified, identifiable (coded), anonymised (unlinked), or anonymous (unidentifiable) :
– In identified samples, information stored with samples includes identifiers such as patient name or number.
– In identifiable samples, unidentified samples can be linked back to identifiers through a coding system.
– In biobanks which samples are anonymised these are kept without any identifiers. This means that they cannot be connected again with those identifiers
– In anonymous biobanks samples, the later are collected without identifiers, therefore the source is impossible to identify.

The purpose of the research and the source of the genetic material affects the nature of the identification used in a given research project. Especially it has to be considered at this stage is the one related with traceability. The development of research with human samples, especially if they could be transferred to a human patient creates new needs of regulation in the field of anonymisation and pseudonimysation. On one side, traceability of tissues and cells should be guaranteed, but on the other side it is absolutely necessary to ensure a certain level of confidentiality to the donor in order to avoid the abusive use of his/her personal data, affecting privacy.

In order to protect both interests it is absolutely necessary to develop different processes so as to ensure the purpose aforementioned. These processes could consist in the anonymisation of the data, which should have the effect of disabling the individual's identification or of avoiding the linking of such data with the person to which they belong. In occasions it has also appeared as an alternative process the pseudonymisation of the data, although it is certain that this last process offers a more limited protection of the data.

Anyway, in the case that an option between anonymisation and pseudonimysation should be made a double purpose is being searched : on one hand confidentiality related to the donor himself, and on the other to ensure traceability of the tissues and cells employed.

* **Anonymisation.** The Directive 95/46/CE does not give a definition on what should be understand under anonymisation, but as it was indicated above we can establish the juridical effects regarding the personal data that have been subjected to such a process, i.e. that are anonymous. Nevertheless, indirectly it can be deduced what the Directive understands when talking of anonymisation. In accordance with the aforementioned Directive, the anonymisation refers to any process which makes no longer possible the identification of the interested person (recital n° 26). This recital seems to entail an absolute impossibility of identification due to the anonymisation process. Art. 2, b seems to follow this same orientation. But, on the other hand, recital 26 also establishes that «to determine whether a person is identifiable, account should be taken of all the means *likely reasonably* to be used either by the controller or by any other person to identify the said person» (the underlined has been added). The word «reasonably» seems to be opposed to the statement of the Directive previously mentioned : with «reasonably» the level of demand of identification impossibility is limited to a certain degree (the «reasonable»).

* **Pseudonymisation** as such does not imply data to be anonymous or to be related to a non identifiable person; it means just data having been codified. In order to know if the data are anonymous or pseudonymised, we have to consider if they require or not unreasonable procedures or disproportionate efforts to achieve the person's identification.

Keeping in mind pseudonymisation procedures that are used habitually, in most of the cases the data will be identifiable person's data and not anonymous data. Consequently, pseudonymised data will be subjected to the principles of protection of personal data. Pseudonymisation or codification could be an adequate mean to be used when in a medical or genetic research it is necessary to maintain the identity of the subjects involved in that research and consequently the anonymisation of the data is not possible.

Data pseudonymised are usually subjected and they should continue being subjected to the regime of protection of personal data. Taking into account that the pseudonymisation is a temporary and reversible system of protection, the data submitted to pseudonymisation have to be considered data of identifiable persons and have to be protected that way, which does not differ from the system of protection established for identified persons.

Related to this aspect the Directive on setting standards of quality and safety for the donation, procurement, testing, processing, storage, and distribution of human tissues and cells, considers essential to ensure the traceability of tissues and cells (art. 10), but on the other hand states «Members States shall take all necessary measures to ensure that all data, including genetic information, collated within the scope of this Directive and to which third parties have access have been rendered anonymous so that the donor and the recipient are no longer identifiable». It seems that the use of the concept of «anonymous» data, as used by the aforementioned Directive does not match with the one set by Directive 95/46/EC. In this case, the Directive on setting standards of quality and safety for the donation, procurement, testing, processing, storage, and distribution of human tissues and cells refers to a pseudonimysation process and not to an anonymisation one.

5. – PRIVACY AND THE GENE

Also the question of ownership and privacy arises. The immense promise of genomic research – rhetorical or not – has often seemed to place a high public and corporate value on genetic information. At the same time, the fact that many people consider genetic information to be the most intimate information that can be revealed by an individual has placed the gene in a highly sensitive category of information that includes such things as health and credit information. While many policies and regulations have evolved in the past century to protect individual privacy in a variety of circumstances, issues around privacy and the gene are often considered to challenge the efficacy of these mechanisms.

This may, in part, be a result of the newness of genetic technologies, an increased awareness or understanding of the technologies, or a combination of these and other factors. Regardless, practices that have provoked scandals in recent years, such as retaining human tissue for research, raised little concern only twenty years ago. Allen (1997) describes the devices that have emerged in the last one hundred years to place the force of law behind what had for centuries only been a philosophical ideal, distinguishing between the informational, decisional, physical and proprietary dimensions of privacy relevant to the genetics debate.

* **Informational privacy** is defined as «the claim of an individual to determine what information about himself or herself should be known by others» (Allen 1997); it is the dimension of privacy most commonly addressed by bio-ethicists. Typically, informational privacy in medical settings has been protected by asking patients to actively provide informed rather than presumed or tacit consent, both of which could be secured simply through an individual's decision to interact with the medical system.

Informational privacy is based on norms that define modernity, in particular the relationship between the individual and society and the tension between «the right to know» and «the right not to know» (Edwards 2002 : 14).

In the sense of physical privacy the right of the individual could be touched if and how far he wants to be tested, screened or observed at all. The fact that DNA can be extracted from very small amounts of tissue has led to concerns about covert DNA sampling and prompted the United Kingdom's Human Genetics Commission to recommend making it illegal to deceitfully gather genetic information for non medical purposes. Current regulations in that country and some American states allow for mandatory testing of some or all categories of prisoners on the basis that it is in the collective interest to violate the physical privacy of criminals.

* **Decisional privacy** concerns the right of the individual and families to make specific choices about information arising from their persons or personal affairs. So, it is important if an individual is allowed to give the information about the results of predictive testing on a foetus to others.

Decisional privacy issues reveal the challenge of trying to regulate collecting genetic information in isolation from other social norms and practices. Funding and supporting pre-natal genetic testing while limiting the range of possible interventions draws the state into an area that was previously in the realm of fate. The mere existence of the capacity to use knowledge to intervene between parents and the fate of their child may well alter current notions of rights and responsibilities.

* **Proprietary privacy** is related to the ownership of personal information, in this case, genetic information. Proprietary privacy raises the question of the individual's right to compensation for commercial products derived from the commodification of their genes, whether and when the individual retains property rights, and to what extent. The Public and Professional Policy Committee of the European Society of Human Genetics (PPPC) recommends different approaches to ownership of samples based on the character of the collection (European Society of Human Genetics 2003); and that the various approaches to ownership should be subjected to multi-party contracts rather than defined in legislation. According to the Committee, only anonymous data should be regarded as «abandoned,» in which case «…the processor and/or Principal investigator should be considered as the custodian of these data…» Otherwise:

> … the subject should always be considered as a primary controller of its DNA and clinical information directly derived from it. Once the information has been processed, it becomes research data (i.e. data) unless there is agreed private ownership. The processor and/or principle investigator of DNA sample[s] and genetic data should be considered as the custodian of the DNA/genetic data.

The former rights include, for example, the right to manage, to exclude others, to sell or lease, and to receive compensation for trespass or loss, as well as a corresponding set of ownership duties, for example, to maintain so that others are not injured. Private ownership of genetic materials and/or information resulting from the analysis of the materials creates the possibility of profit and incentives for distribution, as well as access and investment in research. Commodification is seen by many as problematic, primarily because it may remove respect for things such as humans, gametes, foetuses, human organs or genetic sequences by inappropriately assigning these monetary value and control mechanisms (patents for example).

6. – Autonomy related to the use of samples: the donor's consent

Related to the conditions of donation free, informed and specific consent has to be required, what is clearly stated under the Directive on setting standards of quality and safety for the donation, procurement, testing, processing, storage, and distribution of human tissues and cells. The same criteria are established under the European Convention on Human Rights and Biomedicine of 1997 (including its Additional Protocol from 2002).

At this point, problems could arise in relation with freedom to revoke consent. Even when freedom to revoke consent to the loss of physical integrity, especially in case of donation of a body part, is a long-established and undisputed legal principle (as an essential guarantee of the donor's free will and an expression of the sacred inviolability of the body) this does not mean, that even after donation the donor retains discretionary powers over the dissociated parts/substances of his body, meaning ultimately the power to withdraw his authorization and to reclaim sovereignty over them. On the contrary, the need to adapt traditional thinking on separated body parts to the new context created by recent achievements in biomedicine forces the point that, once donation has occurred on a basis of voluntary, conscious and informed consent, the donor renounces his ownership of, sovereignty over and all other rights regarding the ceded parts, substances or tissue, provided these are used for the purpose which legitimised the donation and in respect of which consent was given. Only where there is a discrepancy between the originally use of body parts and the actual use to which they are put – whether because relevant data were withheld from the donor which might have precluded or conditioned his consent or because such data unexpectedly come to light in the course of events – does the possibility arise of the donor revoking his original consent or claiming compensation for deception or resulting moral damage (without prejudice to administrative or penal measures to penalize dishonest or unlawful behaviour in this field).

On the other side, the eventual subjection of minors or legally incapacitated adults to procedures which compromise their physical integrity should be considered under a restrictive point of view. In principle, and following the general criteria established by European Convention on Human Rights and Biomedicine and by its Additional Protocol from 2002, it seems to be the better option not to authorized (to forbid) any extraction of substances, elements, products and tissue from the bodies of minors and incapacitated adults without any direct therapeutic or diagnostic benefit to the same.

7. – A CHALLENGE FOR INTELLECTUAL PROPERTY RIGHTS?

One further important question is: «Who owns our genes?»

Is it the patient respectively the donor to whom the intellectual property rights belong, or the researcher respectively the pharmaceutical enterprise? The Moore case in the USA solves this question quite clearly: the pharmaceutical enterprise. But we could say: it depends. First of all as we have stated previously the donor keeps the control of the personal information of his sample if it has not been anoymised. By the other hand, in general we can say that tissues and cells are of course individually assigned to the donors before separation into property rights. Traditionally, these rights lose their function as property rights for the donor within the integration into a biobank because of being involved in the bank by default.

In general, the leading opinion states that patients or donors transfer their property rights to the bank, the researchers, or the pharmaceutical industry. Basis is the informed consent. And the question is if all rights could be transferred. Normally, some right remain with the patient or donor, at least to control the data or destruct them as far as they are not anonymised.

The exception is the case that the individual gave a blank consent. The different forms of consent are realized in practice as empty rituals during which the two conflicting sides are lead to their aimed conclusions: One part dispenses and the other is allowed to work for his own, and the benefit of others if research is successful. That is why it has come to a conventional direct reallocation of disposal rights in favour of the pharmaceutical industry and indirectly – concerning the future possibility of medical results – for the benefit of the donors as well. In case of successful drug development, the community of patients will profit from the donation even if the donor himself has no direct earnings at all (this problem comes up again if less-developed-countries or purely indigenous communities are affected.)

If we continue to think along these lines, informed consent (despite its apparently empty significance) brings benefit-sharing with it almost automatically, and that is through its latent structure. In other words: Every time genetic data or tissues are allocated to researchers for another use, there is the chance to share positive results with the whole community on one hand. On the other hand, this positive abnegation of individuals is washed out and apparently limited through the expansion of property rights of the business. «Apparently limited» is supposed to mean that the knowledge about the results is now guided alongside monetary equivalents. The donor gives up his property rights for the benefit of the industrial side of the transaction. From the view of business they fulfil a process of collecting the given material and data because of taking the risk of capital investment.

This is why generally an adequate return of investment may be realized and thus also should be debated under ethical aspects. In this point, we substantially agree with the criteria established on the Directive on tissue banking, contrary to gain a financial gain by the donor, but it could be considered that a system similar to the one set by the UNESCO International Declaration on Human Genetic Data (2003) should be put in place. In its art. 19 the aforementioned declaration states:

«Sharing of benefits. (a) In accordance with domestic law or policy and international agreements, benefits resulting from the use of human genetic data, human proteomic data or biological samples collected for medical and scientific research should be shared with the society as a whole and the international community. In giving effect to this principle, benefits may take any of the following forms:

(i) special assistance to the persons and groups that have taken part in the research;

(ii) access to medical care;

(iii) provision of new diagnostics, facilities for new treatments or drugs stemming from the research;

(iv) support for health services;

(v) capacity-building facilities for research purposes;

(vi) development and strengthening of the capacity of developing countries to collect and process human genetic data, taking into consideration their specific problems;

(vii) any other form consistent with the principles set out in this Declaration.

(b) Limitations in this respect could be provided by domestic law and international agreements».

By establishing one such system we will ensure that one part of the benefits obtained by companies will be devoted to social needs related with groups of patients, medical care, etc., avoiding any economic gain for the donor.

8. – REASONS FOR RESEARCH

So, we can see that biobanks contain a lot of chances and risks that have to be analysed all over the world. In this context the legal questions related to biobanks are important to investigate. For our project the focus on some European and Latin American biobanks is the main important thing. Firstly, we can see how developed biobanks are in Europe and Latinamerica; secondly, the question arises how far biobanks are regulated in these countries; thirdly, we can follow the above described questions and some more important ones and come to a statement about the situation in all these countries, and also what has to be done furthermore.

PART II.

National Reports

LEGAL AND SOCIAL IMPLICATIONS OF CREATING BANKS OF BIOLOGICAL MATERIAL IN ARGENTINA

BY

SALVADOR DARÍO BERGEL

SUMMARY : 1. The facts : Situation of scientific research with human biological samples and biobanks in Argentina. 2. Legal Framework. 2.1. General legislation applicable. 2.2. Specific legislation. 2.3. Reports and opinions by national institutions and bodies. 2.4. Professionals and institutions : quality standards and accreditation requirements. 2.5. Ethics Research Committees. 2.6. Obtaining of samples (invasive intervention in the donor). 2.7. Sample ownership. 2.8. Protection of the subject's privacy (duty of confidentiality and security of data and sample archives). 2.9. Extent of the consent (generic or specific). 2.10. Use of samples obtained for another purpose. 2.11. Specifically issues related with local communities. 2.12. Maintenance : security standards, storage lengths. 2.13. National and international transfer and circulation of samples. 2.14. Property rights. 2.15. Other issues. 2.16. Final comments, conclusions, other reflections, etc.

1. – THE FACTS :
SITUATION OF SCIENTIFIC RESEARCH WITH HUMAN BIOLOGICAL SAMPLES AND BIOBANKS IN ARGENTINA

The remarkable evolution of biology since the second half of the last century has created the need to establish regulatory systems in several areas (for example research involving human beings, organ transplant, biobanks, etc.).

Regulations seem not to have moved forward as expected, and nowadays we find ourselves with a legal vacuum, which needs to be filled either through analogous laws or general legal principles.

Several areas of medical reseach need to use biological samples, which require suitable storage when they are not used immediately.

The samples obtained do not only represent inert collections, but – depending on the purpose of the medical research – may be exchanged with other centres in the country and abroad.

Biological samples represent a biobank's raw material, separate from other similar materials such as germ cells, embryos, foetuses, which are conceived as autonomous units, which does not mean that the cells or tissue removed from them are part of the banks.

As due to their very nature biological samples contain clearly sensitive genetic information, which present a series of problems related to the use and management of such samples, such as the protection of the donor's privacy, the property regime they are subject to, or their use for purposes other than those initially suggested, or their export.

The samples of a person who has been identified are not similar – for obvious reasons – to the ones that belong to a person who can be identified or anonymous samples whose donor's identity is impossible to establish.

To sum up, biobanks became an essential instrument for medical research that requires specific regulation, since the lack of adequate rules can translate into a lack of protection of the first order of legal property.

There is not only a scientific interest, but also an undeniable public interest regarding the adequate management of these banks, since their inadequate use can infringe basic citizens' rights, and also hinder scientific research.

2. – Legal Framework

2.1. – *General legislation applicable*

There are a series of rules of different legal relevance which, given the lack of specific legislation, can guide us to the solution of specific cases.

Among these general rules are:

a) Law 17.132 on medical practice and collaborative work (Official Bulletin 31167), section IV which contains chapter 1 (on clinical analysis) and chapter 2 (on anatomy andpathology examinations).

b) Law 25.326 on data protection, the objective of which is the protection of personal data recorded in files, databases or by any other technical means of data processing.

In accordance with the 2nd article, information related to health constitutes sensitive data. The processing of personal data is illegal when the owner had not given explicit free, and informed consent which will have to be stated in written or by other similar means according to the circumstances (article 5.1).

Sensitive data can only be processed and disclosed when there are reasons of public interest authorized by law (article 7, section 2).

Article 10 states that the person responsible and others who take part in any aspect of the processing of personal data, will be obliged to maintain professional confidentiality.

c) Penal Code. According to article 157 bis anyone who commits any of the following will be liable to imprisonment:

1. accesses a personal database in any way, deliberately and unlawfully breaking confidentiality systems and data security.

2. reveals information stored in a personal databank which he or she is obliged by law to treat as confidential

d) The Blood Law 22.990 (Official Bulletin 21.283) article 75, states that the importation of human blood and derivative components can only take place when authorized by the Executive, with the intervention and at the request of the applicable national authority in the case of properly proven necessity or shortage.

Article 64 states that the exportation of human blood is forbidden, with the exception of those cases where, for security reasons, it is authorized by the Executive .

e) Law 23.511 created the National Genetic Data Bank (NBGD). Although its primary function was connected with determining the descendants of the victims of state terrorism, there are also several regulations related to this subject.

Article 8 states that the records of the NBGD will be preserved in an incorruptible way and in such conditions that will faithfully reflect their content.

2.2. – Specific legislation

No specific law exists on the regime to which biobanks established for research purposes could be subjected.

The closest is resolution 319 of INCUCAI (Instituto Nacional Central Único Coordinador de Ablación e Implante – the Single Central National Institute for the Coordination of Organ Harvesting and Implantion)– an independent body that operates as part of the National Health Ministry. According to the resolution, these banks are governed by this institute.

The INCUCAI was created under Law 23.885 of the 1st of November 1990 and it works as part of the National Health Ministry as a permanent body concerned with public rights, with financial and administrative independence.

Article 26 section f, considers that among its functions is «suggesting rules and to providing technical assistance to those organizations which this law concerns».

Over time, INCUCAI has become the guiding authority of biobanks.

Law 24.193 article 44 authorizes INCUCAI, under the supervision of COFESA (Consejo Federal de Salud- the Federal Health Councilto establish rules for the creation of establishments where medical procedures related to transplantation are carried out and to promote scientific research, exchange information and publish papers/reports.

This law empowered the INCUCAI to establish a National Register of Institutions, transplant equipment and tissue banks.

2.3. – Reports and opinions
by national institutions and bodies

There is no information about this.

2.4. – Professionals and institutions:
quality standards and accreditation requirements

Appendix I of resolution 319/04 contains rules to establish banks of hematopoietic progenitor cells, obtained from umbilical and placental blood. This regime extends – *mutatis mutandi* – to all banks that preserve biological material whether for clinical uses or for research.

The establishments will have to submit the following documentation:

– Identification and authorization.
– Details of the administrator
– A plan showing the location of the bank and its different sections. The bank must have an exclusive physical place in which to carry out its activity. It should have the following sections:
– Administration
– Medical administration.
– Laboratory administration.
– Unit processing laboratory.
– Cryopreservation laboratory
– Unit storage room.
– Laboratory for the screening of infectious/contagious diseases.

2.5. – *Research Ethics Committees*

The Resolution does not contain regulations about research ethics committees. The regulations contained in Resolution 1490/07 (Guide to good practices in clinical research involving human beings) can be used by analogy (Official Bulletin 14.1.07).

In this regard, it was established that the Research Ethics Committee (CEI) must provide an independent, competent and appropriate evaluation of the ethical aspects and quality of the scientific methodology of the proposed tests, and must also evaluate whether the research is based on the latest scientific knowledge (3.1.4).

The CEI must be constituted in such a way as to ensure a competent evaluation and review of the scientific, medical, ethic and legal aspects of the research, free from any risk or influence that may affect its independence (3.2.1).

At least one of its members should not be a scientist and in the case of an Institutional Committee this must also include a lay member. It is essential that some of the members have knowledge of bioethical issues and/or have knowledge of research methodology.

2.6. – Obtaining samples
(invasive intervention in the donor)

According to regulation C 3.300 of resolution 319/04, the collection of the material will take place according to the procedures outlined in the relevant procedural manual. The methods used to collect the samples will use aseptic techniques and valid procedures to provide an acceptable level of viability and the recovery of the progenitor cells.

Once collection is complete, the primary collection bag will carry the following information:

– Numerical or alphanumerical identification of the CPH-SCU unit.
– The collecting centre and the identification of the donor.
– Date and hour of the collection.
– Name and volume of the anticoagulant and other additives.
– In the case of donations, the name of the donor and, if applicable, the name of the recipient and a unique identification of the donor.

2.7. – Sample ownership

The INCUCAI rules do not contain regulations about this, so there is a serious legislative vacuum.

We believe the principles of ordinary law are applicable in relation to this issue, which in the case of anonymous samples the property would belong to the bank. In the other cases (identified or identifiable samples) the donor would keep his rights according to the terms of the informed consent. These should be respected by the bank, otherwise it would be held legally responsible.

2.8. – Protection of the subject's privacy
(duty of confidentiality, data security and sample archives)

Section B 5.380 of the INCUCAI's rules states that the HSC-UCB banks must have a system to keep the identity of the donor and the recipient confidential. This regulation should be applied to all banks that preserve biological material or human genetic material.

On the other hand, Law 21.173 was added to the Civil Code, article 1.071 bis, which protects and extends the right to privacy.

In medical research under the guidelines approved by the Health Ministry's resolution 1490/07, the confidentiality of records will be protected, as long as they can reveal the individual's identity, and the privacy and confidentiality rules will be respected in accordance with the applicable legislative requirements (2.9).

2.9. – *The extent of the consent (generic or specific)*

Section C 1.300 of resolution 319/04, contains several regulations under the title of «Donor Consent».

Section C 1.311 states that the consent for the collection of – hemotopoietic stem cells (HSCs), umbilical cord blood (UCB) will be obtained prior to collection when the HSC/UCB are collected from the plancenta in utero. Section C 1.312 states that the formal procedures for participation by the HSC/UCB bank will be discussed with the mother in a language that is understood by her. Explanations will include at a minimum the general purpose, possible risks, benefits and options in relation to the donation to the mother or the infant, including medical and ethical facts and the mother's right to refuse.

There will be a standard procedure for the mother's informed consent that will include, as a minimum, the following:

– Unconditional donation of the HSC/UCB for use in transplants.
– Discarding or sending of units that do not conform with the storage requirements.
– Interviews about the mother's personal and family medical history.
– Storage of samples for future research.
– Keeping in touch with the donor over the long term, with the objective of notifying the donor/family about infectious or genetic diseases.

An informed consent form is added as an appendix, which establishes:

a) That the donor has received and understood the information provided about the donation of hematopoietic progenitor cells, and has had the chance to ask as many questions as necessary to fully understand the process.

b) That she agrees to donate 20 ml. of her blood in order to determine the RH blood group antigens of the HLA system and for screening for transmissible infectious diseases markers.

c) That she authorizes the use of the placental blood for other research, such as research into blood groups, RH factor, histocompatibility, bacteria and cell culturing, transmissible contagious disease screening, and any other research required to achieve the project's aims.

d) That she can withdraw her consent to the donation of the HSC blood from the placenta up until the moment prior to her child's birth. This will not lead to the mother being penalized in any way.

e) That she renounces the right make any complaint regarding the donated placental blood and gives her approval to communicate the information obtained through the donation in the HSC/UCB bank, and to inform the INCUCAI's HSC donors register of the characteristics of the unit in a strictly confidential way.

2.10. – *The use of samples obtained for another purpose*

This issue is not regulated by INCUCAI's directives.

Nonetheless, the use of the samples extracted with the donor's consent for other purposes different to those stated in the «informed consent» form, is a transgression that would compromise whoever does this, according to the application of the principles of common law.

2.11. – *Specific issues relating with local communities*

Despite the fact that article 75, section 17, of the National Constitution recognizes the existence and guarantees respect for the towns inhabited by the indigenous population, there is no legal or administrative regulation related to this in relation to medical research or biobanks. Our situation differs from that of Bolivia, Peru, Colombia or Ecuador. The few indigenous people who live in Argentina are not organized into local communities.

2.12. – Maintenance: security standards, storage lengths

Item D 7.100 of the guidelines states that establishments where HSC-UCB units are stored will establish policies regarding the duration of storage, storage conditions and the elimination of donations.

Item D 7.531 requires storage facilities to have a continuously active alarm system.

2.13. – National and international transfer and circulation of samples

There are no specific rules about this. Nonetheless, the regulations included in Law 22.990 of December 2nd 1983 (Blood Law) could be applicable by analogy. Article 75 states that the importation of human blood, its components and derivates, may only take place in cases of necessity or proven shortage, if there is express authorization from the Executive as requested by and with the participation of the applicable national authority.

Article 74 prohibits exportation, with the exception of those cases in which it is authorized by the National Executive for security reasons.

2.14. – Property rights

The INCUCAI's rules do not contain regulations regarding this.

2.15. – Other issues

No comments in this section.

2.16. – Final comments, conclusion, other reflections, etc.

Until now – as has been shown – existing biobanks inside the country are governed by INCUCAI's regulations, applied by analogy. Although this fills the existing legal vacuum, it does not represent an appropriate solution.

As we have shown, the banks discussed aremixed since they keep material both for clinical applications and for basic research.

We consider that at a minimum legislation regarding this subject must consider the following:
– The technical characteristics of biobanks.
– The responsible authority.
– The protection of the confidentiality of stored data.
– Obtaining informed consent through transparent procedures.
– A property regime that covers the extracted samples.
– Rules about saving and preserving the samples.
– How controls should function.
– Infringements and penalties for breaking rules.
– How authority should be applied.

LEGAL AND SOCIAL IMPLICATIONS OF CREATING BANKS OF BIOLOGICAL MATERIAL IN BRAZIL

BY

María Fátima FREIRE DE SÁ

Summary : 1. The facts : Situation of scientific research with human biological samples and biobanks in Brazil. 2. Legal Framework. 2.1. General legislation applicable. 2.2. Specific legislation. 2.2.1. Resolution n. 340, dated from July 8th, 2004. 2.2.2. Resolution 347 dated from January 13th, 2005. 2.3. Reports and opinions by national institutions and bodies. 2.3.1. The Genomic Ancestral Project and the National Identity. 2.3.2. About the other biobanks holding investigatory purposes. 2.4. Professionals and institutions : quality standards and accreditation requirements. 2.5. Ethics Research Committees. 2.6. Obtaining of samples (invasive intervention in the donor). 2.7. Sample ownership. 2.8. Protection of the subject's privacy (duty of confidentiality and security of data and sample archives). 2.9. Extent of the consent (generic or specific). 2.10. Use of samples obtained for another purpose. 2.11. Specifically issues related with local communities. 2.12. Maintenance : security standards, storage lengths. 2.13. National and international transfer and circulation of samples. 2.14. Property rights. 2.15. Other issues. 2.16. Final comments, conclusions, other reflections, etc.

1. – The facts :
Situation of scientific research with human biological samples and biobanks in Brazil

In Brazil, although the presence of scientific research Project, aiming at the constitution of human biological sample Banks, there are no specific juridical norms, which aim at the regulation of its obtainment, use and assignment. And such reality is not far from most countries, which bear with the existence of biobanks holding no specific legislation, as for example, it was the case of Spain before the publication of Statute 14 of July, 3rd, 2007, known as BIL – Biomedical Investigation Law.

Otherwise, it is important to point out that there is specific regulation in Brazil, which preserves the protection of non-human biological samples, referring to the genetic wealth existing in the national territory, on the continental platform and in the economic zone exclusive for the scientific research, technological development or bio-prospection. This is due to the fact that the ecosystems raise interests in several areas of the national and international science.

Brazil's 1988 Constitution ensures to all, Brazilians or not, an ecologically balanced environment, being imposed to the public Power and the community the duty to defend it and preserve it for the current and future generations (art. 225, CR/88). And to ensure the effectiveness of this right, it states as being the incumbency of the public power the preservation of the diversity and the country's genetic wealth integrity, besides the surveillance of the entities dedicated to the genetic material researches and manipulation (art. 225, §1º, II, CR/88).

Aiming at abiding the constitutional determination, the President of Republic, at the use of the attribution bestowed by article 62 of the Constitution, edited the Provisional Remedy (PR) n. 2.186-16/2001, whose aim is to establish the rights and duties relating to the Access to the existing genetic wealth component in the Brazilian territory, by creating, in the Environment Ministry scope, the Genetic Wealth Management Council, officially determinative and statutory, whose duty is, among others, to set up criteria for the creation of the database for the information registration on the related traditional knowledge (1).

In accordance with article 7th, I, from such PR, the genetic wealth is defined as «all the genetic originated information, contained in samples of the whole or part of animal, microbian, fungus or plant samples, in form of molecules and substances from the metabolism of such living or dead organisms, found under *in situ* conditions, including domestic, or kept in *ex situ* collections, once they have been collected under *in situ* conditions within the national territory, in the continental platform, or within the exclusive economic zone». At the beginning it is noticed that, by the normative definition itself, the human biological sample is excluded

---

(1) Traditional knowledge associated to the individual or indigenous or local community's information holding potential or real value, relating to the genetic wealth (art. 7º, II, MP 2.186-16/2001).

from the scope of the guardianship of the above mentioned PR. Last, but not least, the 3rd article clearly establishes that such statutory diploma is not applicable to the human genetic wealth.

Due to that, the human biological samples in Brazil need specific statutory guardianship, which establishes, for example, a functional structure of the administrative agencies, holding institutional attributions, aiming at surveying and regulating the creation of such biobanks containing human genetic material, as there are non-human biological samples.

2. – Legal framework

2.1. – *General legislation applicable*

Being Brazil a signer of International Declaration on the Human Genetic Data, approved in the 32nd session of the UNESCO's General Conference, held on October 16th, 2003, the anomy status, until then referred, is not altogether absolute. It is known, however, that this document establishes the general normative directives, as it is the case of principle determination, many already existing in the national judicial disposition, which have their interpretation directed to the specific theme. And this is perfectly visualized in the article 1º, «a» which establishes as being the objective of the Declaration ensure the respect for the human dignity and the protection of the human rights and the fundamental freedom in terms of collection, treatment, use and conservation the genetic human data, in accordance with the imperatives of equality, justice and solidarity.

If in Brazil the concept of non-human biological samples can be spotted in 7º, I, of the Provisional Remedy n. 2.186-16/2001, the concept of human biological samples comes from the International Declaration upon the Human Genetic Data, as it defines as being a biological sample 'any [...] biological material (for example, blood, skin, or bone cells, or blood plasma where nucleic acids are present and which contains someone's characteristic genetic constitution» (art. 2º, IV). As for the bank holders of the human biological samples, there is no regulation.

The need of specific statutes for these scientific procedures is urgent. As it is clearly pointed out on the art. 3º of the International Declaration upon the Human Genetic Data, although each person has a characteristic genetic constitution, someone's identity can not be reduced to his genetic characteristics, as this person is made within an inter subjective sharing context and it implies a freedom element.

Undoubtly, as time goes by, the scientific advances have shown situations never imagined before. If in modernity principles the concern with the people's intimacy and privacy juridical protection referred to the external manifestation of this being Who thinks, acts and chooses, currently, the privacy and intimacy juridical guardianship have taken other directions, turning to the individual's own body constitution to guard his genetic data which are confounded with the rights considered as being personal.

Together with the scientific desires driven by the new Technologies applied to the human life, several problems are recurring, as, beyond the laboratory experiments it is the human being and his whole manifestation, while being the holder of dignity, autonomy and self conscience. Dealing with people is dealing with a being who is able to move himself within a space of inquiries and self assertiveness, besides being constituted by a sensitive basis of vitality called body, which keeps within itself a series of possibilities, some of which still not decoded, able to physiologically identify the own person and to determine the boundaries of his freedom in this self-assertiveness process. And this can not be forgotten.

What we are by nature (human beings) are not confounded with who we are, that is, who we became (human people). While human being is simply belonging to a taxonomic unit, being a human person is to have the freedom to construct a judicially guarded personality. Obviously, this does not imply in the absence of the human being's judicial protection, but it implies differentiated normative guarantees in alike differentiated argumentative scopes, as well as it is attributed singular treatment to *the biological life* and to the *judicially guarded life*. Notwithstanding, invariably, at certain moments, such guardianships will tangent each other, so that the protective norm of the human person implies the protection of the human being and vice-versa.

The way of approaching the human being's protection, results from the way how we deal with the species to which we belong to. Any scientific methods tending to change the species' sensitive structure imply the modification of what we are by nature (human beings). It is in this sense that it is justifiable, for example, the prohibition of reproductive cells manipulation aiming at cloning or even the production of chimeras. In Brazil, the Bio security Statute 11.105/05 was emphatic at prohibiting such practice (art. 6º, IV), classifying it as crime, whose penalty is 2 to 5-year confinement and fine (art. 26).

On the other hand, the human being protection implies the normative guardianship of what the human being is able to become, that is, a subject holder of autonomy and self-conscience, who is able to define the biographic features of his own life within a context of shared living, in which attributes content to his dignity with the other. It is the result of the exercise of the «freedom element» mentioned in the article 3rd, of the International Declaration on the Human Genetic Data.

Concerning the human biological samples, the problems are more and more latent, once the heart of the problem is centered in the fact that the human beings are not directly involved in the research, but in fact, parts of their bodies which have been collected and stored for a determined aim. Such aspect raises one of the biggest problems faced by the modern science, that is, the collision between freedom of research, ensured in the Brazilian Constitution through art. 5º, IX (2), *versus the* protection of the integrity of life and of the human person, resulting from the constitutional guarantee of the free development of the personality. What would be the boundary between the research freedom and the protection of the life integrity and the human being subject to the research?

In Brazil, the researches involving human beings regulations is protected by the Resolutions of the National Council of Health which, although not having the normative Power of the legal provisions (punishment), set up ethical and regulatory directives which relate the researchers to certain prescriptions, as it is the case of the research approval by a determined Ethics Committee.

---

(2) Art. 5º, IX, from CR/88: «the expression of the intelectual, artistic, scientific and communicative activity is free, independently from censorship or permit».

2.2. – Specific legislation

The National Council of Health is a collegiate agency, holding permanent and deliberative characteristics, composed of governmental representatives, renderers of services, health professionals and users, relating to Ministry of Health, whose scope is actuate in the formation of strategies and control of strategies and upon the control of the accomplishment of the health policies, including their economic and financial aspects (art. 1º, §2º from Statute 8.142/90).

The President of Republic Act n. 99.438, dated from August 7th, 1990, which disposed on the organization and attributions of the National Council of Health, was revocated by the presidential Act n. 5.839, dated from July 11th, 2006, which establishes as being the CNS's competence, among others, *the technological and scientific incorporation and development process follow-up in the health area, aiming at observing ethical patterns compatible with the Country's social-cultural development.*

This way, the researches involving human beings in Brazil, besides being obviously submitted to the normative dispositions risen from the 1988 Republic Constitution, are related to the pre-established rules set by the National Council of Health's Resolutions. For the purpose of the current work, are highlighted: Resolutions n. 196, dated from October 10th, 1996; n. 304, dated from August 9th, 2000; n. 340, dated from July 8th, 2004; and n. 347, dated from January 13th, 2005. Among other normative precepts, the promotion of the human dignity and the resolutions of the International Declarations belonging to the national judicial disposition under a new focus (art. 5º, §3º CR/88, added by the Constitutional Amendment n. 45/2004 (3)) are emphasized.

The National Council of Health Plenary approved, in its 59th ordinary meeting held on October 9th and 10th, 1996, the Resolution n. 196, which establishes the directives and statutes for researches involving human beings.

The Resolution incorporated, under the view of the individuals and of the communities, the Bioethics' four basic referential: *autonomy* (III.1, a), non-mal efficiency (III.1, c), *beneficence* (III.1, b)

---

(3) Art. 5º, §3º from CR/88: The international treats and conventions upon the human rights which are approved, in the House of National Congress, in two turns, by three thirds of the respective members' votes, will be equivalent to the constitutional amendments.

and justice (III.1, d), aiming at ensuring the rights and duties which refer to the scientific community, the research subjects and the State. The Resolution states that the researches with *human beings* are all of those which, individually or collectively, involve directly or indirectly such beings, *on their whole or their parts*, including the manipulation of information or materials (II.2), which for sure comprises the use of *human biological samples*.

The procedure for the insertion of the human being in the research implies, at first, the clear and free consent, apart from some critical points, which deserve being highlighted and discussed. According to Resolution 196, the clear and free consent is the subject of the research's or his legal representative's agreement, being that voluntary, free of vices, dependency, subordination or intimidation, after prior detailed and complete explanation on the nature of the research, its objectives, methods, benefits, potential risks and inconveniences which may arise (II.11). The clear and free consent must be kept integrally from the moment the research is started, as well as during the whole of its procedures, specially when related to the possibility of inclusion in a control group or placebo.

Being the research subject's consent on determined term consubstantiate, he is given the freedom to lift his consent, at any phase of the research, under no penalty and any loss of his care, notably when it concerns with the secrecy of the obtained secret.

Concerning the use of the samples, the Resolution states that the biological material and the data obtained in the research shall be used exclusively for the aim of the foreseen purpose in the research protocol.

It also forecasts that researches with human beings shall follow procedures which ensure the confidentiality and privacy, the image protection and the non-stigmatization, ensuring the non use of information in harm of the people, including in terms of self-esteem, prestige and/or economic-financial ones (III.3, i). Concerning the research ownership rights, it is disposed that the protocol to be submitted to the ethical review can only be reviewed if it is instructed with some of the responsible researcher's, the sponsor's and the involved institutions' identification documents (VI e VI.1) and with the research description, which comprises, among other documents, the expression of pre-existing consent relating to the property of the generated information, showing the inexistence of any restrictive clause related to the public advertising of the results, unless when it is for patenting : in this case, the results shall become public, as soon as the patenting phase is finished; declaration that the research results will be public, being them favourable or not. (VI.2, l e m)

In case of researches involving vulnerable groups, a representative shall be invited as an *ad hoc* member of the Committee, to participate in the project's analysis. CEP shall keep the research's project, the protocol and its reports in its database for 5 years after the end of the study.

There is no disposition in this National Council of Health Resolution on the national and international exchange of information.

2.2.1. *Resolution n. 340, dated from July 8th, 2004*

Due to the human genetics research-related technical-scientific advances, the National Council of Health approved the Resolution 340/2004, whose content is restricted to the specific normative for the regulation of research projects in human genetics, considering, in consonance together with the International Declaration on the Human Genetic Data the potential risks to the health and the protection of the human person rights, his fundamental freedom and the human dignity in the collection, processing, use and storage of the data and the human genetic materials.

The Resolution 340/2004 recognises the owner individual of his genetic data, being able to withdraw them from the bank where they are stores at any moment. (III.7).

As for the data to be dissociated from the individual it is necessary to present justification which will be both analysed by CEP and CONEP. The subject must be told about the advantages and disadvantages of such procedure, as well as he must sign up specific consent term for this purpose. (III.8 and III.9).

The information exchange is possible and, being it international, it is necessary to register the opportunities of technology transfer (IV.1, m).

Such researches, by producing a special data category and by containing personal, medical and scientific information, require evaluation on the impact of their knowledge upon the individual, the family and the whole of the group the individual belongs to.

This way, the subject of the research can choose whether to be informed or not about the results of his exams – right to know or not to know (III.4).

The subject of the research has the right to, after being informed about the procedures, authorize the storage of data and materials. The Clear and Free Consent Term shall explain the possibility of the material to be used in a new research project (V.1, e).

The Resolution is clear when it refers to the challenge of the use of the genetic data for other purposes, except for the hypothesis of the obtainment of previous consent from the donor individual or his legal representative, when he does not have plenary capacity do to so. It is necessary, in such cases, the elaboration of a new research protocol, under the approval of the Ethics Committee in Research or the Ethics National Council in Research. In this aspect, the Resolution foresees the possibility of using the material for other purposes, if it is unfeasible the obtainment of the Clear and Free Consent, once there is the Ethics Committee's authorization (III.12).

2.2.2. Resolution 347 dated from January 13th, 2005

On January 13th, 2005 the National Council of Health approved Resolution n. 347 which outlines directives for the ethical analysis of research projects which involve storage of materials or use of materials from previous researches.

In general lines, it has a complementary characteristic to Resolution n. 196/96 once it concerns the use of biological material in other researches and the Exchange of samples, situations which were not foreseen in the cited Resolution.

Resolution 347/05 determines, that, in case of foresight of future use of the biological material in other researches, there must be suitable justification and the donors' consent, with the express authorization for the storage of material (items 1, 1.1 and 1.2). It still establishes that the Project must contain declaration that the new research will be submitted to the institution's CEP as well as to CONEP, the latter, when it is the case (item 1.3).

Concerning the responsibility for the storage of the samples, the Resolution states that the biological material will be stored under the responsibility of the depositary institution, which must have statute or regulation approved by CEP, including the definition of the responsible parties for the guardianship and by the authorization of the use of material (item 2.1); mechanisms which ensure secrecy and respect for the confidentiality (item 2.2); mechanisms which ensure the possibility of contact with the donors for information supply of their interest (for example, exams results, for clinical follow-up or genetic counselling) or for the obtainment for specific consent for the use in a new research project (item 2.3).

It is important to verify that the present Resolution forecasts the possibility of sample exchanges national and internationally wide. The fore situation, it is key the agreement among institutions, aiming at ways of operating and using the stored material. For the international exchange, besides the agreement, the legislation in force for the delivery of material abroad shall be obeyed and the regulation for CEP' s analysis concerning the procedures relating to the second point, above cited (item 5).

In this Exchange, the research and the Brazilian institution are considered as being the quotaholders of the foreign Banks, with the right to reach the material for future researches. This means that the stored material will not be of exclusive ownership of the country or the depositary institution (item 5.1).

Concerning the samples already stored the Resolution conditions the use in new researches to CEP's approval, and, when necessary, by CONEP (item 6.1).

6.2. The research protocols which intend to use the stored material shall include:

a) Justification of the use of material;

b) Description of the collection and storage systematization, with the definition of the start date or duration;

c) Copy of the Free and Clear Consent Term – TCLE – obtained from the date of the research, when the material was collected, including the storage and possible future use authorization, if the storage occurred from the research approved after the Resolution CNS n° 196/96; e

d) Specific TCLE for the new research : in case of the impossibility of obtainment of specific consent for the new research (dead donor, unsuccessful attempts of contract or other situations) the justifications shall be presented as part of the protocol for CEP's analysis, which may authorization or not the individual consent.

It is important, finally, to highlight the complementary character of this Resolution, and the reason why Resolution 196/96's directives shall be taken into consideration, concerning the targeted individuals' consent relating procedures and the specificities of the researches done in groups and vulnerable subjects.

2.3. – Reports and opinions by national institutions and bodies

2.3.1. The Genomic Ancestral Project and the National Identity

Specifically concerning the biological samples aimed at the biomedical research, the biobanks can host material belonging to certain individuals or even to entire families and populations, aiming at outlining the genetic profile of a group or diagnose genetic diseases.

Since 2005, at the Universidade Federal do Rio Grande do Sul, Professor Dr. Francisco M. Salzano has been coordinating a research for the development of a set of European, African and indigenous ancestral genetic markers, able to identify and quantify the individual inter ethnic mixture. The markers can be used in studies of associations between genetic diseases and specific mutations. A AND bank has been constituted to be used in this investigation and the aim of this research is the knowledge of the normal and pathological genomic variability among the Brazilian populations, Latin Americans and alike, and their medical and forensic implications.

Genomic Ancestral and National Identity : biomedical and forensic implications is the title of the research project above cited. It has the following partner institutions and their coordinators :

– Pontifícia Universidade Católica do Rio Grande do Sul, Sandro L. Bonatto;
– Universidade Federal do Paraná, Maria Luiza Petzl-Erler;
– Universidade de São Paulo, Ribeirão Preto, Wilson A. da Silva Júnior;
– Universidade Federal de Minas Gerais, Sérgio D. J. Pena, Fabrício R. dos Santos, Eduardo Tarazona Santos; e
– Universidade Federal do Pará, Sidney E.B. Santos, Ândrea K.C. Ribeiro dos Santos, João F. Guerreiro.

Three subprojects have been set up, as follows :
- Micro-evolution among indigenous populations;
- Dynamics of the genetic flow among non-indigenous populations; and
- Multi factual characteristics and genetic susceptibility

The development of the Project was only possible through the agreement of the Institutional Bioethics Committees, besides the National Council of Ethics in Research (CONEP)'s favourable opinion. The informed consent was obtained after detailed information to the subject of the research. In the case of indigenous populations, there was previous contact with the leaders of the community for the explanation of the proposed aims. Afterwards, when from the material collection, the information was done in an individualized way, giving the subject freedom in the sense of participating supplying his material or refusing to have it collected.

UNESCO's Universal Declaration on Genome and Human Rights, UNO's Declaration on the rights of Indigenous Peoples permeated all the procedures for the obtainment of the research subject's free and clear consent.

As it is stated, the research started in 2005 and the last two and a half years, have been dedicated to the activities of collection, testing and interpretation of the samples and the results in the institutions involved in the research.

According to Professor Francisco Salzano, the criterion for the obtainment of the samples varies a lot, taking each of the three subprojects into consideration. For example, in the subproject *multi-factual characteristics and genetic susceptibility* the study is carried out with sick people, keeping its respective controls : the subproject *genetic flow dynamics among non-indigenous populations* studies, mainly, the urban populations and the obtainment of data for the forensic use. The subproject *indigenous populations micro-evolutions* collects genetic material from voluntary donors in villages.

Each subproject constitutes a biobank which interlinks to the others through a net of associated institutions. Once the sample are collected, which is called by the Project coordinator, «genetics' demonization», it is practically impossible the flow of the samples internationally, also existing strong restrictions at national level.

Currently, when there is the need to study material in a Center different from the researcher's, it is the researcher who moves to the study of stored material in a certain laboratory.

The aim is, as final result, to find information about the Latin American human groups' history along around 20,000 years. Besides the academic value, such researches will help to interpret the present and forecast the biological future of the human species. In the more applied studies the aim is to help the authorities to identify criminals and supply adequate criteria for responsible maternity and paternity. On the other hand, it has been undoubtly set that the human groups show different resistance and susceptibility to diseases and differentiated genetic wealth. The aim is to reach an individualized medicine, with treatments adapted to each person in particular.

2.3.2. *About the other biobanks holding investigatory purposes*

There are two main biobanks kept by the State with investigatory purposes: the ADN National Bank *(Breast Cancer and Genetics Project)*, from Oswaldo Cruz Foundation (FIOCRUZ) and the *Tumours and ADN National Bank,* from Instituto Nacional de Câncer (INCA).

FIOCRUZ's physicians formed a research team on the breast cancer in 1995, setting up a *ADN National Bank* for this study. The project is ongoing and has been financed by furtherance agencies.

The project comprises the following actions:
- Carcinogenesis study and breast cancer prevention among the Brazilian population;
- Comparative study, at the epidemiologic level and tumour biology, in several States in Brazil;
- Studies of women with genetic predisposition (specific genes BRCA1 and BRCA2);
- Methodological development in the genetic counselling area for women holding alterations in BRCA1 e BRCA2;
- Development of bioethics related aspects in the genetic counselling;

— Study of emotional factors involved in the breast cancer sickness process;
— Study of Breast Tumours through the molecular biology (oncogenes and oncogenic suppressive);
— Epidemiologic and clinic study of the Breast Cancer among under 50-year old women. (FARIA, 2007)

Material for research will be collected from risk patients, such as: a) Patients who hold family history of breast and/or ovary cancer for three generations; b) Patients who present breast cancer or bilateral ovary; c) Men who have breast cancer associated to family breast cancer; d) Jewish ashkenazi women who have breast and/or ovary cancer in the pre menopause period; e) Families who hold two cases of breast and/or ovary cancer among first degree under 40 relatives (FARIA, 2007)

This way, the «AND National Bank» project intends the characterization of BRCA1 and BRCA2 specific genes, which will base the cancerous genetic predisposition analysis of each of these patients.

The monitoring of patients holding oncologic familiar history will be done through the clinic-psychological follow-up as well as through genetic counselling.

In another Project, INCA, bound to the Ministry of Health, on May 11th, 2005, the *Tumour and ADN National Bank*, aiming at the cancer research, diagnosis and treatment.

Initially, samples of tumours of higher incidence among the Brazilian population — such as lung, breast, womb, prostrate and esophagus — are stored aiming at elaborating the population's genetic profile, by identifying the important genes for each type of tumour.

In the future, it is expected that the Bank has a laboratory for the extraction of nucleic acids from a high number of tissues, which will allow not only a better quality control, but also will centralize the extraction process, allowing that more investigators are beheld by tissue unit. (INCA, 2005)

INCA's «ADN and Tumours National Bank» holds well defined consistent objectives based on three pillars:

1. Establishment of a net of collection and processing of samples of tumour-stricken and normal tissues, blood and clinic data of the most relevant tumours in Brazil (due to their frequency and mor-

tality) and their transfer to INCA's Research Center. This net will comprise university medical centers, such as cancer hospitals, including INCA's hospitals, totalizing 20 centers in the Five geographical regions in the country. Such centers are selected through their potential in recruiting patients and the availability of trained personal for diagnosis, samples collection and data processing. The protocols for samples collection, identification, storage and transfer for INCA's Research Center, shall be submitted to evaluation and be approved by the local Ethics Committees. All the patients who agree to participate in the Project will be invited to sign up an Informed Consent Term. The team, composed by physicians, nurses, technicians and bio graduates from each selected Center, will be trained by INCA's team to ensure that the protocols previously defined are followed.

2. Establishment of a ADN and tumours Bank at the INCA's Research Center, with accurate identification system, suitable storage and easy recovery of tissues and ADN samples. This bank will hold infrastructure for micro dissection and tissue arrays and ADN.

3. Implementation of a bio computerized unit for the data control and analysis. (INCA, 2005)

The researches are still at the beginning, but it is expected «individualized therapies to be defined, from each patient's regional and ethnical characteristics, improving the efficiency» in the cancer diagnosis and treatment. (INCA, 2005)

The Bank will be a repository of data for the researches developed throughout the country and not only concerning Cancer National Institute's researches. The samples orders will obey the following procedures: a) «Investigator's *Curriculum Vitae delivery*, sources study description and justification, methodology, type of ordered material, ethical considerations and the agreements with the conditions for the use of material»; b) «A limited lot of samples will be sent to the researcher and, after the presentation of the initial data which show the standardization of the proposed methodology and the laboratory capacity for its use, the further samples required can be released»; c) «The patient's material and data will be delivered without identification to the approved projects' coordinators.» (INCA, 2005)

The ADN and Tumours National Bank searches, as research result, allow the development of studies in the area of diagnosis and therapeutic markers; standardize and computerize the sample collection procedures and clinical data.

2.4. – *Professionals and institutions : quality standards and accreditation requirements*

There is no information about this issue.

2.5. – *Ethics Research Committees*

The Ethics Committee in Research is an interdisciplinary and independent collegiate, which must exist in the institutions which perform researches involving human beings in Brazil. It was created to defend the research's subjects' interests in their integrity and dignity and to contribute for the development of research within ethical standards.

Its role consists of : a) evaluate and follow up the ethical aspects of all the researches involving human beings, according to national (Res. CNS 196/96 and complementary resolutions) and international directives (Helsink Declaration, International Directives for the Biomedical Researches involving Human Beings – OMS), aiming at safeguarding the research's subject's dignity, rights, security and welfare; b) exercise consulting and educational role to ensure the continuous education of the institution's researchers and promote the discussion on the ethical aspects of the researches in human beings in the community.

The institutions where the researches are held are responsible for the implementation and operation of the Ethics Committee. The CEP must be registered in the National Committee of Ethics in Research – CONEP.

The Ethics Committee in Research must be constituted by a multi professional and multidisciplinary collegiate, having professionals from the health area, exact, social and human sciences, the ones dedicated to the study of Bioethics, and at least a representative member of the institution's users.

The composition and procedure for the decision taking at CEP shall ensure its fundamental characteristic of independence relating to political, institutional, hierarchical, corporate, financial and economic-market influences.

The participation is voluntary and at least half of its members must hold experience in research.

Projects which shall be presented to CEP:

- Res. CNS 196/96 considers as research involving human beings those done in any area of knowledge and that, directly or indirectly involve individuals or communities, on their whole or parts, including the manipulation of information and materials. This way, it is also taken as researches, the ones involving human beings, the interviews, questionnaires, use of data base and handbooks reviews.
- The submission of a Project to a CEP is independent from the research level, whether being it a graduation course's conclusion work, or being some work from a scientific initiation or from doctorate, being that of academic or operating purpose, once it is in compliance with the definition «researches involving human beings"

Research Protocol:

• Documents necessary for the research Project analysis by CEP:

- Face Sheet: document which gives juridical consistency to the Project, because it identifies the researcher responsible, the institution and CEP – it contains the researcher and institution's term of commitment.
- Research Project: it is through this document that the an analysis is done and through which the research's methodological adequacy is made- the ethical review of all or any research proposal involving human beings can not be dissociated from its scientific analysis: the methodological solidity is an ethical issue in itself;
- Clear and Free Consent Term: written in accessible language by the subjects of the research- this document shows, clearly, the recognition of the research's subject as an autonomous being and the best defender of his interests. The subjects' protection constitutes the CEPS fundamental reason ...
- The TCLE shall be obtained after the research's subject and/or his legal responsible being sufficiently aware of all the possible benefits, risks and procedures which will be done and of all the information pertaining to the research.
- It can not have the connotation of «responsibility exemption term»

- By protecting the research's subject, automatically are the researcher and other involved staff being protected, including CEP, which becomes co-responsible for the research after its approval.
- There are special situations when the TCLE can be exempted, having it to be substituted by a justification about the reasons for the impossibility of its obtainment.
- Detailed budget of the research project: resources, source, and destination, as well as the value of the researcher's wages.

No exam or procedure can be charged from the patient or from the payer agent of his assistance.

The researcher's wages can never be a sum which induces him to alter the risk/benefit ratio for the research's subjects.

The main researcher's and other participants' Curriculum vitae – aims at evaluating the researcher's technical capacity and ethical adequacy for the research accomplishment.

• The list of centers and researchers involved as well as the respective CEPs' approval in multi centric studies.

• If the research is carried out in a health institution, the technical responsible shall be aware and authorize its performance, once he is the one responsible for all the procedures done within the institution.

Research Project Assessment:
- Verify whether the research Project is suitable from the methodological viewpoint;
- Verify whether the necessary measures have been taken to minimize foreseen risks (by taking into consideration the physical, psychological, moral, intellectual, social, cultural or spiritual dimensions);
- Identify likely benefits and verify whether the risks are favourably proportional in relation to the benefits for the research's subjects;
- Verify whether the TCLE provides thorough understanding of the Project and its implications for the research's subjects;
- The TCLE shall ensure the individual the right to refuse to answer questions which may cause any sort of constraints.

2.6. – Obtaining of samples
(invasive intervention in the donor)

There is no information about this issue.

2.7. – Sample ownership

The Resolution 340/2004 recognizes the individual as being the owner of his genetic data, being allowed to withdraw them from the bank where they are stored at any time (III.7).

In order to have the data dissociated from the individual it is necessary to present a justification which will be analysed by CEP and CONEP. The subject shall be warned about the advantages and disadvantages of such procedure, as well as shall sign up a specific consent term for this purpose (III.8 e III.9).

2.8. – Protection of the subject's privacy
(Duty of confidentiality and security of data and sample archives)

The Resolution 196/1996 determines that the researches involving human beings shall ensure the confidentiality and de privacy, the image protection and non-stigmatization, ensuring the non-use of the information in detriment of the people, including in terms of self-esteem, prestige and/or economic-finances. (III.3, i).

2.9. – Extent of the consent
(generic or specific)

There is no information about this issue.

2.10. – Use of samples obtained for another purpose

The Resolution n. 340, dated from July 8th, 2004 voids the use of genetic data for other purposes, except when there is prior consent from the donor individual or his legal representative, in case he does not hold plenary capacity to do so. Anyway, it will be necessary to proceed with the elaboration of a new research protocol, with the approval of the Ethics Committee in Research or of the Ethics National Council in Research. Concerning this aspect, the Resolution forecasts the possibility of using the material for other purposes, if being the obtainment of the Clear and Free Consent impracticable, once it is authorized by the Ethics Committee (III.12).

2.11. – *Specifically issues related with local communities*

The clear and free consent can not always be obtained from the person directly involved in the research, due to any incapacity which inhibits him to undergo the research, it is the case of groups named *vulnerable groups*. According to Resolution 196/96, the researches involving human beings shall be developed, preferably with individuals holding plenary autonomy, so that the individuals belonging to vulnerable groups will participate in a *subsidiary* way, that is, when the desired information can not be obtained through the subjects holding plenary autonomy, unless the investigation may bring direct benefits to the vulnerable (III.3, j).

Although the capacity non-plenitude inhibits such individuals from expressing their free and clear will, the Resolution 196/96 reinforces the need of maintaining the autonomy of these subjects, *according to their possibilities*, as in the researches involving human beings, they shall always be treated in their dignity, their autonomy shall be respected, and defended in their vulnerability (Res. 196/96, III.1, a).

In case the researches involve children and adolescents, it is necessary the authorization of their legal representatives, respected, though, the research's subjects' autonomy in not wanting to participate in the process. On the other hand, being the child or adolescent holder of mental disturbances or disease mental, the researcher shall present clear justification of the choice of the research's subject, which shall be approved by the Ethics Committee in Research, besides the accomplishment of the requirement of the clear and free consent through the so-called vulnerable subjects' legal representatives, «without the suspension of the right of individual information, within the his capacity restraints» (Res. 196/96, IV.3. «a»). The same happens with adults in situation of substantial decrease of their consent capacities.

Within the cultural diversity of the Brazilian people, the indigenous peoples deserve special treatment, situation safeguarded by

Resolution 196/96.Thereforem such issue deserves to be carefully analysed.

The Brazilian indigenous peoples comprise a cultural multifaceted existence which include approximately 227 communities. At first there was strong political trend in the quest for the indigenous integration to the metropolises' culture, fact which invariably deteriorated the maintenance of the typical pluralism of the Brazilian society. Nowadays, such inclusive policies concerning the indigenous communities have abandoned this interactive trait, aiming at keeping the plurality, not integrating the natives in loss of their culture, but including them in a shared reality, where his cultural peculiarities are preserved. Otherwise, there is still a long way ahead to evolve towards this aspect.

And as an example of the need for this evolution, it is necessary to highlight the judicial treatment given to the indigenous populations' capability in Brazil for the practice of acts of the civil life. The Brazilian Civil Code which was in force from 1916 until the beginning of 2003, established being all men able of rights and duties in the civil warrant, but when treating incapable people, established that the wood inhabitants should be treated like relatively incapable people, in need of, this way, legal representatives (FUNAI – Indigenous populations National Foundation) who assisted them at the practice of acts of the civil life.

In 1988 the Republic Constitution delivered specific treatment to the indigenous populations recognizing their social organization, customs, languages, beliefs, and traditions, besides the original rights on the lands which they traditionally occupy. (art. 231, CR/88). It also granted them with the standing to sue, being to their communities or organizations, to sue in defence of their rights and interests (art. 232, CR/88), being the charge of the Public Ministry, whose constitutional attribution is to defend the juridical order, the democratic regime and the social and individual interests available (art. 127, CR/88), intervene in all the procedural acts.

Notwithstanding, although the Republican Constitution has gone further in this aspect, the 2002 Civil Code, which took force at the beginning of 2003, replacing the 1916 Civil Code, established that the indigenous populations' capability would be regulated by a *special legislation*, where the Express forecast of relative incapacity would be withdrawn, as it had been stated in the 1916 Civil Code, masking it through a unique paragraph in the art 4th of the Civil Code, which refers to the relatively incapable subjects.

And the special legislation mentioned in the unique paragraph in the art. 4th of the 2002 Civil Code refers to the Indian Act, Statute 6.001, dated from December 19th, 1973, whose fundamental basis is the 1916 Civil Code. And, being this way, it is necessary for the concession of the civil capability, the demonstration that the Indian is found integrated to a «national community».

The indigenous populations, while being the research's subjects, may be considered as being vulnerable, depending, for this, on the degree of social inclusion in the community and himself as a person. This way, the item IV.3 disposes, «and» from Resolution 196/96 that, in case of researches carried out in culturally differentiated communities, as it is the indigenous populations case, the informed consent shall be obtained together with the prior community consent through their own leaders, not being the efforts for the obtainment of individual consent dispensed.

As a consequence of the need to guard the researches involving such populations more carefully, the National Council of Health approved, on August 9th, 2000, the Resolution n. 304, whose aim was to regulate the researches carried out in indigenous communities, departing from the necessary respect for the way of living of each community and the recognition of the right of indigenous subjects' participation in the decisions which affect them.

The Resolution 304/2000 incorporated the ethical and social demands from Resolution n. 196/96, with emphasis on the detailing on the development of such researches, even warning against their accomplishment in communities with isolated indigenous populations, that is, those «individuals or groups who avoid or are not in touch with the involving society.» (II, 3). Otherwise, the research with indigenous subjects is not prohibited. In accordance with the Resolution, when it is for the development of researches in isolated indigenous communities, it is necessary to present detailed justifications (III, 3), besides, obviously the respect for the social and autonomy restraints of each of the assessed individuals and community.

Whatever it is the research involving the Indian and his community, it is required respect for his view of the world, customs, aesthetical attitudes, religious beliefs, social organization, peculiar philosophies, linguistic differences and political structure (III. 2.1); not accepting the physical, mental, psychological, or intellectual and social exploitation of the subjects involved in the research (III. 2.2); not accepting situations which put the social, mental and physical welfare and the integrity in risk (III, 2.3); the assurance of the equality of the interests involved, taking the involved subjects' vulnerability into account (III, 2.4); besides the informed consent which results from the research's targeted community agreement which can be obtained through their respective indigenous organizations or local councils, without the exclusion of the individual consent.

It must be highlighted Resolution 304/2000's permanent concern on the fact the consent is not only the indigenous subject adscript, while individual subject, but to his community involvement. The first contact and the first authorization are made with the community, then just later it is turned individually to the indigenous subject.

Resolution 304/2000 foresees that it is not allowed the formation of Banks of biological material collected from indigenous populations without the express agreement of the community involved, besides the prior detailed presentation of the purpose in the research protocol to be submitted to the Ethics Committee in Research and to the Ethics National Committee in Research, besides the formal approval of these agencies' express agreement (III, 5). This resolution holds specific norms about the national and international exchange of information. Concerning further points about which there is omission, it is applied what is disposed in Resolution 196.

Thus, it is noticed that, being capable subjects or integrated in groups whose vulnerability is the target of regulatory guardianship the research standing to sue comes from the frankness through which the informed consent is obtained, which shall be free and clear, essential for the research accomplishment.

The Resolution 196 determines that any research involving human beings shall be submitted to the examination of an Ethics Committee in Research. Such committee shall be composed by the researcher institution and if it is impossible to constitute such committee, the institution or the researcher responsible shall submit the project to another institution's CEP examination. It still disposes that in the cases when the research has as object indigenous populations, it is necessary the participation of a consultant acquainted with the communities customs and traditions (VII.7 Res. 196/96), in order to allow that such community participates in the research, but has their own cultural integrity preserved.

2.12. – *Maintenance : security standards, storage lengths*

According to Resolution 347/2005 of National Council of Health, the biological samples will be stored under the Institutional researcher's responsibility, which must have rules or regulations approved by CEP. It must include: a) definition of responsibility on storage and autorization of samples usage (2.1), b) mechanisms of secrecy and confidenciality assurance («codificação») (2.2), c) mechanisms to provide sharing of informational interests with donors or to obtain specific consent for new research appliance (2.3).

The biological samples storage will be authorized for a period of 5 years, if there is a project approval by CEP or CONEP, in specific cases. Renewal can be granted by means of institutional keeper request, based on presented report justifying further development of bio-material research activities extention and description (3).

2.13. – *National and international transfer and circulation of samples*

The Resolution n. 347/2005 determines that, in case there is forecast of future use of biological material in other researches, there shall be suitable justification and the donor's consent, holding the express authorization for the material guardianship (items 1, 1.1 e 1.2). It still establishes that the Project shall contain declaration that the new research will be submitted to the institution's CEP and CONEP, the latter, when it is the case (item 1.3).

The Resolution n. 196/1996 does not forecast any disposition about the national and international Exchange of information.

The Resolution n. 340/2004 states to be possible the Exchange of information and, being them international, the opportunities of technology shall be recorded. (IV.1, m).

The Resolution n. 347/2005 foresees the possibility of Exchange of the samples Exchange national and internationally wide. In the former case, it is necessary the agreement among institutions, explaining ways of operation and use of the stored material. For the international Exchange, besides the agreement, the legislation in force for the delivery of material abroad shall be obeyed and the regulation shall be presented for the CEP's analysis, referring to the procedures relating to point two above cited (item 5).

In this Exchange, the researcher and the Brazilian institution are considered as the quotaholders of the foreign bank, having right of direct Access to the material for future researches. This means that the stored material will not be exclusive property of the depositary institution or country (item 5.1).

2.14. – *Property rights*

There is no information about this issue.

2.15. – *Other issues*

There are no further comments in this epigraph.

2.16. – *Final comments, conclusions, other reflections, etc.*

For the conclusion of the present report, we have opted for two recurring issues which cause us concern when it comes to the researches situation in Brazil, and specifically in relation to the Genetic Samples Banks. They are the lack of control on the creation of Biobanks and their work; the aspects which shall be written in the Clear and Free Consent Terms.

At first, despite the clear absence of specific legislation, we could apparently defend the Idea that the National Council of Health's Resolutions become the capable means to regulate the researches and solve the their consequent impasses.

However, such problems are not as simple as they may seem. In a recent contact with the Executive Agency of the Ethics National Committee in Research, from the National Council of Health, Ministry of Health, we required information about the number of biological samples Banks filed or authorized by CONEP, besides the fact that we wanted to know which ones they would be. The reply meant that our demand extrapolated the public data CONEP's Executive Agency had.

According to the Agency herein, the regulating statute for the storage of biological material shall be authorized by the Institutions' Ethics Councils in Research (item 2 from Resolution CNS 347/05) and not by the Ethics National Committee in Research – CONEP.

Such assertion has caused us perplexity, as it showed the evidence of the lack of control of the national agency in face of the several banks of human biological samples which may appear in Brazil. There are no mechanisms of filing these banks in Brazil. In summary, the biobank shall be created by the researcher institution and its operations will be submitted to the own institution's Ethics Committee in Research itself, being able to be approved by CONEP, when it applies (art. 1.3 of Res. 347/2005). In face of the absolute lack of control of the national agency it is imperative to think about the creation of filing and biobanks control mechanisms by each country's National Committees of Ethics in Research.

Another aspect which deserves to be included as conclusion is the Clear and Free Consent Term which aims at obtaining the necessary consent from the research's subject for the preservation of the several possibilities resulting from the research. We are aware of the population differences and ethnical groups of each country, many of them considered as being vulnerable, and who bring distinct inquiries to each of the Latinbanks Project's participant.

This is the issue. Resolution CNS 196/96, no Item IV.1, determines that the information given to the research's subjects is made through an accessible language and that it includes other aspects, as follows:

a) The justification, the objectives and the procedures which will be used in the research;

b) The expected benefits, the possible constraints and risks;

c) The existing alternative methods;

d) The follow-up and assistance method, as well as their responsible staff;

e) The assurance of the elucidations, before and during the course of the research, about the methodology, informing the possibility of inclusion in a control group or placebo;

f) The subject's freedom to refuse to participate or withdraw his consent, at any phase of the research, under no penalty or loss of his care;

g) The assurance of the secrecy which ensures the subjects' privacy concerning the confidential data involved in the research;

h) The ways of compensation of the expenses resulting from his participation in the research; and

i) The ways of indemnification in face of fortuitous damages resulting from the research.

This way, there is no «model» to be used as template in Brazil, but directives to be followed, taking the particularity of each research into consideration. We highlight the following items in Resolution CNS 347/05, complementary to Resolution CNS 196/1996 :

1) When, in research projects, it is foreseen the storage of human biological materials for future investigations, besides the points foreseen in Resolution CNS n° 196/96, the following shall be presented :

1.2. Consent of the research's subjects who are the donors of the biological material, authorizing the material storage;

6. About the use of the stored samples :

c) Copy of the Clear and Free Consent Term – TCLE – obtained from the research when the material was collected, including the storage and possible future use authorization, if the storage occurred from the approved research after Resolution CNS n° 196/96; and

d) Specific TCLE for a new research : in case of the impossibility of obtaining the specific consent for a new research (dead donor, previous unsuccessful attempts of contact and others) justifications shall be presented as part of the protocol for CEP' s analysis, which may or may not exempt the individual's consent.

In a certain way, we believe it is unfeasible to define previously a consent pattern for these types of research. Each research has its own well outlined objectives, as it can be noticed in the project mentioned in the Brazil's Report. This way, we prefer to sketch the aspects we understand as being necessary for the clear and free consent terms, as reported in Resolutions 196/96 and 347/05, above cited.

Furthermore, differently from the several reported biotechnological researches the biobanks do not refer directly to the human individual while as a whole or part of this human being which have been removed, losing, this way, the integrity Idea, but which continues belonging to his privacy and individuality sphere, what shall be safeguarded and analysed in each concrete case, especially in cases when the collected human biological material remains anonymous.

It can be concluded that, in Brazil, the issues around Banks of human biological samples are stated in a fragile way, beyond the evident insufficiency of public discussions which can legitimate the creation of norms suitable for the access and control of the researches.

LEGAL AND SOCIAL IMPLICATIONS OF CREATING BANKS OF BIOLOGICAL MATERIAL IN CHILE (1)

BY

LORENA DONOSO ABARCA

SUMMARY : 1. The facts : Situation of scientific research with human biological samples and biobanks in Chile. 2. Legal Framework. 2.1. General legislation applicable. 2.2. Specific legislation. 2.3. Reports and opinions by national institutions and bodies. 2.4. Professionals and institutions : quality standards and accreditation requirements. 2.5. Ethics Research Committees. 2.6. Obtaining of samples (invasive intervention in the donor). 2.7. Sample ownership. 2.8. Protection of the subject's privacy (duty of confidentiality and security of data and sample archives). 2.9. Extent of the consent (generic or specific). 2.10. Use of samples obtained for another purpose. 2.11. Specifically issues related with local communities. 2.12. Maintenance : security standards, storage lengths. 2.13. National and international transfer and circulation of samples. 2.13.1. National and international transfer and circulation of samples. 2.13.2. National and International Exchange. 2.14. Property rights. 2.15. Other issues. 2.16. Final comments, conclusions, other reflections, etc.

1. – THE FACTS :
SITUATION OF SCIENTIFIC RESEARCH WITH HUMAN BIOLOGICAL SAMPLES AND BIOBANKS IN CHILE

In the few references we have found to Biobanks in Chile, the concept of Biobanks has been used in terms of Spanish legislation, and they have consequently been referred to as *«non-profit public or private establishments for the collection of biological samples, conceived for the purpose of biomedical diagnosis or research and organised as a technical unit with criteria regarding quality, order and*

---

(1) Acknowledgements : Thanks to Professor Carlos Romeo Casabona and his team for allowing us to participate in the research despite difficulties with local communication.

use» (2). Similarly, the importance of furthering development has been recognised, especially towards *in vitro* research, in support of the development of specific drugs for the treatment of illnesses that may have high incidences in Chile and have not got a high impact on an international level (3).

In any case, it has been warned that the mass storage of biological samples raises complex technical concerns which affect the collection of the sample itself, its transport, identification, traceability, conservation at different temperatures, recovery from storage systems, handling of electronic data, etc. Furthermore, the importance of establishing and implementing quality management systems, both at a public and private level, has been recognised and has been the subject of some legislative development.

In order to learn about the operation of the biological material sample banks in Chile we carried out some studies based on the analysis of *in vitro* samples found (4), such as «*Immortalised Neurons. Instituto de Ciencias Biomédicas [Institute of Biomedical Sciences] (ICBM). Dr. Pablo Caviedes and co-workers*» (5).

With regard to the social and economic impact of Biobanks in Chile, we have warned that Biobanks in Chile have come to attention in three specific areas, namely: a) innovative strategies; b) public policies on prevention, diagnosis and treatment of illnesses which may have some genetic basis; and c) the need to identify people within the framework of legal research.

Another social implication of the development of this matter relates to the innovative strategies, in so far as Chile's inclusion as

---

(2) See the informative note on the radio cooperative web site in relation to this http://www.cooperativa.cl/p4_noticias/antialone.html?page = http://www.cooperativa.cl/p4_noticias/site/artic/20060915/pags/20060915112838.html (visit 02.02.2008).

(3) Such is the case, for example, with research into the early detection and treatment of gallbladder cancer, the primary cause of death in Chilean women, which does not reach significant research levels since it does not have the same impact in developed countries.

(4) Such is the case with the study: «Study of synaptogenesis in *in vitro* spinal neurons. Effects of the blocking of electrical and synaptic activity on homoeostatic plasticity», assigned in 2002 by the Comisión Nacional de Ciencia y Tecnología [National Science and Technology Commission], of which Dr. Luis Gerardo Aguayo Hidalgo is the director in charge at the University of Concepción.

(5) Distinctly basic studies by this group gave rise to the production of immortalised cell lines from adult tissue, by means of a patented protocol. The lines retain stable differentiated functions in culture. Many of these lines are models for *in vitro* studies for the pharmaceutical industry (biological trials for new drugs), as well as eventual sources for cellular therapy in various illnesses. Researchers have also generated an industry for producing serums and supplements for the culture of tissue.

a market supplier of global services is sought, within which, on health matters, especially in relation to the possibility of developing a market for clinical processing of samples for scientific aims. In turn, the possibility has been considered, in the area of processes of greater added value (KPO), of including medical services, related to clinical analysis whether at diagnosis or medical treatment monitoring stage and services linked to biotechnology and pharmaceuticals, such as clinical tests and research in drug development, all of which are in the most recent phases of development in Chile.

Chile has received an opportunity in this regard through which it is estimated that it will fulfil various conditions internationally deemed to be materially relevant, such as political and economic stability, adequate human capital for the provision of services in the health sector, reasonable labour costs, good transport and telecommunications infrastructure. Nevertheless, there have been warnings as to the need to advance in the legal framework of handling personal information, which is central to the development of this type of service at a national and international level.

Therefore, from an innovative viewpoint the strategic approach to Biobanks refers to improving the country's competitiveness index in the global services market, by means of the main way of reviewing personal data handling legislation by determining and implementing such corrective measures required so that the legal framework may offer suitable protection to owners of personal data who provide biological samples.

Likewise this point of view entails the drawing up of practices developed within the health related institutions, in terms of the administration of their Biobanks, in pursuit of standardisation and certification of processes in accordance with internationally accepted standards.

Secondly, with regard to *in vitro* health research for preventative purposes or development of drugs, the studies carried out on population groups of specific ethnicity, in which the rules of informed consent are especially significant, not only for those persons involved in the studies, but also those representatives of said originating populations. Such is the case with the creation of a Biobank of blood samples from the indigenous Mapuche population for *in vitro* research purposes, motivated by the low incidence of bronchopulmonary illness in the aforementioned population. This resulted in a social commotion due to the fact that although the scientists in charge sought permission from the donors of the samples, they did not inform the representatives of the indigenous population (the «loncos»), resulting in their rejection based specifically on the need to protect the genetic heritage of the population and the endeavour to agree systems of financial compensation to these communities for the use of their genetic information in medical and/or pharmaceutical research.

Additionally, information has been found on the operation of Biobanks for purposes other than those assumed in the study. We refer to the creation of banks of stem cells, the creation of a DNA data bank of persons in the commission of violent crimes and the creation of a DNA bank of relatives of detained-disappeared persons, for whom no remains have been found, however these will not be subject to our analysis.

2. – Legal Framework

2.1. – *General legislation applicable*

In this regard we must point out that Chile has adopted and is part of international treaties on Fundamental Rights and specifically those related to the health sector. In any case, although the international legal framework has been incorporated in general terms, only some specific matters have had specific regulatory developments required for the actual application of this legislation at a national level.

In all cases, pursuant to Article 5 of the Political constitution of the Republic of Chile, international human rights treaties underwritten and subscribed to by Chile are applicable even where no specific legislation has been determined (6).

In general, we understand that general legislation on fundamental rights, especially freedom, the right to life, health and privacy generally applies to Biobanks in Chile. In turn the regulations on handling personal health information apply to more specific mat-

---

(6) Article 5 Sec.2 CPR 1980: The exercise of sovereignty recognises, without limit, the respect of essential rights arising from human nature. State bodies are duty bound to respect and promote such rights which are guaranteed by the Constitution, as well as current international treaties ratified by Chile.

ters, within which we can draw special mention to the handling of personal information related to biological samples as well as support of information relative to an identified or identifiable natural person. In addition, the Health Code and a number of executive decrees and resolutions, be these at a centralised or regional level, are applicable to this issue.

A primary need in this regard is that legislation is not consolidated in one regulatory text, the analysis of different regulations of different levels is necessary.

The fundamental regulation on this issue is Article 19 of the Political Constitution of the Republic of Chile, in so far as it establishes, as a fundamental guarantee the right to health (7), primarily in terms that the coordination and management of actions related to health corresponds to the State, including those related to *in vitro* research. Additionally the Constitution establishes respect for the protection of private life as a fundamental guarantee and the honour of the family of the individual (8), which we must consider a basic rule in the regulation of the protection of personal health information, an issue regulated by Law 9.628, which in turn introduces amendments to the Health Code.

It has been generally established in Chile that personal health data is especially protected and is therefore classified as «sensitive information». Therefore, this information may only be used in the manner to which the person has consented or whereby its use is necessary in the determination of health treatment corresponding to the person to whom the data belongs.

Thirdly, the provisions of the Health Code and specific regulations in the area of health are applicable to this issue. The most relevant regulations relate to patient rights, especially protection of

---

(7) Article 19 No.9 CPR 2005. – «The State protects the free and equal access to actions for health promotion, protection and recovery and rehabilitation of the individual.

The coordination and management of health related activities will also correspond to it.

It is the pre-emptive duty of the State to guarantee performance of health actions, be this through public or private institutions, in the manner and under the conditions determined by law, which may establish compulsory contributions.

Every person shall have the right to choose the health system they wish to use, state or private».

(8) Article 19 No.4 CPR 2005.

privacy, informed consent, procedures and regulation of the profession, and shall be analysed in detail later in the corresponding paragraphs.

Another regulation which applies to this issue is Law 20.120, on scientific research on human beings, their Genome, and prohibiting human cloning of September 22, 2006. This law filled a sensitive void in terms of the regulation of research. Among its principal regulations are those relating to the need to have prior authorisation for research, granted by a hospital or administrative authority subject to approval by ethics committees specially regulated by law, which until then had only been subject to statutory regulation (9).

The Law stipulates that a specific breach shall result from failure to comply with the Article 20 requirement for authorisation, which provides that carrying out a biomedical research project on human beings or their genome without the corresponding authorisation required by the aforementioned Law and those carrying out such activities «*shall be sanctioned with a three year suspension from professional practice and full national expulsion from professional practice in the event of repeated violations*».

Additionally, the law establishes the basis for informed consent, regulating in general the requirements for Consent, the levels of information and procedures for attaining information.

The law also recognises the need to consider the ethnic-cultural factor in scientific and genomic research. Law 20.120 specifically developed a person's right to freedom and privacy, in terms of genomic information which can be obtained through scientific and biotechnological research.

Other issues regulated at a statutory level regarding taking, conserving and the eventual use of samples, one of the primary concerns for the regulator being the establishment of rules and protocols regarding the management of hospital waste in general and the final destination of biological materials in specific.

---

(9) The final section of Article 10 stipulates that «All biomedical scientific research must have the express authorisation of the director of the establishment in which it shall be carried out, subject to approval by the corresponding Scientific Ethics Committee, pursuant to regulations».

Other regulated issues are the therapeutic equivalence of pharmaceutical products in Chile, regulated by Exempt Resolution (10) No. 727/05, Published in the Official State Bulletin on November 29, 2005, supplemented by Exempt Resolution No. 159/06, published in the Official State Bulletin on June 8, 2006. This regulation requires that «studies to establish therapeutic equivalence, both 'in vivo' and 'in vitro', will be presented to the Institute of Public Health for approval. In all cases, if this authority rejects a study it must do so by means of a substantiated resolution.»

In so far as we are interested, Study to establish therapeutic equivalence is defined as «*Comparative – clinical, bioavailable or 'in vitro' pharmacodynamic study – between a reference pharmaceutical product and a test product*». Dissolution kinetic studies are defined as «*'in vitro' tests that, under scientifically defined experimental conditions, permit the establishment of a kinetic dissolution profile of an active agent from a solid pharmaceutical form*». Finally, Bioexemption is defined as «*the prerogative of the regulating authority to be exempt from the duty to have to present in vivo studies for the establishment of therapeutic equivalence, which may be demonstrated by means of in vitro studies*».

The regulation also governs, in general terms, the selection criteria for sample participants and establishes the parameters which must be considered in the sample labelling system, which are: age, sex, state of health.

With regard to the experimental conditions of the *in vitro* dissolution kinetic study, «*these must be established in an appropriate manner, selecting the best conditions in order to obtain a suitable differentiator, a prediction of the in vivo behaviour and a possible in vivo-in vitro correlation*».

2.2. – Specific legislation

No specific legislation in Chile.

---

(10) The scope of application of the regulation is defined in the following terms: «*This Regulation is binding in all national territory with regard in vivo or in vitro studies to demonstrate, where applicable, the therapeutic equivalence of products from multiple sources formulated with any of the active principals from the lists approved by the Resolution by the Ministry of Health.*»

2.3. – Reports and opinions
by national institutions and bodies

In the course of the research various professional ethics codes were found in relation to health research, including those involving the taking of biological samples with which we are concerned. These stand out mainly due to the fact that they regulate the issue of «informed consent» for persons who are the source of the data.

Regarding research, the National Science and Technology Commission requires that research projects involving the management of biological samples be subject to ethics committees. Similarly, the document «perspectives on informed consent» (11) has been drafted, which indicates, in the case at hand, that people must be informed in simple and «layman» terms as to what type of biological samples will be taken, what amount of fluids will be extracted, what the purpose of the samples will be and the security measures that will be adopted to guarantee confidentiality. They should also be informed as to the destination of the excess quantities of extracted biological samples and as to the possible personal risks involved in participating in the study.

This document also provides that the samples may only be used for those studies for which the person has consented to and in order to use these in other studies consent must be sought again. In the event that it is not possible to locate the person again, a request must be made to the ethics committee for a decision.

With regard to matters of informed consent, the Health Minister agrees to the Recommendations on informed consent by the World Health Organisation.

It is important to highlight the work carried out by Doctor Fernando Lolas as compiler, who records the principal research related ethical regulations. An electronic copy of this work is attached for analysis by network members.

This work comprises a systematization of the ethics regulations in health research. In so far as we are interested it deals with the need for research to be based on protocols previously approved by the ethics committees established previously, which clearly establish the clinical parameters, establishing, among others, the type of

---

(11) http://www.fondecyt.cl/comite_bioetica/consentimiento_informado.pdf [02.11.2007].

samples to be extracted, the methods to be employed in doing so and what measures shall be taken to minimise the risks associated with the extraction of the samples. Similarly the destination of the samples when the studies have been carried out should be considered, as well as the clinical files associated with each of the samples obtained.

With regard to the conservation of the samples, it is generally considered that upon completion of the study samples need not be conserved and, in any case, it should be established in the information protocol to the source subject of the sample, the records required for the purpose of consenting to possible conservation. This material must also be the subject of a general research protocol.

In the case that samples are conserved, the protocol should indicate the conservation methods and associated security measures.

With regard to informed consent, this manual refers to the ethical and legislative standards recognised at an international level, making them applicable in Chile.

Additionally, in the doctrine contributions of interest to us have been made with regard to the generally accepted practices in the management of biological waste and may be outlined as follows (12) :

– I. – Sharps or glass waste management : This issue is of interest to us in that this type of material often serves as means for collection and analysis of the samples. On this subject, the practices detected indicate that, in general, sharps and glass material (independent of whether or not these are the means by which a medical sample has been deposited for any purpose), must be deposited in puncture resistant containers (drums or thick cardboard boxes), duly identified, separated from regular waste and located in the health centre clinical waste area. These must then be removed on specific days of the week, avoiding compression of the

---

(12) Dr. Alberto Fica C.; E.U. Gloria Ruiz, CIIH.; Mr. Yunes Ali, Logistical Support Manager. Hospital Waste Management Regulations. Draft or review date: October, 2000. Date approved by Intra-hospital Infection Committee (IIH): October, 2000. In the same way, the Joint Position of the Chilean Society for the Control of infections and hospital epidemiology and the Chilean Society for infectious diseases, available in electronic format at http://www.cepis.ops-oms.org/cursoreas/e/fulltext/desechos.pdf [visit : 03.05 2010].

boxes. It is planned that they will be brought to a health waste site in special containers.

– II. – Microbiological waste management: It is also generally planned that as this waste originates from the Microbiology Laboratory and the Immunology Laboratory, they may be: disposed as solid waste if the material is reused; or disposed as solid waste and incinerated prior to their elimination, if these are disposable.

– III. – Management of histological waste (Pathological Anatomy, biopsies, others): Bodies and body parts must be handled with standard (gloves, masks, eye protection and waterproof apron).

Anatomical remains from the Centre, biopsies, maternity and bags from the blood bank must be transported in resistant and waterproof containers until they arrive at the external incineration site, in accordance with current regulations. This is due to legal and cultural reasons and not because they pose greater risk of infection.

The collectors for bodily fluids from the Centre must be eliminated separately from the regular waste. They must not be compacted and will be sent to a health refuse site along with the sharps material.

2.4. – *Professionals and institutions: quality standards and accreditation requirements*

The health sector is a regulated profession in Chile. Law 20.120 requires that personnel who take part in research work involving human beings must comply with the conditions for qualified professionals (Article 10 (13)).

Qualification is regulated in the different General Requirement Guidelines for the operation of laboratories, among which mention should be made of PAS 14 Blood Donation Centre Requirements Guidelines, 2007, by the Ministry of Health, PAS *11, Requirement Guidelines for Pathological Anatomy units, December 2007,* PAS 12 Clinical Laboratory Requirement Guidelines, issued by the Ministry of Health, December 2007, which specify the work and the personnel authorised to work in clinical laboratories, which is the place of preference for taking samples for biomedical research. By combin-

---

(13) Article 10 section 1 provides that «*All scientific research on human beings which involves any type of physical or psychic intervention must always be carried out by qualified professionals in the area, justified in objective and methodology and in line with the law.*»

ing these two references we can learn, who the authorised personnel for carrying out medical research are.

With regard to the operation of the laboratories in Chile, the Official Chilean Standard NCh-ISO17025 of 2001 is of importance, «*Requisitos generales para la competencia de los laboratorios de ensayo y calibración*», «General requirements for the competence of testing and calibration laboratories», Standard declared Official in the Republic of Chile by Exempt Resolution No 529, of December 28, 2001, Ministry for the Economy, Development and Reconstruction, published in the Official State Bulletin on January 22, 2002.

Regarding the certification of personnel to be in charge of taking samples we rely on Decree 1704 of 1993, the paragraph which appears to be of most significance to the work they carry out and provide authorisation to be carried out, the most relevant to us is the part referring to transport of examination samples, this is the official authorised by the Ministry of Health for the exchange of samples between laboratories or banks, for which we now have a regulation, despite the fact that it does not have the status of a law, in which significant reference is made to biobanks, namely the exchange of samples between health institutions.

Decree 1704 of 1993, from the Ministry of Health, ratifies the Regulation for the exercise of auxiliary professions in medicine, dental medicine, chemistry and pharmacy indicated.

Article 3 of the regulation provides that: «*Auxiliary Radiology, Radiotherapy, Laboratory and Blood Bank Paramedic shall be interpreted as the person qualified by means of a training course regulated by the Ministry of Health to carry out the functions attributed to them in accordance with regulations, in the areas of Radiology, Radiotherapy, Laboratory and Blood Banks, under the direct supervision of a corresponding professional.*

In the performance of their work, they shall have the following functions:

1. To collaborate with professionals in charge in the execution of radiological, imaging, radio therapeutic and/or laboratory examinations in haematology, biochemistry, microbiology, parasitology and blood banks for the purpose of diagnosis, prevention and management of the treatment of hospitalised and emergency room patients.

- *To receive examination orders and verify compliance with current regulations.*
- *To prepare, get the patient up and position the patient as required for examination or treatment.*
- *When required, administer contrast medium to the patient orally.*
- *To collaborate with the professional in the application and monitoring of radiotherapy techniques in outpatient and inpatient care.*
- *To prepare material for carrying out examinations.*
- *To take examination samples in accordance with professional guidelines.*
- *To make daily statistics for the receipt of orders for examinations, transfer of examinations taken and delivery of appropriate results.*

2. *To collaborate with the corresponding professional in the preparation of samples for their processing, analysis and the corresponding results.*

- *To receive samples in accordance with regulations and procedures.*
- *To handle, conserve and transport examination samples in accordance with biosafety and quality control regulations and procedures.*
- *To carry out technical preparation of samples for processing in accordance with established regulations.*
- *To manage centrifuging, staining, culture, preparation of stool or other samples for direct live observation, preparation of serological samples, preparation of biological liquids, manual and automated pipetting, sterilisation, general weighing and measuring of volume, developing films, loading and unloading of chassis and others.*
- *To apply and comply with regulations on the prevention and control of intra-hospital infections, both in the execution of procedures, management of materials, organic or inorganic waste and the maintenance of the place of work.*

3. *To collaborate with the professional in charge in the preparation of material for use in the processing of examinations.*

- *To prepare, label, sterilise, order and store culture resources.*
- *To collaborate in the preparation of reagents and other materials.*
- *To prepare equipment and supplies for taking corresponding examinations.*
- *To receive and/or recover, prepare, store and distribute tubes and vials used daily for taking samples.*

4. To collaborate with professionals in charge in educational activities regarding the importance of timely examinations in order to comply with medical guidelines.

– To inform the user or relatives about the preparation, their collaboration and care prior to the radiotherapy examination.

For the purposes of being able to carry out this activity the person must have obtained a professional degree, granted by «*Technical Training Centres, Professional Technical Schools or institutions authorised by the Ministry of Health to provide such education in accordance with the set schedule of 1,600 hours for 1 academic year, 40% of which shall be theory and 60% practical*» (Art. 6) and «*At the end of their training period, in the event that it has been provided by an authorised institution, the interested party must sit a theory and practical competence exam before a commission designated by the Director of the Health Service, a representative of the Deputy Medical Director of the Health Service, a professional specialising in auxiliary training and a professional designated as certifying officer for this purpose*» (Art. 7).

Upon meeting these requirements, by resolution of the respective health service the person shall be authorised to undertake professional activity, which is communicated to all health services in the country.

This seeks to guarantee the qualification of the professional working directly with medical samples.

With regard to suitable places to carry out both *in vivo* and *in vitro* therapeutic equivalence tests, the Technical Regulation which defines the criteria for establishing therapeutic equivalences for pharmaceutical products in Chile, EXEMPT. RESOLUTION (14) No. 727/05, Published in the Official State Bulletin on 29.11.05 and supplemented by : Exempt Resolution No. 159/06, published in the Official State Bulletin on June 8th, 2006 establishes that these should take place «*in laboratories authorised by the Public Health Institute or at WHO recognised centres, the European Agency, EMEA, the Food and Drug Administration, FDA, the Directorate General of Medicines of the Ministry of Health of Canada, The Span-*

---

(14) The scope of application of the regulation is defined in the following terms : «*This Regulation is binding in all national territory with regard in vivo or in vitro studies to demonstrate, where applicable, the therapeutic equivalence of products from multiple sources formulated with any of the active principals from the lists approved by the Resolution by the Ministry of Health.*»

ish Medicines Agency of the Ministry of Health and Consumers, the Japanese National Health Science Institute, the Medicine Control Agency (MCA) in the United Kingdom, the Medical Products Agency (MPA) in Sweden, the Swiss Medical Products Agency (Swiss Medic)».

In accordance with this regulation, the studies it regulates must be carried out according to a written protocol, previously approved by the corresponding Ministry of Health Scientific Ethics Evaluation Committees for the area. Should this organisation not exist in a specific city, ad hoc committees will have to be constituted for the purpose of analysing the protocol conditions.

With regard to the installations, it is provided that *«the infrastructure and the human resources and materials must allow for certification that the institution complies with the basic requirements for undertaking the proposed study and that the site where the study will take place is adequate for the safe and efficient undertaking of the study».* Furthermore *«areas must be available for the storage of biological liquids which guarantee stability, safety, absence of contaminants and limited access».*

2.5. – Ethics Research Committees

Initially ethics committees are regulated in Chile by means of a Permanent Internal Technical Directive from the Ministry of Health (DPTI No. 10, on Ethics Committees), however, a more formal regulation may be found in Exempt Resolution 134 of 1994, from the same Ministry, which was later amended by Exempt Resolution No. 1856 of 1999, from the same State Ministry.

This regulation signifies that these committees are established in order to «learn of and declare the ethical, moral or legal application of medical actions and specific research projects». They are established as multidisciplinary groups of health professionals who fulfil the function of resolving ethical dilemmas which may arise with specific research projects. The regulation provides that there are ethics committees in the main health establishments in the country, in addition to an ethics committee in the Ministry of Health, basically devoted to advising the relevant Minister on the evaluation of the reports and/or records from the medical ethics committees of the Health Services and on the drafting of policies and general regulations as required.

With regard to their duties related to scientific research, regulations provide that «the directors of hospital services will be duty bound to request the decision of the respective Medical Ethics Committees, for the approval and execution of any research project corresponding to their scope».

Additionally, the regulation stipulates that in those instances related to a research protocol comprising the scope of 3 or more health services or when it involves general research, of interest to national health policies, the Ministry of Health may be requested to establish an ad hoc Ethics Committee, comprised of one or two representatives of the Ethics Committees of each of the services involved, as well as a lawyer and a bioethics expert assigned by the Ministry of Health.

As we have seen in the analysis of the law 20.10, of 2006, the lack of such authorisation constitutes a breach, punishable by fine.

Law 20.120 creates the National Bioethics Commission, which pursuant to Article 15, «*shall be comprised of nine professionals, experts in bioethics, designated by the President of the Republic, in accordance with the Senate adopted by two thirds of its members present, in a special sitting convened for this purpose*».

Pursuant to Article 16 of the law, the function of the commission is «*to advise the different State Powers on matters of ethics which arise as a result of scientific and technological advances in biomedicine, as well as on matters regarding biomedical scientific research on human beings, recommending the promulgation, amendment or withdrawal of regulations it governs*».

As regards the manner in which it should act, the law is clear that it should first tend to the patient's well-being, then the good of the health team and lastly the prestige of the establishment and the respective service. In its decisions it must consider the patient's clinical records, the informed opinion of the patient where appropriate and the current national regulations on the issue and existing international recommendations.

Regulations require that the research team submits the following information to the respective ethics committee, in order that it may adopt a decision:

a) Precise statement of research objectives.

b) Clear and sufficient information on the current level of knowledge of the issue to be addressed.

c) Justification of the need to use human subjects.

d) A precise list of the proposed intervention actions, defining the duration of the experience.

e) A statistical plan.

f) A precise definition of the criteria that will determine suspension of the research.

g) Precise criteria for the intake and discharge of human subjects, subject to the research.

h) Submission of information on the safety of the medicines and devices or techniques to be used, supported by prior laboratory or animal experiments.

i) An expression of the gains versus the potential risks to which participating subjects are subjected.

j) A clear expression of the measures proposed to obtain informed consent.

k) Due protection of the participating subjects where these are voluntary, including a Sworn Statement which disclaims liability for the Health Service.

l) Records guaranteeing position as a researcher, certifying or accrediting that they have sufficient installations and resources to carry out the research.

m) Guarantee of confidential management of data.

n) In cases of research in communities, the appropriate information must be submitted to the regional and community authorities service the communities in question.

It is important to highlight that the regulation further recognises that in Chile health practices are regulated by the following ethical guidelines:

a) The Declaration of Geneva, by the World Medical Association (Geneva. 1948; Sydney 1968).

b) International Code of Medical Ethics. (III General Assembly of the World Medical Association at London in October 1949. Amended by the 22nd World Medical Assembly Sydney, 1968; and the 35th World Medical Assembly Venice, 1983).

c) Code for Nurses, ethical concepts applied to nursing (International Council of Nurses, May, 1973).

d) Declaration of Helsinki. Recommendations as a guide to doctors in biomedical research on human beings. (18th World /medical Assembly, Helsinki, 1964. Revised by the 22nd World Medical Assembly, Tokyo, 1965; and amended by the 35th World Medical Assembly Venice, 1983; and the 41st World Medical Assembly, Honk Kong, 1989).

e) Declaration of Lisbon. Patient rights. (Adopted by the 34th World /medical Assembly, Lisbon, 1981).

f) Patient's Bill of Rights. (American Hospitals Association, 1973).

g) Recommendation regarding on the rights of the sick and dying (adopted by the Parliamentary Assembly of the Council of Europe, in the 27th Ordinary Session, 1976).

h) Declaration of ethics in medicine by the Latin-American Association of National Medical Academies (ALANAM). (Ratified by the Latin-American Advisory Committee, Quito, 1973).

i) Code of ethics of the Chile Medical Association.

2.6. – *Obtaining of samples (invasive intervention in the donor)*

Article 10 section two of Law 20.120 establishes the principle of protection of the individual in the following terms: «*Scientific research may not take place if there is information which implies that there is a risk of destruction, death or severe and lasting bodily injury for a human being*». We understand that the regulation does not refer to competency of the proceedings or personnel, because these matters are dealt with specifically by other legal regulations. As such, we understand that this paragraph will incorporate into our legislation the provisions of UNESCO.

Currently, in general terms, with regard to persons who may be sources for specific research samples, Exempt Resolution (15) No. 727/05, Official State Bulletin, November 29, 2005, supplemented

---

(15) The scope of application of the regulation is defined in the following terms: «*This Regulation is binding in all national territory with regard in vivo or in vitro studies to demonstrate, where applicable, the therapeutic equivalence of products from multiple sources formulated with any of the active principals from the lists approved by the Resolution by the Ministry of Health.*»

by Exempt Resolution No. 159/06, Official State Bulletin, June 8th, 2006 requires that the population involved in the taking of sample must be the as homogeneous as possible and clear inclusion and/or exclusion criteria for subjects in the study must be established. Regarding each of the subjects, the samples must be labelled in accordance with the following parameters: age, sex, state of health.

The Ministry of Health has issued a guide which must be implemented by the health institutions on matters of taking and conserving biological samples (16). It is a VETA guide «Guide of Systems for Surveillance of Food borne Diseases (VETA) and the Research of outbreaks». This regulation refers to the suitable tools for the collection of samples and for their conservation, divided according to the type of samples, biological materials involved and the investigative framework in which it takes place.

By way of example, in order to take samples of skin lesions, such as boils, abscesses, general secretions, (mainly on the arms, hands, fingers, neck and face), in the framework of staphylococci research, the following procedure is available for collection of samples:

«*1. Clean the skin with a physiological solution or mild disinfectant to avoid contamination by saprophytic germs.*

2. Put pressure on the lesion using sterile gauzes and collect the sample with a swab, trying to collect as much of the secretion as possible.

3. If the lesion is closed, disinfect the skin and squeeze with a sterile syringe.»

In terms of the conservation and transport of the sample the following is provided:

«*If it is not possible to send it immediately to the laboratory, place the swab or material collected with a syringe in a sterile tube or vessel for transport.*

In the event that it is not possible to send the sample within 24 hours, place in a container with ice, until delivery to the laboratory.»

---

(16) http://epi.minsal.cl/epi/html/software/guias/VETA/E/anexo_c.htm, an integral part of the Virtual Library on Health – Food Safety (http://www.inppaz.org.ar/), coordinated by INPPAZ PAHO/WHO, in the context of the Regional Virtual Health Library project (http://www.bireme.br/) promoted by the OPS through the Latin-American and Caribbean Centre for Information on Health Sciences, BIREME PAHO/WHO. [02.11.2007].

Similarly, we have found a manual on the collection of samples, from the Ministry of Health, Los Lagos in the 10th Region of Chile, Valdivia Health Service, Hospital Base Valdivia (17). This documents deals in detail with both the collection and the conservation of biological samples, in the framework of diagnosis and treatment of patients, with the aim of avoiding personnel involved in the handling of samples getting into a situation whereby they would be at risk of intravenous contamination.

An element, which at this stage of research must be highlighted, is that this document defines the following type of fluids:

«BODILY FLUIDS: Bodily fluid shall be interpreted as all secretions or biological, physiological or pathological liquids produced by an organism: blood, urine, stools, tears, saliva, semen, bronchial secretions, secretions from wounds, optical, nasal and pharyngeal secretions, vaginal secretions, urethral secretions, CSF, pleural liquid, ascitic fluid, articular liquid, amniotic fluid, among others.

HIGH RISK BODILY FLUIDS: This always applies to blood and all other fluids which contain visible blood. The following are also included: semen, vaginal secretions, breast milk and those liquids from normally sterile cavities such as: cerebrospinial fluid, synovial fluid, peritoneal fluid, pericardial fluid and amniotic fluid. These are deemed high risk due to the fact that they are an infection source of the hepatitis B and HIV viruses and other intravenously transmitted agents.

LOW RISK BODILY FLUIDS: This applies to stools, nasal secretions, expectoration, perspiration, tears, urine or vomit, with the exception of those which visibly contain blood. *It must be considered that although these fluids do not present a source of infection for the hepatitis B and HIV viruses and other agents which may be transmitted intravenously, there is a risk that they may transfer bacterial infections upon contact with the skin or mucus membrane of the operator.*»

In each of these cases the collection, custody and treatment procedure is regulated.

---

(17) www.ssvaldivia.cl/hospital/acredita/normas/Manual.doc.

In addition to the aforementioned, the Medical-Legal Institute keeps a «*Record for the collection of samples for laboratory examinations and the start of the chain of custody*». This record refers to the source of the biological material, which in this case may not necessarily be the body of the directly affected individual, it may be from clothing or other objects with which they have come into contact. With regard to the chain of custody, this relates to a delivery/receipt record of the biological material by the various agents who come in contact with the samples, whereby they must record the state of the item every time they receive it, the amount of material received/delivered, and the reason for the transfer.

Exempt Resolution (18) No. 727/05, Official State Bulletin, November 29, 2005, supplemented by Exempt Resolution No. 159/06, Official State Bulletin, November 29, 2006.

With regard to the taking of samples, these must be collected «in sufficient numbers and intervals to characterise the dissolution profile of the pharmaceutical product, using at least four sampling periods, not including time zero, and these must be the same for both profiles.

In both products, when 85% dissolution is obtained, one additional sampling point is sufficient."

Then the frequency of sampling is regulated and the sample quantities adopted to achieve a suitable study.

In terms of the handling of samples, regulation provides as follows:

«*All samples of biological fluid must be treated as potentially dangerous or infectious and be managed according to the applicable biosafety procedures and/or regulations.*

Ideally, the analyst should not know the identity (commercial origin or otherwise) of the analysed products. Samples must be identified and coded in order to safeguard confidentiality.»

In this case, the regulation on taking samples refers to the need to ensure results in relation to the absorption and effects of the

---

(18) The scope of application of the regulation is defined in the following terms: «*This Regulation is binding in all national territory with regard in vivo or in vitro studies to demonstrate, where applicable, the therapeutic equivalence of products from multiple sources formulated with any of the active principals from the lists approved by the Resolution by the Ministry of Health.*»

drugs subject of the analysis. Therefore, the amount of samples, frequency, method and fluids to be analysed are regulated.

Additionally, the regulation deals with the procedure for the transfer of samples as follows: *«the transport of biological samples must take place in accordance with Standard Operating Procedures (SOPs) which considers the type of container, the recording of transport conditions (temperature, humidity and temperature), and the correct identification of the samples»*.

With regard to the receipt, identification, internal distribution, conservation, maintenance, use and storage of samples submitted to analysis must be carried out according to a Standard Operating Procedure (SOP).

The test laboratory must have a documented system for the unequivocal identification of the samples which are to be analysed and ensure that there can be no confusion at any time as to the identity of the samples. Upon receipt, the condition in which the sample is received must be recorded, including any anomaly or deviation from the normal condition (for example, defrosted sample, hemolysate, etc.)

It must be verified that the samples comply with the conditions agreed with the Clinic.

In terms of storage *« The test laboratory must have suitable installations and equipment for the storage of biological samples, appropriate for the quantity of samples and storage conditions required.*

The samples must be stored in conditions which ensure their identification, stability and integrity during their entire period of storage, including the influence of the primary container (possibility of interaction and/or adsorption). The same type of primary container must be used for all samples.

There must be procedures in place for the recording and monitoring of temperature during the period of storage of the samples.

«The test laboratory must have SOPs which address the steps to be followed in handling and storing the biological samples in any eventuality (for example, electrical failures, cleaning services) and for the elimination of biological samples».

There are many manuals on this matter in which patients are informed of the preparatory measures for taking of samples, however they do not explain the internal procedure for treatment or conservation of medical samples.

It is in this way that some studies have been detected on the basis of *in vitro* analysis of biological samples (19), which have procedural manuals, without these referring to these issues.

2.7. – Sample ownership

No provisions regarding this matter.

2.8. – Protection of the subject's privacy
(duty of confidentiality
and security of data and sample archives)

We understand that the biological samples constitute personal data in the sense that these are part of the human body, even when separated from the body they retain codified and non-codified DNA information which is susceptible to being attributed to a determined and/or undetermined person.

Personal data is defined in Chile under Article 2 subsection f) of Law 19.628, of 1999, in the following manner: *«that [information] regarding any information concerning identified or unidentifiable individuals»*. Consequently, the national legislation follows the European concept on personal data and provides as follows:

a) All information: concerns a broad concept, which encompasses images, sounds, even graphology, or physical samples provided in the subject's records.

b) Regarding an individual: Due to the fact that it refers to a quality of personality, directly derived from human dignity, only individuals are subject to personal data protection with legal entities being excluded in Chile.

c) Identified or unidentifiable: Shall be interpreted as personal data susceptible to being linked to a determined or determinable person by means of identification procedures (which may involve various degrees of complexity).

---

(19) Such is the case with the study: «Study of the synaptogenesis in *in vitro* spinal neurons. Effects of the blocking of electrical and synaptic activity on homoeostatic plasticity», assigned in 2002 by the Comisión Nacional de Ciencia y Tecnología [National Science and Technology Commission], of which Dr. Luis Gerardo Aguayo Hidalgo is the director in charge at the University of Concepción.

With regard to health data, in the same Article, under subsection g) of this law sensitive data is defined as *«that personal data referring to physical or moral characteristics of a person or to facts or circumstances of their private or personal life, such as personal habits, racial origin, political ideologies and opinions, religious beliefs or convictions, physical or psychological state of health and sex life»*.

As may be appreciated from the regulation, the listing of sensitive data is not limited, which has presented advantages from the point of view of protection of rights, in that it has permitted the qualification of data as such by means of precedent and according to the specific circumstances surrounding a specific example of data handling. Hence, in so far as we are concerned, we can advise that the legislator considered a priori data which reveals information on the physical or psychic state of health of the person as sensitive. Consequently, the samples collected in the biobanks are not necessarily susceptible to qualifying under this category.

Continuing with our analysis, that personal health data which qualifies as sensitive must be subject to the regulations provided in Article 10 of this law, which provides that: *«Sensitive data may not be handled, except where authorised by law, consent is obtained from the owner or it relates to information required for the determination or granting of health benefits corresponding to the owners.»*

Consequently, in each case legal authorisation must be sought, or (informed) consent provided by the owner of the samples, or it must be accredited that the samples are necessary for the determination or granting of health benefits corresponding to the owners of the samples.

In addition to the above the provisions of Article 11 of Law 19628 is relevant, in so far as it provides that the person in charge of the register or data bank where the personal data is stored prior to recollection must take care for the samples with due diligence and is liable for any damage thereto. This implies the need to implement security measures for the handling of data according to the degree of sensitivity involved. In our opinion biobanks should have security measures of the highest level introduced, in terms of the backup of personal data. On this same aspect, the law provides that persons who work with personal data, both in public and private bodies, are duty bound to keep these confidential when collected from sources not accessible to the public (as is the case at hand) as well as other records related to the data banks, an activity which never stops in this field.

In addition to the above, Article 24 of law 19.628 amended the Health Code, implementing the new Article 27 below : «*Medical prescriptions and clinical laboratory analysis or examinations and health related services are confidential. The content may only be revealed or a copy provided with the express written consent of the patient. Anyone unduly divulging the content or breaching the provisions of the following section shall be punished in the manner and with the penalties established in Chapter Ten.*

The provisions of this Article do not impede pharmacies from revealing the sales of pharmaceutical products of any nature for statistical purposes, including the name and quantity thereof. In no case may the information provided by pharmacies include the names of patients receiving prescriptions or the medications issued to them or any information which may identify them.

Pursuant to this regulation, we estimate that the medical samples may be deemed confidential, based on the fact that the phrase «*health related services*», is sufficiently generic to deem it so.

2.9. – Extent of the consent
(generic or specific)

Law 20.120 governs informed consent, stating that whosoever offers consent must comply with the following requirements :

I. – In terms of Timing : consent must be provided prior to proceedings and after a change in the terms and conditions of the research, whereby the scientific committee deems that the changes are not minor.

II. – In Terms of the Information that should be Provided, the law requires that appropriate, sufficient and comprehensible information regarding the essential aspects of the research is provided, especially in relation to the objective, benefits, risks and procedures or alternative treatments. Similarly, special attention must be drawn to the right not to authorise the research or to revoke consent at any time, and by any means, without liability, sanction or loss of any benefit.

III. – In Terms of the Manner : the law requires that consent consists of a document signed by the person consenting to the research, by the corresponding research director and the director of the centre or establishment where the research shall take place, who, shall also act as certifying officer.

Pursuant to Article 19 of the law, the omission, altering and/or falsification of the informed consent document is punishable by law under the following terms:

I. – Omission or Blatantly Incomplete Preparation of the Document: fine of 10 to 20 monthly tax units (20).

II. – Falsification or Malicious False use of the Document: Minimum length of short-term imprisonment and a fine of 10 to 20 Monthly Tax Units (21).

2.10. – Use of samples obtained for another purpose

According to law 20.120, each time samples are exchanged or there is a change in the principals and/or scope of the research the informed consent of the person who owns the sample or their legal representatives, in the case of children and/or persons unable to provide consent, must be sought again (Art. 10 to 12 law 20.120)

2.11. – Specifically issues related with local communities

In Chile, law 20.120 establishes special regulations for obtaining informed consent, however, these do not refer to obtaining consent from indigenous communities.

Nevertheless, the standard informed consent form by the National Science and Technology Commission requires that the need to distinguish if it is necessary to obtain informed consent according to the customs and/or cultural requirements of the specific community in which the research is to be carried out should be decided on a case by case basis.

This requirement derives from Chile's adoption of the United Nations Declaration on the rights of indigenous populations, in which it confirms as a general principal in Article 19 which provides

---

(20) A Monthly Tax Unit is a unit of adjustability of the Chilean currency (peso), for tax purposes. Its value may be consulted at http://www.utm.cl.

(21) The minimum short-term imprisonment is between 60 and days. This is a sentence which may be paid.

that: «the States shall have consultations and shall cooperate in good faith with indigenous populations through the representative institutions prior to adopting and applying legislative or administrative measures which affect such populations, in order to obtain their prior and informed consent».

2.12. – *Maintenance: security standards, storage lengths*

No comments in this paragraph.

2.13. – *National and international transfer and circulation of samples*

2.13.1. *Transfer of Samples to Other Researchers or Institutions*

According to law 20.120, each time samples are exchanged or there is a change in the principals and/or scope of the research the informed consent of the person who owns the sample or their legal representatives, in the case of children and/or persons unable to provide consent, must be sought again (Art. 10 to 12 law 20.120).

2.13.2. *National and International Exchange*

In Chile this is not regulated, therefore, international exchanges remain subject to international cooperation agreements between researchers who legitimately hold biological samples.

Similarly, having consulted the National Customs Service, it has been confirmed that biological samples are not subject to the customs system as no monetary exchange takes place in the transactions, due to the fact that the samples are free.

2.14. – *Property rights*

There are no specific regulations in Chile with regard to the ownership of body parts and human fluids when separated from the human body as a sample. This leads us to conclude that these samples are subject to the general regulations regarding people (the owners thereof), and consequently they legally remain part of the body. Therefore, the owner shall always be the person from whom they originated. This is independent of the rights which arise for the researcher in so far as they are legitimate holders of the sample.

The reasons that this legal system remains is due to the existence of genetic material which makes anonymity almost impossible and, secondly, because the consequences of the research may affect the persons dignity.

Consequently, with regard to the unnamed samples, we will have to wait for legislative deliberation, however applying the principal of precaution, whilst specific legislation is passed, it will have to be deemed that researchers do not acquire rights of ownership but rather they shall handle the samples as mere holders thereof.

2.15. – *Other issues*

The regulation of Biobanks has been especially difficult in Chile, basically due to the fact that public-private agreements have been achieved for the definition of the make up of the ethics committees which will intervene in their approval and control. This has increased uncertainty for researchers, and has complicated obtaining of information.

2.16. – *Final comments, conclusions, other thoughts, etc.*

– Research on biobanks in Chile has focused on three fundamental areas : a) The Legal System regarding the use of biological samples from human beings in scientific research; b) professional accreditation requirements for those participating in research on human beings; c) Characteristics of informed consent in Chile, generated by the fact that it is a multicultural country wherein there are many indigenous communities.

– An indication is given, in any case, that although a general trend towards the destruction of biological samples obtained upon completion of the health examinations and those obtained for the development of *in vitro* study has been discovered, for which there are no historical sample banks in Chile, some examples of banks of this type of material have been discovered, although they can only be catalogued as collections and do not necessarily apply to the technological concept of biobanks.

- Notwithstanding this, the analysis of some administrative practices developed at laboratory level has been relevant, in respect of which some probing has been carried out as to the experiential function in terms of the protocols established for the collection, handling and destruction of samples, as well as the legal system regulating the personnel working in this type of institution and the application of regulations generally governing health sector institutions.
- A second concern is that Chile has not passed specific regulations governing Biobanks, therefore we had to look to general regulations on medical and pharmaceutical research based on biological samples, handling of personal health data, and generally regarding the function of the health system in Chile and this is what shall be summarised in the following pages.
- Having clarified theses issues, we refer below to the evidence detected regarding the regulation of taking, conserving and handling biological material, in terms of the owner, the purpose and use and the technical procedures followed in handling biological material involved in these activities.
- In this respect we can say that the primary fields in which information has been found are as follows: a) Research linked to epidemiological monitoring; b)Research regarding food risks; c) Research in the pharmaceutical sector or «bioequivalence» studies.
- With regard to regulatory issues, the regulation is systematized both at the administrative and deontological headquarters regarding four fundamental aspects, namely: 1. – Rules regarding handling: designed to avoid contamination of samples on the one hand and the infection of personnel involved in handling the samples on the other; 2. – Rules regarding materials suitable for the conservation of the biological sample; 3. – Ethical rules regarding obtaining and handling biological samples; 4. – Procedural protocols for obtaining results from biological samples, mainly within the framework of a criminal investigation; 5. – Rules regarding the transport and conservation of biological samples; 6. – Rules regarding the treatment of health data.
- Additionally, information has been included on the operation of Biobanks for purposes other than those assumed in the study. We refer to the creation of banks of stem cells, the creation of a DNA

data banks of persons in the commission of violent crimes and the creation of a DNA bank of relatives of detained-disappeared persons, for whom no remains have been found, although these will not be analysed in depth as they are not the focus of our analysis.
– Similarly we will analyse other social consequences of the development of Biobanks in Chile, such as public perception, perception of the authorities, both in regard to health and economy, and the government in general.

LEGAL AND SOCIAL IMPLICATIONS OF CREATING BANKS OF BIOLOGICAL MATERIAL IN COLOMBIA

BY

Emilssen GONZÁLEZ DE CANCINO

Jorge Iván HERRERA MORENO

Carolina FIGUEREDO CARRILLO

AND

Mónica Lizet MORALES NEIRA

Summary : 1. The facts : Situation of scientific research with human biological samples and biobanks in Colombia. 1.1. Scientific Research in Colombia. 1.1.1. University of Antioquia (Medical School). 1.1.2. Pontificia Universidad Javeriana. 1.1.3. Immunology Institute Foundation of Colombia. 1.1.4. National Institute of Legal Medicine and Forensic Sciences. 1.1.5. National Cancerology Institute. 1.1.6. National Health Institute. 1.1.7. Non-University Hospitals. 1.2. De Facto Situation in Colombia. 2. Legal Framework. 2.1. General legislation applicable. 2.2. Specific legislation. 2.3. Reports and opinions by national institutions and bodies. 2.4. Professionals and institutions : quality standards and accreditation requirements. 2.5. Ethics Research Committees. 2.6. Obtaining of samples (invasive intervention in the donor). 2.6.1. From persons. a) Samples stored that have been taken solely and exclusively for biomedical research purposes and effects. b) Samples stored that have been taken as the result of a medical act. c) Samples stored that have been obtained for donation for therapeutic purposes. d) Samples stored that have been taken for judicial investigation purposes and effects. 2.6.2. From corpses. a) Body components of corpses for research purposes when relatives do not come forward. b) Body components of corpses for research purposes when relatives come forward. 2.7. Sample ownership. 2.8. Protection of the subject's privacy (duty of confidentiality and security of data and sample archives). 2.9. Extent of the consent (generic or specific). 2.10. Use of samples obtained for another purpose. 2.11. Specifically issues related with local communities. 2.12. Maintenance : security standards, storage lengths. 2.13. National and international transfer and circulation of samples. 2.14. Property rights. 2.15. Other issues. 2.16. Final comments, conclusions, other reflections, etc.

1. – THE FACTS :
SITUATION OF SCIENTIFIC RESEARCH WITH HUMAN
BIOLOGICAL SAMPLES AND BIOBANKS IN COLOMBIA

1.1. – *Scientific Research in Colombia*

The National Science and Technology System, which was set up under Law 29 of 1990 and developed pursuant to Decree 585 of 1991, was amended recently by Law 1286 of 2009, which changed its name to the National Science, Technology and Innovation System. It is considered to be open because it is made up both of policies, strategies, programmes, methodologies and mechanisms that foster research and innovation and of public, private or mixed organisations which engage in or promote the performance of these types of activities. According to the law, the goals sought by the system are to encourage, foster and consolidate the development of science, technology and innovation as fundamental bases for economic and social development.

Management and coordination are in the hands of the Science, Technology and Innovation Administration Department – Colciencias – which will, in turn, have National Science and Technology Programme Councils, Science, Technology and Innovation Departmental Councils, and the Science, Technology and Innovation Advisory Council.

As guiding body for the System, the Science, Technology and Innovation Administration Department (Colciencias) [1] is responsible for formulating, guiding, directing, coordinating, executing and implementing state policy on scientific and technological research. In view of its administration department legal status, the director of Colciencias will sit on the National Council for Economic and Social Policy (CONPES), and may both speak and vote at its sessions. Pursuant to its functions, Colciencias should foster, coordinate and reinforce scientific, technological and research development; specifically, this goal is to be achieved by creating scientific culture, training researchers, reinforcing scientific and

---

[1] Prior to Law 1286 of 2009, its legal status was that of a public, national establishment attached to the National Planning Department with administrative autonomy and independent equity, and it was called the Francisco José de Caldas Colombian Institute for the Development of Science and Technology (Colciencias). It has now been transformed into an Administration Department, and enshrined in Article 5 in the aforementioned Law 1286 of 2009.

technological capabilities, and drawing up policies on such matters (2).

Every group that engages in research in our country registers the institution it belongs to with Colciencias, together with the research lines declared by the group, the sectors they apply to, the curriculum vitaes of the different members of the group, the projects, and products which result from the research, such as scientific articles, books, seminars, patents, etc.

Now, as far as biobanks are concerned, there is no record of these of any type whatsoever in our country. To carry out the search, therefore, we began by following up on the research groups that are registered with Colciencias, breaking them down by departments (3) and by the subjects of their research projects.

We deduced from the projects that banks or collections of biological samples exist for carrying out the respective research. We are nevertheless not sure whether they perform biobank functions. The vast majority of research topics refer to human genetics, malaria, cancer, the human papilloma virus, and endemic tropical diseases such as dengue and leishmaniasis.

The main promoters of research in Colombia are further education establishments and their hospitals, although a number of private and public institutions and laboratories are also important in this field. The ones we were able to find out about are detailed below.

1.1.1. *University of Antioquia (Medical School)*

This is a public university whose medical school is noted for its experience in scientific research. It has various groups, one of the most outstanding of which is the «Antioquia Neuro-Sciences Group». To carry out its research, the Group formed the first neuro-bank in the country, and this collects and stores biological samples so it can study neurological and neuro-degenerative diseases and neuro-development disturbances. The biological samples that the neuro-bank handles are brain tissue, cerebrospinal fluid, blood com-

---

(2) http://quihicha.colciencias.gov.co/ (Consulted on 18 March 2009).
(3) Regional division of a political-administrative nature.

ponents (plasma and serum) and biopsy material (skin and other organs).

These samples are used in research aimed at understanding brain diseases, so that solutions can be found for treating them, improving the quality of life of sufferers, and, in the best of scenarios, curing them.

The principal diseases researched at the neuro-bank are hereditary and sporadic Alzheimer's disease, attention/hyperactivity deficit disturbance (TDAH), language problems, CADASIL, Huntington, Wilkinson and Parkinson diseases, and ataxias (4).

1.1.2. *Pontificia Universidad Javeriana*

This is a private university whose medical school has a research centre called the Human Genetics Institute. This engages in research, teaching and clinical services in the human genetics field in Colombia (5).

According to information we received from different sources, the human biological material bank closest to the biobank definition proposed for this research is, precisely, that at the Human Genetics Institute, which is run by Dr. Jaime Bernal Villegas. This bank supported the *«Expedición Humana»* Project in 1992, in which around 400 people from different professions and universities were involved and approximately 35 indigenous communities were visited (6).

Its initial aim was to identify the genetic roots of the Amerindian, negro and mestizo races living in Colombia. *«Expedición Humana»* worked in conjunction with the Pontificia Universidad Javeriana Clinical Genetics Unit on categorising proteic polymorphisms and molecular polymorphisms in DNA. The biological material that was gathered from individual persons was processed partly *in situ* and partly in a laboratory in Bogotá. Samples were kept in freezers, although insufficient quantities of this type of organic material are available for studying the molecular markers which

---

(4) www.neurociencias.udea.co (Consulted on 26 October 2007).
(5) www.javeriana.edu.co/Genetica (Consulted last on 2 April 2009).
(6) BERNAL VILLEGAS, Jaime, «Genética y Cultura» (Consulted at www.universia.net.co on 2 April 2009).

define human polymorphism and the genetic bases of these peoples' pathologies either now or in the future.

The samples in the bank were classified in three sections: Serological Bank, Cell Bank and DNA Bank. All samples are available to interested researchers (7). At the time it was set up, this bank received deposits of serum, erythrocytes and leukocytes. Researchers have at their disposal individual classification (RFL or molecular print), sample quality control, and scientific support from the Pontificia Universidad Javeriana Clinical Genetics Unit.

All research processes engaged in at the Institute which involve samples of biological material and Colombian human DNA are governed by internal regulations (8).

1.1.3. *Immunology Institute Foundation of Colombia*

This is run by Dr. Manuel Elkin Patarroyo. It currently has various lines of research, the more notable of which include identifying molecules to be candidates for different vaccinations against transmittable diseases, *in vitro* and *in vivo* studies for selecting those molecules.

The biological samples used in the research come from volunteers. Lymphocytes are obtained from peripheral blood in the manner stipulated by the Institute's Ethics in Research Committee. These samples are not taken until the volunteer has been informed of the aims of the study and told what the samples will be used for. Each volunteer signs the respective informed consent, which is written up by the Institute's Ethics in Research Committee (9).

1.1.4. *National Institute of Legal Medicine and Forensic Sciences*

The National Institute of Legal Medicine and Forensic Sciences is a public, national establishment with its own legal status and equity and full administrative autonomy which belongs to the judicial branch of the public power and is attached to the Public Prosecution Service. Its fundamental mission is to provide technical and

---

(7) GOMEZ, G., Alberto, «El Banco Biológico Humano», *Javeriana Magazine. Christian Thought in Dialogue with the World*, Vol. 118, Bogotá, July 1992, pp. 9-11.

(8) PONTIFICIA UNIVERSIDAD JAVERIANA. Human Genetics Institute, «Regulations governing National and International Research Cooperation with Biological Material and Colombian Human DNA», *Semillas*, No. 10, June 1997, pp. 34 and 35.

(9) www.fidic.org.co (Consulted on 15 August 2007).

scientific support and assistance for the administering of justice throughout the country, in matters relating to legal medicine and forensic science. Not only is it a bone marrow and tissue bank, it also continually coordinates and promotes scientific research (10) and supplies samples for such purposes (11).

The Institute carries out research into genetics and also performs tests to determine genetic profiles for affiliation and individualisation studies of biological samples of human origin by means of «nuclear short tandem repeats (STRs)», using human biological samples such as blood, semen, urine, saliva, hair, bone, dental pulp, soft tissue and epithelium cells (12).

1.1.5. *National Cancerology Institute*

This is a state-owned Social Company whose duties include «advising and supporting the Ministry of Social Protection in the drawing-up, execution, control and evaluation of national policies, plans, programmes and projects relating to cancer research and research into similar diseases» (13). It should also «coordinate, programme and execute clinical, epidemiological and experimental research into preventing and controlling cancer in Colombia».

The aim of the Institute's research policy is to generate the necessary knowledge that will enable the number of cancer cases in the country to be reduced, and to reduce its effects on morbidity, mortality and economic and social costs. The Institute's research lines are cancer load and related factors in Colombia, etiology, molecular and cellular mechanisms, risk control and early detection, cancer diagnosis and treatment in Colombia, oncology services, psychosocial aspects, and political action and cancer (14).

The Institute has records on file of patients diagnosed as suffering from cancer throughout the country, and since it provides med-

---

(10) Law 938 of 2004, Article 33 et seq.
(11) Resolution 0485 of 2002, Article 1 : «*The National Institute of Legal Medicine and Forensic Sciences may, through its Regional or Section Directors, hand over unclaimed corpses and/or body components (organs, tissues, fluids and derivatives thereof) resulting therefrom to further education institutions and scientific, hospital or similar duly-authorised entities which require the same for research or teaching activities...*».
(12) www.medicinalegal.gov.co (Consulted on 27 October 2007).
(13) Decree 1177 of 1999.
(14) www.incancerologia.gov.co (Consulted on 13 April 2009).

ical care and hospitalisation services, it also has a complete bank of samples related to the subject.

The National Cancerology Institute has recently started the necessary procedures for setting up a nationwide tumour bank which will perform all the functions of a biobank.

1.1.6. National Health Institute

The Carlos Finlay Special Studies Institute (15) and the Samper Martínez Laboratory (16) merged in 1962 to form what is today known as the National Health Institute, part of which is a «Virology Group» which acts as a nationwide reference laboratory for diagnosing the HIV infection. It was the first group to isolate this virus in the country, and it also undertook the first studies aimed at measuring the prevalence of AIDS. It consists of several laboratories, in which various pathologies of viral origin are diagnosed and researched, and it has eradication and elimination programmes for diseases like polio and measles. It also acts as a base for watching over diseases which have a big impact on public health, such as yellow fever, dengue, HIV/AIDS, viral hepatitis and rabies. It is also a member of the National Laboratories Network (17).

Samples that are sent to the NHI should be accompanied by a pathological anatomy studies application and all information that might be necessary for guaranteeing the production of records and thus permitting pathological clinical correlation (18).

---

(15) In 1944, the section of the Ministry of Health that did research into yellow fever was given the name Carlos Finlay Special Studies Institute (ICF), in honour of the Cuban scientist. www.col.ops-oms.org (Consulted on 1 July 2008).

(16) The Samper Martínez Laboratory was founded in 1917 with the mission of responding to scientific concerns in health areas of the day by producing rabies vaccine and diphtheria serum and by setting up processes for diagnosing microbe and parasite diseases. www.scielo.org.co (Consulted on 1 July 2008).

(17) Decreto 2323 of 2006, Article 3, Number 10: «The National Laboratories Network is a technical system the aim of which is the functional integration of national reference laboratories, public health laboratories, clinical and other laboratories, and microscope and sampling services, for the performance of public health supervision activities, the rendering of services, quality management and research».

(18) www.ins.gov.co (Consulted on 13 April 2009).

1.1.7. Non-University Hospitals

Health Provider Institutions (IPS) tend to have human biological materials stored, although they act not as banks but as inert collections, which some of them consider to be part of their «scientific heritage» (19).

1.2. – De Facto Situation in Colombia

We pointed out in the first report that no study exists in Colombia into the *de facto* situation as far as human biological material banks for *in vitro* biomedical research are concerned, that neither is there any record or specific regulation governing this, and that in general terms very little is known about their existence and activities. Similarly, no regulation or national doctrine has concerned itself with the legal and ethical aspects of obtaining and storing biological samples and other activities connected with these.

To find more information about these establishments and the activities that go on there with biological samples, we therefore had recourse to the research instrument of the sample.

Those surveyed were, firstly, universities and institutions that are recognised in the country for their scientific research work. Secondly, hospitals that are linked to universities, especially ones with medical schools. And finally, hospitals, clinics and laboratories that are notable for aspects like their level, importance, size, or the fact that they perform some specific activity which in principle implies using human biological samples.

The survey was mailed to 67 of the aforementioned institutions or entities, and by email to a further 41, mostly in Bogotá and the rest in provincial capitals. A letter was attached which referred to the research project and the fact that the survey formed part of that project, and its purpose was also explained.

The survey consists of seventy questions, which enquire about the following points, amongst others. About the biobank: year set up, related to some biobank network, regulations of any nature which govern it, and the existence or otherwise of quality management programmes and an ethics in research committee. About sam-

---

(19) This is how the former Lorencita Villegas de Santos Hospital viewed a number of aortic tissue samples. See Constitutional Court Judgment T394 of 2000.

ples stored in the biobank: type, number, origin, conservation methods, storage time, transportation, means of identification, circulation, import and export, and criteria for organising them.

Further matters surveyed include the informed consent of persons from whom samples come, specific points they are informed of, the protection of information deriving therefrom, the existence or otherwise of databases and information about samples taken from corpses, and how these are obtained.

We received twelve answers. Only six completed the survey. The others argued that they did not have a biobank or that other demands had to be met before they could complete the survey.

We will now proceed to draw a number of conclusions from the surveys that were completed about the activities that Colombian biobanks engage in, related to each point in the report.

2. – Legal Framework

2.1. – *General legislation applicable*

In an attempt to establish what system could apply to biobanks in Colombia and the activities they perform with human biological samples, it is necessary to turn to a wide range of different types of regulation which refer to different aspects of the activities engaged in by biobanks, such as ones which regulate scientific research on humans, the system which applies to using body components, informed consent of the subject and how personal information and medical records are treated.

We will now mention the regulations that we will refer to under the different points in the report.

Law 9 of 1979, «whereby sanitary measures are enacted».

Law 23 of 1981, «whereby regulations are enacted in connection with medical ethics».

Law 73 of 1988, «whereby Law 9 of 1979 is added and other provisions are enacted relating to the donation and transplanting of organs and body components for transplant purposes and effects and other therapeutic uses».

Law 919 of 2004, «whereby the selling of human body components for transplant purposes is forbidden and trafficking therein is classified as an offence».

Law 1164 of 2007, «whereby provisions are enacted in connection with Human Skills in Health».

Law 1266 of 2008, «whereby general *habeas data* provisions are enacted and the handling of information contained in personal databases is regulated, especially financial, credit, commercial and services data and data from third party countries, and other provisions are likewise enacted».

Law 1286 of 2009, «whereby Law 29 of 1990 is amended, Colciencias is transformed into an Administration Department, the National Science, Technology and Innovation System in Colombia is reinforced, and other provisions are enacted».

Decree 3380 of 1981, «whereby Law 23 of 1981 is regulated».

Ministry of Health (now Ministry of Social Protection) **Decree 786 of 1990**, «whereby Heading IX in Law 9 of 1979 is partially regulated in terms of the carrying out of clinical and medical-legal autopsies and viscerotomies, and other provisions are enacted».

Decree 1571 of 1993, «whereby Heading X in Law 9 of 1979 is partially regulated in terms of the functioning of establishments engaged in the extraction, processing, conservation and transportation of total blood or haemo-derivatives thereof, the National Blood Banks Network and the National Blood Banks Council are formed, and other provisions are enacted on the matter».

Decree 1101 of 2001, «whereby the Inter-Sector Bioethical Commission is set up and members thereof are appointed».

Decree 2493 of 2004, «whereby Law 9 of 1979 and Law 73 of 1988 are regulated in connection with body components».

Decree 2323 of 2006, «whereby Law 9 of 1979 is partially regulated with respect to the National Laboratories Network and other provisions are enacted».

Ministry of Health (now Ministry of Social Protection) **Resolution 13437 of 1991**, «whereby hospital ethics committees are set up and the Ten Commandments of Patient Rights are adopted».

Ministry of Health (now Ministry of Social Protection) **Resolution 8430 of 1993**, «whereby scientific, technical and administrative regulations are established for health research».

Ministry of Health (now Ministry of Social Protection) **Resolution 1995 of 1999**, «whereby regulations are established for the handling of medical records».

National Institute of Legal Medicine and Forensic Sciences Resolution 485 of 2002, «whereby the procedure is regulated for handing over corpses and body components obtained therefrom for teaching and research purposes and effects».

Ministry of Social Protection Resolution 2640 of 2005, «whereby Articles 3 and 4, Paragraph 2 to Article 6, Number 10 under Article 7, and Articles 25 and 46 in Decree 2493 of 2004 are regulated and other provisions are enacted», which refer to the national and regional donation and transplant network.

Ministry of Social Protection Resolution 5108 of 2005, «whereby the Good Practices Manual for Tissue and Bone Marrow Banks is established and other provisions are enacted».

Ministry of Social Protection Resolution 2378 of 2008, «whereby Good Clinical Practices for Institutions which Conduct Research with Medicines on Human Beings is adopted».

2.2. – *Specific legislation*

There is no specific legislation in Colombia that refers to operating requirements or the activities that biobanks engage in. As far as research with biological samples of human origin is concerned, Ministry of Health Resolution 8430 of 1993 is the only regulation governing the matter; however, since it is a regulation that was issued in 1993, it should be updated.

No interest can be noted at the present time either by Congress of the Republic or by other bodies with powers to regulate these questions. They have not been dealt with in case law.

2.3. – *Reports and opinions by national institutions and bodies*

Decree 1101 of 2001 set up the Inter-Sector Bioethics Commission (CIB) as a body attached to what was then known as the Ministry of Health, and this Commission was given advisory duties and responsibility for making recommendations and proposing regulatory frameworks in connection with various issues, but especially those relating to ethical queries that were raised by scientific and technological advances when these involved human beings, and with respecting human dignity.

The Committee is made up of the Minister of Justice and the Law or a representative thereof (nowadays the Minister of the Interior and Justice), the Minister of Health or a representative thereof (nowadays the Minister of Social Protection), the Minister of National Education or a representative thereof, the Minister of the Environment or a representative thereof (nowadays the Minister of the Environment, Housing and Regional Development), and the Director of the Francisco José de Caldas Colombian Institute for the Development of Science and Technology (Colciencias). Pursuant to Article 32 in Law 489 of 1998, recognised scientists, some of whom are experts in bioethics, are permanent guests.

CIB is the advisory body to the national government on all matters that are directly or indirectly related to ethical matters in scientific research. It should also give the government advice and make recommendations to it on ethical queries that arise as a result of scientific and technological research on human beings, and on matters connected with research into the human genome, cloning, biomedical research, *in vitro* fertilisation, the extraction and transplanting of organs and tissues and xenotransplants, wit individuals and communities, especially those that are carried out or intended to be carried out on ethnic or racial minorities, children, the disabled, corpses and animals.

This Commission has unfortunately met on only a few occasions, and it has issued only a small number of opinions. Specifically, no document was found relating to research on human biological samples, biobanks or the activities performed by biobanks.

Article 7 in Law 1164 of 2007, which enacted provisions in connection with Human Skills in Health, established that an Ethics and Bioethics Committee should be set up to support the National Human Skills in Health Council, and that this would be coordinated with the Inter-Sector Bioethics Commission in accordance with Ministry of Social Protection regulations.

There is no other state or private organisation in the country that issues reports or opinions of a general nature on these issues, and we therefore cannot say anything under this point. This is notwithstanding work that is done by scientific research centre committees, as their opinions are of a specific nature.

2.4. – *Professionals and institutions: quality standards and accreditation requirements*

As we have already said, there are no specific regulations in Colombia that cover biobanks, and there are therefore no regulations that refer to requirements which might be demanded of them as institutions or of professional staff who work there. However, Law 9 of 1979, which enacted sanitary measures, stipulates in general terms that a Sanitary Licence issued by the Ministry of Health (nowadays the Ministry of Social Protection) or whatever entity the respective function might be delegated to is a requirement for any establishment to open and operate, and that this licence should be renewed periodically. This regulation thus enables us to say that the Sanitary Operating Licence applies to biobanks.

A specific and rigorous system applies to biobanks (20) which store blood samples. In fact, the aim of Decree 1571 of 1993 is to regulate activities connected with the obtaining, donation, conservation, processing, storage, transfusion and supply of human blood and components or derivatives thereof, and with establishments or offices which perform these activities (Articles 1 and 2). And Article 4 therein specifically stipulates that human blood may be extracted and used without profit for scientific research purposes and effects (21).

This Decree has a very wide sphere of application, as does its definition of a Blood Bank (22), since this includes any establishment or office that stores human blood for research procedures; specifically, this would be the case of the biobanks subject matter of this study. Similarly, the definition of a blood donor also includes a person who freely gives a portion of his or her blood for research purposes (23).

---

(20) We refer to biobanks which stock blood samples and supply these to scientific research centres, and which also engage in exchange or circulation activities with other biobanks.

(21) «Article 4 : Human blood may only be extracted and used without profit and for preventive, therapeutic or diagnostic purposes and effects on human beings or in scientific research».

(22) «Article 2 : For purposes and effects hereof, the following definitions are established. Blood Bank : This is any establishment or office which holds a Sanitary Operating Licence for carrying out research relating to the obtaining, processing and storage of human blood for the transfusion of total blood or in separate components, for apheresis procedures and for other preventive, therapeutic or research procedures (...)». (The underlining is ours).

(23) «Blood Donor : A person who, subject to his or her meeting the requirements stated in this Decree, freely and without any economic payment voluntarily gives a portion of his or her blood for preventive, therapeutic, diagnostic or research purposes, freely and consciously». (The underlining is ours).

We therefore restate our view that this Decree applies to biobanks which engage in activities consisting of obtaining, processing, storing and supplying biological samples of human blood. Furthermore because before it can perform any of these activities, the institution or establishment has to obtain a Sanitary Operating Licence (24).

And this Decree also regulates matters like premises, equipment (refrigerators, centrifugal freezers, pipettes, etc.), consumables, technical and scientific staff, ways of marking blood bags, technical management, donor requirements (age, weight, consent, physical appraisal), tests that should be performed on blood units, quality guarantee, bio-security, filing and records, sanitary licence, sanitary safety measures, control and supervision, penalties and procedures.

Meanwhile, in order to regulate Decree 2493 of 2004 on Transplants, the Ministry of Social Protection issued Resolution 5108 of 2004, which establishes the Good Practices Manual for Tissue and Bone Marrow Banks. This Resolution sets out to regulate banks which store as their name indicates – tissues and bone marrow for therapeutic purposes, specifically for transplants. Although the regulations are extremely wide-ranging and complete, they thus do not apply to banks which store biological samples for biomedical purposes. This opinion is shared by the Ministry of Social Protection (25).

As we mentioned earlier, although the only regulations which apply to biobanks are those contained in Decree 1571 of 1993, if the bank stores blood samples, the trend would seem to be to establish a rigorous control over those activities, in terms not only of technical matters and staff but also of state supervision.

---

(24) «Article 5: Human blood may only be obtained and any of the activities referred to in Article 2 in this Decree may only be performed at medical-care institutions, transfusion services and blood banks which have obtained a Sanitary Operating Licence for such purpose, duly issued by the competent sanitary authority».

(25) In response to a right of petition with respect to whether the Good Practices Manual for Tissue and Bone Marrow Banks (Resolution 5108 of 2004) did or died not apply to banks which store human biological samples for bio-medical research, the Ministry of Social Protection replied as follows : «The Good Practices Manual for Tissue and Bone Marrow Banks applies to non-profit institutions which are responsible for obtaining, extracting, processing, preserving and storing tissues and bone marrow for the purpose of conserving them and supplying them for therapeutic or transplant purposes» (the bold is in the original text).

2.5. – Ethics Research Committees

Regulations in Colombia governing ethics in research committees tend to be scattered. Two main regulatory statutes refer to them.

Firstly there is Resolution 8430 of 1993, hereinafter the Resolution on Research in Health, which establishes that these committees are compulsory in all institutions that engage in research on human beings, for settling all issues relating to the subject (Article 2). There is no careful regulation, there is no listing of the general duties that such committees are to perform or of the guiding principles for their work, and there is no mention whatsoever of who should sit on the committees in order to guarantee that decisions are made independently and that there is a suitable balance in the interests involved. There are simply a number of regulations assigning specific functions, such as those listed below.

– To approve the research project of the respective research institution (Article 5, letter g).
– As a validity requirement, to check the informed consent that will be used in the research that the respective institution will carry out (Article 16, letter b).
– To authorise the institution to obtain informed consent without a written form in research where the risk is minimal (Article 16, paragraph 1).
– To authorise the researcher to dispense with the obligation of obtaining informed consent in research where there is no risk (Article 16, paragraph 1).
– To establish the parameters on the basis of which the ability to understand and the reasoning and logic of a subject who is about to grant his or her consent should be evaluated (Article 16, paragraph 3).
– To authorise informed consent to be obtained, in the case of individuals who belong to a community and who do not have the ability to understand the implications of taking part in research, from a person holding moral authority over the said community (Article 19).
– To see that the requirements stipulated for obtaining the informed consent of children and the disabled are met (Article 26).

– To suspend research where the risk is more than minimal when the risk could affect the biological, psychological or social wellbeing of the child or disabled person (Article 28, paragraph 2).

Secondly, we have Resolution 2378 of 2008, which establishes Good Clinical Practices for Institutions which Conduct Research with Medicines on Human Beings (26).

This Resolution states that research institutions should have an Institutional Ethics Committee, which it defines as an «independent organisation whose members are doctors, scientists and non-scientists and whose responsibilities are to guarantee that rights, safety and wellbeing are protected of human beings who are involved in a study by means of, amongst other things, constantly reviewing, approving and checking the study project and amendments to documentation and the informed consent of study subjects».

It goes on to list the duties of these committees : (1) to safeguard the rights of those participating in the research; (2) to evaluate and approve or not approve the proposed research before a start is made on it; (3) to obtain and keep the necessary documentation for each study that is put to it for consideration; (4) to consider the competence of the researchers; and (5) to periodically evaluate progress being made with approved studies that are in progress.

It likewise refers to the make-up of the committees, topics that their regulations should govern, procedures for exercising their different functions, documentation and records, and the way to evaluate each of these aspects. The National Institute for the Supervision of Medicines and Foodstuffs (INVIMA) is the state entity that is responsible for ensuring that institutions meet all the requirements that are stated in the Resolution.

Although regulations governing the committees are scattered around the documents mentioned above, institutions that conduct research on human beings and which are obliged to set up an Ethics

---

(26) The Good Clinical Practices for Institutions which Conduct Research with Medicines on Human Beings were drawn up by the Pan-American Network for the Harmonisation of Pharmaceutical Regulations (REDPARF) at a meeting that was held in the Dominican Republic in March 2005 and which was attended by Colombia in the form of the National Institute for the Supervision of Medicines and Foodstuffs (INVIMA). REDPARF handed the document to the Ministry of Social Protection through the Pan-American Health Organisation (OPS). REDPARF is a forum for harmonising pharmaceutical regulations in which medicine regulating authorities from the region, representatives of regional economic integration bodies, the pharmaceutical industry, consumer groups, academics and other interested parties take part.

in Research Committee draw up their bylaws in such a way as to regulate the make-up and operation of the committee in a detailed manner (27). It can be seen that they establish their regulations through resolutions or minutes which state the number of members, the way in which these are elected, the duties of the committee, and the conditions under which it will meet.

The various institutions all state in their bylaws that committee duties include (a) evaluating research from the scientific, methodological, financial and ethical standpoints, taking into account the risks and the effect it could have on participants or the community, (b) verifying researcher suitability, (c) analysing the informed consent provided in the research in order to check that it has been granted properly, and (d) periodic control of and follow-up on the research (28).

It will thus be seen that institutions which do research on humans are obliged to set up these committees. Institutions that do research using human biological samples are therefore required to have them, and in principle, it is thus not an obligation that biobanks as such should meet, because they support research but do not actually do it.

---

(27) CARDOZO DE MARTINEZ, Carmen Alicia, and others (editors), *Ethics in research : a Social Responsibility*, Pontificia Universidad Javeriana and National University of Colombia, Bogotá, 2008. «The general consensus is that there is an urgent need to appropriate outside reflections, generate internal ones and take on our responsible role with research and the community». These initiatives have been on the increase, stimulated by WHO (World Health Organisation) policies as set out in its operating guides for ethics committees that evaluate biomedical research and in international ethical guidelines for biomedical research on human beings issued by CIOMS (Council for the International Organisation of Medical Sciences). These policies are a persistent wake-up call for improving the implementation of research standards, specifically in matters relating to the accreditation of independent, multidisciplinary, multi-sector and plural ethics committees at national, institutional and local levels; for developing ethical evaluation within countries, and for educating the members of such committees. These guides set out to act as a basis for enabling committees to carry out their own written procedures and thus perform their biomedical research duties.

(28) Regulations of the ETHICS IN RESEARCH COMMITTEE OF THE NATIONAL DERMATOLOGY INSTITUTE (www.dermatologia.gov.co), the BIOLOGICAL RESEARCH CORPORATION (www.cib.org.co), SAN JOSÉ HOSPITAL – HEALTH SCIENCES UNIVERSITY FOUNDATION (www.fucsalud.edu.co), LA SAMARITANA UNIVERSITY HOSPITAL (www.hus.org.co), LOS ANDES UNIVERSITY (www.uniandes.edu.co), UNIVERSITY OF CALDAS (www.ucaldas.edu.co), UNIVERSITY OF CARTAGENA (www.unicartagena.edu.co), POPULAR CATHOLIC UNIVERSITY OF RISARALDA (www.ucpr.edu.co), THE CALI SECTION OF THE UNIVERSIDAD LIBRE (www.unilibrecali.edu.co), NATIONAL UNIVERSITY OF COLOMBIA (www.unal.edu.co) and LA SABANA UNIVERSITY (www.unisabana.edu.co).

2.6. – Obtaining of samples
(invasive intervention in the donor)

Any sample that a biobank stores can come from one of three sources :

I. Persons

II. Corpses

III. Communities (*infra. Letter K : Specific questions relating to local communities* (29))

2.6.1. *From persons*

They may have been taken as part of a medical act or procedure – in a diagnostic test, for example, or solely for biomedical research purposes and effects, as with the Colombian National Health Institute, which sometimes collects samples from people in order to carry out its research, or as donations for therapeutic purposes, as with the tissue and bone marrow banks that operate in Colombia, or as part of a judicial investigation, such as those undertaken by the investigative bodies in each country's penal system, in our case the Public Prosecution Service, or the judicial police, or, for example, as part of family proceedings.

Every activity in which samples are taken of human biological material is governed by specific regulations, in addition to higher-ranking ones such as those contained in the political constitution or in international human rights treaties (Article 93, Political Constitution).

Since this section relates to the taking of samples, we will now examine informed consent regulations governing each of these activities.

a) *Samples stored that have been taken solely and exclusively for biomedical research purposes and effects*

In this case, the institution which undertakes the research approaches people who are of special interest to the specific goal of its project because of the nature of the samples that can be

---

(29) These are really simples that come under number I, but special attention is paid to them in this study in line with international and constitutional regulations.

obtained from them, such as because they come from families with a background of a certain illness or disease. On other occasions, they turn to the general public or to a specific social group in order to gather biological material.

It can happen that the subjects need to participate in the research for long periods, perhaps because samples need to be taken from them at a later date, or careful follow-up needs to be done on them, or information about their state of health needs to be updated periodically, or further samples have to be taken from them.

Measures have to be adopted in both cases in order to guarantee their rights, because the danger exists in each one that these could be violated. Logically, there could be certain particularities in a subject who is involved on a permanent basis in the research, since in some circumstances his rights could be exposed to greater risks.

As we have already mentioned, all institutions in Colombia that engage in the field of scientific research in health are governed by Resolution (30) 8430 of 1993, issued by what is today known as the Ministry of Social Protection (31), «whereby academic, technical and administrative regulations are established for health research» (32), and by Resolution 2378 of 2008, whereby «Good Clinical Practices for Institutions which Conduct Research with Medicines on Human Beings is adopted». These are the only regulations which specifically govern research on human beings in the country.

Article 48 in Chapter VI of Resolution 8430 of 1993, entitled «Research on Organs, Tissues and Derivatives thereof, Products and Corpses of Human Beings», states that while research is being done, not only should the human corpse be respected, the provisions established in the Resolution and in other regulations governing the disposal of human corpses, tissues and organs should be adhered to as well.

Article 47 states that research on human beings also includes research which involves the use human body components and all

---

(30) «Resolution» is one of the names that are given to administrative acts that regulate or develop regulations of a legal nature.
(31) The Ministry of Social Protection was formed in 2002 by merging the Ministry of Health and the Ministry of Labour.
(32) Hereinafter, «Heath Research Resolution».

activities relating to the taking, conservation, utilisation, preparation and final use thereof.

Although the regulation does not refer textually to biological samples, we are of the opinion that the system established therein applies to such samples, because of their similarity to other body components that *are* specifically referred to, since they are all biological materials where the main feature is that they have been separated from the structural unit of the human body. Moreover, in view of the fact that the regulation was enacted in 1993, it is clear that the Colombian legislator of the day did not have – nor does he have today – either the scientific or the legal perspective to decide whether there was a need to add the expression «biological samples», in view of the value that these can have in the field of scientific research and because of their implications as far as the rights of the subjects they have come from are concerned.

In line with this evolutional interpretation, the rules that are stipulated under Heading II, «Research on Human Beings» (33), will apply to all research that involves biological samples that have come from humans. We will now proceed to examine those regulations.

What is of interest to us in the first Chapter («Ethical Aspects of research on Human Beings») is that it states that with all research on human beings, the informed consent should be obtained in writing of the subject of the research or of his or her legal representative (Article 6). In this case, although the research relates to a component that has been separated from the human being, it does not cease because of that to have implications for the subject from which it has been removed.

Article 14 provides a definition of informed consent: «agreement in writing whereby the subject of the research, or alternatively his or her legal representative, authorises his or her participation in the research with full knowledge of the nature of the procedures, benefits and risks that he or she will be subjected to, by free choice and without any coercion or compulsion whatsoever».

---

(33) The different Chapters under this Heading are: (I) Ethical Aspects of Research on Human Beings, (II) Research on Communities, (III) Research on Children or the Disabled; (IV) Research on Women of Fertile Age or who are Pregnant, when Giving Birth, during Puerperium or Lactation, on the Newly-Born, the Use of Embryos, the Deceased and Foetuses, and Artificial Fertilisation, and (V) Research on Subordinate Groups.

The following Article (Article 15) specifically regulates the information that should be given in the document containing the informed consent of the subject of the research (*infra. Letter I : Extent of Consent*).

Furthermore, Article 16 states that for this document to be valid, it should (a) be drawn up by the main researcher and contain the information stated above (Article 15), (b) be checked by the Ethics in Research Committee of the institution where the research is being done, (c) contain the names and addresses of the witnesses and their relationship to the subject of the research, (d) be signed by the subject of the research and by the two witnesses, and (e) have a copy issued specifically for the subject of the research.

Also specifically regulated is the consent of children and the disabled (Article 23 et seq.), with it being stated that in addition to obtaining the informed consent of those who hold parental rights or who legally represent them, a certificate should be obtained from a neurologist, psychiatrist or psychologist as to the ability of the subject of the research to understand and reason. If such a test establishes that the child or disabled person has an adequate mental capacity and psychological state, his or her acceptance should likewise be obtained (Article 26) (34).

Also regulated is informed consent to the research by women of fertile age, pregnant women, women while giving birth and during the puerperium and lactation, and research on newly-born babies (Article 29 et seq.). Additional requirements are established in each case. In the case of women of fertile age who are going to take part in research where the risk is more than minimal, for example, before consent is granted it should be certified that they are not pregnant and that the probability of their becoming pregnant while the

---

(34) In Judgement T-492 of 2006 (Magistrate Marco Gerardo Monroy Cabra), in which the case was studied of a woman who wanted to force a health company to sterilise her daughter who was suffering from a mental problem, the Constitutional Court expressed the view that in the case of persons who are incapable (because they are children or because they are suffering from some mental limitation or other), when acts are going to be performed which will restrict or limit their constitutional rights, such as an operation, the decision of their legal representative or guardian is not sufficient in itself, since a prior judicial authorisation of such act is necessary. The process should demonstrate the need for the measure in the particular case, together with its specific usefulness. If we thus follow the views of the Court, namely that authorisation by the legal representative of an incapable person is not sufficient in instances of operations or other actions which will seriously affect that person's constitutional rights, we can conclude that in the case of research where the risk is more than minimal, prior authorisation by a judge is also required.

research is being conducted is less. In the case of pregnant women, women while giving birth and during the puerperium and lactation, or for research on newly-born babies or the deceased or when embryos or foetuses are to be used, or in the case of artificial fertilisation, the consent of the spouse or partner is also required, and this can only be dispensed with «in the event of disability or when it is manifestly or convincingly impossible for it to be given, or because the partner is not responsible for the woman, or when there is an imminent risk to the life of the woman, embryo, foetus or newly-born baby».

These specific regulations governing research on human beings represent a guarantee that the rights of persons involved in or linked in some way to the research will be protected. They also especially stress matters relating to the document expressing the consent, since it can be concluded from the text of Articles 15 and 19 that apart from warning the donor of the risks implied in the act of taking the sample, he or she should be informed of other matters relating to the issue that concerns us, so that his or her rights can be protected.

In fact, the subject of the research has to be informed of «the guarantee that the person will not be identified, and that information relating to his or her privacy will be treated as confidential» (Article 15, letter (h)). It can be inferred from this that an institution which stores personal information (or supporting documentation containing that information) has to treat it as confidential even after the research has been completed. The sample or the information that is gained from it can thus only be used subsequently for a purpose other than that which the subject of the research consented to if the same confidentiality is guaranteed, as well as other matters. In general terms, therefore, the obligations that an institution and its researchers take on do not get extinguished by the fact that the research work has been completed, as they remain in force and are fully enforceable until the danger of the person's rights being violated ceases – this in principle is when an irreversible dissociation occurs of the sample or the information that is stored in the biobank under the identity of the source subject.

The person also has to be given a justification for the research and be told its objectives (Article 15, letter (a)), and this, in our opinion, means that he or she should be told about the specific research in which the sample or the information that is gained from it is going to be used, and similarly, if it is going to be used simultaneously in more than one research activity or in subsequent research, then he or she should be informed of this. Similarly, a ban derives from this on concealing information about the real purpose for which the sample or the information that is gained from it is to be used, or about the aims of the research in which it is *foreseen* that it will be used.

b) *Samples stored that have been taken as the result of a medical act*

Since we are now in the field of medical activities, we should look at regulations which govern the obtaining of informed consent in this area.

The body of Colombian laws includes Law 23 of 1981, which is the Medical Ethical Code, Decree 3380 of 1981, which regulates that Ethical Code, and Resolution 13437 of 1991, issued by the Ministry of Health (today known as the Ministry of Social Protection), which sets out the «Ten Commandments» as far as patients' rights are concerned.

Articles 15 and 16 in Law 23 of 1981 are important, as these state that the doctor will request the patient's consent before giving medical and surgical treatment which he deems essential and which could have adverse consequences. He should also explain the risks and the possible consequences to the patient or to those responsible for him or her beforehand. Therefore, if doctor liability occurs, this will not be greater than the envisaged risk.

According to Resolution 13437 of 1991, every patient, without restrictions of any nature whatsoever, is entitled to enjoy clear and full communication with the doctor, who will give him or her all information that might be necessary about the illness he or she is suffering from, about the procedures and treatment that he or she is going to be subjected to, and about the risks that these entail.

Points that the patient should be informed of include the nature, aims, advantages, risks and consequences of the diagnostic or therapeutic procedure that is going to be carried out on him or her, and the effects of not carrying it out. When the procedure consists of taking biological samples, the patient should be informed not only of the immediate but also of the mediate goal (35).

And anyway, as Number 8 under Article 1 in Resolution 13437 states, the decision of a patient to either take part or not take part in scientific research should be respected, and he or she should first be provided with full information about it, including the objectives, possible benefits and foreseeable risks. The information about the latter points refers not just to health matters but also to risks to his or her intimate rights, such as privacy.

On numerous occasions (36), the Constitutional Court has referred to the right that a person who is going to undergo a medical procedure or operation holds to be asked for his or her informed consent beforehand. The Court has stressed in this context points like the fact that an individual holds an exclusive right over his or her own body, the inviolability of the human body, that the principles of freedom and autonomy prevail, and that the individual needs to have a sufficient and adequate knowledge of the basic information before he or she makes decisions about medical diagnoses, treatment and research.

It specifically stated the following on this last point: «those involved in research on human beings, which is unquestionably necessary in order to improve the quality of medical treatment, should be particularly strict in obtaining the informed consent of potential subjects, who are entitled to decide whether or not to take part in the scientific undertaking, without any compulsion or deceit, on the basis of an objective knowledge and understanding of all possible risks involved in and benefits of the experiments. As a result of this free involvement in the medical experience, the patient ceases to be an object thereof and becomes the subject of and joint participant in scientific development, with his or her dignity and inviolability thus covered. This therefore explains why Article 7 in the Civil and Political Rights Pact stresses that «nobody shall be subjected to medical or scientific experiments without his or her freely-granted consent». This provision is a direct development of the regulations

---

(35) We have no documentary evidence of one particular concern that certain doctors have expressed to us informally, relating to the existence of a general clause for using a biological sample subsequently for research into DNA.

(36) See the following Judgements, amongst others: T-412 of 2004, T-559 of 1995, SU-337 of 1999, T-1390 of 2000, T-597 of 2001, T-850 of 2002, T-1025 of 2002, T-1021 of 2003, T-1229 of 2005 and T-866 of 2006.

established in the Nuremberg Code, the first principle of which states, precisely, that the voluntary consent of the human subject is absolutely essential in this kind of research (37). (The **bold** is ours).

Although the Constitutional Court has not referred directly to the specific question of biobanks, its pronouncements have thus stressed the fact that the individual is entitled to be given full information before a medical procedure is carried out, *even more so when this is in the context of a research activity*. It can be concluded from this that he should be given full information about any subsequent purpose to which the sample or the information that will be gained from it will be put, before the respective sample is taken, since the subject cannot become a joint participant in science without his or her consent.

The big question arises when, at the time a sample is taken for medical purposes, subsequent use thereof for scientific research was neither foreseen nor foreseeable. We will come back to this point later (*infra. Letter J : Use of Samples Taken for Another Purpose*).

c) *Samples stored that have been obtained for donation for therapeutic purposes*

Specific regulations exist in Colombia governing activities connected with obtaining body components for therapeutic purposes.

The object of Decree 2493 of 2004 (38) is «to regulate the obtaining, donation, preservation, storage, transportation, use and final disposal of body components, and transplant or implantation procedures with respect thereto in human beings». (The underlining is ours).

On the question of obtaining body components, this Decree establishes, amongst other things, a ban on remuneration (Article 15), conditions relating to a live donor and a deceased donor (39) (Article 16), donation mechanisms (Article 17), the tests that should

---

(37) Constitutional Court, Judgement SU-337 of 1998. Magistrate Alejandro Martínez Caballero.

(38) Henceforth, «Decree 2493 on Transplants».

(39) Decree 2493, Article 2 : **Live Donor** : This is a person who is fully acquainted with all the risks that could arise during the procedure and who, after meeting the requirements stipulated in this Decree, makes the donation in life of those organs or part thereof whose function is compensated for by his or her organism in a safe and adequate manner.

be performed in order to guarantee the quality of donated organs and tissues (Article 18), the way to establish a brain death diagnosis (Article 12 et seq.), the way tissues should leave and body components should be received (Article 37 et seq.), and the way in which body components should be removed or rescued (Chapter V).

According to Article 16, if body components are to be used for transplant or implant purposes, then if the donor is a live donor, he or she must be an adult, must enjoy his or her full mental capacities and be in good health, in the case of a female she should not be pregnant, specific informed consent (40) should have been given, and the donor should have been warned of the consequences of his or her decision and of the fact that it is impossible to definitely know all risks that could arise during the procedure.

If a live donor is a child or a pregnant woman, the obtaining of progenitive cells will only be applicable if the informed consent of the person's legal representatives has first been obtained, where applicable.

The regulations stipulated in this Decree are very strict as to the purpose for which the donation is made. Moreover, they are binding regulations that cannot be overruled privately by the parties involved, and the institution or person in charge of extracting the body component should therefore adhere to them closely. Body components that are obtained for therapeutic purposes thus cannot be put to any other use unless an attempt has first been made to serve the immediate purpose.

Varying the purpose – therapeutic – for which tissue or an organ has been obtained is thus not permitted. If it can no longer be used for this purpose and the aim is to use it in biomedical research, the consent should first be obtained of the person from whom it was extracted, since – as has already been said – the law strictly protects the purpose for which it was obtained, and if the possibility of using it for this purpose has been exhausted, any other purpose should be accepted by the source subject (or relatives thereof),

---

(40) Decree 2493, Article 2 : **Informed Consent for Donation, Transplant or Implant :** This is the expression of will by the person who is the donor or receiver of a body component and which has been given freely and expressly after such person has received and understood information relating to the procedure that is to be performed.

bearing in mind furthermore that the altruistic reason (41) that drove him or her (or him or her or his or her relatives) to give the informed consent no longer exists.

d) Samples stored that have been taken for judicial investigation purposes and effects

Institutions exist in the state apparatus of every country whose job it is to carry out judicial investigations. In Colombia there are the Public Prosecution Service and various judicial police bodies, such as the Technical Investigation Group (CTI), the Security Administration Department (DAS), the Judicial and Investigative Police Division (DIJIN), and the Judicial and Investigative Police Sections (SIJIN). All of them have procedures manuals which cover the taking of samples from people and the infrastructure for storing them.

Both in the penal system and in paternity investigation proceedings (42), interested parties can have recourse to the institution that the state has entrusted with the task of performing the respective DNA tests, such as the National Institute of Legal Medicine, or duly-authorised private institutions. These likewise have protocols for taking samples and suitable facilities for storing them.

The only purpose for which these samples may be used is for the respective judicial investigation or proceedings, and they cannot, in principle, be set aside for any other purpose (43).

---

(41) Protection of this altruistic reason manifests itself specifically in the categorisation of the human body component trafficking offence established in Law 919 of 2004, Article 1 in which establishes a ban on any form of payment or compensation for them, since they must be donated or supplied free of charge, with no remuneration whatsoever being received. Article 2 thus goes on to fix a penalty of from three to six years in prison for anyone who markets, sells or traffics in human body components or anyone who removes the same from a corpse without having obtained the corresponding authorisation.

(42) The national government issued Decree 2112 of 2003, «whereby the accreditation and certification are regulated of public and private laboratories which carry out paternity or maternity tests with genetic DNA markers, and other provisions are enacted».

(43) As far as whether or not the willingness of the subject (the accused, the victim or other) should be demanded for taking samples that could be used in evidence in penal proceedings is concerned, serious questions arise in constitutional terms due to the various legal assets that could be at stake. In the Colombian body of laws, the regulations that are enshrined in the Civil Procedures Code were studied by the Constitutional Court in Judgement C-822 of 2005 (Magistrate Manuel José Cepeda), where a number of interesting considerations were raised on the question.

2.6.2. *From corpses*

a) Body components of corpses for research purposes when relatives do not come forward

Chapter VI, «Research on Organs, Tissues and Derivatives thereof, Products and Corpses of Human Beings», in the Health Research Resolution refers to «other regulations relating to the disposal of the organs, tissues and corpses of human beings», which include Decree 2493 on Transplants.

Article 46 in this Decree states that only legally-recognised scientific institutions, universities and health institutions authorised by the Ministry of Social Protection that are registered with the Institute of Legal Medicine and Forensic Sciences are authorised to use unclaimed corpses and body components for teaching and research purposes (44).

DNA samples that are taken by the National Institute of Legal Medicine in paternity and maternity investigation proceedings are also used for population studies, with a view to adapting evidence with genetic markers to Colombian characteristics.

Ministry of Social Protection Resolution 2640 of 2005 furthers Paragraph Two to the abovementioned Article 46, and states that the Institute of Legal Medicine and Forensic Sciences is only entitled to hand over unclaimed corpses and body components that are taken from them if certain requirements have been met.

These requirements, which are set out in Resolution No. 00485 of 2002, consist of a written request by the legal representative of the institution to the Director of the Institute of Legal Medicine and Forensic Sciences, a copy of the authorisation resolution from the Ministry to the official or private entity, and the signing of a commitment certificate «accrediting the obligation to transport and bury the corpses and/or body components or to return them in a dignified and adequate manner, to keep a record which will enable the location and final destination of the corpse and body compo-

---

(44) According to Resolution 2640 of 2005, in order to obtain this authorisation, the application should contain at least (a) a copy of the registration in the census of researchers as a Ministry of Social Protection or Colciencias group or research centre, (b) research protocol, which should set out what is intended to be done, (c) curriculum vitaes and profiles of the professionals or professional responsible for this activity, and (d) approval of the project by the institution's research ethics committee.

nents to be specified, and to inform the Regional Director thereof, in order to guarantee and continue with the custody chain system».

In view of the above, institutions which conduct scientific research can obtain authorisation to use body components from unclaimed corpses, provided that the research project has been approved by the research ethics committee and that other legal requirements are met. It can thus be said that at the present time, a biobank cannot gain direct access to biological samples from unclaimed corpses, since it is not, as such, an institution that conducts scientific research. Biobanks which belong to or are linked to institutions that conduct this type of research can gain access, since in this case it is the latter that would request the samples.

In our opinion, this is an obstacle for independent biobanks, because one of their main functions is to be able to access biological samples for the purpose of storing them in a quality and orderly manner so that they can be made available to institutions or researchers that might require them for their projects, and they could therefore be interested in having part of their stock made up of biological samples taken from corpses. Once again, therefore, we can see the need for specific regulations governing the activities that these establishments engage in.

b) Body components of corpses for research purposes when relatives come forward

This point is regulated in Decree 786 of 1990, «whereby Heading IX in Law 09 of 1979 is partially regulated, with respect to the carrying-out of clinical and medical-legal autopsies and viscerotomies, and other provisions are enacted».

This Decree states that medical-legal and clinical autopsies (45) may be performed for investigation purposes – that is, they may have «pure or applied scientific research goals» (Article 4). And it specifically states that the aim of autopsies may be to perform «viscerotomies» (46), so that organs can be removed or body com-

---

(45) **Article 1.** An AUTOPSY or NECROPSY is deemed to be a procedure whereby information is obtained for scientific or legal purposes by observing, working on and analysing a corpse both internally and externally, and bearing in mind, where applicable, the examination of physical evidence relating thereto and known circumstances both prior to and subsequent to death.

(46) **Article 2.** A VISCEROTOMY is deemed to be a gathering of organs from or a taking of samples of any body components of human corpses, for either medical-legal, clinical, public health, research or teaching purposes.

ponent or liquid samples taken for teaching or research purposes» (Articles 5 and 15).

Article 19 then goes on to say that entities other than those which do medical – legal work can only perform viscerotomies for teaching and research purposes if they have been authorised to do so by relatives of the dead person. This requirement will not be necessary if the viserotomy has to be done for sanitary emergency or public health reasons.

In conclusion, when an autopsy is to be performed on a corpse, irrespective of whether it is a clinical or medical-legal autopsy, the respective body components may not be used for research without the consent of the relatives of the deceased. If they do not come forward to claim the corpse, what is stated under the previous section (letter (a)) will apply.

Now, in this case, since authorisation revolves around consent by relatives of the deceased, it is possible for a biobank to request authorisation from them to remove biological samples from the corpse so they can be stored and used for the other functions for which the biobank was set up, on condition that full, clear and accurate information is provided of things like the place where the sample will be stored, the subsequent use it will be put to, the conservation period, information that can be gleaned from it, the possible risks that their rights could be exposed to, and finally, if any research or investigation is in progress or forthcoming, then all information about it.

2.7. – *Sample ownership*

The human body, taken as a whole, cannot be the subject of real rights, and under no circumstances may it be considered to be a thing. It is the subject of a highly intimate right, and nobody can therefore dispose of a whole body; however, other considerations need to be borne in mind when it comes to components that can be extracted or removed from it (47), without permanently altering the integrity of the subject.

---

(47) VALENCIA ZEA, Arturo, *Civil Law: General and Person Part*, Vol. 1, 15th Edition, Bogotá, 2002.

In view of the lack of specific regulations in Colombia on human biological samples, if we are to opt for a criterion on the point relating to ownership of samples, we need to turn to the body of legal regulations which determine the system that applies to human body components, since these regulations refer to a similar concept, namely biological materials that are removed from the human body, although we should bear in mind the fact that the purposes for which this is done differ.

In Colombia – as under the legislation of most countries in the world – certain legal business is permitted with a number of components of the human body, subject to certain principles and the particular goals sought by the legislation being strictly adhered to. The most notable example of such business is donating organs or tissues for transplant purposes, which is subject to strict rules (48).

These can lead us to conclude that a right of disposal exists with respect to samples, when theses are viewed as biological components separated from the structural unit of the human body which are bearers of personal information, but the disposal acts for them are equally subject to rigorous legal limitations. Moreover, they cannot be viewed as just any sort of thing, because the system which applies to ownership, possession and custody thereof has to take into account their nature, their special characteristics and features, and the purposes they are going to be used for. We can draw the same conclusion if we examine the legal system governing the donation by a man or woman of his or her gametes for reproduction purposes (49).

Based on this view that a disposal right exists, the subject is entitled to pass on this ownership of the sample, subject to the restrictions that are established in the general body of laws. In our case, these restrictions would be dictated – or guided – by the principles established in the system governing transplants (50), since we appreciate that these are useful and applicable to our specific subject. Mainly, these are that it can only be done by means of a free legal arrangement, that it cannot apply to vital or non-pair organs

---

(48) Decree 2493 on Transplants.
(49) Decree 1546 of 1998, Article 43 et seq., in which the minimum conditions are adopted for the operation of Reproductive Biomedicine Units, Centres or similar.
(50) Penal legislation (Law 919 of 2004) contains two types of offence relating to the trafficking of organs which should be taken into account when the legal system for transferring body components is being determined.

or to the whole body, that it cannot endanger life and physical integrity, that it cannot be done for illegal purposes or for ones which contravene public order, that the consent of the subject is required, and that the goals consented to should be strictly adhered to.

Following this line of thought, a subject may – subject to these principles being adhered to – consent to transfer or donate his or her biological samples for *in vitro* biomedical research purposes.

In line with the above, it is possible in our opinion to view the sample as a thing from the moment it is completely separated from the human body, and an ownership right can thus be bestowed on it that is initially held by the source subject. A system should then be established that regulates ownership, possession and custody of the sample, one which takes not only the principles referred to in the preceding paragraphs into account but also the consequences of considering the sample to be a biological element and information support.

The result of this dual nature has been said to be that although the subject has transferred or donated his or her sample to research, the entire system relating to the protection of personal data will apply for as long as the sample goes on being associated with him or her (51). Nicolas thus maintains that, as information support, the subject the sample comes from continues to hold rights with respect to the sample, as if it were a data card (52).

Thus, even if the subject transfers his or her ownership of the sample, and even if no irreversible procedure has been carried out for making the sample anonymous, then subject and sample will not be totally separated, and the subject will still hold powers deriving from his or her ownership of the information residing therein. Logically, the scope and extent of those powers would have to be determined, as far as the sample is concerned.

Whether, for example, if information gathered from the sample has been used without authorisation, the subject can or cannot ask

---

(51) The consideration by the Constitutional Court in Judgement T-729 of 2002 is relevant here, since the Court states that one of the characteristics of personal data is that «ownership thereof resides exclusively with the holder, a situation which does not alter when it is obtained by a third party either legally or illicitly».

(52) Nicolás Jiménez, P., «Los Derechos del Paciente sobre su Muestra Biológica: Distintas Opiniones Jurisprudenciales», *Revista de Derecho y Genoma Humano*, 19, 2003, p. 208.

for it to be destroyed or handed over; or in another hypothetical situation, if a person or group of persons can request that biological samples from a relative that are stored in a biobank be handed over for genetic analysis, so that information can be obtained that will be useful for establishing a diagnosis or selecting the most convenient form of treatment.

Passing on ownership of the biological sample is thus no hindrance to considering that the source subject (or third parties) holds powers or rights over it by virtue of the data it contains. A further consideration here is that ownership is not an absolute right, rather that by virtue of the law – or by agreement between the parties – limitations can be established on it in view of the rights that are at stake. It is thus not illogical to reason that even if the subject transfers right of domain to the sample, it can anyway hold powers to request that it be returned or destroyed.

A paradigmatic case surrounding this dual nature of the biological sample arose in Colombia in the Constitutional Court, although no specific reference was made, unfortunately, to the issue which concerns us.

In the case that was studied, a husband and wife authorised a necropsy to be performed on their daughter, who had died one month after birth, so that tests could be performed to determine the cause of death. The hospital handed over the necropsy report, but not the biological samples. The parents later claimed that the document did not contain information about the aortic tissue cut colouring, which was needed for a genetic study, and asked for the samples to be handed over. The hospital refused, claiming that it could only do so if the parents obtained a court order.

The parents then turned to the state organisation responsible for supervising health institutions (Superintendency of Health), which refused on the grounds that, amongst other things, the sample could not be handed over because it formed part of the *scientific equity of the hospital*.

Faced with this refusal, the parents filed a civil action for the protection of constitutional rights, claiming that their fundamental rights to *habeas data*, to health and social security, and to responsibly having a family, had been violated, because the refusal to hand over the samples prevented them from gaining access to information that would enable them to find out the possible problems that their future children would be born with, and whether these were remediable or not.

Finally, the civil action for the protection of constitutional rights reached the Constitutional Court, which stated that in the case in question, the refusal by the hospital to hand over the samples violated various fundamental rights, because it «prevented the couple who wanted to have a family in a responsible manner from knowing what health dangers their children might have to face, or even possibly the couple themselves», and it also restricted «the possibility of obtaining information about genetic patterns which might have a negative influence on the health of the petitioners, which could in turn interfere with the free development of their personality, insofar as the lack of full information could negatively condition their decision to have children, merely because they would be afraid to see another of their children die» (53).

For these reasons, the Constitutional Court ordered the aortic tissue sample from the dead baby to be handed over to the parents.

It will be seen that «the debate revolved around the *corpus material*, the specific biological materials separated from the body of a person who had died prematurely, around something incorporeal, namely protecting personality rights, and around the consequences that would result from not having access to information contained in the material support and about which no written record yet exists» (54).

And it should be noted that although the Court made no reference to the claim by the hospital that the samples were part of its scientific equity, it anyway stated that the parents were entitled to be given the samples because of the benefits the information contained in them could bring to their own health and perhaps to that of children they might have in the future.

All this shows the powers that a subject can retain with respect to his or her sample even if he or she has voluntarily agreed to donate it to research, in view of the information that can be extracted from it. Thus, even if the research institute is deemed to own the sample because it has «acquired» it legally from the subject

---

(53) Colombian Constitutional Court, Judgement C-394 of 2000. Magistrate José Gregorio Hernández.
(54) GONZÁLEZ DE CANCINO, Emilssen, *Muestras Biológicas Humanas y Derecho*. Roman Law Conference, Morelia (Mexico), August 2006.

it was taken from, rights anyway derive from the ownership by the subject of the information contained in the sample with respect both to the personal data (e.g. *habeas data*) and the physical sample itself (possession, destruction, use).

2.8. – *Protection of the subject's privacy (Duty of confidentiality and security of data and sample archives)*

Article 15 in the Colombian political constitution enshrines the right that everyone holds to personal and family privacy and to his or her good name. It also establishes the right to *habeas data* (55), the right that everyone holds to know, update and rectify information about him or her that has been gathered in databanks and in the files of public or private entities.

The right to privacy is enshrined in the Colombian political constitution as a fundamental right, one which protects «that sphere or area of private life which cannot be arbitrarily interfered in by other people, which is an essential element of the human being and manifests itself in the right to be able to act freely in that sphere or group and to exercise personal and family freedom with no limitations beyond the rights of others and the law» (56).

One area which the right to privacy protects concerns the way that personal information held in databanks is treated. The administration of information can, in fact, conflict on occasions with that right, since the information can relate to aspects of the person which, because of their nature, solely concern that person and therefore cannot be gathered, stored, known, used or transferred by others without prior authorisation, or only for reasons specifically enshrined in the law.

One way of protecting the right to privacy is enshrined in the fundamental right to *habeas data*, which «grants the holder of per-

---

(55) In Judgement C-877 of 2005, Magistrate Jaime Córdoba Triviño, the Constitutional Court stated the following: «On the question of the essential content of habeas data, the Court has said that this consists of the right to informative self-determination, which consists in turn of the power that people have to authorise information about them to be used, kept and circulated, in accordance with legal regulations, and of the general and particularly economic freedom, when this is violated due to information that is untrue or unauthorised by the person concerned being circulated».

(56) Constitutional Court, Judgement C-692 of 2003. Magistrate Marco Gerardo Monroy Cabra.

sonal information the power to demand that personal data administrators include or exclude data, grant access to it, or correct, update, certify or add to it, together with the power to restrict the dissemination, publication or transferral thereof, based on personal database administration process information principles» (57).

Pursuant to it exercising prior constitutionality control of statutory laws (58), the Constitutional Court recently passed Senate Bill 27 of 2006 – House of Representatives Bill 221 of 2007 (59). This Bill has already been approved by Congress of the Republic and passed by the President of the Republic, and has now become Law 1266 of 2008, whereby general *habeas data* provisions are enacted and the handling of information contained in personal databases, especially financial, credit, commercial and services information and that originating in third party countries, is regulated.

According to this, although the law refers especially (60) to financial, credit and commercial information, it includes certain generally-applicable precepts that we could use for the issue which concerns us.

One example is Article 3, which includes a number of definitions, one of the more notable of which is the concept that the holder of information is the private individual or legal entity to which the information refers that is in a databank and subject to the right to *habeas data* and other rights and guarantees established in the law. A further definition is of personal data, which is defined as being any information that is associated with one or more specific or specifiable persons or that could be associated with a private individual or legal entity. According to the law, personal data can be classified as public, semi-private or private. Public data is data which has been classified as such in the law or the political constitution. Semi-private data is data that is not of a private, confidential or public nature and where knowledge or dissemination thereof

---

(57) Constitutional Court, Judgement T-729 of 2002. Magistrate Eduardo Montealegre Lynett.
(58) Article 152 in the political constitution states that Congress will regulate the fundamental rights of the person through statutory laws. For this type of law to be passed, an absolute majority of Congressmen voting in favour is required, together with a previous constitutionality control by the Constitutional Court.
(59) Constitutional Court, Judgement C-1011 of 2008. Magistrate Jaime Córdoba Triviño.
(60) In the opinion of Nelson Remolina, as quoted by DEL PILAR ROCHA, Andrea, in «La ley de habeas data, más alla de la información financiera», *Ámbito Jurídico*, it deals superficially with issues like handling sensitive information that warrants more careful regulation in line with worldwide directives.

could interest not only the holder but also a group or sector or society in general. And private data is data that is relevant to the holder by virtue of its intimate nature.

However, in Judgement C-1011 of 2008 the Court expressed the opinion that the Bill – which is now Law 1266 of 2008 – is a partial or sector regulation of the *habeas data* fundamental right, in that it only regulates the handling of personal data of a financial nature for purposes of calculating credit risk.

The Court concludes by saying that the legislator is entitled to make regulations that cover only sectors of a right, and that this specific case relates to a Bill which refers solely and exclusively, both in its general part and in its individual provisions, to the *habeas data* right in financial matters and does not regulate the right in its entirety.

Despite this, before it enacted the law the Constitutional Court had already established the features of personal information, when it stated that such information «(i) relates to matters which are exclusive to a private individual, (ii) enables a person to be identified to a greater or lesser extent by virtue of the overall view that is achieved therewith and with other information, (iii) ownership is held exclusively by the holder thereof, something which is not altered when it is obtained legally or illicitly by a third party, and (iv) treatment thereof is subject to special rules (principles) governing the way it is obtained, administered and disseminated» (61). It had also established certain obligations and duties that arise for the administrators of such information.

Biobanks perform activities which involve dealing with information that is protected under the constitution, as when there has been no process aimed at making information irreversibly anonymous, data that can be extracted from the samples stored in them is considered personal, since it is or could be associated with a private individual. We can say that the term «personal information» is similar to identified information and to that which has been made irreversibly anonymous, respectively. Meanwhile, no parameter is established for establishing when the identity of a person is «determinable», or in other words, when we should be deemed to be in the realm of pseudo-anonymity rather than full anonymity.

---

(61) Constitutional Court, Judgement T-729 of 2002. Magistrate Eduardo Montealegre Lynett.

Apart from storing human biological samples, they are therefore administrators of personal information by virtue of the data that can be obtained from those samples, using a technical and scientific procedure, when it is or could be associated with the subject from which it has been taken. This is clearer if the establishments already hold information about the subject that has been obtained from the sample, mainly genetic data and information about his or her state of health, or other types of information such as age, physical or family characteristics, clinical background, habits or customs, or the population group or community to which he or she belongs.

When the biobank provides other institutions with samples or enters into exchange agreements, and if no procedure exists for making samples irreversibly anonymous, then when the biobank hands those samples over, it is potentially also handling over personal information, since the recipient institution could, for example, obtain information about the congenital pathologies or predispositions to certain illnesses that are associated or associable with a specific person. This problem could also be examined at ethnic or population group level.

The aforementioned Law 1266 sets out a number of principles for administering data, notable amongst which are the principle of purpose, which refers to the fact that there must be a legitimate purpose, in accordance with the law and the constitution, that the holder should be informed of prior to or at the same time as the authorisation is given, the restricted circulation principle, according to which circulation should be subject to limits deriving from the nature of the data, the information temporality principle, which establishes that information about the holder may not be supplied to users or third parties when it is no longer of use for databank purposes, the comprehensive interpretation of constitutional rights principle, which refers to the fact that the law should be construed as ensuring that the constitutional rights of the holder are covered, the security principle, which refers to the fact that all technical measures which might be necessary should be employed when handling the information in order to prevent it getting adulterated, lost, or consulted or used in an unauthorised manner, and he confidentiality principle, according to which everyone involved is obliged to guarantee that the information will be treated as confidential, even after its link to the work being done has ended. These, in fact, are principles that are recognised not only for financial databanks in doctrine and case law.

On the question of biobank activities, we would like to stress first of all the purpose principle. According to the Court, this principle «implies that (i) gathering personal information without establishing the reason for including it in the databank, and (ii) gathering, processing and disseminating personal information for a purpose other than that initially envisaged and authorised by the holder of the information, are prohibited (62).

In the case of biobanks, the subjects from whom the samples come, who are at the same time the holders of the information, should have been told beforehand both the initial and later purposes for which the information or the sample that could be obtained from it is to be used.

Secondly, and following on from the security principle, the personal data administrator – the biobank – should adopt the necessary technical measures for preventing unauthorised access to the information and for guaranteeing that it will be treated as confidential, even after the purpose for which it was obtained has ended. Thus, if the information that is held in the biobank (already taken from the samples, which could be taken from them, or relating to them) has been used in the research for which it was obtained, the confidentiality duty will still remain in force.

Additionally, other praetorian principles apply, such as the principle of liberty, according to which «activities involving the recording and dissemination of personal data may only be performed when the holder of such information, namely the subject concerned, has expressed his or her specific and free consent beforehand» (63), and the principle of necessity, according to which «the personal information concerned should be that which is strictly necessary for achieving the purposes of the databank» (64), which in turn implies that every database should adequately identify the purpose of gathering the personal information and the treatment it is to be given.

---

(62) Constitutional Court, Judgement C-1011 of 2008. Magistrate Jaime Córdoba Triviño.
(63) Constitutional Court, Judgement C-1011 of 2008. Magistrate Jaime Córdoba Triviño.
(64) Constitutional Court, Judgement C-1011 of 2008. Magistrate Jaime Córdoba Triviño.

And anyway, irrespective of whether or not there is any legal obligation, biobank activities should respect the constitutional rights of the subjects from whom the samples have come, especially the right to *habeas data*, to good name, to privacy and to information which, because they are fundamental rights, are covered by a direct protection mechanism in the Colombian body of laws, namely the civil action for the protection of constitutional rights (65).

Now, apart from the fact that information that is obtained from samples is personal, it also comes into the private information category. We will refer specifically to genetic information and information of a medical nature.

As far as the first of these is concerned, the Constitutional Court had undertaken a classification of personal information before Law 1266 was enacted, based on data contained in public information or information that is in the public domain, semi-private information, and confidential or secret information.

As far as the latter is concerned, it stated that it is «information which is of interest only to the holder because it is closely linked to protecting his or her rights to human dignity, privacy and liberty; such is the case with data about people's sexual inclinations, their ideological or political creed, their genetic information, their habits, etc.» (66). And it added that this information, which case law has grouped together into the «sensitive information» category, «cannot be accessed by third parties other than in an exceptional situation, where the confidential information is relevant evidence in a penal investigation and, in turn, is directly related to the aim of the investigation» (67).

---

(65) Article 86 in the Colombian political constitution reads as follows: «Everyone shall be entitled to file a civil action for the protection of constitutional rights before judges in order to claim immediate protection of his or her fundamental constitutional rights, either him or herself or through someone acting on his or her behalf, anywhere and at any time, by means of a preferential, concise procedure, whenever such rights are violated or threatened as the result of any act or omission by any public authority. Protection shall consist of an order for the person in question act or refrain from acting. The award, which should be complied with immediately, may be objected to before a competent judge, who shall anyway pass it on to the Constitutional Court for review. This action shall only apply when the affected party has no other means of judicial defence, apart from that which is used as a transitory mechanism for avoiding irreparable damage».

(66) Constitutional Court, Judgement C-1011 of 2008. Magistrate Jaime Córdoba Triviño.

(67) Constitutional Court, Judgement C-1011 of 2008. Magistrate Jaime Córdoba Triviño. The Court pointed out that «the restriction on divulging data of a private and confidential nature applies notwithstanding the existence of restrictive internal hypotheses, as would happen, for example, if the data contained in clinical records were to be circulated in a hospital for purposes

The Constitutional Court classifies genetic information as «sensitive information», recognises that it is closely linked to rights of a fundamental nature (68), and accordingly classifies it as confidential, thereby granting it the greatest protection possible for information of a personal nature.

Turning now to the second point, medical data, the Constitutional Court has stressed that everyone is entitled to have information about his or her state of health treated as confidential. It is because of this right that medical secrets and medical records are inviolable. This protection of medical data moreover «has a clear *raison d'être* in a constitutional order that is based on human dignity and personal autonomy (political constitution, Article 1), since if certain information about a person's clinical situation is divulged, it could result in that person being subjected to discrimination and to his or her free development being hindered (political constitution, Articles 13 and 16)» (69).

Thus, the Court states, «if a person's medical information is to be circulated, the person must specifically consent thereto. Only exceptional circumstances, in which the fundamental rights of third parties are clearly affected or endangered, could justify any interference in this intimate and private area of a person, and then provided that there are no other suitable means of offsetting the danger» (70).

This protection of medical information is restated in Resolution 1995 of 1999, «whereby regulations are established for the management of medical records», which states that «the medical record is an obligatory, *confidential* private document which chronologically

---

of ensuring adequate medical care. These modalities are permissible, provided that the holder has granted his or her specific authorisation and that internal circulation is aimed at serving constitutionally legitimate goals».

(68) One example of the close relationship between genetic information and various fundamental rights is to be found in the civil action for the protection of constitutional rights case that was resolved by the Constitutional Court in Judgement T-394 of 2000, Magistrate José Gregorio Hernández. This referred to a couple who asked a hospital to hand over biological samples taken from their daughter – who was stillborn – in the necropsy, so that a genetic study could be undertaken that would enable the risks to be established to the health of a future child. The Court expressed the view that «the controversy in question involves other fundamental rights – life, health, information, free development of the personality, and the right to have a family in a responsible manner» – and it proceeded to study these.

(69) Constitutional Court, Judgement T-212 of 2000. Magistrate Alejandro Martínez Caballero.

(70) Constitutional Court, Judgement T-212 of 2000. Magistrate Alejandro Martínez Caballero.

records a patient's state of health, medical acts and other procedures carried out by the health team involved in his or her care. *This document may only be seen by third parties when the patient so authorises, or in the cases stipulated in the law*». (*The underlining is ours*).

Similarly, Resolution 13437 of 1991, which was issued by the Ministry of Health (nowadays the Ministry of Social Protection), enshrines the following as a right of the patient : «4. his or her right to have all medical record reports treated as confidential and secret, and to have such reports divulged only when he or she has granted the respective authorisation».

We have given details of the regulations relating to medical records on the understanding that the protection which the body of laws provides them with derives from the fact that they are considered to be supporting documentation containing personal information relating to health, as does a biological sample, but with the proviso that with the latter, a technical and scientific procedure is required in order to extract that information. In the absence of specific regulations in Colombia relating to considering a biological sample as providing support for personal information, it is therefore plausible to turn to principles which guide how other health information is to be treated. Thus, as in other cases, the nature of the information is a determining factor in establishing the legal system governing the supporting element.

In conclusion, according to the protection system indicated for genetic information and for the medical data of a given subject, and since such information is private, the prior informed consent is required of the person from whom such information comes for management purposes and effects (gathering, storage, treatment, use and circulation).

Furthermore, as far as the issue which is of interest to us is concerned, since biological samples (which have not been irreversibly dissociated) carry that information, then any handing-over of such samples implies that that information can potentially be transmitted, and in principle, therefore, the prior consent of the holder, in other words the person from whom the information was obtained, is required before it can be disposed of.

To all the foregoing can be added what is stated in regulations governing research on human beings in Colombia. The Health

Research Resolution, in fact, states that when research is being conducted on humans, the privacy will be protected of the subject of the research, with the person only being identified when he or she so authorises. This informed consent should contain the information that is referred to in Article 15, which should be explained fully and clearly to the subject of the research.

Decree 2493 on Transplants states that information relating to the donor, the receiver and the donation process is to be treated as confidential, and that it may only be divulged for purposes of meeting the obligations to supply information which are stipulated in that Decree, or when so ordered by a competent judicial authority.

Meanwhile, the Good Practices Manual for Tissue and Bone Marrow Banks sets out a number of specific safety measures for guaranteeing confidentiality. These include measures relating to materials, specifically packing materials, which should be stored safely in order to prevent unauthorised persons having access to them. As far as documentation is concerned, the bank should keep a record of all action taken and completed; data may only be entered or altered by authorised persons, and a record should be kept of all such actions; access to the system should be restricted, and passwords or other safety mechanisms may be used for this purpose. On the question of extracting or rescuing bone marrow and tissue, each donor will be assigned a separate identification code or number, in order to ensure confidentiality.

De Facto Situation

We can draw the following conclusions from the surveys with respect to the security measures that are used for protecting samples and information obtained from or associated with them.

– The sample is protected in most cases by a reversible system for making it anonymous. In other words, the sample is assigned a code which associates it with data identifying the person it comes from (5 out of 6). An alphanumeric code is always used (6 out of 6), and in most cases this is assigned manually (3 out of 5).

– Information resulting from the analysis of the biological sample is protected by a reversible system for making it anonymous (6 out of 6). In other words, the information obtained from the sample possesses a code which associates it with data identifying the per-

son it comes from. In two cases, some samples are associated with data enabling the person they come from to be identified.
- The mechanisms detailed below are also used for protecting data obtained from samples or associated with them.
- Access to databases is restricted.
- Persons having access to such data are required to sign a confidentiality document.
- Databases never give first names or surnames.
- Information is centralised.
- The main researchers or research coordinators have access to the data, together with the other joint researchers or assistants in some cases (2). If people not involved in the research want to gain access to data, they have to request authorisation first from the institution's Ethics in Research Committee.

2.9. – *Extent of the consent (generic or specific)*

The Health Research Resolution states that all research which involves using human biological samples, including all activities relating to the obtaining, preservation, preparation and final use thereof, should adhere to the regulations established under the «Research on Human Beings» Heading and other Articles connected with the disposal of organs, tissues and corpses of human beings (Article 47). Articles 14 and 15 under this Heading refer to informed consent as the written agreement whereby the subject of the research or his or her representative freely and without any force whatsoever authorises him or her to take part in the research, provided that he or she is fully acquainted with the nature of the procedure and the benefits and risks he or she will be subject to. The Articles also list the information that should be given in the informed consent document.

On the question of informed consent, the Resolution specifically regulates certain hypotheses, such as research with minimal risk where, subject to Ethics in Research Committee authorisation being granted, consent may not be required to be given in writing; in the case of research with no risk, the researcher may dispense with obtaining consent at all; with research on communities, health and other civil authority approval will be required in addition to the consent of the subjects included in the study; in the case of research on children or the disabled, in addition to the informed consent of whoever holds parental rights or legally represents the child or disabled person in question, a certificate should be obtained from a neurologist, psychiatrist or psychologist stating that the subject is capable of understanding, reasoning and using logic; and with research on pregnant women, women while giving birth and during the puerperium and lactation, and in research on live or dead newly-born babies or relating to the use of embryos, dead babies or foetuses or for artificial fertilisation, the informed consent should be obtained of the woman and her spouse or partner – except in the event of disability or when it is manifestly or convincingly impossible for such consent to be given – once they have been given information as to the risks to the embryo, foetus or newly-born baby in each case.

Decree 2493 on Transplants defines informed consent as a free and specific manifestation of will by a person who is donor or receiver of a body component that is given after such person has received and understood information relating to the procedure that is to be carried out. It also establishes that before body components can be used for transplant or implant purposes, specific informed consent should have been given in the form of a sworn statement before a notary public, with a period of at least 24 hours elapsing between the signing of the document and extraction of the organ, and the subject should have received information about the consequences of his or her decision and the fact that it is impossible to be sure of all risks that could occur during the procedure, since unforeseeable circumstances could arise.

In Resolution 5108 of 2005 (71), «whereby the Good Practices Manual for Bone Marrow and Tissue Banks is established and other provisions are enacted», it is stated that before stem cells are extracted from bone marrow, all matters relating to the procedure and the risks it could entail should be explained to the donor in terms that he or she can understand, and specific informed consent should be granted, with a period of at least 24 hours elapsing between the signing of the document and extraction of the bone

---

(71) Hereinafter «Good Practices Manual for Bone Marrow and Tissue Banks».

marrow, and with the provisions stipulated in Article 16 in Decree 2493 of 2004 being taken into account.

As stated under other points, there are no specific regulations in Colombia governing what matters the source subject should be informed of when a biological sample is going to be taken form him or her for storage in a biobank. The information that the subject should be provided with in such cases is very particular, in view of the unusual situation, and specific regulation by the legislator or the corresponding regulatory authority would be required.

This hypothesis is not entirely similar to research with human beings that is regulated in the general Colombian body of laws, since in this case the object of the research is an item that has been separated from a human body and whose main importance lies in its being considered to be information support, and therefore, although there is a real risk that the rights of the subject will be affected, it is anyway different from the potential extent to which health can be affected when the research is conducted directly on the subject.

In view of the lack of regulations, we have mentioned under this point those matters which subjects should be informed of under the terms of our legislation in the case of research on human beings and the disposal of body components, because they indicate what common points information should be provided on and their relative degree of specificity, and in general terms, they give an idea of the guarantee that should exist in the integration of information.

De Facto Situation (numbers 2 and 4)

– The samples taken by those institutions which completed the survey all came from live donors, specifically and exclusively for research purposes. Moreover, in only one case did the samples (contra-samples) come from paternity tests as part of jurisdictional proceedings.
– No samples have come from corpses.
– All institutions always asked the person to consent to the sample being used for these specific, exclusive research purposes.
– Consent was expressed in a written document at all the institutions.

- When requesting consent, apart from pointing out that the sample will be used for research purposes, potential donors are generally told about other matters (specific consent), such as what data it will be possible to gain from the sample, the place where it will be stored, the name of the institution conducting the research, the name of the director or person in charge, the goal and the use to which the information obtained from the sample will be put, and the potential donor is also told that he or she is entitled to raise any other query he or she might have.
- Three of the six institutions do not tell the subject how long the sample will be stored, and no reference is made to any right to ask for it to be destroyed. Nor is authorisation requested at two of the six institutions for the sample to be used in other research or for it to be passed on to other institutions. One of the six institutions does not request consent for the sample to be stored, and no reference is made to the right to be told of the information that is obtained from the sample.
- Information obtained from samples is kept indefinitely.

2.10. – *Use of samples obtained for another purpose*

Under the previous point (obtaining samples), we examined the possible sources of biological samples that are stored in the biobanks of different kinds of institutions, such as scientific research institutions, hospitals or state research entities.

It was shown that all activities resulting in the obtaining of samples are performed with an immediate goal in mind, such as diagnosing an illness, obtaining genetic information for health research, or performing a test for judicial proceedings. However, once this immediate goal has been achieved, or if it proves impossible to achieve it, questions arise as to what should be done subsequently with the sample: should it be destroyed, should it be kept and stored indefinitely or as long as is biologically viable, or should it be used for some other purpose, such as biomedical research? And if information is extracted from it, the question also arises of it possibly being used later in other activities.

No specific regulations exist in Colombia for answering these questions, and with a view to finding a solution, recourse should therefore be had to the general guiding principles behind our body of laws, rights of a constitutional nature and regulations governing the different activities in which biological samples are obtained, and in general terms, answers should be deduced in the direction of protecting the rights of the subjects involved.

A query arises mainly in cases where a change occurs in the purpose initially envisaged for the sample or the information obtained from it. We can, in fact, put forward two hypotheses.

The first of these is when an alternative subsequent use is presented to the donor or other subsequent purposes are established during the process of obtaining the sample, either for it or for the information that might be gathered from it. In institutions which not only provide hospital services but also carry out research, for example, the document requesting consent to carry out the procedure of obtaining a sample for diagnostic purposes – or preferably a separate document (72) – could also request authorisation for the biological sample or the information that is obtained from it to be used subsequently in biomedical research, or for it to be stored in the institution's biobank or in some other one.

Under this hypothesis of there being both an immediate and a mediate goal at the time a sample is taken, the regulations governing each of these respective activities should apply. In the example mentioned, when an institution in Colombia is taking a sample, it should adhere to regulations governing the practising of medicine, especially those relating to informed consent which are contained in the Medical Ethics Code (Law 23 of 1981) and regulatory decrees thereon. And the regulations governing research on human beings – which include, as has already been mentioned, research where human biological samples are used – that are established in the Health Research Resolution should also be adhered to.

The two activities (medicine and research) have principles or rules in common, such as informing a person of the risks involved, indicating what information can be gained about his or her health, the confidential treatment that the information will be given in

---

(72) The importance of the consent by the subject from whom the sample is taken being given in a separate document lies in the fact that the biobank should set out to deposit on its own premises the documents accrediting the informed consent of subjects from whom it has extracted samples that are stored, so that when the sample is physically handed over to another biobank or institution, those documents can be handed over at the same time.

accordance with the purpose for which it was obtained, and the right to not know that the person is suffering from certain illnesses or is likely to suffer from them. In view of the nature of research activities, however, there are further requirements that can be stipulated, namely that information be provided about the aims of the research, the possible benefits to the person, the right to know the results, the institution that is conducting the research or the name of the researcher in charge of it, how long information or the sample will be stored for, or whether it will be used in other research or by other institutions.

Finally, we repeat that whenever it is foreseen or foreseeable at the time the sample is taken that it will be used subsequently for a purpose other than that for which it is going to be taken, the subject should be informed in the fullest and most comprehensible and specific manner possible of all matters relating to that mediate purpose, and since in our case this is biomedical research, he or she should be told things like the goals (economic, commercial or purely scientific), the powers the subject retains with respect to the sample and information that might be obtained from it, the fact that the confidentiality obligation remains, and the rights the subject holds with respect to any benefits that might be obtained.

The second hypothesis is more problematic, namely when there is no more than an immediate goal for the sample or the information that is obtained from it at the time the sample is taken, but when this has been achieved (or when it becomes impossible to achieve it), either the sample or the information is to be used for some other purpose that was not consented to by the source subject who, at the same time, owns the personal information contained in it.

We will refer in this report to samples that could currently be held in biobanks for *in vitro* biomedical research but which were initially taken for some other purpose, which was the only one that the source subject consented to. This takes on importance when the sample or the information obtained from it was not subjected to an irreversible procedure for making it anonymous and it is neither convenient nor beneficial to do so for its subsequent use.

It is basically a question of two extremes: the interests of biomedical research, and the fundamental rights of the subject from whom the sample comes. And the fact cannot be ruled out that economic, industrial or commercial interests could also be involved.

As far as the first of these extremes is concerned, Colombia's political constitution guarantees freedom of research (73), and grants it fundamental right status.

The Colombian Constitutional Court has said that «freedom which consists of expressing and reflecting human rationality is part of a person's fundamental rights, and the natural tendency in this to search for the truth in different fields necessarily leads to new areas of knowledge being incessantly explored» (74). Moreover, various articles in the constitution (2, 70 and 71) commit the state to promoting and fostering research, especially by further education establishments.

The Constitutional Court has also said that the right to freedom of research includes a general interest commitment, one which «takes on greater importance in the case of research which studies the human being, since the implications that its results could have in the sphere of human dignity (political constitution, Articles 1, 42 and 70) mean that the state's supervision duty and the researchers' level of responsibility should be that much greater» (75).

And it went on to say the following: «the fact that the prevalence of the fundamental right to research necessarily implies that no restriction of a general nature can be imposed on it does not mean that this guarantee has no social commitment attached to it. On the one hand, the state retains the legitimate power to control and supervise any such activities that private individuals carry out in this field through its authorities, but at the same time, those private individuals are obliged to behave in a responsible manner as far as handling the results of their research is concerned» (76).

Thus, although the right to free investigation is guaranteed constitutionally, it is not a right that can be exercised without any lim-

---

(73) Article 27. The state guarantees freedom of teaching, learning and research.
Article 69, paragraph 3. The state shall reinforce scientific research in official and private universities, and shall provide special conditions for this to be done.
Article 70, paragraph 2. Culture in its different manifestations is one of the cornerstones of nationality. The state recognises the equality and dignity of everyone living in the country. The state shall promote research, science, and the development and dissemination of the nation's cultural values.
(74) Constitutional Court, Judgement T-172 of 1993. Magistrate José Gregorio Hernández Galindo.
(75) Constitutional Court, Judgement C-505 of 2001. Magistrate Marco Gerardo Monroy Cabra.
(76) Constitutional Court, Judgement C-505 of 2001. Magistrate Marco Gerardo Monroy Cabra.

its whatsoever. The basic principle on which it is based is that the first limit on any right is the rights of other people, with special consideration being given to constitutional rights of a fundamental nature.

If we follow this line of thought, any research activity in Colombia, such as that which is conducted on the human body or which implies using any of its components, should adhere to the principles, values and rights that are enshrined in the political constitution. It should thus respect human dignity, the fact that the general interest prevails over private interests, the prevalence of a person's inalienable rights, the principle of protecting ethnic diversity and the principle of protecting the nation's cultural and natural riches, and the extensive catalogue of rights which likewise impose a limit on research and on all activities associated with it (77).

As far as the specific question is concerned of using samples for *in vitro* biomedical research that were initially to be used for some other purpose, the rights that are in special danger of being violated are the right to free development of the personality, the right to personal and family privacy, the right to freedom and autonomy, and the right to freedom of thought.

This practice would be licit as long as the rights of the subject from whom the sample is taken were guaranteed, but it is impossible to establish precise rules. Rather, the way in which the conflict between the rights and interests that are at stake, irrespective of whether these are personal, scientific, economic, ethical, etc., is to be resolved should be determined in each case. The use of samples left over from diagnostic tests for biomedical research, for example, is not something that can be judged beforehand.

This practice would, in fact, be illegal if the patient became a subject of research as a consequence of the results obtained from an analysis of the samples taken in the clinical context. Thus, if no consent was requested at the time the sample was taken for it to be used subsequently in research, the patient could not be forced to

---

(77) Heading II in the political constitution is entitled «Rights, Guarantees and Duties». The Heading is, in turn, subdivided into three Chapters: «Fundamental Rights», «Social, Economic and Cultural Rights», and «Collective and Environmental Rights». And the procedural measures were also established for guaranteeing that those rights are respected: the civil action for the protection of constitutional rights, to ensure that fundamental rights are respected, and the people's action for the protection of collective rights and interests.

take part later in research that he or she had never been informed of. The patient could not be transported from a medical environment (where the sample was taken) to a research environment, unless he or she had known this and accepted it.

Similarly, if it was intended right from the start to use the sample for research in the pharmacological or industrial field, the patient should have been told this, since concealing economic goals in order to get round ethical and legal imperatives is not justifiable.

If, on the on the hand, surplus samples are used in health research and the right to information and confidentiality has been guaranteed from the start, with no interference in the patient's private life and no disguising of real interests, there can be no reproach from the patient's rights angle.

Paradigmatic cases can arise where special considerations are warranted. For example, with samples that have been stored for a long time and where it is impossible or would involve an excessive effort to contact the source subject in order to request his or her consent to the new goals sought (78).

In our opinion, in that specific situation – unlike that which arises when it is possible to contact the source subject – they can in principle be used in the field of biomedical research if, firstly, it was not foreseeable that they would be used for that purpose at the start and the consent of the subject for this was therefore not requested, since – and we repeat – under no circumstances can the concealing of information from the source subject that the institution or the researchers had or should have had knowledge of at the time the sample was taken be condoned, favoured or encouraged. And secondly, if it is not advisable in the research to subject them to a process of making them irreversible anonymous, they can be used, provided that there is no danger of the subject's fundamental rights being violated and that his or her life is not affected in any way (his or her privacy, everyday life, peace and calm, etc.).

Furthermore, according to the Health Research Resolution that is in force in Colombia, institutions which conduct research on humans, which includes that which is conducted using body com-

---

(78) If it is a question of subsequently using information about the subject relating to the samples, what was stated under the point relating to protecting the subject's privacy should apply.

ponents (Article 47), «should have an Ethics in Research Committee which has the job of dealing with all issues that might arise on the subject» (Article 3), and so decisions relating to these and other particularly problematic questions should be submitted to it (79).

The internationally-recognised principle relating to the rights of the person prevailing over those of society or science should anyway be remembered.

De Facto Situation

From the information we were provided with in the survey, all the institutions that answered it obtained samples specifically and exclusively for research purposes.

2.11. – *Specifically issues related with local communities*

Heading II, Chapter II, of the Health Research Resolution refers to research on communities.

It states that human health research on communities will only be permitted when the expected benefit to those communities is reasonably certain, and when previous studies, conducted on a small scale, have determined that there are no risks (Article 17). Before any such research can be conducted, approval should be obtained from the health authorities and the respective authorities in the community, together with the informed consent of the individuals who will be taking part in the study (Article 18) (80). Participation will be entirely voluntary.

---

(79) There is a gap in Colombian legislation with respect to regulations governing these committees, one which can be seen, for example, in the fact that the general guiding principles are not established for the few functions the committees are assigned or for what members should sit on them in order to guarantee independence in decisions that are made and an adequate balance between the interests that are at stake.

(80) It should be stressed that indigenous and Afro-Colombian communities have been campaigning very actively to ensure that the rights and guarantees they are granted under the terms of the political constitution are protected. This is reflected, for example, in Judgement C-030 of 2008, which declares the Forestry Law (Law 1021 of 2006) unenforceable because indigenous groups were not consulted about it beforehand, and according to Law 21 of 1991, whereby ILO Agreement 169 was approved, governments are obliged to consult indigenous or tribal peoples about all legislative or administrative measures that are likely to affect them directly. The Court based itself on the same arguments in Judgement C-175 of 2009 when it declared Law 1152 of 2007, which enacted the Rural Development Statute, unenforceable.

It likewise states that if the individuals who make up the community are not capable of understanding the implications of taking part in the research, the Ethics in Research Committee of the entity to which the main researcher belongs, or of the entity where the research will be conducted, may grant authorisation for the informed consent of the subjects to be given through a reliable person who holds moral authority over the community (Article 19).

In the event of experimental research, the research institute, in addition to having an Ethics in Research Committee, should first request authorisation from the Ministry of Social Protection and also undertake toxicity studies and other tests, depending on the characteristics of the products and the risks they imply top human health (Article 20).

Finally, it states that all research on communities should include practical measures for protecting individuals and ensuring that valid results are obtained (Article 21), and that ethical considerations applicable to research on humans should be extrapolated from the research on communities (Article 22).

2.12. – *Maintenance :*
security standards, storage lengths

We have not found any regulations in the body of Colombian laws which relate to the length of time that a sample may be kept after it has been extracted. However, in view of the considerations mentioned under the point relating to informed consent, the institution may keep samples for as long as the subject has authorised. This period should be determined on the basis of criteria like the maximum length of time that the sample can be kept without deteriorating and how long the research it will be used for will last.

De Facto Situation

As far as the length of time that a sample may be kept is concerned, there is no uniform criterion : one bank keeps samples for as long as the research lasts, while another says it keeps them indefinitely, and the remaining institutions did not answer the question.

2.13. – *National and international transfer and circulation of samples*

We have not found any regulations in Colombia which specifically regulate the transferring or exchanging of biological samples for research purposes, and research institutions that store biological samples or biobanks cannot therefore be ordered to meet any specific legal requirements. This perhaps explains why it can be seen from answers to the questions on the survey which referred to this issue that some national research institutions occasionally transfer their samples to international institutions without this being controlled or supervised in any way by any state entity.

It has been said in this text, in connection with the guarantees that the subject should be given in terms of his or her rights, especially at the time his or her informed consent is obtained, that if it is foreseen (or foreseeable) at a given institution that samples will be used for more than one research activity at the same time or for further research at a later date, the consent of the patient should be obtained first, with authorisation being specifically requested for those purposes.

The danger of the subject's rights being violated is clearer where samples are transferred between different research institutions or biobanks, since the establishment which, in principle, holds custody of the samples and is responsible for administering information connected with them changes. The source subject should therefore be asked to authorise the institution to hand such samples over to another institution. If the name of this second institution is known, it should be stated specifically, but if not, a general authorisation should be requested. All institutions which could potentially hold the samples and information relating to them should also offer the subject the same guarantees in terms of his or her rights, as stated in the initial informed consent document.

The only regulations that exist in Colombia do not provide a satisfactory answer on this issue.

On the one hand, Decree 2493 of 2004 on Transplants states that «bone marrow or tissue may only be exported from the country by way of donation for transplant or implant purposes on grounds of human solidarity and on a non-profit basis, after authorisation therefor has been given by the National Institute for the Supervision of Medicines and Foodstuffs, INVIMA. They may only be exported from the country through Tissue Banks or Bone Marrow Banks» (Article 37). And as far as importing is concerned, Article 39 refers to there being a therapeutic need for the body component.

Decree 1573 of 1993, meanwhile, prohibits the exporting of total blood or components or derivatives thereof, and states that «only for reasons of a serious public calamity or on grounds of international solidarity, and providing national needs can be met, may the Ministry of Health authorise blood or components thereof to be exported on an occasional basis, and then solely for therapeutic purposes and on a non-profit basis» (Article 8).

It will be seen that the regulation restricts the exporting and importing of blood and human body components to when grounds exist for international solidarity, and this could lead to the hypothesis being deduced that it would not be possible to import and export them merely for research purposes.

However, we have not found any provision in the general body of laws that prohibits the exporting or importing of biological samples or human body components for scientific research purposes. In our opinion, therefore, we cannot deduce that the abovementioned regulations constitute a ban on this activity, and it should accordingly be stated that such a hypothesis is not regulated in Colombia, and it thus does not constitute illegal conduct, at least in principle.

It is perhaps because of this lack of a ban that institutions stated in some surveys that they had sent human biological samples abroad, certainly on the principle that guides relations between the state and its associates, namely that what is not specifically prohibited is permitted.

De Facto Situation

On the issue of transferring samples to other researchers, we have the information that was given in the surveys, from which we can conclude that three of the institutions surveyed do send samples, two of them abroad, under joint research agreements with other research institutes, educational establishments and industrial, commercial or pharmaceutical companies. It is impossible for us to determine whether samples have been transferred at national level, since the necessary information was not given in the survey.

The survey also asked whether banks contained samples that had come from other countries, and the general answer was «no».

2.14. – Property rights

This point will deal with the question of the possible economic benefits of scientific research that is conducted using human biological samples, since, as stated in the definition we have based ourselves on, samples contain genetic material (nucleic acids) that is deemed to be biological material and they are an important source of information which could lead to economic gain in the context of bio-technological progress. The main issue that will be studied is whether human biological material can be patented.

Colombia is governed by the industrial property system that was set up under Andean Community of Nations Decision 486 of 2000 (81). The requirements for it to be possible for an invention to patented are the same as those that are generally stipulated anywhere else in the world: newness, inventiveness and industrial application, with the particularities there might be in terms of understanding each one.

The Decision also contains a list of what is not considered to be an invention, from which we mention the following: «(a) discoveries, scientific theories and mathematical methods, (b) all or part of living beings as found in nature, natural biological processes, biological material that exists in nature or which can be isolated, including the genome or germoplasma of any natural living being».

This is the base regulation for starting the discussion of what can be patented in Colombia in our field of interest, or to put it another way, which bio-technological inventions the Colombian patents

---

(81) The Andean Community of Nations (CAN) is a regional organisation of which Bolivia, Peru, Colombia and Ecuador are currently members. The four countries are home to almost 100 million inhabitants, in a surface area of 3,798,000 square kilometres. The Andean Integration System (SAI) consists of all organisations and institutions in the Andean Community, and its purpose is to allow for effective coordination between member countries so as to make Andean sub-region integration that much closer, to promote the sub-region abroad, and to reinforce action connected with the integration process. SAI is made up of the following organisations and institutions: Andean Presidential Council, Andean Council of Ministers of Foreign Affairs, Andean Community Commission, Andean Community General Secretariat, Andean Community Court of Justice, Andean Parliament, Business Consultancy Council, Labour Consultancy Council, Andean Development Corporation, Latin American Reserves Fund, Simón Rodríguez Agreement, Andean Health Organisation – Hipólito Unanue Agreement, and Simón Bolívar Andean University. For further information go to www.comunidadandina.org

office would grant the privilege of a patent to and which ones it would not (82). Clearly, other regulations in the Decision which refer to requirements for an invention to be patentable, application requirements and the nullity system must also be met.

For various authors, under the terms of the CAN Decision and especially Article 15 therein transcribed above, genes, proteins and polypeptides cannot be patented in Colombia, since they imply identifying something that already exists in nature (83). It is nevertheless debatable whether or not, in the light of this regulation, a similar position could be adopted to that taken up in the European Directive, according to which the total or partial sequence of a gene that has been isolated or has been obtained by means of a technical procedure can be patented, even though the structure of the said element is identical to that of a natural element (Article 5.2) (84).

On the other hand, it is fairly clear that it is possible in Colombia to patent biological material (genes or gene sequences) that has been isolated or obtained using some other procedure and then modified or transformed, for example by re-combining DNA techniques, and also is of use industrially.

This does not mean that the same questions are not asked in Colombia as elsewhere in the world – albeit with less intensity. It should moreover be remembered that different interpretations with varied scopes and contents can be made of the body of regulations governing the industrial property system, especially on the question of patents, and that intellectual property is anyway one area of law where the greatest efforts are being made to establish a common, worldwide system, as evidenced by the trend in Europe (Directive 98/44/CE, for example) and the OMC Agreement on Aspects of Intellectual Property Rights relating to Trade (ADPIC).

Many different issues have been discussed on the question of the patentability of human genetic material, and many and varied have been the answers that have been given by national and supra-

---

(82) One function of the Superintendency of Industry and Trade is to deal with everything to do with issues like processing patent applications, granting compulsory licences and exploitation licences, filing and registering patents, decreeing expiry of the rights patents confer.

(83) ARCHILA PEÑALOSA, Emilio José, «Radiografía de patentamiento del genoma humano», *La Propiedad Inmaterial*, No. 1, 2001, pp. 81-101. Similarly, GONZÁLEZ DE CANCINO, Emilssen, «Patentes sobre genes humanos», *Derecho y Vida*, No. XXXVIII, 2004.

(84) In favour of an affirmative answer, GONZÁLEZ DE CANCINO, Emilssen, *op. cit.*, p. 3.

national patent offices, bearing in mind that to the purely legal component must be added the political, environmental, ethical and, above all, economic aspects of the question. We will now briefly refer to some of these topics that Colombian doctrine has studied, in connection with protecting human genes using patents law.

Firstly, it is claimed that the newness requirement is not met, since the gene or gene sequence is an element that is found in nature. Traditionally, patents law has protected inventions. This is why, under the hypothesis of vindicating genes or gene sequences, discussion revolves around whether the object of the patent is an invention or a discovery. The tendency in industrialised nations is to extend protection to discoveries, because some people say that nowadays discovery involves merit, effort, work and research (85).

To the above can be added the view that what we have is an invention – not a discovery – when the gene or gene sequence can not only be isolated and produced but also have an industrial application, and in that case there can be no doubt as to its patentability. Thus if, in addition to identifying the gene or gene sequence, the protein or polypeptide that codes and the function they perform are found, the gene or gene sequence could be the vindication of the patent.

And with respect to this industrial application, arguments are also going on about what the scope of it should be or how it is to be understood, particularly since it is claimed that the gene and the protein or polypeptide that codes are known, but the practical application that could be developed is not; occasionally, however, it has been considered that «it is sufficient to demonstrate a reasonable chance of success in the proposed industrial application for the requirement to be deemed to have been met» (86). It should be pointed out that granting a patent on a gene or gene sequence with a very flexible analysis in terms of the usefulness to industry requirement could result in scientific research being blocked or coming to lack any stimulus, since companies would not conduct research on a gene or gene sequence that has already been patented, bearing in mind the economic risk that this would entail if someone else held such an ample exploitation right.

---

(85) RENGIFO GARCÍA, Ernesto, *Propiedad intelectual. El moderno derecho de autor*, 2nd Edition, Ed. Universidad Externado de Colombia, Bogotá, 1997, p.292.
(86) GONZÁLEZ DE CANCINO, *op. cit.*, p. 2.

As far as the inventiveness requirement is concerned, arguments also rage as to whether the privilege that the patent grants really is a reward for human ingenuity : for some people, this ingenuity cannot be seen in the mere identification of genes or gene sequences, especially as the technique has advanced so much that machines are nowadays used for undertaking the routine work of identifying gene sequences. Others, on the other hand, recognise that identifying a gene and the protein or polypeptide that codes is a long and time-consuming task, one which requires creativity and human intellect, and that it therefore deserves to be patented.

Finally, in systems where the morality clause (87) is included, some people argue whether the patents office can prevent the privilege being granted to genes or gene sequences by applying this clause. Behind this are arguments of a political, ethical, economic and social justice nature all around the world.

Apart for the above considerations, it should be stressed that because of the particular characteristics and features of the population make-up in Andean Community of Nations member countries, Decision 486 establishes certain regulations in the patents system for protecting indigenous, Afro-American and local communities, and these have important legal effects.

The general protection principle is set out in Article 3, which states that «Member Countries shall guarantee that when the protection conferred on elements of intellectual property is granted, the biological and genetic heritage and the traditional knowledge of their indigenous, Afro-American and local communities shall be safeguarded and respected. The granting of patents on inventions resulting from material which has been obtained from such heritage or such knowledge shall accordingly be subject to the said material having been acquired in accordance with the international, community and national body of laws» (88).

---

(87) Article 20 in Decision 486. «The following shall not be patentable : (a) inventions where commercial exploitation thereof in the territory of the respective Member Country must of necessity be prevented in order to protect public or moral order; to this end, commercial exploitation of an invention shall not be deemed to contravene public or moral order simply because a legal or administrative provision exists which prohibits or regulates such exploitation (...)».

(88) Decision 391 was issued by the Andean Community of Nations, and this establishes the «common system for access to genetic resources» : Article 4 in this Decision excludes from its sphere of application human genetic resources and products derived therefrom. This explains why we have not mentioned the Decision when studying this point.

And, following on specifically from this point, it states that if the legal requirements governing access to the genetic resources which resulted in the procedure or product patent being developed were not met when such resources were obtained, this constitutes grounds for absolute nullity (89).

2.15. – *Other issues*

It should be noted that some Decisions of the Constitutional Court related to this matter have been identified:

2.15.1. *T-559 of 1995*

Twenty-ninth (29) November, Nineteen Ninety Five (1995).
Magistrate Rapporteur: Dr. ALEJANDRO MARTINEZ CABALLERO.
Issue: Informed consent of patient.

2.15.2. *SU-337 of 1999*

Twelfth (12) May, Nineteen Ninety Nine (1999).
Magistrate Rapporteur: Dr. ALEJANDRO MARTINEZ CABALLERO.

Issues: Grounds, definition and scope of informed consent in medical treatment. Operating on minors and informed consent: in cases where the consent of parents or guardians does not apply. Legal problems associated with «hermaphroditism» or forms of «gender disguise». Family autonomy in medical matters and risks of social discrimination against persons with ambiguous genitalia: the need for qualified and persistent informed consent of parents.

2.15.3. *T-394 of 2000*

Sixth (6) April, Two Thousand (2000).

---

(89) Article 75. The competent national authority shall decree, either officially or at the request of any person and at any time, absolute nullity of a patent when: (...) (g) if applicable, a copy has not been submitted of the access contract, when the products or procedures for which a patent is sought have been obtained or developed from genetic resources or products deriving therefrom originating in any Member Country; (h) if applicable, if a copy has not been submitted of the document accrediting the licence or authorisation to use the traditional knowledge of indigenous, Afro-American or local communities in Member Countries, when the products or procedures for which a patent is sought have been obtained or developed from such knowledge originating in any Member Country (...).

Magistrate Rapporteur: Dr. José Gregorio Hernández Galindo.

Issue: Duty to provide medical information (retention of tissue samples).

2.15.4. *T-1390 of 2000*

Twelfth (12) October, Two Thousand (2000).

Magistrate Rapporteur: Dr. Alejandro Martinez Caballero.

Issue: Reiteration of the constitutional doctrine on informed consent in cases of ambiguous genitalia or «hermaphroditism».

2.15.5. *C-505 of 2001*

Sixteenth (16) May, Two Thousand and One (2001).

Action challenging the constitutionality of Act [*Ley*] 22 of 1984 wherein «*Biology is recognised as a profession, its practise is governed in this country and other provisions are prescribed*». The provisions challenged are declared ENFORCEABLE.

Magistrate Rapporteur: Dr. Marco Gerardo Monroy Cabra.

2.15.6. *T-597 of 2001*

Seventh (7) June, Two Thousand and One (2001).

Magistrate Rapporteur: Dr. Rodrigo Escobar Gil.

Issue: The scope of the principal of informed and qualified consent in the absence of certainty as to the intent or experimental nature of a health service.

2.15.7. *T-729 of 2002*

Fifth (5) September, Two Thousand and Two (2002).

Magistrate Rapporteur: Dr. Eduardo Montealegre Lynett.

Issue: The content and scope of constitutional law with regard to the protection of personal data and to informational self-determination.

2.15.8. *T-850 of 2002*

Tenth (10) October, Two Thousand and Two (2002).

Magistrate Rapporteur : Dr. RODRIGO ESCOBAR GIL.
Issue : Informed and qualified consent.

2.15.9. *T-1025 of 2002*

Twenty-seventh (27) November, Two Thousand and Two (2002).
Magistrate Rapporteur : Dr. RODRIGO ESCOBAR GIL.
Issue : Informed consent with regard to medical treatment of gender assignment of minors.

2.15.10. *T-412 of 2004*

Sixth (6) May, Two Thousand and Four (2004).
Magistrate Rapporteur : Dr. MARCO GERARDO MONROY CABRA.
Issue : Appropriate medical treatment. Informed consent of patient.

2.15.11. *C-877 of 2005*

Twenty-third (23) August, Two Thousand and Five (2005).

Action challenging the constitutionality of Article 60 of Act [*Ley*] 610, 2000 and section 3 of Article 2 of Act [*Ley*] 901, 2004. *The provisions challenged are declared ENFORCEABLE.*
Magistrate Rapporteur : Dr. JAIME CÓRDOBA TRIVIÑO.

2.15.12. *T-1229 of 2005*

Twenty-eighth (28) November, Two Thousand and Five (2005).
Magistrate Rapporteur : Dr. JAIME ARAÚJO RENTERÍA.
Issue : Informed consent. Importance with regard to medical – surgical procedures.

2.15.13. *T-492 of 2006*

Twenty-ninth (29) June, Two Thousand and Six (2006).
Magistrate Rapporteur : Dr. MARCO GERARDO MONROY CABRA.
Issue : Permanent sterilisation of disabled women.

2.15.14. *T-866 of 2006*

Nineteenth (19) October, Two Thousand and Six (2006).

Magistrate Rapporteur : Dr. JAIME ARAÚJO RENTERÍA.

Issue : Informed consent of patient. Reiteration of jurisprudence.

2.15.15. *C-030 of 2008*

Twenty-third (23) January, Two Thousand and Eight (2008).

Magistrate Rapporteur : RODRIGO ESCOBAR GIL.

Action challenging the constitutionality of Act [*Ley*] 1021, 2006 «*Which issues the General Forestry Act*».

2.15.16. *C-1011 of 2008*

Sixteenth (16) October, Two Thousand and Eight (2008).

Review of the constitutionality of the Statutory Law Project No. 27/06 Senate – 221/07 Chamber (Acum. 05/06 Senate) «*whereby the general provisions for protection of personal data are prescribed and the handling of information contained in personal data bases, especially financial, credit, commercial, services and information from other countries, in addition to other provisions.*"

Magistrate Rapporteur : Dr. JAIME CÓRDOBA TRIVIÑO.

2.15.17. *C-175 of 2009*

Eighteenth (18) March, Two Thousand and Nine (2009).

Magistrate Rapporteur : Dr. LUIS ERNESTO VARGAS SILVA.

Issue : Action challenging the constitutionality of Act [*Ley*] 1152 of 2007 «*which prescribes the Statute for Rural Development, reforms the Colombian Institute for Rural Development (INCODER), in addition to other provisions*».

2.16. – *Final comments, conclusions, other reflections, etc.*

In view of the issues we have encountered in gathering full, exact information both about applicable regulations and about the de facto situation with biobanks in Colombia, we are of the opinion that it would be advisable to have a systematic and specific body of regulations on the subject. This would benefit research, as it would help to encourage progress and build confidence in those who are part of it, and would also provide researchers and research subjects with legal certainty, thus, making it easier to form a community of researchers for a specific area.

The legal regulations must ensure that the authorization, inspection and control systems, with relation to the quality of equipment and facilities used by the researchers are accurate; and also that the procedures are able to secure the rights of the individuals involved with the investigation.

It would be advisable to create a biobank system in which public and private institutions could be part of, and that would guarantee the following principles :
– Dignity and human rights
– Access to scientific progress
– Intellectual honesty and integrity
– Protection of Public Health
– Solidarity and International cooperation
– Assessment of risks and benefits
– Autonomy and individual responsibility
– Privacy and confidentially
– Fairness, justice and equality
– No discrimination
– Cultural diversity and pluralism
– Social responsibility, amongst others.

As part of the biobank structure, it is important to create an ethics committee that would analyze the ethical implications and would facilitate the decision-making process in those cases proving particularly troublesome and controversial.

The human health researches on indigenous and Afro-Colombian communities have a particular importance in our country because the political Constitution grants them special protection. For that reason, the regulations should be very clear with relation to the acquisition of informed consent from individuals who make up the community in order to ensure respect for their rights. Biobanks cannot obtain samples by abusing these regulations. Therefore, nothing in that regulation could be interpreted as an exit for biobanks to allow researchers the acquisition and use of the samples, without the individual and communitarian control.

On the other hand, the absence of a specialized bibliography could indicate a lack of concern about the topic in the academic world. This is another issue that we should bear in mind and attempt to remedy in the future.

LEGAL AND SOCIAL IMPLICATIONS OF CREATING BANKS OF BIOLOGICAL MATERIAL IN COSTA RICA (1)

BY

Carlos VALERIO

SUMMARY : 1. The facts : Situation of scientific research with human biological samples and biobanks in the country. 1.1. Cellular and Molecular Biology Research Center (CIBCM). Universidad de Costa Rica. 1.2. INISA. University of Costa Rica. 1.3. Newborn Screening Program. 1.4. National Children's Hospital. 2. Legal Framework. 2.1. General legislation applicable. 2.1.1. General Health Act N° 5395 of October 30, 1973. 2.2. Specific legislation. 2.2.1. General Regulations for the Operation of Health Establishments and Related Establishments, issued by means of Executive Decree N° 30571-S of June 25, 2002, published in La Gaceta N° 138 of July 18, 2002. 2.2.2. Costa Rican Association of Microbiologists and Clinical Chemists Act and its Regulation No. 771 of October 25, 1949, Act No. 5462 Statute of Microbiology and Clinical Chemistry Services, Code of Ethics of the Microbiologist and Clinical Chemist, Executive Decree N° 12 of September 30, 1957. 2.2.3. Norms for the authorization of Immunohematology Departments and Blood Bank». N° 30697-S of September 23, 2002. 2.2.4. Regulations for Biomedical Research in assistance activities of the Costa Rican Social Security Fund of November 17, 2005. 2.2.5. Investigator Brochure. Guide to procedures for research in human beings in the University of Costa Rica. 2006. 2.3. Reports and opinions by national institutions and bodies. 2.4. Professionals and institutions : quality standards and accreditation requirements. 2.5. Ethics Research Committees. 2.6. Obtaining of samples (invasive intervention in the donor). 2.7. Sample ownership. 2.8. Protection of the subject's privacy (Duty of confidentiality and security of data and sample archives). 2.9. Extent of the consent (generic or specific). 2.10. Use of samples obtained for another purpose. 2.11. Specifically issues related with local communities. 2.12. Maintenance : security standards, storage lengths. 2.13. National and international transfer and circulation of samples. 2.14. Property Rights. 2.15. Other issues. 2.16. Final comments, conclusions, other reflections, etc.

---

(1) Acknowledgements : Dr. Henriette Raventos (Research Centre on Cell and Molecular Biology – University of Costa Rica), Dr. Jorge Azofeifa (School of Biology – University of Costa Rica) and Dr. Rafael Jiménez (Bioethics Committee – Children's National Hospital).

1. – THE FACTS:
SITUATION OF SCIENTIFIC RESEARCH WITH HUMAN BIOLOGICAL SAMPLES AND BIOBANKS IN THE COUNTRY

There are several subject areas where human biological samples have been used for biomedical research in Costa Rica.

1. Biochemistry and Molecular Biology: includes the molecular analysis of microorganisms and toxins, as well as the structural characterization of proteins and other macromolecules related to agents that cause various pathologies.

2. Human Genetics: several groups have contributed to the study of the genetic and molecular origin of different inherited disorders. In this sense, there has been a very important international collaboration component.

1.1. – *Cellular and Molecular Biology Research Center (CIBCM). Universidad de Costa Rica*

The Cellular and Molecular Biology Research Center of the University of Costa Rica shows an interesting development in research with humans, for which it has DNA databases to research on mental illnesses and other types of inherited disorders.

The CIBCM has the following banks:

1. DNA bank of subjects in schizophrenia, bipolar disease, deafness, migraine, alcoholism, and Alzheimer's dementia studies. The goal of these studies is to determine genotypes. These samples are kept in freezers at the CIBCM and are generally in duplicate at the foreign associate's laboratory.

2. Plasma banks for research at the CIBCM on the role of infectious factors in bipolar disease and schizophrenia.

3. Serum banks for research at the CIBCM on viruses that may lead to human cancers.

4. Bank of live frozen lymphocytes. These are samples which were not sent to the corresponding cell line laboratory in the United States. Therefore, they are stored in a medium that keeps them frozen and alive to create immortal cell lines in the future or carry out *in vitro* studies. They may be used for a future transformation with Epstein Barr virus (EBV) to make them immortal (inexhaustible source of DNA).

5. Bank of cell lines from Costa Rican subjects in the United States. They are cell lines transformed with EBV from Costa Rican subjects to later extract the DNA and carry out the genetic studies mentioned above. There are approximately 100 immortal cell lines from the deafness study subjects in Seattle, 1500 from schizophrenia in the University of Texas in San Antonio and in the Repository of the National Institute of Mental Health of New Jersey, and approximately 200 bipolar disease samples in New Jersey. In addition, in the study carried out by the Costa Rican National Center of High Technology (CENAT) on bipolar disease, there are approximately 2000 cell lines in the University of California, in Los Angeles. These samples are used to carry out functional studies in *in vitro* live cells; for example, in Texas, the expression level of a specific gene is being measured (measuring mRNA and protein) in the cell lines of these patients. Other Alzheimer's dementia study samples are kept in Mount Sinai in New York.

6. A brain sample bank is being created in the Hospital San Juan de Dios to study dementia.

1.2. – *INISA. University of Costa Rica*

In the Health Research Institute of the University of Costa Rica, there is not a formal data bank. Samples are often taken for a particular investigation and if it were necessary to preserve them, they are stored in the INISA.

In most cases, the samples are used for infection studies or other genetic studies, cancer and aging markers.

In this sense, the INISA has a cooperation agreement with the Central American Population Center to carry out the CRELES Project (Longevity and Healthy Aging Study) for health research.

Generally, the INISA shares the samples it may have with other research organizations, as long as it has the approval of the UCR's Scientific Board.

There are no internal guides or norms for taking, storing, transporting and using the samples.

1.3. – Newborn Screening Program

This Program's main objective is to prevent mental retardation and other disabilities caused by inherited metabolic diseases and related disorders, through detection and early treatment.

The National Newborn Screening Program started in 1990 and is formed by the Costa Rican Social Security Fund, the National Children's Hospital and the Costa Rican Association for Newborn Screening and Disability Prevention in Children.

The diseases currently included in massive newborn screening are: inherited metabolic diseases such as phenylketonuria, maple syrup urine disease, galactosemia and hormone deficiencies such as congenital hypothyroidism and congenital adrenal hyperplasia.

The lab analyses performed to the blood sample drawn 4 days after birth by puncture of the newborn's heel («dry blood spot») are centralized in the National Laboratory for Newborn and High Risk Screening, ascribed to the Quality Assurance Program of the Center for Disease Control in Atlanta, Georgia, United States.

The samples, which are later used in *in vitro* research, are few; some of them are transferred to the National Children's Hospital for such purpose.

1.4. – National Children's Hospital

For being part of the Newborn Screening Program, the National Children's Hospital has samples for research, which are stored until they are used, provided that the sample is distributed into several studies and is later exhausted.

Likewise, there are DNA samples to study thrombotic markers.

It is worth mentioning that the National Children's Hospital does not have a biobank; it holds some collections for specific purposes.

2. – LEGAL FRAMEWORK

There is not a specific law on biological sample banks. The existing law makes reference to blood banks and other banks, which are analogously applied to the country's existing banks or collections.

Costa Rican law does not regulate the manipulation of human samples. It is not included in the Biodiversity Act or in the General

Health Act. There is only an agreement from the National Health Research Council (CONIS) of February, 2006 (2) (CONIS 103-06), which forces researchers to apply for the Health Ministry's blood and tissue exportation permit.

2.1. – General legislation applicable

2.1.1. General Health Act N° 5395 of October 30, 1973

The General Health Act sets forth the requirements to operate health laboratories and the restrictions such activities are subject to. Article 83 defines Microbiology and Clinical Chemistry laboratories, which comprises, among others, Blood Banks, which are defined as an entire establishment where human blood and blood derivatives are obtained, stored, manipulated and supplied.

This law mentions the requirements to operate blood banks as well as the restrictions such activities are subject to. For example, paragraph 90 sets forth that any individual or legal entity wishing to install and operate a Blood Bank needs, previously authorized by the Association of Microbiologists and Clinical Chemists, to be registered in the Ministry.

Article 91 provides that in order to establish and operate blood banks, the interested parties must state, when registering in the Ministry, the nature and technique of the processes they intend to carry out and submit the background information certified by the Association of Microbiologists and Clinical Chemists, crediting that the establishment meets the regulatory conditions required for its due operation, basically regarding the person who will technically respond for the operation, the adequate facilities and equipment for its elaboration, manipulation, classification and storage of the blood and its derivatives, as well as the identification, health condition and registry of blood donors. The Association of Microbiologists and Clinical Chemists will be responsible of supervising these establishments, notwithstanding the Ministry's control and surveillance capacities.

Paragraph 93 provides that human blood, plasma or its derivatives may only be used for medical-surgical and therapeutic pur-

---

(2) CONIS 103-06.

poses and under medical prescription. In case of national disaster or emergency, the Ministry may use blood reserves or blood derivatives in public and private blood banks.

Finally, paragraph 94 provides that it is forbidden for private establishments to export human blood, plasma and their derivatives, except in case of emergency, and to the Ministry's criterion.

2.2. – Specific legislation

2.2.1. General Regulations for the Operation of Health Establishments and Related Establishments, issued by means of Executive Decree N° 30571-S of June 25, 2002, published in La Gaceta N° 138 of July 18, 2002

Since the General Health Act requires that those individuals or legal entities operating health establishments or related establishments be registered in the Health Ministry and obtain the permit or authorization from that body to be authorized to install and operate, these regulations provide which legal requirements must be met in order to obtain such authorization.

The regulations define this authorization as the mandatory observance procedure carried out by the State to authorize health establishments and related establishments, public, private and mixed, through which the users are guaranteed that they comply with the structural requirements in order to provide the service they explicitly offer, with an acceptable risk for the users. The establishments must meet the following requirements: physical plant, human resource, material resource, equipment and organization.

These regulations include those establishments devoted to auxiliary, supplementary or support actions for medical care: all those providing services or supplying special material assets, necessary to attain such purposes. This category includes, among others, laboratories for microbiological and clinical chemical analysis, blood banks and image diagnosis service and pathology laboratories.

These regulations include those establishments carrying out research in humans, those with Blood Bank Services and those with Tissue Bank Services.

2.2.2. Costa Rican Association of Microbiologists and Clinical Chemists Act and its Regulation No. 771 of October 25, 1949, Act No. 5462 Statute of Microbiology and Clinical Chemistry Services, Code of Ethics of the Microbiologist and Clinical Chemist, Executive Decree N° 12 of September 30, 1957

Said regulations deal with the creation of this professional association and establish the norms that will govern its operation and the exercise of microbiology as a profession in Costa Rica. Ethical norms are established for professionals in Clinical Chemical Microbiology to follow.

2.2.3. Norms for the authorization of Immunohematology Departments and Blood Bank». N° 30697-S of September 23, 2002

These regulations establish the requirements for the authorization of services to be provided by an immunohematology center and a blood bank. It also sets forth the requirements to apply for such authorization. This norm aims at specifying the conditions and requirements an Immunohematology Department and Blood Bank should meet. Such specifications must be met in order to obtain the Health Ministry's authorization, which entitles the operation of these establishments.

The scope of application of these regulations is national and applies to all Immunohematology Departments and blood banks, public, private and mixed.

This decree defines blood bank as a service created to collect and store human blood components, which may later be used to treat other individuals.

2.2.4. Regulations for Biomedical Research in assistance activities of the Costa Rican Social Security Fund of November 17, 2005

These regulations basically govern drug trials. However, Article 9 establishes requirements for genetic research, providing that the performance of clinical genetics studies without gene therapy, studies on population genetics and behavioral genetics will be authorized.

Thereafter, this norm provides that the collection, manipulation, use and storage of genetic data, human proteomic data and biological samples must be compatible with the international right regarding human rights.

The norm also provides that this data is property of the Costa Rican Social Security Fund (CCSS).

Whenever the analysis or storage of human genetic data, human proteomic data or biological samples is carried out by another national or foreign institution, a biological material transfer agreement must be subscribed between the CCSS and such institution.

Human genetic data, human proteomic data and biological samples obtained for biomedical research purposes should not be associated with an identifiable person. Even if they are dissociated form a person's identity, the necessary precautions must be adopted in order to guarantee the security of those data or those biological samples. They may only be associated with an identifiable person if needed to carry out research and under the condition that the person's privacy and confidentiality of the data or of the biological samples at issue will be protected in compliance with the country's laws.

In these investigations, the informed consent must specify the purpose behind obtaining the genetic data and human proteomic data, as well as the place where these data will be used and stored. These data cannot be used for a purpose that is different from the one indicated in the original consent.

2.2.5. *Investigator Brochure. Guide to procedures for research in human beings in the University of Costa Rica. 2006*

As a way to make sure human samples are used correctly, the University of Costa Rica, upon request of the Scientific Ethics Committee, requires from all the institution's researchers who, for various reasons must transfer human biological material from one unit to another, within the institution or to any other institution outside the University, national or international, the document Biological Material Transfer Agreement (MTA). This document must be signed by the researcher who receives the samples and the one who provides them and by the legal advisors of both institutions.

The document must clearly specify: a) the origin of the material, b) that it will only be used for scientific research purposes, c) that it will not be transferred to third parties under any circumstance,

d) that the person receiving the sample must always recognize the source of origin of the sample in any publication or media in which the material is involved.

In addition, the informed consent must clearly specify if the samples will be transferred.

The samples may only be used for the purposes provided in the informed consent.

The main goal of the MTA is to guarantee the rights of the subjects, protect the researcher, and protect the researcher's and the institution's intellectual property.

2.3. – *Reports and opinions by national institutions and bodies*

Public and private institutions associated with this issue in Costa Rica have not delivered any legal, social or ethical criteria concerning this matter.

2.4. – *Professionals and institutions: quality standards and accreditation requirements*

Resolutions regarding quality standards and requirements for responsible institutions and professionals are described within the section on applicable legislation in this report.

2.5. – *Ethics Research Committees*

The Costa Rican National Council for Health Research (Consejo Nacional de Investigación en Salud [CONIS]) was created by Executive Decree N° 31078-S, as a consultation entity under the Minister of Health with regard to research with human participants. This decree is valid since 2003.

At present, there are seven accredited committees. Public committees are ascribed to the University of Costa Rica (UCR), the Costa Rican Institute of Nutrition and Health Research and Education (Instituto Costarricense de Investigación y Enseñanza en Nutrición y Salud [INCIENSA]), the Institute for Alcohol and Drug Addiction (Instituto sobre Alcoholismo y Farmacodependencia [IAFA]), the Costa Rican Social Security System and the National University.

There are two private committees ascribed to the University of Medical Sciences (Universidad de Ciencias Médicas [UCIMED]) and the CIMA San Jose Hospital.

The main committee responsible for approving the type of research discussed in this report is the Scientific and Ethics Committee at the University of Costa Rica, which is governed by the «Scientific and Ethics Regulations of the University of Costa Rica for Research with Human Subjects», dated June 22nd, 2000.

Six UCR members, one of whom is an ethics specialist, constitute this committee. Each member is selected according to his or her credentials and the Vice-Rector of the University then ratifies their appointment for a period of two years. There is an additional member in the committee who represents the community, is recruited via mass media and is not linked to the institution. This Committee is independent with regard to its evaluation, advice and decision-making processes.

2.6. – Obtaining of samples
(invasive intervention in the donor)

Normally, most of the samples kept in DNA and serum banks are blood samples; therefore, they are collected by peripheral venipuncture. Some exceptions are: collection by finger puncture or by scraping the buccal mucosa (mucous membrane inside the cheek), when finding the vein is difficult in the case of children or if preferred over other procedures. But in these cases, permanent cell lines cannot be created as an inexhaustible source of DNA.

2.7. – Sample ownership

As mentioned before, in the context of the Costa Rican Social Security Fund (CCSS), the sample belongs to this Institution.

In the case of the UCR, in theory, the ownership rights belong to it, but in practice, the senior investigator has control. Nevertheless, this does not seem to be very clear, because it is also established that when the subject withdraws his/her consent, the ownership is his/hers and the UCR keeps the custody. In the case of samples sent to the repository of the National Institutes of Health, this is a resource of the federal government for all researchers.

In Costa Rica, some investigators believe that the subject has ownership rights over the sample.

2.8. – *Protection of the subject's privacy (Duty of confidentiality and security of data and sample archives)*

All the samples and clinical information are codified at their arrival to the laboratory. The codes are kept separately. All clinical information is kept in locked files in private offices, and only the study staff has access to it. Moreover, the staff in charge of interviewing and collecting samples has received training in research ethical norms.

Informed consents usually indicate to the patient that his/her DNA sample and results will be kept in a specific place.

The person is informed that the study's code number will be replaced with a new code number. Once the study's code number is removed from the sample, there will be no way of establishing a relationship between the sample and the person's identity. The person will no longer be linked to his/her sample.

In private studies, the Sponsor will keep the DNA files in a separate file. The DNA files will not be considered part of the medical file kept by the study doctor. The study doctor keeps the signed files for the DNA tests.

In private studies, the Ethics Committee of the University of Medical Sciences (CEC-UCIMED), and in all the cases, the National Health Research Council (CONIS) of the Ministry of Health and other health authorities (such as the FDA, the United States Food and Drug Administration) may review these files.

The access to the results will be limited to whatever is necessary to ensure the study's adequate development. Privacy will be protected. The research associates will not use or reveal the DNA results to anyone. Security measures will be taken to protect the DNA results; these include: keywords for databases and controlled access to the buildings.

Unless required by law, the results will not be delivered to the employees, insurance companies or to the public. The results of the DNA tests may be published anytime and may also be presented during scientific meetings. The subject will not be identified in any publication or presentation of the research results. Normally, the subject or his/her study doctor will not receive the test results.

The DNA results will only be identified using code numbers. They will not include the name or address, or any other data that may establish a relationship with the subject.

In general terms, in clinical research, the samples are sent with the initials and sometimes with the subject's date of birth; the information used to know their identity can only be found in the investigation site. The pharmaceutical company may review the patients' clinical files, but it cannot take the lists of patients with full names. In addition, such lists will not be accepted if the site sends them.

On the other hand, in pharmacogenomic studies where certain clinical data is requested in order to make the analyses, the laboratory relabels the samples and the data that correlate to that subject using different codes; the laboratory makes the analyses, correlates and finally destroys this code.

If the data is stored digitally, it must comply with Chapter 11 of the Code of Federal Regulations, which provides the security mechanisms for digital information. All reports must be sent via fax to those numbers having private faxes, and these, as well as everything related to the subject's information, must be handled as a confidential document.

2.9. – *Extent of the consent (generic or specific)*

In most cases, the consent is specific, when the subject answers the following questions:
– What is the purpose of the study?
– What am I being asked to do?
– How will my identity and test results remain confidential?
– Who may have access to my results?
– What will happen if I eventually change my mind?
– What are the benefits?
– What are the risks?
– How will my sample be stored?
– Will I see the results of my DNA tests?
– Will I be paid for my participation?

– Will I be paid for the use of my results?

– Contacts for questions :

The Cellular and Molecular Biology Research Center has a general form required by the respective scientific ethics committee that includes mandatory sections, but it is modified according to each study. This committee recommends its inclusion if the subject consents that his/her sample be used in the future in other studies and also if he/she prefers that the sample be destroyed if he/she withdraws from the study.

2.10. – Use of samples obtained for another purpose

The information is only used for research purposes.

The Cellular and Molecular Biology Research Center does not uses samples for studies that have not been specified in the informed consent form, except if the samples are anonymized and the Scientific Ethics Committee of the University of Costa Rica (UCR) grants the respective authorization, but only in the case of anonymous samples.

2.11. – Specifically issues related with local communities

Costa Rica does not perform this kind of research with special local communities, e.g. aborigines.

2.12. – Maintenance : security standards, storage lengths

Normally, they are conserved forever. In clinical trials sponsored by companies, the information is destroyed after some time. But this generally depends on each study.

2.13. – National and international transfer and circulation of samples

As it will be mentioned in the introduction, in the UCR, the assignment may only take place after a MTA (Material Transfer Agreement) is signed or when the samples are sent to a Repository where they lose identity, but are still used for the research they were collected for.

As indicated in the first section, the University of Costa Rica participates in an important number of trials sponsored internationally, in particular from the United States. Therefore, national and international exchange rules are stipulated by specific agreements in each study, as well as the signed MTA referred to in the above section.

2.14. – *Property Rights*

Except for UCR resolutions mentioned in this report, specific regulations on this matter do not exist in Costa Rica. This results in regulation of sample property rights according to the sponsor's dispositions in each particular study.

2.15. – *Other issues*

There are no any import issue to discuss in such matter

2.16. – *Final comments, conclusions, other reflections, etc.*

Costa Rica is a small county with obstacles for development in some areas. In particular, research has been a highly debated topic for many years, in particular by the Social Security System, which has lead to very limited state funded/public research, with the exception of important breakthroughs in Genetics by the University of Costa Rica.

For this reason, and because genomic research is not a political priority, there are no legislation or policies for support and development of biobanks. There are some collections at the UCR, but many samples are taken to the United States where most research studies have been funded. It is of crucial importance to settle matters dealing with patent law and intellectual property, as well as fair distribution of benefits. In addition, it should be noted that currently there is no academic or intellectual development on this topic.

On the other hand, public debate is limited and thus the population is scarcely aware or knowledgeable on these topics. Furthermore, certain influential Catholic groups continue to fight and condemn research with the human genome, cloning and *in vitro* fertilization.

Under this state of affairs, studies on biological samples and generation of biobanks at present are unstimulated activities. The private sector and in particular the UCR are among the few institutions performing research on biological samples in Costa Rica. Nevertheless, the country stands out for its participation in important global studies related to human biological samples.

LEGAL AND SOCIAL IMPLICATIONS OF CREATING BANKS OF BIOLOGICAL MATERIAL IN FRANCE

BY

Myriam BLUMBERG-MOKRI

AND

Laurène ALARD

Summary : I. Introduction. 1.1. Definition and stakes of biobanks. 1.2. The lay out of biobanks. II. Legal Framework. 2.1. General legislation applicable. 2.2. Specific legislation. 2.2.1. Denominations of biobanks in the French law. a) The Biological Resource Centre. b) Other denominations of biobanks. 2.2.2. The Law of August 6, 2004. a) The categories of biobanks. b) The necessity of representatives. c) The procedures of declaration or authorization. 2.2.3. A late regulation. 2.3. Reports and opinion by national institutions and bodies. 2.3.1. Opinion from the National Ethics Advisory Committee for the life sciences and health. 2.3.2. Reports from other institutions and bodies. a) The National Commission for Data Protection and Libertie. b) National Academy of Medicine. 2.4. Professionals and institutions. 2.4.1. The professionals. 2.4.2. Institutions. 2.5. Ethics Research Committees. 2.6. Obtaining of samples. 2.6.1. General provisions. 2.6.2. Nature of the sample. a) Blood. b) Organs. c) Tissues, cells, human body products and their derived. 2.6.3. Sanctions. 2.7. Sample ownership. 2.7.1. The principle. 2.7.2. Sanctions. 2.8. Protection of subject privacy. 2.8.1. Coding : the principle. 2.8.2. Exceptions. 2.9. Extent of Consent. 2.9.1. Non-opposition. a) General provisions. b) Specific provisions. 2.9.2. Express consent. 2.9.3. The consent and non-opposition forms. 2.10. Use of samples obtained for another purpose. 2.11. Specifically issues related with local communities. 2.12. Maintenance. 2.12.1. Guarantees of security. a) Control a priori by Authorities and Ethics Review Committees. b) Security standards. 2.12.2. Conditions of storage. 2.12.3. Duration of storage. a) Specific provisions. b) The absence of general regulation. 2.12.4. destruction of samples. 2.13. National and International transfer and circulation of Samples. 2.13.1. Conditions of assignment. authorization. 2.13.2. Forms of assignment. 2.13.3. Transmission of personal data to states outside the European Union. 2.14. Property rights. 2.15. Final comments, conclusions, other reflections.

1. – INTRODUCTION

1.1. – *Definition and stakes of biobanks*

Biobanks, still called «biothèques» (1) are private or public collections which store elements of the human body such as DNA, cells, tissue biopsies, gametes, and blood. Biobanks are structures dedicated to the collection, preparation, aliquotage, cryopreservation, and management of biological resources for use in biomedical research. They can either be independent or part of a network. Biobanks stand at the intersection between health professional structures, where samples are taken, and research laboratories, where samples are analysed.

The use of the term «biothèque» has advantages over the use of the term «biobanks.» First of all, «biothèque» is more inclusive than the term «biobank». It encompasses different types of biobanks, from simple collections of samples to the real biobanks. Furthermore, according to the National Ethics Advisory Committee for the life sciences and health «a word such as «biothèque» (...) highlights the notion of archiving. The conservation of books and documents was considered to be for the common good» (2).

According to Mrs Cambon-Thomsen, in biobanks activities «several elements of tension are emerging:
– Rights of Persons (autonomy, confidentiality, protection of the private life) versus the rights of researchers;
– Non-commercial use of body parts versus development of commercial products derived from samples;
– Maximum quality samples preserved versus ease of use and economic utility;
– Transparent and optimal use of samples and data for the rapid advancement of knowledge versus prioritizing the rights of researchers and companies: how to protect the interest of

---

(1) Expression of CAZE DE MONTGOLFIER, S., in *Collection, storage and use of the products of the human body within the framework of the researches in genetics: historical, ethical and legal inventory; practical analyze within the biothèque*, University of Paris V Decartes, (dir.) Herve C., 2002, p.28. It is forged by associating "Bio", living, with "theke" trunk point discharge.

(2) THE NATIONAL ETHICS ADVISORY COMMITTEE for the life sciences and health, opinion n° 77 *on Ethical issues raised by collections of biological material and associated information data*, March 20th, 2003.

researchers and populations while ensuring the dissemination of information and data ? » (3)

This report attempts to explain how French biobanks deal with these tensions in practice and how French legislation regulates this activity.

1.2. – *The lay out of biobanks*

Biobanks can store different kinds of samples. Although samples can have vegetal, animal or human origins, this report only concerns human samples. However, within the category of human samples, subdivisions are possible.

Indeed, there are subdivisions created by the French law: such as blood, organs and tissues, cells and human body products. There are also relevant subdivisions which have emerged from practice: the DNA biobank, tumorobanks, tissue banks, etc. Thus, subdivisions can be based on either the nature of the sample or the purpose of the storage.

Determining how many biobanks exist is a tedious task, especially because there are different types of biobanks in France. Indeed, nowadays, it is difficult to estimate how many biobanks there are in France and nobody has the same number. For instance, in an international survey taken in 2001, some authors believed there were 67 human biobanks in France (4) even though only 9 human biobanks are recorded on the website of the French Consultative Committee on Biological Resources (5). In an interview, Georges Dagher, representative of the biological collections at the National Institute of Health and Medical Research and member of the French Consultative Committee on Biological Resources, said that there are «between 40 and 50 well structured biological resource centres» which first appeared between 2001 and 2006 (6).

It is difficult to check how many biobanks exist in France in part because France did not regulate biobanks until relatively

---

(3) CAMBON-THOMSEN, A., «Biological samples bank: ethical and legal aspects. General introduction», in the *Review of epidemiology and public health*, 2003, vol n° 51 p. 99-126.

(4) HIRTZLIN I. DUBREUIL, C, CAMBON-THOMSEN and al., «An empirical survey on biobanking of human genetic material and data in six EU countries», *European Journal of Human Genetics*, 2003, p. 475.

(5) www.crbfrance.fr/.

(6) Interview of DAGHER, Georges by CABUT, S., «Biobanquier un metier d'avenir», *Liberation*, November 25th, 2006.

recently (7). Indeed, while biobanks have existed for decades, regulations first appeared only about ten years ago. The French law now requires biobanks to make a declaration or seek authorization. Since many biobanks pre-existed this law, some biobanks never fulfilled these formalities.

Another consequence of the fact that regulation of biobanks is relatively new in France is that there is a stark difference between theory and practice. The law sets up many conditions that biobanks should respect. However, because many biobanks have operated for a long time without any regulatory framework in place, some old practices can still be observed, particularly with concern to obtaining consent.

Despite the inconsistency between regulation and practice, the French law is slowly changing the biobanks system in France. It aims to achieve better control and oversight over this activity.

2. – Legal Framework

2.1. – *General legislation applicable*

The issues raised by biobanks implicate some of the essential principles set forth in the French law. Indeed, this activity is sometimes in tension with the conception of the human body as well as the requirement of obtaining informed consent from the biomedical research participant.

With the Law on bioethics of 1994, the French legislature established in the first part of the Civil Code several principles in order to protect the human dignity through the protection of human body. Indeed, all of these principles are illustrate the right to respect for the human body, which is affirmed in the article 16 of the same Code.

As biobanks' activities involve samples collected from the human body, an overview of some of these fundamental principles is helpful. In France, two important principles related to protection of the human body are connected to issues surrounding biobanks: the unavailability of the human body and the integrity of the human body.

---

(7) Cf *infra*, p. 10.

The unavailability of the human body is a principle which asserts that a person is not the owner of his body and that in fact nobody is. This principle is very close to the principle of non-marketability of the human body, according to which patrimonial value should not be conferred upon the human body. These two principles are affirmed in many ways throughout the first part of the French Civil Code.

Indeed, under the terms of the article 16-5 of the Civil Code «Agreements that have the effect of bestowing a patrimonial value to the human body, its elements or products are void». The article 16-6 goes further and says that «No remuneration may be granted to a person who consents to an experimentation on himself, to the taking of elements off his body or to the collection of products thereof».

The second principle related to issues raised by biobanks is the principle of integrity of the human body. It is illustrated by the article 16-3 of the Civil Code, which stipulates that «There may be no invasion of the integrity of the human body except in case of medical necessity for the person or exceptionally in the therapeutic interest of others» and that «The consent of the person concerned must be obtained previously».

Thus the necessity of requiring consent emanates from the principle of integrity of the human body. The necessity of obtaining consent from a patient is affirmed in many places in the French law and the medical deontology. It also is linked to another important right – the patient's right to information. These two fundamental rights of the patient are relevant to the activities of biobanks. Indeed, they must be respected during the collection of the sample and they also influence the rights of the patient with regard to his or her sample.

Thus, some fundamental principles asset forth in general legislation have links to the activities of biobanks. However, these principles are not sufficient to regulate this such activities. Specific legislation is required.

2.2. – *Specific legislation*

The specific problems posed by biobanks have been treated by the French legislature only recently. The first provisions about biobanks were adopted into law on July 29th 1994 (8) but were very minimal. Even though biobanks were first established in France at the end of the 1980s, the debate about them began in earnest in the French legislature at the beginning of the twenty-first century.

The questions surrounding the topic of biological samples and specimens reached the international stage in 1999 with the OECD's work on biological resources, and with the creation of the Euro-BioBank network in 2001 ... After this, it became imperative for France to address the issue of biobanks and regulate them. The minister of research created the French Consultative Committee on Biological Resources in 2001 and an important law was passed in 2004 (9).

2.2.1. *Denominations of biobanks in the French law*

a) *The Biological Resource Centres*

In 1999, The Organization for Economic Co-operation and Development organized the Tokyo Workshop on Biological Resource Centres (BRCs). France adopted the definition of Biological Resource Centres that was agreed upon at the workshop. Biological resource centres are «an essential part of the infrastructure underpinning life sciences and biotechnology. They consist of service providers and repositories of the living cells, genomes of organism, and information relating to heredity and the functions of biological systems. BRCs contain collections of culturable organisms (e.g. microorganisms, plant, animal and human cells), replicable parts of these (e.g. genomes, plasmids, viruses, cDNAs), viable but not yet culturable organisms, cells and tissues, as well as databases containing molecular, physiological and structural information relevant to these collections and related bioinformatics» (10). This is a broad definition of Biological Resource Centres. It is not only limited to human biological samples.

In 2001, the minister of research created the French Consultative Committee on Biological Resources. Its mission is to create and

---

(8) *Law n° 94-654 of July 29th 1994 relating* to donation and use of elements and products of the human body, to assisted reproduction and to prenatal diagnosis.
(9) *Law n° 2004-800 of August 6th 2004 relating* to bioethics.
(10) OECD, «Biological Resource Centres: underpinning the future of life sciences and biotechnology», 2001.

maintain a constantly evolving list of the biological resource centres in France. According to a member of this committee, the number of human biological resource centres in France could grow to between 80 and 100 in three years. The French Consultative Committee on Biological Resources monitors the activities of biobanks, in particular the management and quality of the services. However, there are no clear criteria which govern the classification of these centres. Classification is done in an ad hoc manner.

b) *Other denominations of biobanks*

Biological Resource Centres is one of several terms used to denote biobanks in France. French law also refers to biobanks as 'collections' and 'banks.'

Collections : The term 'collection' appears in the part of the Public Health Code intitled «Preparation, storage and use of tissues, cells and their derived». Under the terms of its article 1243-3, the collection of human biological samples designates «the reunion for scientist purpose of biological sample taken on a group of persons identified and selected». Thus, according to the French law, 'collections' are established only for Scientific purposes. Entities which collect samples for therapeutic purposes and entities which transfer samples are not included in this category.

Banks : Another term used in the French law is the term banks. The decree of December 29th 1998 (11) which approves the rules of good practices relating to conservation, to transformation and to transport of tissues of human origin used for therapeutic aims gives a definition of tissue banks which seems applicable to all biobanks. Accordingly, a 'biobank' is «a service or a department of a public establishment of health or an organism assuring the transformation, the storage, the distribution and the cession» of human biological samples.

Therefore, French law makes a distinction between collections, banks and biological resource centres (12). However it is important

---

(11) Decree of December 29th 1998 which approves the rules of good practices relating to conservation, to transformation and to transport of tissues of human origin used for therapeutic aims

(12) CAZE DE MONTGOLFIER, S. in *Collection, storage and use of the products of the human body within the framework of the researches in genetics : historical, ethical and legal inventory; practical analyze within the biothèques, op. cit.*

to note that despite the use of these three terms in the French law, they do not constitute the accepted criteria for determining the different regimes of biobanks.

2.2.2. *The Law of August 6, 2004*

This law established three categories of biobanks and set up new procedures to be followed by biobanks.

a) *The categories of biobanks*

The French law makes a distinction between three categories of biobanks :
- Organisms which prepare, store, distribute and transfer the samples for a therapeutic purpose (article L.1243-2 of the Public Health Code) : → Authorization.
- Organisms which prepare and store the samples for a scientific purpose (article L.1243-3 of the Public Health Code) : → Declaration.
- Organisms which prepare and store the samples with the aim of their cession for a scientific activity (article L.1243-4 of the Public Health Code) : → Authorization.

Even though the first category (biobanks which contain samples that will only be used therapeutic purposes) is outside the scope of this report, mention should be made of this category since the purposes for which samples will be used are liable to change.

b) *The necessity of representatives*

The first category of biobanks needs to identify a representative for the medico-technical activities (article R. 1243-12 of the Public Health Code). The second and the third categories need to identify a scientist representative or a scientist representative coordinator when there are several research sites (articles R.1243-57 and R.1243-63 of the Public Health Code). It is from great interest to notice that these provisions were taken after two opinions had been adopted, one by the National Academy of Medecine, the other by the National Ethics Advisory Committee, which insisted on that point (13).

c) *The procedures of declaration or authorization*

The first category of biobanks needs to be authorized by the French Agency of Sanitary Security of the Health Products after a prior opinion of the Agency of Biomedicine, which was created by the Law relating to bioethics of 6th, 2004. The authorization is given for five years and is renewable.

If there is a substantial change in the activities of the organism, a new authorization will be required. For minor changes in the organism's activities, a simple declaration to the director of the French Agency of the Sanitary Security of Health Products is sufficient. When biobanks in this category operate without authorization, they are liable to a sanction of 2 years' imprisonment and a fine of €30 000 for natural persons, and also incurs the additional penalty of prohibition, for a maximum period of ten years, to undertake the social or professional activity in the course of which or on the occasion of which the offence was committed. (article 511-8, 511-8-1 and 511-27 of the Penal Code). This maximum amount of fine applicable to a legal person is five times that which is applicable to natural persons which means for this offence a maximum fine of €150 000 and also possibility of penalties as dissolution, prohibition to exercise, placement under judicial supervision, permanent closure or closure for up to five years of the establishment, disqualification from public tenders, prohibition to make a public appeal for funds, prohibition to draw cheques, confiscation of the thing which was used or intended for the commission of the offence, posting a public notice of the decision or disseminating the decision in the written press (article 131-28 of the Penal Code).

Biobanks falling under the second category have to be declared to the Minister of Research. When the organism is a health institution, the institution makes the declaration not only to the Minister of Research but also to the director of the Regional Agency of Hospital Cares. Before the declaration, the opinion of the Human Pro-

---

(13) THE NATIONAL ACADEMY OF MEDICINE, *The Biological Resource Centres in medical institutions*, Bourel-Ardaillou Report, 2002.
THE NATIONAL ETHICS ADVISORY COMMITTEE for the life sciences and health, opinion n° 77, *op. cit.*

tection Committee is required. Both the Minister of Research or the director of the Regional Agency of Hospital Cares, can suspend or forbid the activities of the organism with the prior opinion of the French National Commission for Data Protection and Liberties. When these biobanks operate without a prior declaration or when the Minister responsible for research has objected to suspended or forbidden their activities, natural person of biobanks may receive a punishment of 5 years' imprisonment and a fine of €75000 (article 511-5-2 of the Penal Code) and (five times for a legal person if the biobanks is convicted of this offense). Indeed, the penal provision of 6 August 2004 states that it is an offence punishable by five year's imprisonment and a fine of €75,000 for natural person to keep and transform for scientific purposes, including purposes of genetic research, any organs, tissue, cells or blood, or its components or products derived from it without having made in respect of it the preliminary declaration required by article L. 1243-3 of the Public Health Code; where the Minister responsible for research has objected to these activities, or has suspended them, or forbidden them. The same penalties apply to keeping or transforming any organs, tissue, cells or blood, or its components or products derived from it, with a view to handing them over for scientific use, including purposes of genetic research, without having first obtained the authorisation required by article L. 1243-3 of the Public Health Code, or when this authorisation has been suspended or withdrawn.

Finally, the third category of biobanks needs to be authorized by the Minister of Research after a prior opinion of the French National Commission for Data Protection and Liberties. When the organism is a health institution, it needs to be authorized by the Minister of Research and the director of the Regional Agency of Hospital Cares. When these biobanks operate without authorization, they face a potential punishment of 5 years' imprisonment and a fine of €75000 as seen above (article 511-5-2 of the Penal Code).

Sometimes the same biobank falls under to two different categories. In that case, the procedures related to both categories will have to be followed.

2.2.3. *A late regulation*

The law of 2004 imposes the obligation of filing a declaration or seeking. Though there was a framework for biomedical research in place before this, there were not specific procedures related to biobanks and many biobanks existed without any oversight by the government. Thus, it could be possible that some biobanks are still not allowed by the authorities.

Because of this possibility, a decree (14) was adopted by the government, in August 2007 to encourage the biobanks to comply with the formalities. This decree establishes the model for filing for a declaration or making the request for authorization to prepare or store for scientific purpose elements of the human body (15).

2.3. – Reports and opinion by national institutions and bodies

In France, the National Ethics Advisory Committee for the Life Sciences and Health has made the most important contribution to the regulation of biobanks. However, other national institutions and bodies have also made more modest contributions.

2.3.1. Opinion from the National Ethics Advisory Committee for the Life Sciences and Health

The mission of the National Consultative Ethics Committee on Health and Life Sciences is «to give opinions on ethical problems and societal issues raised by progress in the fields of biology, medicine and health» (16). This Committee was created 26 years ago, in 1983, and the French law is always committed to ensuring its freedom, independence, and the legitimacy of its recommendations. Its purpose is to provide the referring authority with an in-depth recommendation, allowing everyone to formulate their own opinion.

This committee produced its first opinion linked to biobanks early in its history. Indeed, in May 1985 it propagated the opinion 4 on «Medical registries for epidemiological and preventive studies,» (17) which insists on the importance of guaranteeing medical confidentiality and requiring consent to collect and to process

---

(14) Decree of August 16th, 2007, fixing a model of file for the declaration or the request of authorization for preparation or storage for scientific purpose of elements of the human body.
(15) Cf. Annex.
(16) Law n° 94-654 of July 29th 1994 relating to donation and use of elements and products of the human body, to assisted reproduction and to prenatal diagnosis.
(17) THE NATIONAL ETHICS ADVISORY COMMITTEE for the life sciences and health, opinion n° 4 on medical registries for epidemiological and preventive studies, May 6th, 1985.

information. According to the committee these guarantees will flow from the accreditation of qualified organisations, the scientific and moral stature of their managers, and restricted access to the information.

This was the first of several opinions related to the issues raised by biobanks. Only three years later, the committee issued a second opinion on «problems arising because of the development of methods using human cells and their derivatives» (18). This time, the Committee focused on the financial consequences of human cellular «donations» and reaffirmed the principle of non-marketability of the human body. However, it also stated that remuneration is permissible for the work involved to obtain a product from the sample :

«Later use of the sample, which must remain strictly anonymous, may fall into two categories :

a) the product is a substance (a molecule, or a segment of a DNA molecule, for instance) which has required sometimes considerable effort to develop or isolate (interferon, erythropoietin as in the case considered, monoclonal antibodies);

b) the product is a cell which is used as a laboratory reagent. It must however be cultured, sometimes cloned or even modified to achieve indefinite replication (immortalisation).

It can be argued that there is less development work in the latter case, but payment is acceptable for the work that is involved.

The commercial product which may be the outcome of development work must be considered separately. It becomes part of normal distribution circuits.

The result of these considerations is that the person from whose body the cells were sampled has no rights over the consequences of their processing and use, and that his heirs cannot have rights over these cells and their derivatives which he did not have himself.

However, if the cells are to be used for purposes other than diagnosis, therapy, or cognitive» (p. 1).

Thus, the person from whose body the cells were taken away has no right to determine how they will be processed or used after. However, the Committee disapproves if the cells are intended for a purely economic use.

This particular topic raises several ethical issues and was tackled many times by this Committee during the last decades. On three other occasions the French Committee reaffirmed the principle of

---

(18) THE NATIONAL ETHICS ADVISORY COMMITTEE for the life sciences and health, opinion n° 9 on problems arising because of the development of methods using human cells and their derivatives, February 23rd, 1987.

non-marketability of the human body (19) which is stated in French Civil code.

Another issue raised by biobanks is the question of genetic data. On this topic, the National Consultative Ethics Committee on Health and Life Sciences provided in June 1991 an «opinion regarding the application of genetic testing to individual studies, family studies and population studies (Problem related to DNA 'banks' and computerisation)» (20). In this opinion the Committee reiterates the necessity of accreditating qualified organisations and restricting access the information, the importance of which it already acknowledged in the opinion 4. However, it also added the requirement of specific provisions allowing any interested party to control his own personal data. The Committee also insists on principles of confidentiality and respect for privacy by specifying that any investigation into an individual's genotype should be undertaken only if he has specifically given his consent. He may well question the extension of research into areas unrelated to that for which the authorisation was given at the time of sampling (for instance due to the length of time DNA can be preserved).

Over the years several other opinions on biobanks were made. The National Consultative Ethics Committee on Health and Life Sciences expressed opinions on some topics which could be related with biobanks or at least with some issues connecting with this matter as :

– «the re-examination of the law on bioethics»;
– «the creation of human embryonic organ and tissue collections and their use for therapeutic or scientific purposes»
– «Umbilical cord blood banks for autologous use or for research»
– «Informed consent of and information to persons accepting care or research procedures»
– «Ethical questions arising from the transmission of scientific information concerning research in biology and medicine»

---

(19) THE NATIONAL ETHICS ADVISORY COMMITTEE, opinion n° 21 that the human body should not be used for commercial purposes, December 13th, 1990, opinion n° 27 that the human genome should not be used for commercial purposes, December 2nd, 1991, and opinion n° 93 on commercialisation of human stem cells and other cell lines, November 17th, 2006.
(20) THE NATIONAL ETHICS ADVISORY COMMITTEE, opinion n° 25 regarding the application of genetic testing to individual studies, family studies and population studies (Problem related to DNA 'banks' and computerisation), June 24th, 1991.

– «Questions for the Estates General on Bioethics»

All of these opinions are related to the ethical issues raised by biobanks.

Among all of these opinions, the most important one with regard to biobanks is the opinion 77 (21) of 2003 on «ethical issues raised by collections of biological material and associated information data : 'biobanks', 'bioltheques'» («biolibraries»). This opinion touches upon all of the ethical considerations surrounding biobanks in one general report. The French Committee has unlighted : «several causes of tension due to the creation of these large banks affect the rights of individuals. They are related to the evolution of the notion of informed consent, its adaptation to cope with the durable nature of the banks and repeated use of their contents, possible contradiction between security and protective measures and abusive use of the items collected, and finally, the view that individuals may have of their rights over such items» (p. 14). On this occasion the Committee declared itself in favour of :

– a clear definition of the contents of the function of conservators or curators and their obligations including :
– the need to subject their activity to authorization and to standards for quality, security and monitoring;
– the set up of an independent mediating body to deal with the several rights and obligations linked to biobanks;
– the conditions of payment for the cost of conservation;
– the reinforcement of the demands connected to personal consent;
– some form of contracting procedure to structure relations betweens researchers and between researchers and banks;
– the reaffirmation of non-tradability of the collected samples;
– the need to share the benefits;
– the need to put this system in the hands of a regulating authority.

This opinion takes in account that the «rules governing the accumulation and use of such collections must respect two principles, which are sometimes contradictory. One is that they should be put to optimal use to serve the community, particularly for scientific, medical, and public health purposes; the other is that in so doing,

---

(21) THE NATIONAL ETHICS ADVISORY COMMITTEE for the life sciences and health, opinion n° 77, *op. cit.*

such collections should not be simply treated as though they were public property that could be somehow incorporated into the social and public fabric, or on the contrary, treated like merchandise. In other words, donors must be informed in broad terms of the type of study which their donations will be used for, and of the framework in which these studies will be undertaken» (p. 15).

Even though all of these opinions are not legally binding, the National Consultative Ethics Committee on Health and Life Sciences advised the government and the regulating authorities to ensure that the French legislation and practice on biobanks is not unethical.

The National Consultative Ethics Committee on Health and Life Sciences was the principal author of reports on biobanks, but some other institutions and bodies produced their own reports as well.

2.3.2. *Reports from other institutions and bodies*

a) *The National Commission for Data Protection and Liberties*

This Commission, established by the law of January 6, 1978, is an independent administrative authority protecting privacy and personal data. The Commission has provided one important recommendation on treatment of information about personal health data for research.

Indeed, in February 1997, the Commission set forth its first recommendation on «personal health data process» (22) which highlights the necessity of guaranteeing the medical confidentiality, deidentification (anonymization), and authenticity of data.

Even though this recommendation does not refer directly to biobanks, its provisions are clearly applicable to biobanks because they involve health data processing.

b) *National Academy of Medicine*

The Academy of Medicine, which was instituted to respond to the requests of the government on all subjects relating to public health, works as an independent observatory and a high ranking network

---

(22) THE NATIONAL COMMISSION FOR DATA PROTECTION AND LIBERTIES, recommendation n° 97-008 on personal health data process, February 4th, 1997.

of expertise on medical evolution. Within the framework of this mission, the Academy of Medicine published two reports on Biological resource centres.

In «the biological resource centres in medical institutions report» (23), written in 2002, the academy insisted on the necessity of an independent statute with a scientific council and its own funding.

In the second report, written in 2009, the academy focuses on the «changes needed in biological resource centres regulation» (24). Thus, the academy recommends:
– a clear definition of the BRCs statutes including a guarantee of independence;
– a simplification of the BRCs functioning involving easier conditions of consent, cession or genetic studies;
– to pursue the inventory of the existing BRCs.

A significant part of all of these opinions and reports provide advice about issues related to biobanks. The government and the legislature are not bound by these documents but will certainly consider them in the regulation process.

2.4. – *Professionals and institutions*

Some of the opinions and reports named above insist on the importance of accreditation of qualified organisations and the scientific and moral stature of their managers. To ensure that these considerations are respected, the French law includes some provisions about the criteria that the professionals and institutions should meet.

2.4.1. *The professionals*

The law requires the presence of a doctor during sampling, storage, and research.

First, the law specifies that some samples must be taken only by a doctor or, in the case of samples such as blood or cells, under the

---

(23) THE NATIONAL ACADEMY OF MEDICINE, *The Biological Resource Centres in medical institutions, Bourel-Ardaillou Report», op. cit.*

(24) THE NATIONAL ACADEMY OF MEDICINE, *The changes needed in biological resource centres regulation*, 2009.

direction and responsibility of a doctor (25). The French law also affirms that biomedical research must be conducted under the direction and the supervision of a doctor (26).

Moreover, the French law mandates that it is necessary for a doctor to control the storage of specimens. Indeed, the article R1243-13 of the Public Health Code requires that representatives of biobanks must have a diploma in medicine or pharmaceutical studies or a PGD in the area of science of life and health.

Furthermore, the article R1243-15 of the same code requires that the abilities and qualifications of the biobanks' workers are in conformance with the requirements for good practices.

Thus, the people working at every stage of the biobanks process must be professionals of medicine, pharmaceuticals, or of the science of life and health. This requirement helps to guarantee quality, security, and monitoring. It is also likely to lead to more respect for donors' rights.

2.4.2. *Institutions*

The French law does not address the statutes of biobanks. A biobank can be found within a hospital, a pharmaceutical laboratory or a patient association. The law does not require that biobanks be a public institution to collect, store and use biological samples. Indeed, the decree of December 29th, 1998 designates biobanks as «a service or a department of a public establishment of health or an organism (...)» without specification.

The CCNE considers that «in France, at this time, the system is virtually part of the public or non-profit sector. This is because the sources of most of the «premium collections» were in the public hospital system. However, associations have now gained significant ground in this respect. The question arises of exchanges of material and information with foreign operators whose mode of operation is commercial. In the same way, public institutions do not hesitate to claim intellectual property rights or to file for patents in connection with research based on these banks. The question of whether a bank can be a private institution.

---

(25) Article L1221-8-1 of the Public Health code.
Article L1232-1 of the Public Health code.
(26) Article L1121-3 of the Public Health code.

The question of whether a bank can be a private institution is solved in the affirmative in major countries where genetic research is very advanced. There is an international trend in that direction. In the last five or six years, the big pharmaceutical companies have been setting up DNA and data banks as part of their clinical research. Others have gone even further with the constitution of specific banks for research on therapeutic targets or to constitute cell lines of embryonic stem cells» (CCNE, Opinion n° 77, p. 22) (27).

However many provisions set up a specific system which applies to biobanks. As noted above (28), the French law requires that every biobank file a declaration with or seek authorization from French authorities before they collect and store biological samples. The requirement of an a priori declaration or authorization was not always followed in practice because many biobanks pre-existed the law which imposed this requirement.

2.5. – Ethics Research Committees

Biomedical research must be authorized by the responsible authority (29) and approved by a Research Ethics Committee. Such Research Ethics Committees are called Human Protection Committees in France. A Human Protection Committee is accredited for six years by the Minister of Research on the recommendation of a prefect of the region. There are forty of these committees in charge of the ethics review of biomedical research protocols throughout France and its territories.

Despite public subsidies, these committees are funded in part by the fees paid by the biomedical research investigators.

In order to ensure the independence of the committees and the legitimacy of their decisions, a notice (30) provides criteria for the composition of committees. Thus Human Protection Committees are composed of two boards.

The first one (the scientific board) includes :

---

(27) THE NATIONAL ETHICS ADVISORY COMMITTEE for the life sciences and health, opinion n° 77, op. cit.
(28) Cf supra p. 9.
(29) Either the French Agency of Sanitary Security of the Health Products or the General Direction of Health
(30) THE REGIONAL DIRECTION ON SANITARY AND SOCIAL MATTERS Notice n° DGS/SD1C/2006/259 related to the set up of Human protection Committees.

– Four persons with great experience in biomedical research (at least two doctors and one person qualified in biostatistics and epidemiology)
– One general practitioner
– One hospital pharmacist
– One nurse

The second one (the scientific and ethics board) includes:
– One person qualified on ethical issues
– One psychologist
– One social worker
– Two persons qualified on legal aspects
– Two representatives of patients' associations

According to the article R1123-12 of the Public Health Code, the Human Protection Committee opinions are passed by a majority vote. Any member of the committee can ask to have a secret ballot. Finally, when there is a tie, the president's vote is the deciding factor.

2.6. – *Obtaining of samples*

The first step in the establishment of a biobank is collecting samples. Sampling conditions vary depending on whether the samples are intended for a private or a public biobank. Indeed, most of the time a public biobank is part of a hospital while a private biobank does not have such an analogous structure to collect its samples. When the biobank is part of the hospital, taking the sample is easier because the staff and the equipment are at easy disposal. When the biobanks are private, such as those created by patients' associations, they need to collaborate with doctors, researchers, or directly with hospitals.

2.6.1. *General provisions*

Under the terms of article L.1211-2 of the Public Health Code «The sampling of elements of the human body and the collection of its products cannot be practised without the prior consent of the donor. This consent is revocable at any time». The article L.1211-4 of the Public Health Code also forbids the remuneration of the person «who takes part in the sample of elements of his body or in the collection of its products».

Obviously, these articles refer to general principles of donation and use of elements of the human body in link with the articles 16-1 and 16-3 of the French Civil code:

> «Everyone has the right to respect for his body.
>
> The human body is inviolable.
>
> The human body, its elements and its products may not form the subject of a patrimonial right.» (art. 16-1 Civil code)
>
> «There may be no invasion of the integrity of the human body except in case of medical necessity for the person or exceptionally in the therapeutic interest of others.
>
> The consent of the person concerned must be obtained previously except when his state necessitates a therapeutic intervention to which he is not able to assent».

In addition to these general provisions, in France there also are specific provisions tailored to the nature or the purpose of the sample.

2.6.2. *Nature of the sample*

The sample can be of different types:
- Blood
- Organs
- Tissues, cells, human body products and their derived elements

a) *Blood*

The article L.1221-8-1 of the Public Health Code allows the sampling of blood in order to create a collection. Taking samples of blood must pose only minor risks. Moreover, the sample can be taken only by a doctor or under the direction and responsibility of a doctor. Biological analyses and screening tests for transmissible diseases have to be done.

b) *Organs*

The Public Health Code does not refer directly to the collection of organs but allows scientific research on organs. Thus, the conservation of organs in a biobank until the time the research is conducted seems permissible.

Organs can only be removed from the deceased for scientific purposes as long as the deceased did not refuse to allow his organs to be extracted before his death. According to the article L.1232-3 of the Public Health Code research protocols which include the removal of organs must be submitted beforehand to the Agency of biomedicine. The Minister of Research can suspend or reject such protocols when the necessity of organ removal is not sufficiently demonstrated or the relevance of the research has not been adequately established.

c) *Tissues, cells, human body products and their derived*

The sampling of tissues, cells, or human body products from a living person for a scientific purpose is permissible (article L.1241-1 of the Public Health Code). It is also possible to take such samples from the deceased. In such cases, the provisions about organ removal have to be respected (article L.1241-6 of the Public Health code).

Taking samples of embryonic and foetal cells and tissues for scientific purposes is allowed only after an abortion (article L.1241-5 of the Public Health Code).

2.6.3. *Sanctions*

For all types of samples, consent is necessary before sampling according to L.1211-2 of the Public Health Code. Thus, when sampling is undertaken without the consent of the patient, the Penal code imposes sanctions.

«The removal of an organ from a living adult without obtaining the person's consent pursuant to the conditions set out by article L. 1231-1 of the Public Health Code, or without authorisation being provided under paragraphs two and five of that provision, is punished by seven years' imprisonment and a fine of €100,000, even when done for therapeutic purposes. The same penalties apply to the removal of an organ from a living minor donor, or a living adult donor who is the subject of a protective guardianship order, without complying with the conditions referred to under articles L. 1241-3 and L. 1241-4 of the Public Health Code» (article 511-3 of the Penal Code).

«The removal of human organic tissues or cells, or the collection of a bodily product, from a living adult who has not expressed his consent as provided for by article L. 1241-1 of the Public Heath Code is punished by five years' imprisonment and a fine of €75,000. The removal from a living minor or from a living adult who is the subject of a protective guardianship order of any red blood-producing cells from the bone marrow without complying with the conditions laid down by, as applicable, articles L. 1241-3 or L. 1241-4 of the Public Health Code, is punished by seven years' imprisonment and a fine of €100,000.s» (article 511-5 of the Penal Code).

«The taking of samples for scientific purposes from a deceased person without having transmitted the protocol required by article L. 1232-3 of the Public Health Code is punished by two years' imprisonment and a fine of €30,000.The same penalties apply to using a protocol that has been suspended or forbidden by the Minister responsible for research» (article 511-5-1 of the Penal Code).

As mentioned above, the amount of fine for a legal person can be five times.

2.7. – Sample ownership

2.7.1. The principle

According to article 16-1 of the Civil Code, «The human body, its elements and its products may not form the subject of a patrimonial right».

Indeed, pursuant to article 16-6 of the Civil Code «No remuneration may be granted to a person who consents to experimentation on himself, to the taking of elements off his body or to the collection of products thereof». Furthermore, under the terms of the article 16-5 of the fundamental code, «Agreements that have the effect of bestowing a patrimonial value to the human body, its elements or products are void».

Thus, it seems that a sample of human origin cannot be sold and that a patient donor cannot be remunerated. However, «the value added conferred to the sample can be rewarded» (31).

---

(31) THE NATIONAL ACADEMY OF MEDICINE, *The Biological Resource Centres in medical institutions*, Bourel-Ardaillou Report, op. cit.

According to Professor Thouvenin (32), it seems that nobody can be the owner of elements of the human body neither the person from whom the sample has been taken, nor the organisms which conserve the samples. Once the elements are extracted from the human body, they are independent and an organism can prepare, store, or transfer them. However, they can only be exchanged for payment when value added has been added to them.

This view seems to be shared by the National Consultative Ethics Committee on Health and Life Sciences (33) and the legislature.

«In any event, curators are the keepers of a collection which in France cannot have been legally bought; it is governed from the outset by the rules of unavailability of the human body and is not marketable. CCNE suggests that this line of reasoning should be complemented by stating clearly that the collection contributes to the constitution of a collective asset, that this resource must be collectively managed in a spirit of solidarity. This certainly does not signify that the work done to maintain that resource should be unpaid, nor that if a work of invention is completed and leads to the creation of a test or of medicinal drugs, that the normal financial consequences of this activity should be denied because the material was banked.

However, the need to organise this sequence of connected events adds fuel to the notion that any bank must be part of an accredited system. Such a system, which requires in-depth legal analysis, must deal openly with the matter of remunerating the conservation activity, and of the financial consequences of later uses. These consequences do not rest on the principle that the collection may be sold; the law must therefore intervene to lay down a compromise solution» (CCNE, Opinion n° 77, p. 23) (34).

This principle does not seem to be subject to any limitation, even with the genetic data. Indeed, the French law does not establish a principle of property in such cases. It only requires express consent for the examination of genetic characteristics.

---

(32) THOUVENIN D., «Tissues and organs banks: the words to say it, the rules to regulate them», *Petites Affiches*, 18 février 2005, p. 39.
(33) THE NATIONAL ETHICS ADVISORY COMMITTEE for the life sciences and health, opinion n° 77, *op. cit.*
(34) THE NATIONAL ETHICS ADVISORY COMMITTEE for the life sciences and health, opinion n° 77, *op. cit.*

2.7.2. *Sanctions*

Under the terms of article 511-2 of Penal Code : «Procuring from another person any of his organs in return for a payment, in whatever form, is punished by seven years' imprisonment and a fine of €100,000. The same penalties apply to acting as an intermediary to facilitate the obtaining of an organ for payment, or the supply for payment of an organ belonging to another person's body.

The same penalty is applicable where the organ procured in the conditions referred to under the first paragraph comes from a foreign country».

The article 511-4 of Penal Code says that, «Procuring from another person human organic tissues, cells or body products in return for payment in whatever form is punished by five years' imprisonment and a fine of €75,000.

The same penalties apply to acting of as an intermediary to facilitate the procuring of human organic tissues, cells or human products in return for any form of payment, or supplying human organic tissues, cells or products of the body of others for payment.»

The non-marketability of the human body is clearly established in the French law. It is manifested in the Civil Code and the sanctions which apply in cases of transgression.

2.8. – *Protection of subject privacy*

Associating personal data with sample data requires compliance with the Law n° 78-17 of January 6th, 1978 (amended in 2004), which governs data processing and freedom. Indeed, even though the law was not passed to regulate the specific issues related to biobanks or medical records, it must be applied to personal data linked to samples.

CNIL (Commission Nationale de l'Informatique et des Libertés –

2.8.1. *Coding : the principle*

One of the conditions which must be respected in the treatment of data is coding. Before carrying out data processing of personal information, it is necessary for the organization in possession of such data to make a declaration to and seek authorization from the

French National Commission for Data Protection and Liberties Commission Nationale de l'Informatique et des Libertés (CNIL) (National Information Technology and Civil Rights).

According to the article 25-14 of the decree of May 9th 1995 (35) «The request for authorization, signed by the person who is qualified to represent the public or private organization which implements the treatment, is addressed to the commission in three specimens».

The commission then has two months to issue a decision. The authorization must mention any exemptions granted for coding data (storing data in the form of a list of names with information about the persons concerned). Authorization ultimately must be given by the CNIL after the opinion of the national Consultative Committee on data processing .

On the other hand, «a declaration and a request for authorization are not necessary when the treatments of data have the aim of the individual therapeutic or medical follow-up of patients» (36).

In other cases, the patients whose data are taken must be preliminarily informed about :
- The nature of transmitted information;
- The finality of the data processing;
- The identity of the recipients and the extent of their access to the information :
- The patient's right of access and their right to oppose at any time the use of their data. They must give their explicit assent for the use of personal data which makes it possible to identify them.

Under the terms of article 40 of the law governing data processing and Freedom «Any individual providing proof of identity may ask the data controller to, as the case may be, rectify, complete, update, block or delete personal data relating to him that are inaccurate, incomplete, equivocal, expired, or whose collection, usage, disclosure or storage is prohibited».

---

(35) Decree n° 95-682 of May 9th, 1995 modifying decree n° 78-774 of July 17th, 1978.
This decree was taken for the application of the Chapter V (a) of law n° 78-17 of January 6th, 1978 governing data processing and Freedoms.
(36) DUGUET, A.M., BEVIERE, B., BOUCLY, G., RIAL, E. and CAMBON-THOMSEN, A., «Rights of patients and bio sources –The use of elements of human body», *Journal of forensics and medical law*, 2007, Vol. 50, N° 1-2, p. 61.

When the data are about genetic information, additional safeguards are recommended, particularly for data pertaining to ethnic origin (37).

On January 5, 2006, the CNIL adopted a methodology of reference (MR001) for the treatment of personal data collected in the context of biomedical research. In this methodology, the CNIL suggests that a patient be identified by a number. If this is not possible, the CNIL states that at a minimum, the patient should be identified by their initials. Coding excludes the use of the patient's full name and social security number.

In one public hospital in Paris, data processing is done using national data-processing software created by the ministry of health. This software is readily accessible to biobanks as it is free of charge and has been placed at their disposal. The hospital practices anonymization as it is conceptualized in Europe. The term has a different meaning in America. In Europe, 'anonymization' means that it is possible to link the patient with his sample. Such anonymization procedures are used in the hospital mentioned above because the hospital's biobank was set up not only for research but also for therapeutic pursuits. Therefore, maintaining such a link is essential.

A biobank of a patient's association used the same method for anonymization, which ensures that it is always possible to identify a particular patient's sample. This choice was made because preserving the link between the patient and sample allows the patient to revoke his assent to its use at any time and offers a better protection of his or her rights. It also allows researchers to consult the clinical file when it is necessary to do so and to communicate the results of the research to the patient. Even so, personal data are protected via encrypted files.

However, traceability is not possible in all biobanks. Several biobanks in France chose the total anonymization approach. There is not national harmonization on this matter.

Some public biobanks called tumorobanks (because they all work on the same research topic) set up a national catalogue containing descriptions of samples based on 44 criteria. This catalogue allows tumorobanks to network. Tumorobanks all are equipped with sys-

---

(37) DUGUET, A.M., BEVIERE, B., BOUCLY, G., RIAL, E. and CAMBON-THOMSEN, A., *op. cit.*, p. 57.

tems allowing them access to biological, anatomopathological and clinic data. The National Institute of Cancer recommends the use of this national catalogue to every hospital tumorobank.

More specifically, the National Catalogue of data (38) includes:
– Information on the site of tumorobank;
– Information on the patient;
– Information on the illness;
– Information on the sample;
– The biological type of samples preserved;
– Further information.

2.8.2. *Exceptions*

Under Article 55 of Law governing data processing and freedoms, derogation of the principle of coding data is possible:
– When data processing is associated with «studies of pharmacovigilance».
– When data processing is associated with «research agreements concluded in the context of national and international co-operative studies.»
– «If a particularity of the research required it.»

An authorization from the CNIL is required.

2.9. – *Extent of Consent*

The article L.1211-2 of the Public Health Code clearly requires consent for the sampling stage. Yet, it still is necessary to explore whether consent is required for the storage and the use of samples.

2.9.1. *Non-opposition*

a) *General provisions*

The same article also requires the absence of opposition when a sample will be used for a different medical or scientific purpose than the purpose for which it was originally intended. Sometimes, the

---

(38) NATIONAL INSTITUTE OF CANCER, *Tumorobanks in hospital, Recommendation to clinicians and searchers*, November 2006, p. 111-120.

scientific purpose for which a sample is intended is simply storage in a biobank. According to this article, consent is not always necessary when a sample is used for scientific research. If the sample is being used for a purpose other than that for which it was initially intended, only absence of opposition will be required after information is conveyed to the patient about the modified use of the sample.

The law n° 2004-800 of August 6th, 2004 requires non-opposition. Before this law was implemented, the French legislation did not say anything about the purpose of the sample. Consent was only required for genetic analysis of the sample (39). This provision was enacted to protect the security of patients and to simplify the procedure that doctors and researchers follow. However, in practice the law did not lead to a streamlined process because securing non-opposition of a patient is just as complicated.as obtaining consent. Even if consent is not required, the non-opposition is valid only if relevant information was conveyed to the patient. Supplying the patient with this information takes as much time acquiring consent.

b) *Specific provisions*

– A person under guardianship : when the sampled person is underage or an adult under guardianship, non-opposition must be obtained from the person who has parental authority or the guardian (article L.1211-2 of the Public Health Code).
– An absent person : when the sampled person is nowhere to be found, transmiting information and securing non-opposition is not obligatory and the sample can be used. However, there is an exception when the sample is made of germinal tissues or cells. In that case, the use of the sample without obtaining non-opposition after information is duly conveyed is strictly forbidden.
– A deceased person : when the sampled person is deceased and when the sample is made of germinal tissues or cells, the intended purpose of the sample cannot be changed. Taking a sample from the body of a deceased person is possible only if the doctor asks the near relatives about the deceased's wishes and informs them about the purpose of the sample. Beforehand, the Agency of bio-

---

(39) Cf. *supra*, p. 11.

medicine is informed of any sampling for therapeutic or scientific purposes.
- A person who takes part in biomedical research: when the sampled person takes part in biomedical research, the Human Protection Committee can decide that conveying information about modifications to its intended use will not be necessary. However, when the sample consists of germinal tissues or cells, the use of the sample without securing non-opposition and exchanging information is strictly forbidden.

2.9.2. *Express consent*

Under the terms of the article 16-10 of the Civil Code, «The examination of the genetic characteristics of a person can be undertaken only for medical aims or for scientific research. The express consent of the person must be obtained in writing before the examination and after the person was duly informed about its nature and purpose. Consent must mention the purpose of the examination. It is revocable at anytime». This article existed even before the law of August 6th 2004 but it was supplemented by this law – especially by the informed consent provisions concerning purpose. It is impossible to depart from this provision. Even when the person is deceased, the consent has to be signed before the death.

Thus, when there is a sample intended for genetic research in a biobank, the express consent of the patient is necessary while non-opposition is sufficient for other types of samples.

2.9.3. *The consent and non-opposition forms*

According to the directive 2004/23/EC of March 31st 2004, the donor or their relatives should receive appropriate information (40). In France, most of the biobanks and hospitals which participate in research already have the forms required to document information transmission as well as consent or non-opposition (41). Most of the time, the provisions about information and non-opposition or information and consent are in the same form.

---

(40) Directive 2004/23/EC of March 31st, 2004 on setting standards of quality and safety for the donation, procurement, testing, processing, preservation, storage and distribution of human tissues and cells. Cf. annex.
(41) Examples of documents in annex.

All the non-opposition forms specify that the sample can be stored by a biobank and used in biomedical research. However, some of the forms do not specify the purpose of the research. Therefore, the donor has to accept any research that will be conducted using the sample and cannot authorize use of his sample for only one type of research. With a non-opposition form, the signature of the patient is not mandatory. Only the signature of the doctor who witnessed the non-opposition is required.

The consent forms specify that the sample can be stored by a biobank and used in biomedical research involving genetic examination. This form must be signed by the patient.

Some biobank overseers (42) recommend describing all contingencies in the forms and asking if the patient consents to :
– The research which is underway
– Genetic experimentation
– The storage of the sample
– Other research on the same theme
– Other research on a different theme
– Commercial valorisation.

The patient just has to tick the boxes and sign the consent form.

Thus, there is no standard practice with regard to consent or non-opposition forms. Some biobanks ask for the consent of the patient in all cases, while others ask only for non-opposition in some cases.

Despite these forms already prepared by some biobanks, the consent or the non-opposition of the patient is not always duly obtained. In practice, when the patient received the information, he or she can be just informed that the sample will be used by biomedical research without any other specification. Beside, this information is rarely given by a doctor. Unfortunately, there is a stark difference between theory and practice.

---

(42) Such as Mme Di Donato ex-overseer of AFM-Genethon biobank.

2.10. – Use of samples obtained for another purpose

Samples can be used for diagnostic and therapeutic purposes or in fundamental, epidemiologic or clinical research. Moreover, it could also be used for judicial matters such as the identification of a suspect or tests of paternity.

The French law allows samples to be utilized for purposes which deviate from those for which they initially were intended. The French law, places samples stored to be used in biomedical research into three classifications:
- Sample taken directly from a person taking part in biomedical research (article L.1211-2 and articles L.1121-1 and next of the Public Health Code).
- Samples taken from a patient for a diagnostic or therapeutic use and then repurposed for research (article L.1211-2 of the Public Health Code).
- Samples which come from surgical waste (article L.1245-2 of the Public Health Code).

French legislation makes a distinction between samples obtained for diagnostic, therapeutic, and scientific purposes. Nevertheless, there are conditions which have to be respected if the sample is deposited in a collection or a biobank and subsequently used for scientific research, whatever the origin of the sample. Under the terms of the article L.1211-2 of the Public Health Code, «the use of elements or products of the human body for a medical or scientific purpose other than the one for which the sample was takien is possible». Therefore, it is possible to conserve a sample in a biobank even if it was not originally intended for this purpose, though some conditions about consent have to be respected pursuant to the article L.1211-2 of the Public Health Code.

2.11. – Specifically issues related with local communities

The principle of non-discrimination is written at a universal level into the Universal Declaration of Human Rights of 1948, and at a regional level into the Charter of Fundamental Rights of the European Union of 2000, and basically into the European Convention of

Human Rights of 1950 is directly applicable in national law and in front of the courts.

Those considerations which focus on «local communities» do not apply in France because of the principle of non-discrimination.

Discrimination comprises any distinction applied between natural persons by reason of their origin, sex, family situation, physical appearance or patronymic, state of health, handicap, genetic characteristics ...

The non-discrimination is registered in the fundamental legislation of France through the Declaration of Human Rights and citizen of 26 août 1789, included into the «bloc de constitutionnalité», i-e in the French Constitution of the Fifth Republic.

According to this principle the French law may not distinguish between individuals based on any ground such as sex, race, colour, ethnic or social origin, genetic features, language, religion or belief, political or any other opinion, etc. Therefore, this principle also applies to local communities and the French law make no distinction on biobanks regime ...

2.12. – *Maintenance*

2.12.1. *Guarantees of security*

a) *Control a priori by Authorities and Ethics Review Committees*

When samples are collected and conserved in biobanks to respond to research needs, the declarations made by biobanks allow the responsible administrative authorities to verify before and during biobank activities that legal requirements are satisfied. The Human Protection Committee is consulted before the declarations are filed and it makes recommendations about the use of these samples.

Storage of samples is one of the essential activities of biobanks. The stored samples are preserved in the form of spangles of serum. A code makes it possible to link the spangle to the file of the patient.

b) *Security standards*

Biobanks have to respect the ISO standard 9001 : 2000, set up by the International Organization of Standardization. This standard addresses the topic of management systems to be used in any organization. However, it is also applicable to the collection and storage of biological samples.

Some public institutions such as the National Institute of Health and Medical Research or the Welfare Services of Hospitals of Paris have written ethical charters on the collection, storage, preparation, use and transfer of biological resources of human origin. These principles are binding on the staff of both institutions.

2.12.2. *Conditions of storage*

Biobanks in France store samples using two methods. Samples can be stored either with liquid nitrogen at -160° C or in a freezer at -80° C. For some types of samples, such as tumors, there are specific recommendations from the National Agency of Accreditation and Valuation of health (43) (now called the High Authority of Health).

2.12.3. *Duration of storage*

In France, there are no general provisions that regulate the duration of storage for biological samples. Some specific situations are, however, regulated by law, decree, or application.

a) *Specific provisions*

In cases of assisted reproduction, embryos are conserved for at least five years, except if the parents specifically request that they be destroyed (article L.2141-4 of the Public Health Code). This provision sets parameters for the duration of storage of the embryos only before scientific research commences. Such research is not always allowed in France. However, when this type of research is allowed, the duration of the research and the storage cannot exceed five years (article R.2151-2 of the Public Health Code).

In cases of biomedical analysis, the decree of 26 November 1999 sets up the «Guide of good execution of biomedical analysis». This

---

(43) NATIONAL AGENCY OF ACCREDITATION AND VALUATION OF HEALTH, *Recommendations for the cryopreservation of tumours cells and tissues in the aim to practice molecular analysis*, May 2000.

guide recommends that samples be stored for one or three years depending on the tests to be performed on the sample.

Finally, when there is a sample for pathological anatomy and cytology, storage by private doctors is regulated by the article R.6211-44 of the Public Health Code. Such samples must be stored for ten years.

The last two situations do not fall under the umbrella of scientific research. However, these two examples help elucidate how long samples intended for research should be stored because there are no general provisions that regulate this point.

b) *The absence of general regulation*

There is no general regulation governing the duration of storage of biological samples. Therefore, biobanks can decide how long they want to store the samples. However, most of the time, when samples are stored for a therapeutic or diagnostic purpose, storage terminates when it is no longer in the therapeutic or diagnostic interest of the patient.

When samples are stored for a scientific purpose, storage should last the duration of the research, particularly when the samples were specifically taken for a particular research enterprise. Nevertheless, some patients agree that their samples can be used for any number of research projects. In such cases, if the sample can be useful for other research endeavour, it should be stored longer. The decree of 16 August 2007 outlines four possibilities for the treatment of samples at the conclusion of the research:

– The storage of the sample can be prolonged
– The sample can be transferred to another research team belonging to the same organism
– The sample can be transferred to another organism
– The sample can be destroyed

Biobanks usually store samples for a long time and not only the duration of a specific research project. For instance, «Plan cancer» tries to encourage the development of tumorobanks in France and wants to store at least 100,000 tumours (44). The tumorobank of

---

(44) NATIONAL INSTITUTE OF CANCER, *Tumorobanks in hospital, Recommendation to clinicians and searchers*, November 2006, p. 7.

the hospital Hôtel Dieu in Paris stores 10,000 samples (45) and the tumorobank of the hospital Saint-Louis adds 5000 samples each year.

2.12.4. *Destruction of samples*

The provisions which regulate the destruction of human biological samples also regulate the destruction of hospital care waste (46). There are two types of waste (47):
– Waste which carries a risk of contagion has to be burned.
– Anatomical elements have to be cremated (incinerated in a crematorium)

2.13. – *National and International transfer and circulation of samples*

2.13.1. *Conditions of assignment; authorization*

A structure which stores biological samples can be asked or can decide to transfer some of them to other institutions or agencies to allow them to purpose their research aims. In such cases, the structure transfers to agencies the collections of biological samples which are necessary for them to carry out their research goals.
– An authorization is necessary for transfer of samples. According to article L.1243-4 of the Public Health Code, authorization is delivered by the Minister of Research for the commercial transfer of samples. When the organism is an establishment of health, «authorization is delivered by the Minister of Research and the director of the Regional Agency of Hospital Cares».

Authorization is also required under the same conditions for transfers for which no money is exchanged.
– The opinion of the Human Protection Committee is also required.

---

(45) http://www.e-cancer.fr/.
(46) Articles R.1335-1 to R.1335-14 of the public health code.
(47) WELFARE SERVICES OF HOSPITALS OF PARIS, *Collect, store and use human biological samples in hospital*, March 30th, 2008, p. 50-5.
http://www.drrc.ap-hop-paris.fr/ressources_biologiques/document_types_rb.php.

2.13.2. *Forms of assignment*

The assignment can take several forms :
- Cession : when the assignment does not occur within a research partnership,
- Agreement to make samples available : when the assignment occurs within a research partnership,
- Subcontract : when an aspect of the conservation activity or preparation of samples is entrusted to another organism without transferring the responsibilities of conservation and preparation of the samples.

In all cases, the establishment which transfers the sample has to define the conditions of the assignment.

A contract for transfer of biological samples («Accord de Transfert de Matériel» or «ATM») must be drawn up. The contract must indicate whether the transfer will be made free of charge or will require payment. It must also delineate the procedures for verifying declarations of storage, whether samples will be anonmyized, transport conditions, and the procedures for changing the purpose for which the sample is intended during the assignment.

Considering the diversity of forms of assignment of biological materials within the AP-HP (some may involve transfering complete collections of samples while others may involve transferring one or a few samples), material transfer agreements must be signed by :
- the director of the hospital housing the collection of samples after consulting the person in charge of the collection or the research platform, the pole or department head. Beforehand, the Department of clinical research and development must be informed;
- In the absence of the hospital director, the transfer agreement must be signed by the person responsible for the collection or the research platform, or by the head of pole or the chief of service.

Moreover, there are often special recommendations which are promulgated for specific types of biobanks or specific biobanks. For instance, the National Cancer Institute recommended that tumorobanks transfer or release biological material only when :
- a research partnership programme exists (including the establishment of care or research depositories of the samples);

– the partner organism does not have exclusive rights over the samples.

Samples can be transferred to:
– researchers working within the framework of the public research;
– industries concerned with developing screening tests or experiments which will validate the safety and efficaciousness of a treatment.

According to a report by the National Academy of Medicine (48), when the transfer involves biological resource centres, the project will be examined by the scientific council of the centre before it is approved. The scientific council must:
– require that the purchaser will not transfer these samples to a third-person without prior agreement;
– require that the anonymity of the data related to the samples is maintained;
– ensure that exclusive rights to the samples are not granted and that other research projects will not be prevented.

2.13.3. *Transmission of personal data to states outside the European Union*

The transfer of samples entails the transfer of data. According to articles 68 and 69 of the law governing Data processing and Freedoms, the person in charge of the treatment of data must:
– Make sure that the State provides a sufficient level of protection of individuals' privacy, or
– Obtain the express consent of the person.

The law prohibits transferring health data which make it possible to identify the sampled person without payment (Article L. 1111-8 of the Public Health Code).

2.14. – *Property rights*

The fact that a person cannot be the owner of elements of his body does not mean that a scientist cannot have an intellectual property right in his discovery. Indeed, scientists can patent the

---

(48) THE NATIONAL ACADEMY OF MEDICINE, *The Biological Resource Centres in medical institutions, Bourel-Ardaillou Report*, 2002, p. 7.

method or technique used upon elements on the human body (for instance, the method used to isolate a gene). Thus, the results of research can be protected by the French law.

However, the use of biological samples during the research raises issues linked to biotechnologies. The Convention on Biodiversity defines the biotechnology as «Any technological application that uses biological systems, living organisms, or derivatives thereof, to make or modify products or processes for specific use» (49). And yet, an important debate took place in France and Europe in order to decide the conditions of patent issuing when biotechnologies were involved.

In Europe, after 10 years of discussion the Directive 98/44/CE was finally adopted. However, the debate which existed in Europe also appeared in France.

The transposition of the directive within the French Law is the result of several years of discussion. In 2004, the France was fined by the Court of Justice of the European Communities because of an infringement proceeding. Therefore, the French legislator ensures finalized the transposition within the Law of August 6th, 2004 on bioethics and the Law of December 8th, 2004 on the protection of biotechnological invention.

The Directive 98/44/CE, including article 5 has to be applied. Under the terms of article 5 «The human body, at the various stages of its formation and development, and the simple discovery of one of its elements, including the sequence or partial sequence of a gene, cannot constitute patentable inventions». However «An element isolated from the human body or otherwise produced by means of a technical process, including the sequence or partial sequence of a gene, may constitute a patentable invention, even if the structure of that element is identical to that of a natural element».

Thus, samples on themselves are not patentable but an element isolated or otherwise produced by means of a technical process can be a patentable invention. Once again, the value added is necessary to involve property or payment.

---

(49) CONVENTION ON BIOLOGICAL DIVERSITY, Rio de Janeiro, June 5th, 1992.

Helped by samples, researchers take advantage of their invention and are the only ones have benefit from the samples. Indeed, the donor cannot invoke any property rights because of the non-marketability of the human body. However, since the law of August 9th, 2004, the person who takes part in biomedical research has the right to be informed about the general result of the research (article L.1122-1 of the Public Health Code).

2.15. – Final comments, conclusions, other reflections

Biobanks in France have existed for several years and the number of them has increased significantly during the last decade with the rise of international projects such as the Human Genome Project. The law finally regulates this activity and creates a specific regime which addresses several aspects of biobanks.

However, some gaps in regulation can still be observed. Because regulation did not exist until relatively recently, the activities of biobanks are not yet sufficiently transparent. Indeed, the exact number of biobanks in France and its territories is unknown. The French authorities involved in the regulation and control of biobanks are still trying to list all of the institutions with operating biobanks, particularly by encouraging them to declare themselves.

Another issue which remains to be ironed out in the law is the distinction between obtaining consent and non-opposition, which, as seen above, is difficult to apply.

However, these difficulties may be resolved soon. Indeed, the French law on bioethics of 2004 was intended to be revised within five years. In preparation for this revision, the Agency of Biomedicine organized the Estates General on Bioethics in 2009 in order to have public debates on sensitive topics. As a result of this, many French agencies and institutions prepared reports on important topics in bioethics. Of all the institutions that participated in this debate, only the French Agency of Sanitary Security of the Health Products tackled the issues raised by biobanks. In a report (50) published in February 2009, this agency, underscores the complications emanating from the French distinction between consent and

---

(50) FRENCH AGENCY OF SANITARY SECURITY OF THE HEALTH PRODUCTS, *Contribution to the General Estates on Bioethics*, February 2009.

non-opposition (51) and the difficulties of the proof of a non-opposition. The Agency insists on the necessity to revised the provisions on consent and non-opposition.

Beside this complication, the French Agency of Sanitary Security of the Health Products highlights some other complications in its report :
– The importance of delineate the necessity of a declaration or an authorization concerning the maintenance activities involving samples when the biobank was build only on a scientific purpose;
– The change of purpose;
– If the patient change his or her mind during the process and decide to refuse the storage and the use of samples, should they be destroyed?
– Is the change of the situation of a patient (A minor becoming a major for instance) can allow changing the consent given initially?

Therefore, the French Agency of Sanitary Security of the Health Products underscores many issues still existing in biobanks activities. And, with the future revision of the French law, some changes can be expected.

---

(51) Cf *supra* p. 28.

LEGAL AND SOCIAL IMPLICATIONS OF CREATING BANKS OF BIOLOGICAL MATERIAL IN GERMANY

BY

Jürgen W. SIMON

AND

Rainer PASLACK

Summary : 1. The facts : Situation of scientific research with human biological samples and biobanks in Germany. 1.1. Preliminary remarks. 1.1.1. Technical remark. 1.1.2. General remark. 1.2. Criteria for selecting biobanks for this report. 1.3. Legal forms of establishing biobanks. 1.4. List of German Research Biobanks. 1.4.1. Publicly promoted biobanks. 1.4.2. Biobanks at Universities. 1.4.3. Other Biobanks at Public Institutions. 1.4.4. Biobanks of Foundations and Charitable Organizations. 1.4.5. Commercial Biobanks. 2. Legal Framework. 2.1. General legislation applicable. 2.2. Specific legislation. 2.3. Reports and opinions by national institutions and bodies. 2.4. Professionals and institutions : quality standards and accreditation requirements. 2.4.1. Personal equipment. 2.4.2. Laboratory equipment. 2.5. Ethics Research Committees. 2.6. Obtaining of samples (invasive intervention in the donor). 2.6.1. Collection for diagnosis/therapy reasons. 2.6.2. Collection for certain research projects. 2.7. Sample ownership. 2.7.1. Contract for treatment and diagnosis. 2.7.2. Contractual agreement. 2.7.3. Abuse. 2.7.4. Change of purpose. 2.7.5. Return request for samples so far used properly. 2.7.6. Person-related data. 2.7.7. Research results. 2.7.8. The role of anonymization with regard to the right of return or destruction. 2.8. Protection of the subject's privacy (Duty of confidentiality and security of data and sample archives). 2.8.1. Data protection infringement. (a) Anonymous sample. (b) Person-related sample. 2.8.2. Opposing rights of the donor. (a) Anonymized sample. (b) Pseudomized samples. 2.8.3. Civil Code Claims. 2.9. Extent of the consent (generic or specific). 2.10. Use of samples obtained for another purpose. 2.11. Specifically issues related with local communities. 2.12. Maintenance : security standards, storage lengths. 2.13. National and international transfer and circulation of samples. 2.13.1. Ownership rights of the donor transferred to third parties. 2.13.2. Transferral of utilization rights. 2.13.3. International transfer. 2.14. Property rights. 2.14.1. Who is the owner of a sample collected in a biobank ? 2.14.2. Ownership of biomaterials in a biobank.

2.14.3. Ownership transferral. (a) Priority for obligation of storage. (b) Lack of intent to waive ownership rights. (c) Conclusion. 2.15. Other issues. 2.15.1. Who is the owner of a biobank?. 2.15.2. Claims to patent rights. 2.16. Final comments, conclusions, other reflections, etc.

1. – THE FACTS:
SITUATION OF SCIENTIFIC RESEARCH WITH HUMAN BIOLOGICAL SAMPLES AND BIOBANKS IN GERMANY

1.1. – *Preliminary remarks*

1.1.1. *Technical remark*

In the run-up to this report we have identified all German biobanks which are collecting and storing human samples for research purposes, and we have conducted interviews with some of them. For the questionnaires we could refer to two former reports we have prepared for the «TMF – Telematic platform for medical networks» (Berlin) (1) and the «TAB – Office of Technology Assessment at the German Parliament» (Berlin) (2), dealing with the legal situation and the ethical implications of German biobanks.

1.1.2. *General remark*

Biobanks worldwide are playing an increasingly important role within the field of modern biomedical research. So they do in Germany. The importance of biobanks for several scientific and medical purposes is closely tied to the outstanding importance of DNA-samples and genetic data in the diverse activities of biobanks. Especially the handling of genetic material and information gives rise to a great number of ethical and legal questions and issues particularly concerning the protection of the involved donors. The reason for making biobanks legally and ethically problematic is that biobanks as a whole function as data custodians in order to protect the rights and interests of the donors. Biobanks are institutions of safeguarding by acting on behalf of the people, who altruistically donate physical samples and medical data for scientific uses. It is an essential task of the process management of biobanks to regulate, coor-

---

(1) Book-Publication: SIMON et al. (2006).
(2) TAB – Office of Technology Assessment at the German Parliament (2006).

dinate and control all processes within the biobank insuring a high level of donor protection according to the given legal framework and the ethical standards. All possible risks of an unintended donor re-identification outside of the biobank have to be avoided or at least to be minimized. The internal biobank activities – in particular the recruitment of donors, the storage and management of samples and data, including their transfer to external researchers – must be organized on the highest level of quality and quality control. The term «quality» in this context means more than «quality assurance»; it also covers the aspect of donor protection on the basis of informed consent and the valid legal regulations for data protection.

According to §1, German Federal Data Protection Law the individual is to be protected from harm to her or his personality right through the use of one's person related data. Precondition for the collection, handling and use of person related data is the permission or ordinance by the Federal Data Protection Law or another regulation or the permission of the person in question, according to §4 Federal Data Protection Law. This applies to the data gained from genetic diagnoses as well as for all other areas. A distinction must be made between the material gained from genetic diagnoses and data gained from them. This becomes critical in particular in the realm of biobanks as both the material is procured and processed for research as well as the data are generated in this manner of the donor. They are a central component of molecular oriented medical research. So they are of considerable importance with regard to data protection regulations, because biobanks are the main procurement, collection and distribution institution for results gained from genetic diagnoses on a national and international level. The thus possible fabrication of detailed personality profiles would make an application desirable not only for the health care system, but also for the pharmaceutical industry, the government and certainly the donor or patient.

Considering the involved danger potential, high demands must be made to the education of the persons involved. Anonymization of data for the protection is in the foreground of procurement, storage and application of data. At the same time, however, the interests of the donors in their examination results must be considered in that a pseudonymization might be more suitable for their long-term interests.

1.2. – *Criteria for selecting biobanks for this report*

This national report is dealing only with research biobanks: biobanks for storing and preparing samples of human tissue and data for medical or population genetic research purposes. Biobanks for other purposes, i. e. for diagnostic or therapeutic purposes, are excluded.

The German National Ethics Council (3) has defined research biobanks as «... collections of samples of human bodily substances (e.g. cells, tissue, blood or DNA as the physical medium of genetic information) that are or can be associated with personal data and information on their donors». Similar definitions can be found in other contexts including, for example, the 2006 report of the European Strategy Forum for Research Infrastructure (ESFRI).

It is important to see, that collections of human samples and associated data in the sense of biobanks are established explicitly for medical *research* purposes and not for therapeutic goals like e.g. collections of tissues or organs for transplantation purposes.

Furthermore: for a facility to qualify as a biobank, the data and sample collection should not be focused exclusively on a single scientific project but rather, this material should be intended for use in the pursuit of future, probably as yet unknown research goals. In this respect, biobanks are different from individual context related clinical resources.

In Germany there are no large-scale biobanks like the national biobanks in the United Kingdom or in Estonia or in Iceland. Rather there are more than 40 smaller biobanks, engaged in medical research with a specialisation in certain diseases or epidemiological especially population genetic questions.

1.3. – *Legal forms of establishing biobanks*

The most German biobanks are currently operated by public institutions such as university clinics, institutes or departments.

---

(3) Nationaler Ethikrat (2004).

There are only a few private biobanks in Germany. But, in principle, a biobank run as a private company can assume any legal status as long as this status does not require the biobank to be a trading entity. Therefore the most suitable organizational forms for a private biobank are the registered society, the limited company and the chartered foundation. Registered societies are generally recognized by the public as being trustworthy because most such institutions are tasked with jointly pursuing a non-material goal. Several research collaborations in Germany currently operate as registered societies. The most prominent disadvantages of registered societies, however, are frequent inefficiencies in internal organization and the significant legal liabilities imposed upon their boards of directors. Limited companies, by contrast, provide their members with considerable protection against financial ruin because the liability of the company is limited to its common stock. On the other hand, this limitation can render the acquisition of investments on the financial markets both difficult and cumbersome. In the following list one can find examples for all legal forms in which biobanks can be established.

1.4. – *List of German Research Biobanks*

1.4.1. *Publicly promoted biobanks*

The large part of the German biobanks belongs to publicly promoted competence networks which partners are mostly institutes of universities or university clinics.

1. *GEPARD – Competence Network on Parkinson's Disease*

Established at the University of Bonn (the main center) and at the Universities of Dresden, Luebeck, Marburg and Tuebingen (subcenters). The goal is to research neuro-psychiatric diseases (especially the Parkinson's disease). Hitherto circa 3000 samples have been collected, which can be given to third parties in an anonymized form.

http://www.kompetenznetz-parkinson.de

2. *SEPNET – Competence Network on Sepsis*

Established at the University of Jena: it is planned to build up a big sample bank for examining genomic, proteomic and molecular biologic questions. Medium-term with this a quick and safe diagnostic shall be made possible as well as demonstrate new therapeutic ways (risk assessment, target-identification). Until now approx. 7.000 samples of approx. 500 patients were collected.

http://www.kompetenznetz-sepsis.de

3. *Competence Network Malignant Lymphomas*

A decentralized organized biobank with several thousands of samples. In the competence network, with its head office in Cologne, the leading researcher groups and supply institutions in Germany, which are working in the field of malignant lymphoma have joined together. Their goal is to guarantee the optimum treatment, care and information for all lymphoma patients.

http://www.lymphome.de

4. *Competence Network Paediatric Oncology and Haematology (POH)*

Established at the Universities of Cologne and Freiburg: approx. 10.000 samples. The main objects of research are the tumor diseases and diseases of the blood in children.

http://www.kompetenznetze.de/navi/de/root,did=28412.html

5. *Competence Network Chronic Ulcerative Colitis (CED)*

A decentralized joint venture of three biobanks:
– University of Kiel (DNA-bank: ca 4.000 samples)
– University of Regensburg (serum bank: ca 3.600 samples)
– University Charité Berlin (Colon-biopsy bank: ca 1.700 samples of 400 patients)

http://www.kompetenznetz-ced.de

6. *Competence Network Hepatitis*

A Serum- and DNA-bank at the University Essen; a issue-bank is located at the University Cologne; a register of hepatocellular carcinomas is kept at the University Duesseldorf.

http://www.kompetenznetz-hepatitis.de

7. *The Dementia Competence Network*

DNA-biobanks in Bonn, Hamburg and Munich. DNA-samples of ca. 4.800 patients as well as blood and liquor samples of ca 1.000 patients are collected.

http://www.kompetenznetz-demenzen.de

8. *Competence Network Stroke*

A nationwide network of physicians, scientists, self-help associations and other organizations. DNA-samples of ca 2.500 stroke patients and 2.500 healthy control persons (one part of the samples is stored at the Max-Delbrueck Center in Berlin Buch).

http://www.kompetenznetz-schlaganfall.de

9. *German Research Network on Schizophrenia in Bonn and Munich*

Established at the centers Bonn and Munich: each with ca 400 recruited patients for obtaining DNA-samples and certain cell lines.

http://www.kompetenznetz-schizophrenie.de

10. *Competence Network HIV/AIDS*

A research affiliation, which maintains several collections of material:
- DNA-bank at the University Essen;
- Tissue-bank (lymph nodes) at the Bernhard-Nocht-Institute in Hamburg;
- Serum-bank at the Robert-Koch Institute in Berlin;
- Tissue-bank (intestinal mucous membranes) at the Charité in Berlin;
- Tissue-bank (spinal liquor) at the University Wuerzburg

http://www.kompetenznetz-hiv.de

11. *Competence Network Rheumatism*

At present ca 4.000 samples in Berlin, Bochum, Erlangen, Freiburg and Hannover

http://www.rheumanet.org

12. *Competence Network Heart Insufficiency (Berlin)*

Goal is the collection of blood, serum, plasma, DNA and tissue of heart patients, in order to find new ways for the treatment of heart insufficiency. Samples of 6.000 patients were already registered.

http://www.knhi.de

13. *Competence Network Acute and Chronic Leukaemia*

No specific information could be obtained about the scope of the Leukemia cell bank, which delivers samples on request of study groups.

http://www.kompetenznetz-leukaemie.de

14. *PopGen*

A population based DNA-collection for the purpose of researching of popular diseases in the regions of Northern Schleswig-Holstein with its residence at the University of Kiel. At present ca 35.000 samples as well as accompanied clinical data of ca 3.500 patients and ca 3.500 control persons. The biobanks is member of the National Genome Research Network (NGFN).

http://www.popgen.de

15. *Brain-Net*

A decentralized brain tissue-bank with eight brain-bank-centers, each orientated to specific themes. At present ca 2.500 samples total (with ca 25 data points per patient).

http://www.bain-net.net/

16. *Network Muscular Dystrophy (MD-NET)*

Established the Ludwig.Maximilian-University (LMU) in Munich. At present the Cell- and Tissue-bank holds ca 1.500 cell cultures (approx. 250 new samples are obtained yearly).

http://www.md-net.org

17. *German Network of Hereditary Movement Disorders (GEN-MOVE)*

A central DNA-bank at the University Clinic in Tuebingen, which coordinates the communication between the clinical senders and research groups. DNA-samples (the scope is unknown) are produced and forwarded on request to research groups.

http://www.genemove.de

18. *Addiction Medicine Research Association of Baden-Wuerttemberg*

A DNA-bank (extracted from blood samples) at the University of Mannheim : ca 3.000 samples.

http://www.zi-mannheim.de/630.html

1.4.2. *Biobanks at Universities*

19. *Study of Health in Pomerania (SHIP)*

A population based (epidemiological) collection of blood-, urine- and saliva samples for the research of numerous popular diseases (heart- and circulatory diseases?, diabetes mellitus, dental diseases etc) in the region of Vorpommern (Pomerania), carried out by the University of Greifswald (in pseudomized form). Until now ca 80.000 samples (of ca 4.000 persons between 20 years and 80 years, at follow-ups in a five-years-interval). The samples are not only at the disposal for the research affiliation «Community Medicine» of the University of Greifswald but also for cooperation partners as well as for third parties on request.

http://www.medizin.uni-greifswald.de/cm/fv/ship.html

20. *Laboratory for Molecular Medicine at the University of Erlangen*

A gynecological oriented tissue-tumor-bank with 3.000 tissue pieces and over 4.000 genomic DNA-samples from the peripheral blood of patients and control persons.

http://www.frauenklinik.klinikum.uni-erlangen.de/e2201/e162/index_ger.html

21. *Interdisciplinary Network Heart Insufficiency*

At this biobank, established at the University of Wuerzburg, samples and medical data of about 1.000 patients for the epidemiological research of chronic heart insufficiency are registered.

http://www.medpoli.uni-wuerzburg.de

22. *Therapy Study ALL-BFM 2000*

The Therapy Study (started ca 30 years ago) serves the monitoring of the therapy in the pediatric oncology, especially the «acute lymphoblastic Leukemia» (ALL). At the University of Kiel ca 30.000 samples obtained for the ALL-BFM 2000 are stored in form of cell material and DNA.

http://www.uni-kiel.de/all-studie/All_stu_l.htm

23. *LURIC – Ludwigshafen Risk and Cardiovascular Health Study*

Since 1997 the LURIC GmbH and Aventis Pharma Germany, now Sanofi-Aventis are cooperating. The essence of the scientific cooperation is the LURIC-study, which was carried out between 1997 and 2003 by the Clinic Ludwigshafen and the Universities of Freiburg and Ulm and covered a period of ten years total. The main financiers are Aventis and the EU («Bloodomics»). The study aims to research the influence of genes and environmental factors on genesis and course of popular diseases as diabetes, heart- and circulatory diseases or thrombotic disorders; issue is the exploration of the functional relation between gene variation and biochemical phenotype as well as between gene variation and medication. Over 3.500 patients already have participated in this study. Since 2004 a follow-up with these participants is carried out.

http://www.luric.de

24. 2EPIC European Prospective Investigation into Cancer and Nutrition (Heidelberg)

Heart of this institution is the nutritional epidemiological workgroup at the University of Heidelberg, which has gathered blood samples from ca 25.000 persons from Heidelberg and surrounding communities for the «European Prospective Investigation into Cancer and Nutrition» (EPIC)-Study. Also data were obtained through several surveys concerning eating habits, physical activities, pathogenesis and medication. Goal is an assessment of the risk of developing cancer (breast cancer, lung cancer, cancer of the colon, prostate cancer) due to different exposition factors. Inter alia by means of the blood samples biomarkers for the ingestion are determined. The work is promoted by the European Commission Sanco and by the «Deutsche Krebshilfe e.V.»

http://www.dkfz.de/de/klepidemiologie/arbeitsgr/ernaerepi/ee_p01_epichd.html

25. EPIC European Prospective Investigation into Cancer and Nutrition (Potsdam)

This project is part of the «European Prospective Investigation into Cancer and Nutrition» (EPIC)-cohort study (with ca 520.000 study participants from 10 EU-countries) and is undertaken by the department Epidemiology of the University of Potsdam. The EPIC-Potsdam-study, started in 1994, is laid out as a long-term study with a time frame of 20 years. For the epidemiological study from Potsdam and surroundings over 27.000 participants were recruited, from which a blood sample was requested between 1994 and 1998. The aim is the cognition of relations between eating habits and the development of chronic diseases as cancer, diabetes mellitus and cardiovascular disorders. From 5.000 blood samples of newly diseased persons an extract of DNA was taken in order to research the variability of the genetic information and its relation to special biomarkers as well as the disease risk. The obtained data will be evaluated on European level from scientists of the 23 administrative EPIC-centers of the ten countries involved.

http://www.dife.de/de/index.php?request=/de/forschung/projekte/epic.php

26. *Nephroblastom SIOP 2001 / GPOH (Saarbruecken)*

Samples and data are collected from children for a prospective multicentral study for optimizing the therapy of the nephroblastom. More than 100 pediatric clinics in Germany, Austria and Switzerland are involved. The study is part of an international nephroblastom study of the SIOP (International Society of Pediatric Oncology).

http://www.kinderkrebsinfo.de/wilms

1.4.3. *Other Biobanks at Public Institutions*

27. *KORA-gen: Cooperative Health Research in the Region of Augsburg*

A collection of data for the population based «Cooperative Health Research» in the region of Augsburg for the exploration of genetic and molecular questions in the fields of cardiovascular diseases, adiposity, allergies, asthma and different cancers. Supporter of the biobank, which is located in Neuherberg, is the Helmholtz-Center in Munich (HMGU, previously GSF). Since 1984 the KORA-platform has carried out population representative cohort studies. Within the four health surveys and its succession surveys ca 18.000 adult test subjects were examined. The in that course obtained biosamples serve among others as a basis for the assessment of genotype frequencies in the population.

http://epi.gsf.de/kora-gen/

28. *Blood Donor Biobank (Munich)*

Midyear 2006 the biobank was established by the Bavarian Red Cross (BRK) and serves for the determination of the prognostic value of the so-called metabolism biomarkers, which are important for the development of new diagnostic tools and therapies. The stock of samples of the biobank of the blood transfusion services amounts at present ca 3 millions of plasma samples. Hereof ca 100.000 samples of 5.000 diseased donors (after receiving their consent) and of 5.000 healthy persons were taken into the blood donor biobank. An enlargement of the sample stock of the biobank (also by cooperation with other departments in other federal states of the DRK) is planned.

http://biobank.blutspendedienst.com/home.html

29. *Clinical Research Group of Molecular Neurogenetics (Munich)*

A DNA-bank at the University of Munich for the elucidation of the pathogenesis (hereditary dispositions) of neuro-genetic disorders and the development of new therapeutic approaches.

http://www.nefo.med.uni-muenchen.de/Forschungshauptseite/experimentelle_nro /molekulareneurogenetik

30. *Research Institute for Health Protection at Workplace (BGFA)*

The GBFA in Bochum wants to explore occupational illnesses of the respiratory tracts, allergic disorders and chemical-biological effects of hazardous substances at the workplace. The sample bank, built up since 1957 in the DDR, merged 1992 with the principal trade association. At present samples (and data) of ca 30.000 persons are stored. Samples are principally not forwarded to third parties, but analysis data.

http://www.bgfa.ruhr-uni-bochum.de

31. *National Center for Tumor Diseases (Heidelberg)*

The NCT is located at the University of Heidelberg resp. at the German Cancer Research Center (DKFZ) with the assignment to support their biomedical projects. The purpose of the tissue bank is the collection, characterization, registration, archiving and the preparation of tissues and tissue extracts in high quality for scientific exploration in tumor research. Information about the exact size of the sample bank was not available.

http://www.klinikum.uni-heidelberg.de

32. *Heinz Nixdorf Recall Study*

Until 2007 the University Clinic Essen carried out a study with citizens of the cities Bochum, Essen and Muehlheim a.d. Ruhr about heart and circulatory system diseases, in order to test new methods for predicting heart attacks and cardiac death. Blood samples of 4.500 persons were collected; one part of the blood samples is stored deep-frozen for future research in the central laboratory of the University Clinic Essen.

http://www.recall-studie.uni-essen.de/recall_info.html

1.4.4. Biobanks of Foundations and Charitable Organizations

33. PATH – Patients Tumorbank of Hope

PATH was founded 2002 as a non-profit foundation and is determined to contribute with tissue donations to improve the treatment possibilities of cancer patients. In 2003 the first PATH-Center at the Clinic in Kassel was put into commission. Similar centers were founded in Bonn, Marburg and Dortmund. Pharmaceutics companies as Roche Pharma, AstraZeneca Onkologie, Bayer HealthCare and Novartis could be won as sponsors. The tissue bank is replenished continually by the storage of clinical course data. Samples and data can be forwarded in a controlled manner to interested researchers.

http://www.stiftungpath.org/

34. Pseudoxanthoma Elasticum (PXE)

PXE is a rare but severe impairment of the eyesight right up to blindness. According to the American example the German PXE self-help group has founded a biobank in Freudenberg (Bethesda Clinic). The basis is the donation of one sample of each member of the self-help organization to the clinic. Blood samples of ca 150 members are stored also at the heart- and diabetes center NRW in Bad Oeynhausen.

www.pxe.org/

35. German Collection of Microorganisms and Cell Cultures (DSMZ)

Supporter of the DSMZ, founded in 1969, are the Federal State Niedersachsen and the «Wissensgemeinschaft G : W. Leibnitz» located in Braunschweig. Especially cell lines from tumor cells are collected there and linked with personal and clinical data. The collected samples are national and international and sent in to the

DSMZ in a pseudomized form. The biobank contains among others ca 550 human and animal cell lines, which can be ordered for a fee for non-profit purposes.

www.dsmz.de

36. CRIP : Central Research Infrastructure for Molecular Pathology

This facility at the Fraunhofer-Institute in Potsdam does not collect samples, but places between pathological institutes, which are collecting tissue samples and potential users from research projects.

http://www.ibmt.fraunhofer.de/fhg/ibmt/biomedizintechnik/biodatenbanken_crip/

1.4.5. Commercial Biobanks

37. GENOMatch

This sample- and data bank supports the pharmacological research of the Schering Inc. Especially the effectiveness and the tolerance of new drugs are to be explored.

http://www.tembit.de/web/de/genomatch.asp

38. Indivumed Inc. – Center for Cancer Research at the Israelite Clinic Hamburg

This company was founded in 2002 at the Center for cancer research at the Israelite Clinic in Hamburg. Indivumed operates its own research laboratories with the goal to promote the development of individualized medicinally treatment methods for tumor patients. The company offers (among others) an «Integrated Analysis Platform» (IAP) for the identification and validation of target molecules as a service. Hereby samples (tissue, serum, plasma, urine) of tumor patients are linked with an extensive internet based data bank. At present ca 5.000 samples of ca 8.000 patients are stored in the biobank of Indivumed. Services (analysis) but no samples are sold to third parties.

http://www.indivumed.com

2. – LEGAL FRAMEWORK

2.1. – *General legislation applicable*

With regard to the use of biological materials, there is a great need for clarification of the legal ramifications. And since procuring and storing bio materials is becoming an increasingly important point for answering molecular-genetic questions within medical research, finding an answer soon for the related legal and organisational questions is extremely important.

In Germany intensive discussions have been held about the legal and ethical aspects of biobanks. Nevertheless, many questions remain unanswered which concern particularly the core of the mentioned points, i.e. options of use and disposition of biomaterials passed on.

Modern medical research is undergoing a «cultural change» these days in that cooperative research structures are being formed which are geared toward long-term cooperation. Within this usually supra-regional cooperation, often central data and bio banks are installed. Bio materials are valuable starters for research since they contain molecular-genetic information which allows multiple uses independent of the original purpose at the point in time of their collection. This information, however, is so very specific again that the materials may always be connected to their respective donor. Thus, a new step of ethical and personality rights related problems is reached.

But so far, in Germany there are no laws regulating specifically the use of bio materials. Some of the leading medical research networks («competence networks») have begun with the support to clarify the ramifications for a lawful set up and operation of bio material banks.

One central task when setting up and operating a biobank is protecting the property and personality rights of the donors. Further, in particular, the question regarding long-term use for at first undetermined research purposes may be answered only after an intensive analysis of the respective personality rights. These legal questions are somewhat covered up by questions of ethical principles which gain great importance especially in connection with patient consent.

2.2. – Specific legislation

At present in Germany no special legislation exists, which would regulate the handling with samples and data in biobanks. However, there are several laws, which apply to numerous aspects of biobanks. This pertains especially to the regulations of the German constitution concerning the personal rights, which are also to be followed with the donors of bodily material, or to the German Civil Code and the German Criminal Code to possible physical injury, which can occur during the withdrawal of bodily material. Also the regulations in the Federal Data Protection Law accrue, which is only applicable to personalized data though, as well as the different Data Protection Laws of the Federal Countries, which content is mostly congruent with the Federal Data Protection Law. Finally the Hospital Laws, which have been passed by several Federal countries, are also applicable, in so far as the samples and data, which find their way into biobanks, were obtained in a clinical context. Also in some respect the Medical Law and the law on medicines (AMG) are of some relevance, the in some Federal States existing Post Mortem Laws as well as the Law for protection against infection and the law on medical products.

The shortcoming consists in a lack of cross-linking the different law fields concerning the complex activities of biobanks. Usually only single aspects of the activity of a biobank are acquired, so that these are still in a legal grey zone to a large degree. Correspondingly, there are no regulations concerning the auditing resp. the certification of biobanks in Germany yet. Also the Gene Diagnostic Law, which is in course of preparation as well as the Tissue Law won't provide for consistent regulations for the work of biobanks.

2.3. – Reports and opinions by national institutions and bodies

Different commissions and counseling boards already have in part taken a very detailed stand on certain questions in connection with biobanks. It is remarkable that the dealing with this theme concentrates on ethical questions around the «informed consent» and on the personal rights: the focus lies on the embodiment of the informational right of self-determination, the right of nescience etc.

Whereas questions concerning the property rights are almost not dealt with.

Especially two statements have influenced the German biobanks discussion widely:

(1) German National Ethics Council (200): «Biobanks for Research», Berlin

(2) Enquête-Commission (2003): «Law and Ethics of the Modern Medicine», final report, Bundestagsdrucksache 14/9020, Berlin

(3) Central Ethics Commission (2003): «The (subsequent) Use of Human Body Material for Medicinal Research Purposes», Berlin

Ad (1): The position paper of the National Ethics Council is the most extensive statement and discusses biobanks predominantly from the ethical viewpoint, whereas aspects of Personal Rights are in the foreground. Some of the crucial points are:

- A general requirement for an official approval is not needed. Worth considering, however, might be a license requirement for big biobanks.
- The legally required internal control should be replenished by an external control, for which in the public sector data protection officers are responsible.
- The donors should be informed before their consent about all circumstances, which could be cognizable relevant for their decision about consent or rejection. Donors had the right to recall their assent for the use of their samples and data at any time. This right should not be dispensed.
- Furthermore it should be possible to make an agreement with the donors, that, in case of a revocation of the consent, samples and data only could be anonymized and not have to be destroyed.
- Concerning the biobanks the claim for rigid periods for the storage and use would be counterproductive. If it should be avoided that once established biobanks are devalued within a short time, the possibility should be granted, that donors can agree to the use of their samples and data for undefined only in the future to be defined research projects.
- An unspecified consent of the donor for the passing on usually should be defined in such a way that it is only allowed to pass on the material to the same kind of institutions. Except for legal exceptions the transfer only should be made in an anonymized

and encoded form that prohibits the receiver to access the code. Samples and data from biobanks should not be allowed to be passed on and used for other than research purposes. Therefore it would be needed to establish a legal research secret in order to rule out unauthorized (other than for research purposes) access on samples and data.

– More consequently as customary in the past biobanks should be established and maintained according to homogenous scientific standards (Quality assurance).

Ad (2): The statement of the Enquête-Commission mainly deals with the scope of «informed consent» as the «central data protection law problem»; also questions of a «multistage pseudomizing procedure» are discussed.

Ad (3): In the statement of the Central Ethics Commission questions concerning personal rights and data protection rights are discussed: especially strict requirements for informing and consent of the donors are set up. However, no generalized regulations concerning the duration of the storage of human tissue samples are suggested.

There are two further works, in which the authors of this report are also involved:

(3) J.W. SIMON, R. PASLACK, J. ROBIENSKI et al. (2006): «Biomaterial Banks – Legal Framework», ed. by TMF – Telematic platform for medical networks, Berlin

(4) TAB – Office of Technology Assessment at the German Parliament (2006): «Biobanks for the human medicine Research and Application», Workreport No. 112, Berlin.

Ad (3): This as a book published report seeks to acquire all relevant laws and other regulations, which are relevant for the operation of biobanks and to develop recommendations for areas lacking regulations or not having distinct ones: especially the advantages and disadvantages of the different possible legal forms for biobanks are discussed as well as questions of personal protection and property rights on the samples, all legally relevant aspects with regard to the ascertainment and the storage as well as the transmission of samples and data, the relevance of the Medical Law and the Labour Law and the possibilities of research secrecy.

Ad (4): Besides the legal framework in the TAB-report a categorizing and systematic of biobanks are made as well as their scientific and research political meaning discussed. The conflicting priorities of «privacy» and «policy» due to the collision of different parties are pointed out.

2.4. – *Professionals and institutions: quality standards and accreditation requirements*

In Germany, professional and laboratory standards play an important role in the operations of biobanks. Although there are no legal obligations for obtaining permission to create a biobank nor registration is required, the biobanks set great value upon the adherence to technical standards. Moreover, the operations of a biobank are liable under the Data Protection Law and it is mandatory that all medical operations (e.g. as the extraction of samples) are medically supervised. Even without the obligation for biobanks to be certified, the operators of biobanks strive to maintain a high level of professionalism in the processing of samples and data. And all activities concerning data protection (e.g. declaration forms about a patient's consent) are examined by an ethics committee. Within the framework of the voluntary quality assurance, attention is paid to the continual advanced training of the staff as well as the warranty of a high technical standard with all laboratory processes. If nothing else, voluntary certifications of the laboratory operations serve to enhance the donors' confidence in biobanks. There is growing interest on the part of the biobanks in auditing data protection matters as well.

2.4.1. *Personal equipment*

Most of the German biobanks are located at universities or hospitals. In so far as they are not only collecting samples and data, but also obtaining them, also a medical doctor belongs to their staff, who is allowed to collect the samples. For storing data and data editing mostly a computer scientist is available, who is as any other biobank employee bound to secrecy in terms of the Data Protection Law. For the protection of the personal data of the donors and the codes for the pseudomization of the data, normally a special data trustee is responsible, who can be located internal or external to the biobank. Often a biobank includes an ethics-commission into its activities, which assists especially in the composition of the informed consent and the valuation of research projects for which samples and data are requested of the biobank.

A data protecting auditing of biobanks only has taken place in a single case (GENOMatch). Also rules and regulations for the certification of biobanks are still missing.

2.4.2. *Laboratory equipment*

In so far as the biobank treats the obtained samples (e.g. extract DNA from it), carries out certain analyses (such as determination of certain biomarker) or even conducts research on its own, it maintains moreover its own laboratory, which has to follow the rules of «best practice».

Concerning the storage and the transport of material special regulations do not exist. However, the peculiarities of the material to be stored and the state-of-the-art of storage and transport of the material have to be taken into account. That means for every type of biomaterial appropriate receptacles for storage and transport need to be held ready so that a destruction, deterioration or change of the material will be prevented. As this is a technical question, an appropriate code of practice or a customer requirement specification for storage and transport of biomaterials should be developed in cooperation with biologists and biotechnicians. This customer requirement specification has to include the specifics for the storage and transport for every biomaterial, i.e. temperature, storage medium (paraffin block, liquid nitrogen, etc), maximum utilization periods in the environmental air or in certain temperature scopes etc.

The compliance with these technical requirements is of particular importance, if the biobank transfers – for money consideration – the biomaterial for research purposes to third parties. In case the biomaterial is no longer usable because of failures of the biobank during storage or transport, the biobank in this respect is obliged to warranty and damages where applicable.

In case the defectiveness of the biomaterial is detected immediately, the claims of the addressee will be confined essentially to an additional delivery of faultless biomaterial – as far as possible.

Whilst it is not feasible to estimate possible claims for damages from the addressee, if only after months of research emerges that the research results do not bear any significance because the delivered biomaterial was defective. In this case the addressee could have the right of compensation for his useless research expenditures – namely personnel costs, material expenses etc. These costs can be significant. Therefore measurements for quality assurance constitute an important need for biobanks.

2.5. – *Ethics Research Committees*

Ethics committees overseeing the biobanks' affairs serve to protect the donor against misuse of data and to guarantee the donor's informed consent. They advise biobanks on all questions concerning data protection and in this way contribute to a legal quality assurance. Ethics committees are often called by biobanks in cases of doubt regarding data protection questions. All interviewed German biobanks maintain either their own ethics committees (especially when they conduct research) or maintain contacts with the responsible data protection officer of the state. However, there is no legal obligation to appeal to an ethics committee, if the elicitation and collection of samples/data only serve research purposes. Normally it is demanded of the external research scientists who want to obtain samples and/or data from biobanks, that they first submit their research projects to an ethics committee and obtain its approval.

2.6. – *Obtaining of samples*
(invasive intervention in the donor)

Most of the body materials kept in DNA- and serum banks are blood samples obtained from living donors. Mostly the donors are adults. The collection of other tissues, cell lines or even solid organs is more an exception.

Various constellations may be defined in which the collection of body materials from the donor is done (4).

– Collection for diagnosis/therapy reasons within the scope of a contract for treatment
– Collection within in the scope of a particular research project

---

(4) Comp. Statement of the Zentrale Ethikkommission (2003).

- Collection for the purpose of storing samples for later unspecified research
- Other collection reasons (criminal law suits, donation of one's own blood, etc.)

Subject of the report on hand is exclusively the collections, which were created for research purposes. Nonetheless the large part of the samples, which are stored in biobanks, were gained in a clinical context, where they first were collected for diagnostic and therapeutic purposes and only afterwards were put at the disposal for research. Or these are samples for later medical tests («Rückstellproben») as in the case of the Bavarian «Biobank of Blood Donors»: the samples here are obtained during a normal blood donation and have to be stored for five years for legal reasons.

Two contexts, in which samples and data are obtained, which are collected in biobanks, will be briefly discussed here:

2.6.1. *Collection for diagnosis/therapy reasons*

A large portion – if not in fact the major portion – of samples stored in biobanks was collected within the scope of medical treatments, whether in a hospital or in a doctor's practice. The collection is done with the consent of the patient usually exclusively for diagnostic, sometimes for therapeutic purposes. The samples comprise, for example, tissue from medically indicated biopsies of various organs. In such a case, tissue is collected from living or dead persons for reasons of diagnosis. Usually, the diagnosis is not or not exactly known prior to the operation. The volume of tissue is limited.

Another source of tissue is taken during operations (for example tumors from various tissue types, amputation material, organs in connection with transplants). Usually, large volume tissue is collected while only portions thereof are needed for further histological examinations. Usually, the diagnosis is known in advance. There is tissue left over (left-over materials).

Finally, there may be body materials which are not «collected», but «happen to come about», such as with the afterbirth (placenta, umbilical cord). This category includes also body secretions and other «waste materials».

2.6.2. Collection for certain research projects

A proportion of samples is taken for purely research purposes within the scope of certain studies without having a concrete treatment as a goal. Usually, these are specialized studies regarding specific diseases. The goal of these research projects is to examine causes and treatment methods for certain diseases which the donor might also suffer from. Recently, broad sample collections have been initiated without knowing whether a specific disease occurs. These collections were executed with the goal to research whether and to what extent a certain disease occurs in the population (5).

A further manner of collection may be done in that body materials (for example tissue or blood) are taken with the consent of the patient in addition for scientific research reasons in the course of an otherwise medically indicated removal of body materials.

It is important that the collection of samples will not take place against the will of the patient. A consent must be present. Otherwise according to §223 German Criminal Code (StGB) battery could be constituted. It makes no difference, whether the sampling carried out by a physician takes place because of research- or treatment reasons.

Also the collection (or drawing) of blood in a treatment context principally is battery, which is only healed by the given consent of the patient. The «medicasl proviso» («Arztvorbehalt») applies in this context principally also to non-invasive samplings. §1 Law regulation practitioners of alternative medicine states that the practice of medicine is allowed only for medical doctors or with an authorized permission. However, the doctor is allowed to delegate parts of his work to non-physicians. This requires that the assigned task is principally delegable.

Not delegable are tasks which require medical know-how because of the difficulty, danger or because of possible unpredictable reactions; therefore these have to be carried out personally by the physician (6).

These are in particular:

– all (surgical) operations

---

(5) STUHRMANN-SPANGENBERG and SCHMIDTKE (2005), p. 128.
(6) LAUFS (1993), Rdnr 519.

- difficult injections
- infusions
- taking blood samples
- medical examinations
- medical information and consultation of the patient.

Also all invasive operations for diagnostic purposes, especially also injections with contrast media and biopsies, and finally the decision about necessary therapeutic measurements belong to the non-delegable services.

Non-invasive samplings (for example the removing of skin, hair and the saliva sample) are very simple procedures, so that it is justifiable to delegate these to non-medical assistants. Taking blood is only allowed for specially qualified assistants. Biopsies and similar samplings of tissue are not allowed to be carried out by non-medical assistants.

2.7. – Sample ownership

In case the donor has not transferred his sample ownership to the biobank, he has a right to request the return or the destruction of his sample. Whereas donors can waive the proprietary ownership of their samples this doesn't apply with personal rights, which are connected with the utilization of the samples (and data) by the biobank. However, the donor's proprietary rights to the samples depend on the proposed uses of the samples and the context in which they were obtained. Samples often accrue in the clinical (diagnostic and therapeutic) context prior to their further utilization for research purposes. Occasionally samples are collected specifically for research projects. Therefore, different cases need to be distinguished.

2.7.1. Contract for treatment and diagnosis

After termination of contract (or after early termination) the donor may request the return or destruction of the collected samples provided that the body materials have been collected within the scope of a contract for treatment or diagnosis with a doctor.

A limitation arises only if the doctor or the clinic is obligated to destroy the sample for other reasons (for example a contaminated sample).

2.7.2. *Contractual agreement*

The contractual basis for the rights of the biobank may be either a donation contract or usufruct, if a transferral of ownership was not planned.

If the ownership of the sample moves to the biobank, it has an unlimited right of utilization. A legal recall right usually does not apply here (the collection of the body materials will hardly lead to poverty of the donor).

Only if the obligation contract («schuldrechtlicher Vertrag») must be retro-acted upon due to a right of withdrawal or valid contesting by the donor, the donor may request the return of his body materials in the course of this retro-action. If the donor – as provided for in the declarations of intent discussed here – was permitted by the collecting agency that he «... may request at any time the return or destruction of the sample ...», then we are dealing with a contractual right of return or destruction.

2.7.3. *Abuse*

In the case of abuse of the sample, the rights thereto having been legally and with intent transferred to the biobank, the donor may file a claim for cease and desist as per §§823, 1004 German Civil Code (BGB). This claim to cease and desist may even be converted to a claim for destruction or return, if the abuse may not be prevented by other means.

2.7.4. *Change of purpose*

If the purpose of a research project permits or if the project is finished, the donor will have the right to request the destruction of the sample.

2.7.5. *Return request for samples so far used properly*

Should the request of the donor to destroy the sample apply only for the future, there will be no effect on the already stored data and research results. The evaluation and processing executed up to the date of the recall was legally proper. However, this will usually entail the obligation of the research institute to anonymize the person-related data as far as possible.

2.7.6. Person-related data

Should person-related data be gained from a sample, these must be deleted at the request of the donor. No data may be stored against the will of the donor. This is already stipulated as per the Federal Data Protection Law (BDSG). This applies even more so if the data have been collected unlawfully.

2.7.7. Research results

Should the research results have commercial value, the donor may have a claim to gain from the point of view of unjustified enrichment. The research results themselves may not be requested to be handed over. One may have to consider the claim of the donor for preventing publication of the research results.

2.7.8. The role of anonymization with regard to the right of return or destruction

If a sample is completely or even only factually anonymized in the sense of §3 Abs. 6 BDSG, a return or destruction of the sample is impossible. This applies also in case of a factual anonymization, because the effort for identification would be so high as to make it unreasonable for a biobank to make this effort. Since a link from the sample to a person is not given any longer, the rights of the donor are hardly touched by it. Therefore, the donor may at best make a claim for damages. Differing from the sperm case decision by the Federal Civil Court (BGH), the donor will not have a claim for compensation for personal suffering. Since the sample is separated for good from the body and was not intended to be reunited with it, any personality rightful link is missing.

2.8. – *Protection of the subject's privacy*
(Duty of confidentiality
and security of data and sample archives)

All biobanks reviewed have established a system to keep the confidentiality of the donor (and her/his relatives). If the samples and data should be used not in an anonymised manner, they become pseudonymised. The codes are kept separately and protected by an independent internal or external data custodian. The personal data will be strictly separated from the clinical data. Furthermore the clinical information is kept in locked files, and the access to it is restricted to a few staff (as well as to the samples which are in containers, refrigerators and ultra freezers locked). In the most German biobanks the study's code number will be replaced with a new code. Often a second replacement of the code takes place before data or samples are transferred to researchers outside of the biobank. In all cases the measurements for donor's protection – especially the receiving of the informed consent and the transfer of data and/or samples – are controlled by guidelines and an ethic committee.

2.8.1. *Data protection infringement*

In research with human body substances, person-related data are collected, processed and used. Therefore, data protection regulations apply on principle. These regulations are stipulated in the federal data protection laws (BDSG), in the particular state data protection laws and in various special regulations such as the law for doctors, the cancer registry law etc. (Medical Law, Cancer Registry Law [Krebsregister-Gesetz]). Since the specific state data protection laws include mainly the same basic principles and regulations as the BDSG/federal law, we shall refer mainly to the federal regulations in the following. For the question whether data protection regulations apply, we need to distinguish between the tissue sample as such and the data gathered from it. With regard to tissue samples, we are dealing on principle with non-person related data (§3 Abs. 1 BDSG) (7).

---

(7) HALÀSZ (2004), p. 263; BREYER (2004), p. 660.

a) *Anonymous sample*

If the tissue samples are completely anonymous, i.e. the reference sample does not show a person's name either, data protection regulations do not apply (8).

If one represents the opinion that tissue samples must be considered data carriers from which genetic and other medically individualized information may be deduced, this does not oppose this opinion. Some of these genetic and other medically individualized findings are person-related data, but only until or as long as the sample itself has not yet been anonymized.

In objection it is argued that an absolute and secure anonymization may hardly be achieved. By means of an identified reference tissue sample or results from other genome analyses a tissue could be related again to a particular person or to a family related person, even if otherwise no information is known about the respective person. The first version of objection requires that the sample itself is personalized. Should that not be the case, relating it to a particular person does not occur.

It is correct that results from other genome analyses in theory allow for classifying the sample. However, this is considered at present to be too much of an effort so that we may assume that a relationship to a person is not possible as per §3 Abs. 6 BDSG.

In Germany, we understand a purely factual anonymization when we speak about «anonymization». Therefore, §3 Abs. 6 BDSG shows a definition by law of an anonymization: Anonymizing means changing person-related data such that individual information about personal or material relationships may not or only with unproportional large efforts of time, cost and labour be linked to a particular or specified natural person.

Samples which are only factually anonymized do not usually allow as per this definition – at least for the time being– conclusions as to the donor (9). Therefore, it is highly improbable that the data protection rights of the donor are violated (10).

With regard to the option of transferral of ownership to a third party this means that a sample which was anonymized as per §3

---

(8) BREYER (2004), p. 660.
(9) Comp. also WELLBROCK (2003), p. 78.
(10) NATIONALER ETHIKRAT (2004), p. 32; SPRANGER (2005), p. 1086.

Abs. 6 BDSG, i.e. which cannot be personalized in any way, may have its ownership rights transferred to a third party at any time and without limitations from a data protection point of view.

b) *Person-related sample*

Should the sample be labelled for the purposes of identifying it with personal data of the donor, a personal reference is given as per §3 Abs. 9 BDSG (11). Since the tissue sample is considered a carrier of highly sensitive information (12), the personalized sample must fully comply with data-protection regulations as do the person-related data gathered from the sample (13). Thus, the following applies:

In principle, collecting person-related data is only permissible if it is permitted by a legal stipulation (Cancer Registry Law) or by a consent given by the person in question.

Person-related data generally must be deleted (according to §§20 Abs. 2, 35 Abs. 2 BDSG), if their storage is not permissible or if their information is not/not any longer required by the data processing office. An impermissible storage is given if the purpose requiring the information had been achieved.

Within the scope of medical treatment or diagnosis measures, this point in time is the end of the medical measures, unless there is an obligation for maintenance. With research projects this point in time would be the end of the research project. Even if a consent of the donor was given as per §4a BDSG, this consent is usually limited to a particular research project, thus the person-related data must be deleted according to the same principles.

Data collected for research purposes are bound completely to this purpose. They must not be used for other purposes than research according to §40 Abs. 1 BDSG.

Under certain circumstances, further processing may be permissible for another than the original research purpose. However, this requires either a new consent of the donor or a positive answer when weighing the interests of research against the protection of

---

(11) BREYER (2004), p. 660.
(12) BREYER (2004), p. 660.
(13) BREYER (2004), p. 660.

the personality. Here, we are faced with a high level of preconditions (14).

Further, one must observe to anonymize data, but as a minimum to pseudomize them as per §40 BDSG as soon as the research purpose permits this. Pseudomizing is permitted only if anonymizing is not possible.

Handing over person-related data constitutes a form of transmittal in the sense of §3 Abs. 4 Nr. 3 BDSG. Corresponding regulations are found in state data protection laws.

2.8.2. *Opposing rights of the donor*

The rights of the donor to oppose the use or certain uses of his samples vary concerning the manner the sample was operate within the biobanks or in respect to its transfer to researchers outside of the biobank.

a) *Anonymized sample*

Should a sample be completely or at least factually anonymized, it appears impossible at first sight that general personality rights of the donor be infringed. Since the general personality right is expressed in particular by the right to informal self-determination, an infringement in the case of anonymization is not possible.

However, recent literature represents the opinion that without exception even in cases of anonymization consent must be given, independent of the data-protection question (15). This means that whenever a donor has not consented to a particular form of use and utilization, the same is not permissible. Should the donor for example in the declaration of consent be given the right to request return or destruction of his sample without indication of reasons, an anonymization is not permissible, thus also passing on the anonymous sample is not permissible. If the sample were to be anonymized in order to pass it on to a third party, the will of the donor could not be met.

Even if the donor gives his express consent to the utilization of his body materials for particular research goals, a transmission of

---

(14) DEUTSCH and SPICKHOFF (2003), Rdnr.194 m.w.Nw.; LG KÖLN (1995), p. 1621.
(15) VON FREIER (2005), p. 324.

ownership to a third party is not permissible if the third party has deviating research goals or purposes or even aims at commercial purposes (16). The same applies if the donor expressly stipulates in his declaration of consent that a passing on of his materials is not permissible or only permissible to a particular recipient. In all of these cases, the «right of personal body self-determination» (Recht auf leibliche Selbstverfügung) would be infringed (17).

A transferral of ownership to third parties with good intentions will be possible, thus leaving the donor at best a right to damages. There may be a case of penal offence on the part of the acting or responsible party. Therefore, the declaration of consent should include a passage indicating that a right to return or destruction of completely or factually anonymized samples does not exist. Further, the consent to the passing on of anonymized samples to third parties should be included – independent of the person or research purpose of the third party.

b) *Pseudomized samples*

Pseudomized samples are stored under a pseudonym or an assumed name, thus, at first are not linkable to an identifiable person by the recipient. Transferral of ownership of these samples to a third party appears to be possible on principle.

However, since the donor may still be identified, the risk of having his data protection rights infringe upon remains. With regard to pseudomized samples, person-related data are processed. Any passing on of pseudomized samples to third parties, therefore, may be done only under observation of the known data protection regulations.

Moreover, in dealing with samples which are only pseudomized, the general personality right of the donor, in particular his right to informal self-determination is affected.

The transferal of ownership of only pseudomized samples is, therefore, only permissible under observation of the respective data protection regulations, and usually only if the donor has given his consent to the transferal of ownership of his pseudomized sample.

---

(16) DEUTSCH and SPICKHOFF (2003), RdNr 613.
(17) VON FREIER (2005), Fn 50; SPRANGER (2005), p. 1086 f.

This means that samples which were received due to a dereliction on the part of the donor (if this is even possible based on the above explanations), may usually be passed on only in an anonymized version. The reason is that personality rights may absolutely not be given up or abandoned by way of dereliction. In this respect, there must always be an express declaration of the donor.

Therefore, the data protection law and the general personality right of the donor, which superimposes the object ownership of the sample, do limit the absolute right of disposition of the biobank as the sample owner.

2.8.3. *Civil Code Claims*

Should a doctor receive more than a small remuneration for his efforts when transferring the sample, one will generally assume that this must be reprimanded as commercialization without permission (18). Whether and to what degree this applies to a biobank remains a question, because in this case the specific ethics of doctors do not apply in that manner. However, this may interfere with the principle of research freedom connected with non-profit research which should not be confused with the freedom to make profit.

According to Taupitz, contractual concerns of the patient he is entitled to may be affected by a commercial utilization «... if the body materials of the patient are of extraordinary high value, because they may be of a particularly rare type.» (19) This might make it necessary to consider claims for damages or even compensation for personal suffering. The amounts payable would be low, because they would be set according to the level of effort compensation which is paid for the collection of body materials.

With regard to a participation in the gain from utilization of the sample we should state «that a marketable product is based mostly on the substantial contribution made by participating doctors and research institutes. Thus, the contribution by the materials' donor to the marketable product is usually quite low.» (20)

---

(18) SPRANGER (2005), p. 1085.
(19) TAUPITZ (1991), p. 201 (217).
(20) SPRANGER (2005), p. 1085.

2.9. – *Extent of the consent (generic or specific)*

Collection of body materials is done in such cases on the basis of a declaration of intent by the donor («informed consent»). The consent must be granted in written form and before the material collection. The donor's declaration of intent refers usually to the consent to have the collection as such done, i.e. the medical operation. Further, the consent includes the use of body materials within the scope of a certain research project, in part even a specific subject of the research. Additionally, the consent usually refers to the collection of certain person-related data.

In addition to the consent, a special contract dealing with the legal rights concerning the body materials is made with the patient in only few cases.

The consent to using body materials for research is usually given free of charge. Only in exceptional cases (for example in the case of blood donation – this being a special case) is a remuneration paid (21).

The available declarations of consent and the patient information coming with it show that the patient has the right as a rule to withdraw his consent at any time and without giving reasons.

Further the donor sometimes has the option to have his samples destroyed (22).

In other cases, the declaration of consent does not deal with this point except that the general withdrawal of consent is permitted. The question of transferral of ownership rights of body materials or further use of already collected body materials after withdrawal of consent – even in the case that the destruction of the samples is not requested – is not even mentioned.

2.10. – *Use of samples obtained for another purpose*

The samples and data collected in biobanks (as here defined) are only used for research purposes. There are two types of research

---

(21) Nevertheless, a blood donation is mainly considered to have the legal characteristics of a donation or gift.

(22) As expressly in the patient information and consent declaration for the competence network HIV/AIDS.

related to biobanks: Mostly, the research projects – conducted by the biobank itself or by the research institutions, which got samples and data from the biobank – are focused to different diseases; in some cases the biobank conducts or supports population orientated investigations.

On completion of the prevailing research study, for which the samples and data were provided by the biobank, the data are in general to be deleted by the researcher or the remaining samples are to be destroyed, i.e. they are not to be used for further purposes.

2.11. – *Specifically issues related with local communities*

In Germany there are no specific issues related with local communities.

2.12. – *Maintenance: security standards, storage lengths*

Normally, the samples and data are conserved forever. They are stored – in accord with the given «informed consent» – not only for a single research project, but for further research projects of the same or similar kind. In some cases biobanks obtain even blank consents, which concede to them far-reaching uses of the samples and data.

The duration of the storage of the samples for therapy purposes as well as for research purposes is an issue which needs to be led out of the grey zone for the donors. There is e.g. in §12 par. 1 of the Hessian Hospital Law (HKG), which refers to §12 par. 4 Hessian Data Protection Law (HDSG), the requirement to inform the patient about the use of his data and his rights. This would include the duration of the storage as well. At present, however, in practice this is handled differently.

With regard to the use of the samples obtained and stored for therapy purposes in research projects the Hessian data protection registrar holds the opinion, that according to §12 par. 3 HKG and §33 par. 1 and 2 HDSG this applies only for actual research projects and that the transfer of samples for general research projects (biobanks) cannot be legitimized by it.

Regarding the use for general research projects a clear and definite legal basis needs to be established, which according the statement of the National Ethics Committee concerning the establishment and maintenance of biobanks in March 2004 (23), the propositions of the data protection registrars in 2001 and the catalogue of requirements from the data protection registrars in Hamburg and Hessen (24) in terms of data protection should include the following information:

– «the for the samples and data permanently accountable office,
– duration and method of the storage (pseudomized/anonymized),
– quantity of the stored data,
– circle of the persons and offices, which can achieve knowledge of the personal, pseudomized and or anonymized data/samples,
– possible occasions for re-identification of the donors by pseudomized storage,
– information of the voluntariness of the consent and that the persons concerned will experience no disadvantages from their rejection of the consent,
– information of the donor's right to revoke the consent in the future and require the delivery and the destruction of his sample,
– notice about possible information of the donor about research results.» (25)

It is emphasized that the informed consent on a form only refers to this information and needs to be stored apart from the databank, that a strict appropriation and adequate organizational-technical data protection measurements are required, which protect against unauthorized access from third-parties. The samples must be separated from the treatment data/samples and have to be securely pseudomized, and finally in the case of especially sensitive samples/data even a data fiduciary bound to observe confidentiality should be consulted (26).

In the case of sole research projects the information and consent of the test person has principally to be obtained. Explicit legal reg-

---

(23) NATIONALER ETHIKRAT (2004), p. 35.
(24) Comp. DER HESSISCHE DATENSCHUTZBEAUFTRAGTE (2001) Chiff. 27.14.
(25) DER HESSISCHE DATENSCHUTZBEAUFTRAGTE (2004), p. 87 f.
(26) DER HESSISCHE DATENSCHUTZBEAUFTRAGTE (2004), p. 88.

ulations concerning how long samples, obtained exclusively for research purposes, are permitted to be stored do not exist.

Basis for answering the question of the storage duration is the BDSG. The BDSG is valid for all private research projects as well as for projects of federal public offices.

In the case of tissue samples there are no personal data according §3 I BDSG. They are rather viewed as data carriers, from which genetic or other medical individualized findings (personal data) can be deduced.

Special data protection regulations for the storage or destruction of the tissue samples, obtained for research purposes, do not exist. The general data protection regulations are applied. According to §§20 II, 35 II BDSG data are to be deleted, if their storage is illegitimate (or became illegitimate) or their knowledge is no longer necessary for the data processing office for carrying out their tasks. The destruction of the tissue samples entails the deletion of the included personal data.

Also storage is illegitimate if the processing purpose has been accomplished; i.e. with research projects usually after their completion. According to §40 par.1 BDSG for research purposes obtained data are subject to a strict appropriation. Therefore it is not allowed to utilize these for any other than research purposes. As far as the informed consent of the test person, (§4 a BDSG) is restricted to an actual research project the data or samples have to be destroyed after the completion of the project.

If an informed consent is present not only for an actual research project but also for specific research questions by one office or several sufficient precisely defined offices, a longer or even «eternal» storage can be considered. In these cases the demands on the information of the test person and on the determination of the consent are very high. In the interest of the personal protection in such cases special safety measurements are also necessary, the more so as with such multifunctional data supplies the risk of abuse is increased.

2.13. – National and international transfer and circulation of samples

Purpose of a biobank is to provide samples and data for the research. Those usually take place exterior of the biobank. Therefore of particular importance are the so-called «Material Transfer Agreements» (MTA) between the biobank and the addressee of the samples and data. A MTA has to abide by the determinations which were arranged with the donor in the informed consent. Furthermore the biobank has to ensure that the transferred samples and data are only given to reputable researchers, who will abide by the stipulations of the MTAs (e.g. the solely use for research purposes the donor has agreed upon) and do not try to re-identify the donor. However, at present distinct legal terms of reference for the selection and control of the addressees and the formulation of MTAs do not exist. Also it is legally unclear what the transfer to third parties means concerning the property rights on the samples.

2.13.1. *Ownership rights of the donor transferred to third parties*

According to §903 BGB the owner of an object may do with it as he pleases, provided the law or rights of third parties are not infringed. Transferral of ownership according to §929 ff. BGB is one of the rights the owner has. Therefore, a biobank may on principle transfer ownership rights of a sample as per §903, 929 BGB (agreement and transferral) to a third party without problems, if the transferring biobank has the ownership rights of the sample (27).

It is controversial whether the transferral of ownership infringes upon the law or rights of third parties. With regard to samples, this may be possible since two peculiarities need to be observed. First, we need to note that together with the samples for the biobank usually person-related data are gathered. Often, the sample itself has a person's name or is related to a particular person. In addition, information was or is to be gathered from the sample. As mentioned before, data protection regulations, in particular the pertinent federal or state data protection regulation, must be observed as far as

---

(27) In this case, this would mean, deviating from the opinion presented here, that not only a usufruct takes place but that also a transferral of ownership has been agreed on.

they apply. The data protection regulations are laws which may be infringed in the sense of §903 BGB.

Further, we must note that the Federal Civil Court and the leading opinion assume that the object ownership of separated body materials is superimposed or covered by the general personality rights of the donor and the more so the more conclusions one may draw as to the person of the donor (28).

In recent literature, this general personality right is defined in more detail as being a right to bio-ethic or bio-material self-determination, as compared with the right to a self-image or the right to informal self definition (29).

In which manner one describes it in more detail, the general personality right of the donor on principle is a law of a third party to be infringed. Since the general personality right as such may not be waived, one may not assume that consent is a complete waiver.

In this context, the question arises whether in a transferral of ownership one needs to distinguish between entirely anonymous, only factual anonymous, pseudo-anonymous samples or those where the person-related information may not be reduced.

2.13.2. *Transferral of utilization rights*

In light of the opinion represented here to the fact that no transferral of ownership takes place, the question arises whether the biobank is permitted to transfer the right of utilization to third parties. If we assume usufruct, we find first of all that as per §1059 S. 1 BGB usufruct as such may not be transferred. According to §1059 S. 2 BGB, the practical application of usufruct may be left to a third party.

The bio materials bank may transfer the utilization rights to a third party (other biobanks for example), provided and only as far as it has the utilization rights itself and has the permission to transfer such rights to third parties. The permission for transferral of utilization rights may be given in the declaration of intent. For reasons of legal clearness, the phrasing should be included that the donor transfers to the biobank all known utilization rights. It is rec-

---

(28) LIPPERT (2001), p. 407.
(29) Comp. HALÀSZ (2004), p. 82 ff.; LIPPERT (2001), p. 408.

ommended to include a very detailed listing of all commercial and non-commercial types of use.

Conclusion: Anonymized samples may be transferred to third parties at any time, provided the donor has not explicitly forbidden it or provided the donor has not expressly been given the right to request return or destruction of the sample at any time.

2.13.3. *International transfer*

Some German biobanks transfer samples and data abroad. Because the biobank is often partner of an international scientific network or cooperate with international corporations. Recently, special rules for making «material transfer agreements» (MTA) across the borderlines don't exist.

2.14. – *Property rights*

A central aspect in the discussion on an international level is the rights of ownership and personality right with regard to the collected samples.

2.14.1. *Who is the owner of a sample collected in a biobank?*

As per §903 BGB (German Civil Code), the owner has all rights of use which are legally permitted, unless a law or rights of third parties are infringed (30). An infringement of the owner's rights may come under penal law or create the basis for a civil code liability for damages. Therefore, it is of the utmost importance for the individual doctor, researcher or operator of a biobank what his rights are regarding a sample.

The leading opinion has it without question that the body of a living person considered as res extra commercium as well as his organs and the firmly attached body parts or aids (heart pace maker, tooth gold filling) are not considered things in the meaning of the law. Therefore, there is no ownership here (31). A person nev-

---

(30) With regard to the relevancy of this limitation of owner rights in view of human biomaterial there will be more in the following.

(31) SPRANGER (2005), p. 1085 (1084); HALÀSZ (2004), p. 13 f. (with an overview over several theories); PALANDT and HEINRICHTS (2005), §90 BGB RdNr 3; TAUPITZ (1991), p. 1089.

ertheless has an «ownership-like right for decision» as a result from his general personality rights (32).

In Germany, samples are things or objects as defined by §90 BGB, because they are body materials separated for good without the intention to be reunited with the human body.

The question arises how ownership may be argued considering the ruling law about separated body materials. Court rulings and the leading opinion in Germany assume that the object characteristics of body materials are defined after separation from a body analogue to §953 BGB in favour of the person from whose body the separated materials came, and that includes ownership (33).

Ownership and personality rights have the same function to protect absolute rights from infringement by third parties. This results in the authority as per §953 BGB to grant the former *carrier* of separated body parts the same rights as to the owner of an object from which parts are separated. The legal relationship of a person with his body is a much more intensive one than the right to power over an object by its owner. However, if the ruling regarding separated object parts is such that they are part of the ownership of the object owner, then this must certainly also apply for separated body parts. Therefore, personality rights are reduced to ownership rights (34).

The human body as such and thereby also all of its parts and components have already undergone an ownership-like classification. The general personality right of the donor/patient continues to stay with the separated body part. Therefore, the donor/patient continues to be the owner of the separated body materials for the time being (35). There is no automatic transferral of ownership for the collected sample to a third party (36).

Ownership of collected body materials (samples), therefore, moves automatically to the person from whom the body materials have been taken.

---

(32) HALÀSZ (2004), p. 40.
(33) BGH/NJW 1994, 128 (127); VON FREIER (2005), p. 322 (321); FREUND and WEISS (2004), p. 346; LIPPERT (2004), p. 158; TAUPITZ (1991), p. 208; SCHÜNEMANN (1985), p. 86 ff.
(34) BGH/NJW 1994, 128 (127) VON FREIER (2005), p. 322 (321); HALÀSZ (2004) p. 20 ff.
(35) FREUND/WEISS (2004), p. 316; BREYER (2004), p. 661 (660); LIPPERT (2001), p. 407.
(36) LIPPERT (2002), p. 408 (406).

2.14.2. *Ownership of biomaterials in a biobank*

After it has been determined that the ownership of the collected body materials for the time being resides with the person from whom the materials were taken, the question now arises whether this legal situation also applies to body materials which are stored in a biobank or whether and how the ownership of these body materials is transferred to a third party.

The question is whether there is consent about the transferral of ownership. Precondition for this is consent between donor/patient and the biobank or a relevant third party (for example a doctor) which states that the ownership of the sample is to be transferred (37). Precondition for the consent are two concurring declarations of intention (offer and acceptance) each of which becomes valid upon receipt of the declaration by the recipient.

Provided an express offer of ownership transferral was received by the donor/patient, it is no problem to assume a transferral of ownership. Precondition for this is, though, that the donor/patient expressly declares that he offers the collecting party to transfer ownership of the body materials taken from him and that the collecting party in fact accepts this offer.

Such an expressed agreement about ownership transferral usually does not exist. Usually, only the agreement about having samples collected and about having procedures executed with it (diagnosis, research, etc.) is available. The agreement as such, however, is no declaration of intent (38). The mere agreement of the donor/patient as to the collection of body materials is per se no agreement about the transferral of ownership (39).

There may be the option of a conclusive or silent declaration of intent, in particular by means of conclusive actions (40).

2.14.3. *Ownership transferral*

Once the treatment is finished, the bio material which is left over remains with the doctor or the hospital where it was collected. An express agreement according to which ownership of the body mate-

---

(37) HALÀSZ (2004), p. 60.
(38) BGHZ 24, 33; LIPPERT (2001), p. 408 (406).
(39) LIPPERT (2001), p. 407 (406) sees herein no consent to do research.
(40) PALANDT and BASSENGE (2005), §929 BGB, RdNr. 2.

rials is to be transferred to the doctor/clinic is not available. Such cases do not constitute a conclusive agreement to ownership transferral.

The leading opinion (41) – which in particular also includes the German National Ethic Council - assumes rather that the patient waives his ownership rights by leaving behind his body materials without comment. Thus, we assume a case of dereliction (disclaimer/waiver of ownership). The clinic or the doctor should then be able to take up ownership for the body materials which is then without owner. This opinion has met with firm opposition in recent publications (42). According to this opinion, the intent is the source of the idea. This more recent opinion should be followed for these reasons :

a) *Priority for obligation of storage*

If a patient does not demand his body materials back on his own accord, the doctor must examine after the end of the treatment and, thus, the contract for treatment whether storing the body materials is obligatory. The reasoning as to storage is founded partially on a direct and partially on an analogue application of §10 MBO-Ä (43). In accordance with this section, the doctor is obligated to store examination results and documentation of treatments. However, the collected body materials are neither examination results nor part of the treatment documentation but are examination objects. Therefore, the obligation for storage of body materials is considered a minor obligation of the contract for treatment with the doctor, and its duration lasts only as long as it is deemed medically necessary for the patient's healing process – for example with regard to follow-up examinations. Should it be in the interest of a successful treatment – albeit unknown to the patient – to continue to store the body materials, there must not be the assumption that the patient would waive his ownership rights of the collected body materials.

---

(41) Comp. NATIONALEN ETHIKRATES (2004); SPRANGER (2005), p. 1085 (1084).
(42) VON FREIER (2005), p. 326 (321); FREUND and WEISS (2004), p. 316 (315); LIPPERT (2001), p. 407 (406), in conclusion probably also BREYER (2004), p. 660 f., since he considers even a longer storage period to be unlawful.
(43) BREYER (2004), p. 662 (660).

b) *Lack of intent to waive ownership rights*

Only if storing the body materials is not or not any longer considered necessary from a medical point of view, the question arises again whether the patient waived his ownership rights, thus enabling the doctor to gain ownership of the body materials. But even then we do not arrive at a different result.

As already explained, ownership waiver or disclaimer is a one-sided disposition. It comprises, according to the leading opinion, a declaration of intent not requiring a recipient and an action, the waiver of proprietorship. The declaration of intent must be concerned directly with the waiver/transferral of ownership. Further, the intention to waive rights must be recognizable.

This intention to waive rights is supposed to have been expressed in that the patient leaves his body materials behind without comment. This is supposed to constitute a waiver of ownership rights. The underlying assumption for this is that the superfluous and not needed body materials are considered to be waste by the patient and, therefore, he waives his ownership rights in order not to have to deal with the disposal.

This reasoning shows a certain closeness to the so called «bulky trash cases». The ruling in such «bulky trash» cases assumes an ownership waiver by the person who puts out objects to be picked up as bulky trash. From this point of view, the reasoning can be followed at first. However, different from the bulky trash cases, the patient does not give his body materials to the doctor/clinic right away with the intention or wish for disposal thereof, but for the purpose of diagnosis and treatment.

Further, even the Federal Civil Court (BGH – Bundesgerichtshof) in the bulky trash cases has indeed not always assumed a waiver to ownership rights which corresponds to the right of taking possession by some third party.

If an artist puts out paintings made by himself, this is not considered a waiver of ownership, but a declaration of intent toward the carrier of the trash removal to have the paintings destroyed (44). In the case of forgotten objects there is no waiver to ownership rights due to the lack of intent to waive (45).

However, a formal declaration is not always necessary. Alone from a waiver of proprietorship one may conclude a waiver of ownership. In the rulings so far this is assumed only in the case of objects which are not discernibly personal (diaries, personal notes, self-made paintings).

Since the rulings assume for separated body materials which cannot be reattached to be property which is covered to a large extent by the general personality rights of the person from whose body the body materials come (46), one may assume that the property right of body materials is assumed to be purely personal. Thus, a dereliction may be considered only if an express declaration of the donor/patient was given (47).

This presupposes, however, that the patient is aware of left-over body materials. Usually, this will not be the case since he has no idea of how the body materials are processed within the scope of diagnostic measures nor that body materials are in fact left over. Without this awareness one may not assume, with a view on the mentioned ruling of the BGH, that the patient waives his ownership rights of his remaining body materials.

c) *Conclusion*

If the collection of body materials is done on the basis of a contract for treatment, the doctor is obligated to destroy the body materials or hand them out to the patient once the necessity for storing body materials has ceased to exist. A silent agreement about ownership transferral may not be considered (48). Only if the patient declared expressly – prior or after the treatment – that the ownership of his body materials is to transfer to the doctor in charge or the clinic, only then a transferral of ownership rights has been effected.

---

(44) LG RAVENSBURG (1987), p. 3142.
(45) HEFERMEHL, Rdnr. 2.
(46) BGH NJW 1994, p.128 f.
(47) It needs to be pointed out that this opinion is contrast to the above-mentioned ruling opinion. However, it seems to be more consequent.
(48) VON FREIER (2005), p. 322 (321); FREUND and WEISS (2004), p. 316 (315); LIPPERT (2001), p. 407 (406).

2.15. – *Other issues*

Of the numerous further questions, which arise in the context of biobanks, at least two shall be discussed briefly:

2.15.1. *Who is the owner of a biobank?*

Considered owner is the natural or legal person who has the ownership rights of a biobank. This person is the operator of a biobank.

We need to note the following particularity with biobanks: «Biobanks are collections of samples of human body materials... which are or may be linked to person-related data and information about the donors» (49). This makes a biobank a connection for several independent objects which, therefore, are to be seen as a class or entirety in itself on the one hand, and which need to be considered a systematic collection of data which may qualify as a databank in the sense of copyright law (UrhG).

Object classes are also legal objects. Although they are gathered under the same term in legal matters, they are not objects capable of doing business. Their value and their functionality are determined by their completeness and functional connection. Objects of disposals may only be individual objects.

If we assume – as before – that the ownership of body materials does not usually transfer to the collecting institute, then this means that the carrier of the biobank, i.e. the doctor, the clinic or a research institute, is the owner of the necessary operating means for the biobank (storage means, examination means etc.), however, he is not the owner of the body materials. With regard to these, he only has the right to utilization.

Person related data only have a function of classification. Data are no objects and, thus, cannot be owned. Only if the data of a biobank achieve the quality of databank, there may be an exclusive right to utilization in favour of the biobank as per §87 UrhG (copyright law).

---

(49) Term definition of the NATIONAL ETHICS COUNCIL (NATIONALER ETHIKRAT) in its statement *Biobanken für die Forschung*, 17.03.2004, p. 11.

2.15.2. Claims to patent rights

One might consider the case of a missing consent prior to the collection of the sample. In such a case, no patent rights may be granted as per §2 Nr. 1 Patent Law (PatG) if the publication or utilization of the invention would offend public order or is against good manners. In literature, we find this opinion also to apply to achieving the invention in the first place, thus considering the manner of collecting the sample as a severe breach of law (50).

However, if the donor has given his consent to collecting and processing the sample, he may make any further claims.

2.16. – Final comments, conclusions, other reflections, etc.

To summarize the current situation of German biobanks in a legal perspective six points should be emphasized:

1. Body materials taken from a living person remain usually the property of that person according to this opinion. Only if a clear, preferably written declaration of the donor/patient is available showing that he transfers the ownership of the materials to the collecting party (doctor, clinic, biobank etc.), a lawful transferral of ownership has in fact taken place.

Even though literature shows a strong opinion that the ownership of the materials transfers on the basis of a conclusive declaration of intent, one may not exclude the possibility that a court of law will not follow this opinion. In order to exclude the risk of punishability or of code of law claims for damages, it is recommendable to include a passage both in the patient information as well as the declarations of intent to the effect that the ownership of the body materials transfers to the collecting party. As an alternative, the explicit – though limited – usufruct of the body materials may be agreed upon. This may actually be preferable under certain circumstances. This could be the case particularly if the donor/patient is to be granted the right to request the return or destruction of the body materials at any time. – In case of an old sample which was collected during a contract for treatment for the purpose of making a diagnosis or was collected as a «by- or waste product» during

---

(50) KREFFT (2003), p. 106; OHLY (2003), p. 417 (421).

treatment, the obligation for the disposal of the body materials is given unless as an exception it is necessary to store the sample for medical-therapeutic reasons. Doing research with these body materials is usually not permitted without prior consent of the donor. Therefore, old samples should not be used for research purposes. One aspect has not been cleared to satisfaction whether a complete anonymization is to be set equal to destruction, thus allowing research thereafter.

2. Even after the ownership of the body materials has been transferred to the biobank, the personality rights of the donor/patient superimpose the ownership rights. Therefore, the biobank may not do at lib with the body materials in an unlimited manner. In particular, the general personality rights and the data protections law limit the rights derived from the ownership of the body materials. A mostly free disposal of the body materials is usually only possible if the sample has been absolutely or at least factually anonymized.

3. Provided the biobank is the owner of the body materials, it may pass it on to third parties under observation of the rights of the donor and of the data protection stipulations. Therefore, an unlimited passing on to third parties is only possible, if the body materials do not show any further person relationship, i.e. have been anonymized. In this case, a protective conveyance is possible. Passing on pseudomized or body material not at all reduced in it person-relationship is permissible only with the consent of the patient/donor. If the donor objected to the passing on of his body materials, even an anonymized transferral may be prohibited. It is certainly recommendable to include a regulation in the declaration of intent allowing the BB to pass on body materials – at least once it is anonymized.

4. As a precaution, the declaration of intent should include a passage allowing the biobank to anonymize body materials at any time. At the same time, the patient information must note that if that were the case, the patient/donor may not make a claim for return or destruction of the materials since identification would be impossible after anonymization.

5. The donor/patient, on principle, may not waive his general personality rights. At best, he may consent to interventions in his general personality rights after having been completely and fully

informed. Therefore, the information and declaration of consent of the patient play a central role.

6. The donor usually does not have the right to make claims of any kind as to research results, if he has transferred the ownership of his body materials to the biobank and has consented properly to research being done thereon. This applies particularly for commercial utilizations. The patient must be informed in this respect by means of the patient information brochure. The declaration of intent should include correspondingly a passage to the effect that the donor agrees to the biobank using the research results commercially at their own risk and for their own benefit.

LEGAL AND SOCIAL IMPLICATIONS OF CREATING BANKS OF BIOLOGICAL MATERIAL IN MEXICO (1)

BY

INGRID BRENA SESMA

SUMMARY : 1. Situation of the scientific research with biological human samples and biobanks. 2. Legal framework. 2.1. General legislation. 2.1.1. Personal data protection. a) Political Constitution of the United Mexican States. b) Federal Law of Transparency and Access to Government Public Information. c) Guidelines for the Protection of Personal Data. d) Protection of Personal Data Law for the Federal District. e) Penal Code for the Federal District. 2.1.2. Monitoring and control of biobanks. a) General Law on Health. b) Oficial Regulation. 2.1.3. Applicable Regulations on human samples. a) General Law on Health. b) Regulation of the General Law on Health in the matter of sanitary control of the availability of human organs, tissues and corpes. 2.1.4. Research with human samples. a) Title Fifth of the General law on Health. b) General Health Rules on matters of Health Research. 2.1.5. Informed consent. a) General law on Health. b) The General Health Rules on matters of Health Research establish the way in which the informed consent must be obtained. 2.2. Specific legislation. 2.3. Reports and options from various institutions and other organizations. 2.4. Institutions and professionals : quality standards and accreditation requirements. 2.4.1. Institutions and professionals. 2.4.2. Accreditation requirements. 2.5. Research Ethics Committees. 2.6. Samples. 2.6.1. Different types of sam-

---

(1) First, I would like to thank Dr. Jürgen Simon and Dr. Carlos Romeo Casabona, for inviting me to participate in this important project whose objective is to uncover the situation of biobanks that work in human samples for research in Latin American and European countries. This project is not merely a descriptive one, but it also intends to formulate recommendations that allow different States to know about the existence of international instruments that, although not binding, can be considered as sources of Law and may also serve as a source of inspiration for legislation on biobanks in the near future.

I would also like to thank the Legal Research Institute of the National Autonomous University for its logistic support that enabled me to fulfill this investigation and be the hostess of the Latinbank meeting in Mexico City.

I very specially thank my assistant Karla Lefranc for her unconditional devotion to the project. Her findings, investigations and logistic support allowed me to lead the ship to safe port and to prove Mexican hospitality once more.

I also thank the Spanish group, Pilar Nicolás Jiménez, Iñigo de Miguel Beriain and Emilio José Armaza Armaza, who always paid attention to my questions quickly and efficiently, and who organized the logistics of the whole project.

Finally, I also thank all the researchers in charge of biobanks for devoting their time into giving the information necessary for this research. Their information made this report possible.

ples. 2.6.2. Donors. 2.6.3. Sample Collection. 2.7. Sample Property. 2.8. Subject privacy protection. 2.9. Informed consent. 2.10. Use of samples collected for different purposes. 2.11. Specific issues concerning local communities. 2.12. Mantainance. 2.12.1. Security standards. 2.12.2. The storage period of the samples varies according to the different biobanks surveyed. 2.13. National and international circulation and sample ceding. 2.13.1. Transference of the sample to other researchers or institutions. 2.13.2. National and international circulation of samples. 2.14. Property rights on investigation results. 2.15. Other issues. 2.16. Final comments, conclusions, other reflections, etc. 2.16.1. Biobanks situation. 2.16.2. Legislation.

INTRODUCTION

This research encompasses the results from several investigations. First, we verified the existence of *in vitro* human sample biobanks for research in Mexico with the intention of determining the form they operate and detecting the main problems they face with the intention of optimizing their operation. Secondly, we went on to study and analyze the sanitary legislation to detect the existence of a specific norm, or at least a general one, that could be applied to the installation and operation of biobanks. Finally we examined the possible existence of any specific bibliography on this subject in the country.

1. – SITUATION OF THE SCIENTIFIC RESEARCH WITH BIOLOGICAL HUMAN SAMPLES AND BIOBANKS

The Law of Science and Technology (2) established CONACYT (its Spanish acronym) (3), the National Council for Science and Technology, as the entity in charge of organizing and promoting Mexico's science network, integrated by different groups and research institutes. This science network has certain responsibilities related to human samples and biobanks, among these tasks, it has to define strategies, joint programs and articulate actions that allow the efficient use of human and financial resources to create the necessary infrastructure for national development in this area. It also

---

(2) Published on the *Mexican Federal Official Journal* on June, 5, 2002.
(3) Throughout the article we'll keep the Spanish acronyms.

has to design study programs that focus on research, and by doing so increase the number of scientists and research institutions, which in turn will promote networking in this strategic scientific area. Private, public, independent or ascribed to other education institutions can become part of this network.

As such, CONACYT was used as a primary source of information to contact researchers and institutions working on human samples and biobanks. Several questionnaires were sent to CONACYT but we received no answer.

A second source of information was used given the lack of any biobank, biorepository or sample collection registry. By means of personal contacts we identified several biobanks in the National Health Institutes, the Social Security Institution, Universities and Technological Institutions. Researchers working in these institutions informed the existence of other biobanks, although this information turn out to be insufficient.

In order to make quick progress, we sent a first questionnaire to the Federal Institute of Access to Information (IFAI) to detect which public institutions had biobanks and what were their objectives. Through this information we contacted fifty one institutions or official organizations which apparently had biobanks of human samples for research, among them were national health institutes, universities, research centers and hospitals. As a first result, we discovered the existence of thirty eight biobanks. Consequently a second survey was sent to the institutions that had a biobank to obtain specific information for our project.

Furthermore, given that the IFAI can only provide information from public institutions, we also sent the survey to twelve private hospitals, forty eight pharmaceutical laboratories and five clinical laboratories we believed could have biobanks. As a result of this survey, we found out that clinical labs do not have *in vivo* human samples as they dispose all biological material once it has been processed. Only twelve pharmaceutical labs answered the survey, giving a negative answer to the question of having biobanks and none of the private hospitals replied to the survey. The following report summarizes the information obtained by the survey and also includes a brief review of Mexican legislation regarding human samples for *in vitro* research biobanks.

In order to comply with the Latinbank project we sent over fifty questionnaires to public and private institutions to try identify which institutions had biobanks (4). Unfortunately, we only obtained sixteen answers. However, once we detected the biobanks we sent a second questionnaire which was fully responded most of the time. It's very important to point out that some biobanks perform only one research while others carry out several investigations and as a result they use several samples. This is the reason why throughout the report not all the answers match with the number of biobanks surveyed.

2. – Legal framework

2.1. – *General Legislation*

There is no specific legislation in Mexico concerning biobanks of human samples for *in vitro* research, so we're presenting a summary of a general norm related to personal data protection, classification, specification and handling of hazardous residues as well as bio infectious residues. Furthermore, there is no legislation concerning organ, tissue and human cells used in research nor donation that applies to biobanking or about informed consent.

2.1.1. *Personal data protection*

a) *Political Constitution of the United Mexican States*

The Political Constitution of the United Mexican States in its sixth article sets the framework for the protection of personal information stating that «The information concerning the private life and personal data shall be protected in the terms and with the exceptions provided by the law. Every person, without the need to demonstrate a given interest or justify a certain use, shall have free access to public information, his personal data or their rectification».

---

(4) It's important to clarify that all the institutions consulted aren't strictly biobanks but rather simple reservoirs due to the fact that they do not carry out all the activities that a biobank should perform.

b) *Federal Law of Transparency and Access to Government Public Information* (5)

The objective of this Law is «To guarantee the protection of personal data in possession of legally bound subjects (6)»; for the effects of this ordainment, personal data is defined as: «the information concerning an identified or identifiable individual, regarding ethnic or racial origin, or that referring to physical or emotional characteristics, physical or mental states of health, sexual preferences, or any others that affects his personal privacy». We consider that the information contained in the human samples falls under this description.

c) *Guidelines for the Protection of Personal Data* (7)

Based on the Federal Law of Transparency and Access to Government Public Information, the Federal Institute for Access to Public Information issued the «Guidelines for the Protection of Personal Data». The objective of these guidelines is to establish the general policies and procedures that the Federal Public Administration must observe to guarantee the right of each individual to take his or her own decisions regarding the use and destiny of personal data. These set of guidelines seek to guarantee the adequate usage to the dignity and rights of the affected individual and to prevent its illicit and harmful transmission. Nevertheless, given that this is federal regulation, the protection of personal data in the different states public institutions is beyond its scope. Personal data protection is only guaranteed if the state issues its own legislation in this subject matter, as is the case of the Federal District. Another important gap is the lack of protection for data collected and stored by the private sector, as there is no regulation applicable to that information either.

Among the relevant provisions in the IFAI Guidelines are the minimum conditions and requirements to be followed for the correct handling and safekeeping of data systems. They also give a set of principles to be considered in the protection of personal data, and

---

(5) Published on the *Mexican Federal Official Journal* on June, 11, 2002.
(6) Article 18 of the Law.
(7) *Mexican Federal Official Journal* on September, 30, 2005.

some of them are applicable to the data contained in samples and information stored in a biobank.

In the processing of personal data, the different branches and organizations of the Federal Administration must observe the principles of legal control, quality, access and correction, information, security, safekeeping and consent for its transmission; exact, suitable, pertinent and non-excessive processing.

The processing of personal data for statistical purposes must take place by means of the dissociation of the data. When third parties are hired to carry out the processing of personal data, the corresponding contract must stipulate the implementation of safety measures and safekeeping envisaged in the Guidelines, and in the applicable regulation of the contracting branches and organizations, as well as the imposition of conventional penalties that would be caused by its breach.

Personal data can only be transmitted when it is expressly foreseen by law and through the expressed consent of the rightful owners. In order to provide security to the personal data systems, the heads of government branches and organizations must adopt the pertinent measures listed in the Guidelines regarding personal data on paper, in the automated personal data systems or in networks.

The supervision of the protection of data is the responsibility of the Federal Institute for Access to Information and Protection of Personal Data. Therefore, the government branches and organizations must allow civil servants of the Institute, or third parties previously designated by it, the access to the places where the personal data systems are found and operated, as well as the technical and administrative documentation, in order to supervise the compliance with the Law, its Regulation and the Guidelines.

In case that the Institute determines that a civil servant may have borne responsibilities for the breach of the Guidelines, the corresponding internal control agency will be informed in order to determine the legal responsibility, based on the statute on responsibilities and penalties established in the Federal Law of Administrative Responsibilities of Civil Servants.

d) *Protection of Personal Data Law for the Federal District (8)*

Recently, on October 3, 2008, the Federal District issued a Law for the protection of personal data in possession of public entities of the Federal District. This law defines personal data as information concerning an identified or identifiable individual, and that regarding ethnic origin, physical characteristic, state of health, and DNA.

The mentioned ordainment establishes that personal data systems cannot have purposes contrary to the Law or to public morality, and in no case the data may be used for different or incompatible purposes with which motivated their procurement. The subsequent process of such data for historical, statistical or scientific aims is not considered incompatible (9).

Personal data is non- aivable, non-transferable and cannot be distributed, such that they cannot be transmitted except by legal order or by the consent of the rightful owner and this duty will remain even after the relationship between the public entity and the rightful owner of the personal data comes to an end (10).

The person in charge of the personal data system or the users may be released from their confidentiality agreement by judicial resolution and by grounds regarding public security, national security or public health. The data must be stored in a manner suitable for the exercise of rights to access, rectification, cancellation and opposition by the interested party (11).

Personal data must be destroyed when no longer necessary or pertinent to the aims for which it had been collected. An exception to this rule has been established for subsequent processing of the data for statistical or scientific objectives and the dissociation procedure has been carried out previously. Personal data can only be kept in a complete and permanent manner and subject to processing for historical purposes (12).

Each public entity must publish the creation, modification or withdrawal of its personal data system in the Official Journal of the

---

(8) Official Gazette of the Federal District, October 3, 2008.
(9) Article 5 of the Law.
(10) *Idem.*
(11) *Idem.*
(12) *Idem.*

Federal District and these systems must be listed in the registry authorized by the Institute for Access to Public Information of the Federal District (13).

It stands out that the last part of article 10 very textually expresses: «The dissociation procedure will not be necessary with regards to scientific studies or public health.» Whereas article 9 of the International Declaration on Human Genetic Data recommends «When human genetic data are collected for medical and other scientific research purposes, the data must not be associated with an identifiable person, that is to say, they must be irreversibly dissociated».

The processing of personal data will require the unequivocal and expressed consent in writing by the interested party except when the transmission takes place between governmental entities and for the subsequent processing of the data for historical, statistical or scientific purposes, or when regarding personal data relative to health that are necessary for reasons of public health, emergency, or for carrying out epidemiological studies.

Consent may be revoked when just cause exists and retroactive effects are not attributed to it. The processes of personal data systems regarding health, is governed by that stipulated in the General Law on Health, the Federal District Law on Health and other regulations derived from them. The process and cession of this information obliges the preservation of the personal identity data of the patient, apart from those of a clinical character for medical attention, in such a way that the confidentiality is maintained, unless the individual patient has given consent to the contrary. The exception to this rule is for cases of scientific research, public health or judicial aims, where the unification of the identifying data with the clinical information is considered essential. Access to the data and documents related to the health of individuals is strictly limited the specific purposes of each case (14).

The processed personal databases that have been processed must be withdrawn once the period for conservation established by the applicable laws has expired, or when they are no longer necessary for the intended purposes.

---

(13) Article 7 of the Law.
(14) Article 18.

In case that the processing of the systems has been carried out by a person not from within the public entity, the corresponding legal document must establish the term of conservation by the user up to the date when the data must be returned in their totality to the public entity, and who must guarantee their trusteeship or proceed, in such case, with their withdrawal (15).

In the case that consignees of the data are institutions belonging to other federal entities, they must be able to guarantee a level of protection, equivalent or superior, to that established in this Law and in regulations of the public entity in question.

In order to guarantee that the security and protection levels envisaged in the present Law are observed in foreign countries, the consignees of the data are responsible for carrying the cession of information according to what is established in the applicable federal legislation (16).

The head of the public entity will designate the person responsible for the proper use of personal data systems. This person is entitled to use the data only when it bears a relation to the purpose for which they had been obtained (17).

The Institute for Access to Public Information of the Federal District is the agency in charge of directing and monitoring the compliance of this Law, as well as of the regulations derived from it; this agency will be the authority in charge of guaranteeing the protection and the correct processing of personal data.

e) *Penal Code for the Federal District (18)*

This Code establishes a penalty of prison (ranging from six months to two years) and a monetary fine (ranging from twenty five to one hundred minimum daily salaries) to be imposed «to whom that without consent by the holder of rights to grant them, reveals a secret or reserved communication, that has been trusted or become known by any means, or uses this information to obtain direct or indirect benefits».

---

(15) Article 19.
(16) Article 20.
(17) Article 21 fraction VI.
(18) Article 23.

If the agent knew or received the secret or reserved communication for the motive of employment, position, profession, art or office, or if the secret is of scientific or technological character, the prison term will be increased by half and the exercise of the agents profession, art or office shall be suspended for six months to three years. When the agent is a civil servant, destitution and disqualification of six months to three years shall be additionally imposed» (19).

These sentences would be applied to those who handle data contained in the human samples destined for research and do not respect the privacy of the subjects involved.

2.1.2. *Monitoring and control of biobanks*

In order to exercise the monitoring and the control of the biobanks, the general character of regulations on monitoring and control must be applied to facilities that handle blood, tissues and cells.

a) *General Law on Health*

The Health Agency, through a decentralized agency denominated the Federal Commission for Protection against Sanitary Risks, COFEPRIS for its Spanish acronym, exercises the authority of sanitary regulation, control and promotion of the facilities and procedures referred to in the General Law on Health. This Commission is responsible, among others activities, for preparing and issuing the official Mexican regulations regarding products, activities, services and establishments under its authority. The biorepositories handle human samples for research and, as such, fall under the supervision of COFEPRIS:

It is the responsibility of this agency to prepare and issue the official Mexican regulations regarding products, activities, services and establishments, under its authority, to issue official certificates on sanitary conditions of processes, products, methods, facilities, services or activities related to the matters under its authority; to exercise sanitary control and monitoring the regulations of human organs, tissues and cells and their components, their import and

---

(19) Article 213.

export, the establishments assigned to the process of these products and the health institutions. It is also the agency's responsibility to exercise the sanitary control and the monitoring of the donation and transplanting of human organs, tissues and cells, to exercise the authority that the Law and its regulations confer upon the Health Agency in the matter of international health, and to impose penalties and apply safety measures within the scope of its authority (20);

b) *Oficial Regulation*

The Mexican Official Regulation of biological infectious dangerous residues prepared by COFEPRIS defines a biological sample as: «An anatomical part or fraction of organs or tissue, excretions or gathered secretions of a human being or animal, alive or dead, for their analysis» and dangerous residues as «Materials generated during medical attention services of which contain biological-infectious agents according to that defined by the Regulation and that can cause injurious effects on health and the atmosphere.

For effects of the Regulation, biological infectious dangerous residues are considered to be: the blood, tissues, organs and parts that are extirpated or removed during post-mortem examinations, surgical interventions or any other type of operation, and biological samples for analysis.

This Regulation classifies the establishments that generate biological infectious dangerous residues, but in its classification it does not include the biobanks. Nevertheless, we must assume that when these establishments handle samples that could be considered as biological infectious dangerous residues they must comply with the Official Regulation.

2.1.3. *Applicable Regulations on human samples*

Within the sanitary legislation there are regulations regarding the donation of human organs, tissues and cells for research; these organ or tissue samples, therefore, fall under that regulation.

---

(20) Article 17*bis* of the same law.

a) *General Law on Health*

Under the title regarding the transplant of organs and tissues defines the donor as a person that, according to the terms of the corresponding law, decides about their body or any of its components while still alive and after its death (21).

In view of one who donates a sample, a part of the body, so that it may be used in research, falls within the definition of donor. The places where the sample is obtained as well as the procedures to be carried out are analyzed.

Sanitary authorization is required by the health institutions dedicated to the extraction, analysis, conservation, preparation and provision of organs, tissues and cells (22) and the organ, tissue and cell banks. Therefore, it is our opinion that biobanks require sanitary authorization.

The expressed donation shall be made in writing and is to be expanded upon when it refers to the entire body or limited when granting certain components only. It shall be possible for the donor to indicate certain people or institutions as benefactors. Also the donor shall be able to express the circumstances of manner, place and time and anything else that conditions the donation, and shall be able to revoke his consent at any time, without responsibility on his or her part (23). The informed consent for the donation of samples for research must cover these requirements.

The commerce of organs, tissues and cells is prohibited (24) and for the use of corpses, whole or in part of known persons, for research purposes, the consent of the donor is required (25).

For the transfer of organs, tissues and cells from one country to another, the Title of the General Law on Health dedicated to International Health is applied, but the transfer of human tissues outside national territory, including blood and its components and progenitor, hematopoietic and hemo-derived cells that can be the source of genetic matter (desoxyribonucleic acid) with the intention

---

(21) Article 314.
(22) Article 315.
(23) Article 322.
(24) Article 327.
(25) Article 350*bis* 3.

to carry out studies of genomic population, will be subject to the following requirements:

I. – To comprise part of a research project approved by a Mexican institute of scientific research and meeting the regulations for research on humans and other applicable regulation.

II. – To obtain a permit sent by the Health Agency, in coordination with the National Institute of Genomic Medicine which, in its nature of advisory body of the Federal Government and national center of reference in the matter, will register the permits

III. – For effects of this Law, the study of genomic population is understood by one which has the purpose of the analysis of one or more genetic markers in unrelated individuals that describe the genomic structure of a determined population, identify an ethnic group or identify genes associated to a characteristic, a disease or the response to pharmaceuticals.

b) *Regulation of the General Law on Health in the matter of sanitary control of the availability of human organs, tissues and corpses*

It is the responsibility of the Health Agency to issue the technical standards to which, throughout the national territory, the availability of human organs, tissues and their derivatives, products and corpses shall be subject (26).

This Regulation emphasizes the will of the donor, so in no case organs, tissues and their derivatives, products and corpses, shall be available against the will of the original donor (27).

If the human samples assigned for research are obtained from corpses, the special regulation which envisages corpse availability is applied for the effects of research or teaching. This may only be done after death certification and the availability of unidentified corpses, and shall be subject to the opinion of the district attorney's office. This office shall take into account the same Regulation and the technical standards that the Health Minister issues to that effect (28).

The expression of will by the original donor must include the subjects general information and in the case that the subject is

---

(26) Article 4th.
(27) Article 9th.
(28) Article 60.

deceased, the mention of this fact, the name of the educational institution that is the beneficiary of the corpse, the date of reception of satisfactory information on the use of the corpse and, where appropriate, its final destiny (29).

Secondary donors shall be able to permit a corpse to be assigned to research even if the original donor would not have done so while still alive if contrary testamentary disposition (30) does not exist. In case of unidentified corpses provided to educational institutions by the district attorney's office, the special requirements established in the law shall be observed.

Educational institutions that possess corpses for the purpose of research or teaching and the vehicles that are used for the transfer of the corpses or their parts shall require a sanitary license (31). The Health Minister shall be able to demand a sanitary control card from the people who carry out or who take part in some of the acts of disposition of organs, tissues and their derivatives, products and corpses, when there is risk of disease propagation (32).

The Health Agency will dictate diverse safety measures such as the suspension of work, the securing and destruction of objects, products or substances a of sanitary nature that could cause to health risks or damages (33). Violations of the orders of the Regulation will be administratively sanctioned by the Health Minister without effect on the corresponding penalties when they constitute crimes (34).

2.1.4. *Research with human samples*

a) *Title Fifth of the General Law on Health*

In health institutions, under the responsibility of the directors or their respective heads in accordance with the applicable regulations, will be constituted: a research commission and an ethics commission in the case of investigation on human beings (35).

---

(29) Article 80.
(30) Article 81.
(31) Article 90.
(32) Article 116.
(33) Article 129.
(34) Article 130.
(35) Article 98.

Research on human beings shall adopt the scientific and ethic principles that justify medical research, especially when referred to the possible contribution to the solution of health problems and the development of new fields of health science (36). Whoever makes research for health that includes the use of human beings, as well as the use of disease borne microorganisms or biologic material that contain them, the construction and handling of recombinant nucleic acids, radioactive isotopes and the use of devices generating ionizing radiation, and the securing and destruction of objects, products or substances; electromagnetic, that go against legal regulations and the rulings of health research, will bear the sanctions established in the Law, and the penalties they may incur when considered crimes (37).

The General Law on Health on the subject of research on human beings was recently amended (38). The law states that this research may only be performed by health professionals in health institutions under surveillance of the proper health authorities. It also states that genomic studies on population should be part of a research project.

For the purposes of this law, a genomic study on population is the one whose purpose is to analyze one or more genetic markers in non related individuals that describe the genomic structure of a specific population, identify an ethnic group or identify genes associated to a characteristic, a disease or the response to medication.

b) *General Health Rules on matters of Health Research*

In any research where a human being is the subject of study, the criteria regarding respect towards his dignity and the protection of his rights and wellbeing shall prevail (39). In research with human beings, the privacy of the individual subject of research shall be protected. He would only be identified if the results require it and with the prior authorization of the individual (40).

This regulation provides that research with embryos, corpses, fetus, stillborn, fetal matter, cells, tissues and organs extracted

---

(36) Article 100 fraction I, General Law on Health.
(37) Article 130.
(38) Article 100, Published on the *Mexican Federal Official Journal* on July,14, 2008.
(39) Article 13 from the regulation.
(40) Article 16 from the regulation.

from them, shall be made in accordance with the General Law on Health (41).

2.1.5. *Informed consent*

a) *General Law on Health*

This law provides that research on human beings shall have the written consent of the subject of such investigation, or his legal representative if the subject is legally disabled, once the objectives of the research and the possible positive or negative consequences for his health have been fully explained (42).

b) *The General Health Rules on matters of Health Research establish the way in which the informed consent must be obtained*

By informed consent is understood the written agreement, in which the subject of research or, in a given case, his legal representative authorizes his participation on the research with full knowledge of the nature of the proceedings and the risks he will be submitted, through free choice and without coercion (43).

For the informed consent to exist, the subject of research or, in its case, his legal representative shall receive a clear and complete explanation, in a way he can understand, at least, the following aspects:

a) The causes and objectives of the research, the proceedings to be used and their purpose, including the identification of experimental proceedings.

b) The expected discomforts and risks; the benefits to be observed; the assurance of a response to any question and the explanation of any inquiry about the proceedings, risks, benefits and other matters related to the research; the liberty to withdraw its consent at any time and to stop his participation in the studies, without causing any damage to his care and treatment; the assurance that the subject will not be indentified and that the confidentiality of the information related to his privacy will be kept; the commitment to provide updated information obtained during the

---
(41) Article 55 from the regulation.
(42) Article 100 fraction IV, General Law on Health.
(43) Article 20 from the regulation.

research even though it could affect the will of the subject to continue participating; that if additional expenses should rise, these shall be paid from the research budget (44).

The informed consent shall be made in writing and shall meet the following requirements:

It shall be elaborated by the main investigator, indicating the information previously described, according to the technical regulation issued.

It shall be examined and, in its case, approved by the Ethics Commission of the health institution;

It shall indicate the names and addresses of two witnesses and their relationship with the subject of investigation. It shall be signed by both witnesses and the subject of investigation or its legal representative, if that is the case. If the subject of investigation cannot sign, he shall use his fingerprint, and a person he designates shall sign for him, this procedure will be made by duplicate, one of the originals shall be given to the subject of research or his legal representative (45).

In minimum risk researches, such as blood extraction by puncturing of a maximum volume of 450 ml and a maximum recurrence of twice a week, or by saliva, the Ethics Commission, by justified reasons, will be able to authorize that the informed consent be obtained without written paperwork, like in researches of no risk that do not require any deliberate intervention or modification of the physiologic, psychological and social variables of the individuals; in such cases, the researcher is exempted from obtaining the informed consent (46).

When the subject matters are students, laboratory and hospital employees, employees, members of the armed forces, prison inmates, and other special groups of the population for whom the informed consent may be influenced by some authority (47), the research shall be considered research with subordinate groups. Hospital patients should also be considered subordinate groups.

---

(44) Article 21 from the regulation.
(45) Article 22 from the regulation.
(46) Article 17 and 23 from the regulation.
(47) Article 57 from the regulation.

When research with subordinate groups is held, one or more members of the population subject of study, capable of representing the moral, cultural and social values of the group shall participate in the Ethics commission and monitor that the participation as well as the refusal to participate or the withdrawal of the consent during the study will not affect the work or military situation or the judiciary process they are following, and that the result of such research may not be used against the participants (48).

2.2. – Specific legislation

In Mexico there is no specific legislation that refers to biobanks.

2.3. – Reports and opinions from various national institutions and other organizations

The Bioethics National Commission, in charge of preparing the guidelines that the Research Ethics Committees must adopt, was consulted and informed us that guidelines for biobanks that use human samples *in vitro* for research had not been prepared. Consultations with several Ethics Committees were prepared but none of them has responded to date.

2.4. – Institutions and professionals : quality standards and accreditation requirements

2.4.1. Institutions and professionals

Ten of the sixteen biobanks surveyed carry out their activities in public hospitals or national health institutes, five of them carry out their activities in universities and one in a Public Research Center which is a company with state participation.

2.4.2. Accreditation requirements

Presently, Mexican regulation does not require accreditation for biobanks, and as such it is important to consider that the responses refer to the requirements that where met by some biobanks before

---

(48) Article 58 from the regulation.

initiating their operations, but not those imposed by national regulations.

Ten biobanks require a bioethics committee to approve their research protocols.

Three biobanks declared to have asked for direct authorization from the Health Agency.

Two biobanks met the requirements established in foreign guidelines, and other two followed the regulations established by the hospital or institute to which they are ascribed to. Only one biobank mentioned that it operates according to its own procedures manual, approved by its ethics committee. All of the surveyed biobanks claimed to observe the Official Norm on classification, specifications and handling of dangerous infectious biological residues.

2.5. – Research Ethics Committees

The Bioethics National Commission provided the list of research ethics committees registered to find out if they use some regulation to resolve the cases that appear before them, but even though we sent queries to the registered committees, none of them responded.

Only through the responses sent in by the biobanks, we could asses, that some of them require approval of their protocol and their informed consent documents on the part of the research ethics committees. Nevertheless, once the research is underway, the committees, in most cases, do not carry out any supervision of the biobank or the research.

2.6. – Samples

2.6.1. Different types of samples

The way to obtain the samples varies according to the type of investigation. Blood samples are the most common followed by tissue samples. Two biobanks use cerebral tissue, one uses heart tissue and two other biobanks use skin cells. Others use blood plasma, cerebrospinal fluid, DNA and RNA, immortal lymphocytes, cellular lines and bone marrow fluid.

2.6.2. Donors

In fourteen of the biobanks the sample is obtained from live donors, whereas two obtain them from deceased individuals. From the sampled biobanks, nine of them get their samples from adults, three from minors or infants and three did not specified the age of the sampled individuals. Biobanks handling infant samples differ on the age range of their samples: one handles samples from individuals up to ten years-old while the other handles samples from individuals twelve to eighteen years-old.

2.6.3. Sample collection

Researchers working in hospitals or National Health Institutes have more access to obtain samples while those not interacting with patients have more difficulties in doing so. Such is the case of researchers that work with cerebral tissue of deceased people because even when a donor has granted his consent to donate an organ his family and in some cases, even the hospital, may refuse to cooperate with the researcher.

Depending on the number of investigations taking place on a given institution, some biobanks request only one sample from each donor while others ask for more.

2.7. – Sample Property

Of the surveyed biobanks only fourteen answered questions concerning the ownership rights of the sample and the answers varied among them. Eight biobanks considered that the samples were owned by the research center while three of them pointed out that the donor is the owner of the sample and may withdraw his consent and the sample at any time. Three biobanks believed that there is no ownership on the sample, and two of them considered the laboratory as the recipient or guardian of the sample and one biobank claimed that the research center becomes the owner of the sample once it has been processed.

2.8. – Subject privacy protection, (confidentiality duty, archives and data security of samples, privacy of subject)

In respect to the biobanks that answered the questionnaire, twelve stated that they have protection systems for the private data and samples. Only one stated that they didn't keep any specific protection «since the samples are disassociated from the moment they are immortalized, and become established cell lines»; the other three did not answer the section on confidentiality.

Most biobanks disassociate the sample from the donor, they store it and assign a numeric code. The registry which links the sample with the name of the donor is kept either in a computer under a code or in physical archives with a key. Access to these registries is restricted and controlled. Two biobanks disassociate the samples when the project is finished, the rest of them keep the information until the samples are discarded. The reports of the biobank that makes population research keeps the name of the community linked to the sample.

Concerning the existing regulation on privacy, one biobank mentioned that they control and protect all the data obtained from the samples by a Institutional Safekeeping Information System, and only one biobank stated that they comply with the requirements from the Guidelines for the Protection of Personal Data made by the Federal Institute for Access to Public.

2.9. – Informed consent extension (generic or specific)

Fifteen biobanks present informed consent protocols for the donors, and the only one that doesn't produce one is because they receive their samples from another biobank.

Thirteen of those biobanks make specific informed consents and two make a general one. Only two of them explain to the donor the procedure of how they will take the sample and the objectives of the investigation. In the same way, only two explain the risks involved in the taking of the sample. Three biobanks explain to the donor that their refusal to donate a sample does not influence his medical attention. And, only seven biobanks let the donor revoke his consent at any time, as long, as they do not disassociate their data from the sample.

In thirteen biobanks, the consent must be in written form, in six of them they require two witnesses to sign the document. Specially, when the samples are obtained from underage children, the consent must be written. It draws our attention to see that one bionbank expressed that the consent could be oral or written.

Only one biobank gives the donor detailed information about the research and the disease researched, and only if the patient asks for more information, it is given to him. Only two biobanks give out contact information such as a telephone number or an email so that the donor may contact the researcher in case he has a doubt or question.

2.10. – *Use of samples collected for different purposes*

Eleven biobanks only use the sample with the finality agreed by the donor, and which is the specific one for the project. Two mentioned that they may use the sample for an investigation, different from the original to which the consent was given, but with no more specifications.

2.11. – *Specific issues concerning local communities*

Investigations concerning human health in communities shall only be admissible when the benefit that is expected, can be reasonably expected, and when the small scale studies have not reached conclusive results (49).

Researchers in local communities should obtain approval of the health authority as well as from the civil authorities of the community where the research will take place. It should also obtain the informed consent letter from every individual registered in the study, giving all the information that the regulation requires (50).

When the individuals from a community don't have the necessary capacity to fully understand the implications to take part in

---

(49) Article 28 from the regulation.
(50) Article 29 from the regulation.

an investigation, the Ethics Commission from the Institution the head researcher is part of may or may not authorize that the written informed consent from the individuals may be granted by an individual with moral authority over the community. If the Ethics Commission does not authorize it, the research should not be carried out. On the other hand, participation from individuals shall be entirely voluntary and everyone must have the liberty to either not participate or withdraw his or her participation at any point of the study (51).

2.12. – Maintenance

2.12.1. Security standards

Twelve biobanks guard the samples taken and these may only be handled by the people working in the laboratories. The samples are kept in containers, freezers and ultrafreezers; the access is restricted by either key or lock.

2.12.2. The storage period of the samples varies according to the different biobanks surveyed

Two biobanks mentioned that the samples can be preserved for an indefinite time and only degraded ones are discarded. Five biobanks indicated they stored the samples «for some years», without any other specifications. Two mentioned that the period of conservation «depended on each study» and only five biobanks established strict periods of one, five and ten years to destroy the sample.

2.13. – National and international circulation and sample ceding

2.13.1. Transference of the sample to other researchers or institutions

Six biobanks transfer their samples to other biobanks, whether by protocols or collaborative or institutional agreements. Six

---

(51) Article 30 from the regulation.

biobanks, on the other hand, make transfers of the samples and one more biobank receives samples from another biobank.

2.13.2. *National and international circulation of samples*

Eleven of the biobanks surveyed did not export or import samples. Four biobanks export and import samples due to agreements with research projects from various foreign academic institutions, mainly from the United States and Great Britain. The last biobank surveyed imports samples sent in by an American firm.

2.14. – *Property rights on investigation results*

Property rights on the sample are resolved in the clause 2.7. In relation to the possibility of patenting or commercializing the sample, the biobanks surveyed did not give any answer.

2.15. – *Other issues*

It is important to mention that, although it was not a part of the outline in the presentation of the works, we asked the surveyed biobanks if they did or did not give fringe benefits to the source subjects. Only one of the surveyed biobanks answered that the benefit given to the donor is the results of his levels of glucose, cholesterol, and of the blood biometry obtained from his of her blood sample.

2.16. – *Final comments, conclusions, other reflections, etc.*

2.16.1. *Biobanks situation*

It is interesting to comment that of the biobanks surveyed, only the ones ascribed to public institutions agreed to send their answers.

Through the answers given to the questionnaire we sent, we could detect the difficulties that researchers not associated with public hospitals face in order to obtain the samples needed for their research. Because of a lack of specific regulations, the import or export of the samples is a major source of concern for researchers, although it is expected that the July 2008 reforms to the General

Law on Health will alleviate this situation. The procedures for the transference of samples are not fully established and a sense of insecurity causes the transfer of samples not to be a common practice, even though these procedures are essential for the operation of biobanks.

Since there is no standardized model for obtaining the informed consent, each biobank makes its own format according to its own criteria. It is not clear if there is any kind of supervision or careful watch on the application of these consents or on the information that the researcher discloses to the donor about the procedures of sample collection, personal risks, objectives of the investigation and the possibility to revoke the consent, when the data has not been dissociated. In the case of population investigations, the consents are secured in accordance to the General Law on Health and the Rulings on Health Research. Nevertheless, the transmission of information to a population of low educational levels or from a different culture should follow an adequate and accurate methodology.

Regardless of the small size of the sample obtained in the survey, the scarcity of uniform standards in relation to the protection of private and confidential data, and the disregard of biobanks towards the prevailing legal norms, is widely observed. Specially, in relation to population investigations, it is not clear how the privacy and confidentiality of data of an entire community is protected.

Furthermore, the almost lack of benefits given to the donor draws significant attention. Only one biobank provides such benefits, and they are merely the delivery of certain information obtained from the blood samples donated, such as the blood biometry, or the levels of cholesterol and glucose.

In respect to the property rights of a sample, there is also a variety of interpretations. In some cases, the sample is considered the property of the bank, in others, it is considered a property of the donor. There is also the suggestion that while the investigation is taking place there is a sort of «judicial limbo», since there is no «true» owner of the sample. This situation is solved after the research ends, when the sample becomes the property of the investigator. This information shows the need of a uniform criteria to be observed by the biobanks.

2.16.2. *Legislation*

In validation of the initial hypothesis, there is no legislation in Mexico that specifically regulates biobanks. Nevertheless, there are general laws that can be applied. The lack of regulation awareness by the biobanks personnel brings a feeling of insecurity to the staff, since they do not know if they are acting correctly or failing to observe a law.

From these general norms, it is important to pay particular attention to the one that concerns personal data, which is protected by the Constitution. The Law to Access to Information and Protection of Personal Data, and the Guidelines derived from this Law, can solve the cases of investigations in public federal institutions; those taking place in the Federal District are under the Distrito Federal Law of Protection of Personal Data.

But this legislation is clearly insufficient, since it does not regulate the protection of personal data in private institutions or in public entities of different states in Mexico where no specific legislation exists.

On the other hand, the protection of personal data is aimed at protecting the privacy and confidentiality of individual subjects. However, the question arises about the protection of data concerning entire populations. Are they likewise protected? The current norms refer only to individual personal data but they do not mention the data shared by communities in their entirety. This shortness in the scope may lead to discrimination, or at least, to the stigmatization of ethnic groups.

In regards to other aspects, in the investigation with protected human samples, the norms adjudged in Mexico are the General Law on Health and its regulations, and the official Norms issued for specific situations.

In our opinion, based on the norms that have been studied, the regulation and control of biobanks and their work is under COFEPRIS (Federal Control Commission for Sanitary Risks), the decentralized agency dependant on the Health Agency. The General Law on Health and the Ruling of Organs, Tissue and Cell Donation and Transplant regulate the securing, handling, and transfer of the samples, especially those of dangerous residues from living donors or corpses.

Even though the informed consent is clearly described for health investigations, certain precisions are missing in the consents obtained from communities. In Mexico, as well as in other Latin American countries, population researches are under way, and they deserve special attention. The informed consent in communities differs from the individual consent, and we may add that the cultural differences between the researcher and the research subject require special techniques to transmit the information to individuals with very low educational levels.

For the reasons stated above, we recommend that instruments be created, to serve as guides to inform the biobank operators about the norms needed for the establishment and functioning of biobanks. Also, proper registration should be compulsory for biobanks. The control and vigilance of their operations would belong to the Health Agency, but the ethic aspects must be the responsibility of the Ethics committees. Overall, these guides should indicate the way of obtaining the informed consent, individual as well as communal, in the case of population research.

As a conclusion, there is an urgent need to establish Guides that indicate in each case the current legislation that applies to biobanks. Where there are no legislations, the recommendations based upon International Declarations that should be implemented.

LEGAL AND SOCIAL IMPLICATIONS OF CREATING BANKS OF BIOLOGICAL MATERIAL IN PORTUGAL

BY

Helena MONIZ

AND

Sónia FIDALGO

Summary : 1. Biobanks and scientific research with biological material in Portugal. 1.1. Objective of the report. Parameters of the study. 1.2. Existing Biobanks in Portugal. 2. Legal aspects regarding biobanks. 2.1. General legislation. 2.2. Specific legislation. 2.2.1. The concept of health information. 2.3. Reports and opinions of national institutions and other entities. 2.4. Institutions and professionals : quality standards and accreditation processes. 2.5. Ethics Committees. 2.6. Collection of specimens. 2.7. Property of the specimens. 2.8. Protection of privacy. 2.8.1. The general duty of confidentiality of the medical staff, non-medical researchers and assistants. 2.8.2. Specificities regarding biobanks. 2.9. Consent. 2.10. Use of specimens for objectives in variance to those of the collection. 2.10.1. *Excursus* : reference to a biobank created on the basis of specimens used to carry out the PKU test («teste do pezinho») : legal recognition of the database. legal recognition of the biobank ?. 2.11. Specific questions concerning to local communities. 2.12. Length of specimen storage. 2.13. National and International transfer and circulation of specimens. 2.13.1. Guarantee of the custody chain. 2.13.2. Transfer of samples or collections of biological materials to other national or foreign entities. 2.14. Rights on research results 2.15. Another questions. 2.15.1. Subsidiary application of the LPPD. a) The processing of medical data. b) The processing of genetic data. 2.15.2. The Deliberation n° 227/2007 of the Portuguese National Commission for Data Protection. 2.16. Conclusions.

1. – BIOBANKS AND SCIENTIFIC RESEARCH WITH BIOLOGICAL MATERIAL IN PORTUGAL

1.1. – *Objective of the report. Parameters of the study*

In this report, we are only going to briefly focus on the existing Portuguese regulation about the creation of biobanks, or biological material banks, dedicated to biomedical research. For this reason, we are not going to refer to any of the Communitarian and/or International legislation that may exist on this subject.

Exactly because we only propose to provide information on the rules regarding biological materials banks constituted with the objective of carrying out biomedical research, we consider that this study does not include all the regulation regarding to biological material collected for transplants (1), or for medically assisted reproduction (2) that, in the Portuguese system have specific rules. We also exclude any reference to biological material collected with the intention of obtaining ADN for criminal investigation purposes (3).

1.2. – *Existing Biobanks in Portugal*

In Portugal there are some collections of biological material in many of the pathological anatomy departments in the central Portuguese hospitals. Nevertheless, it does not exist a national registration of the existing biobanks, and it also does not exist a registration of the collections of the biological material. And even concerning to the biobanks which were created after the Law nº 12/2005, of 26 January 2005 (Law on personal genetic information and health information), in Portugal we still do not have a national registration of these biobanks. There is only a national registration of the databases of personal data associated to the biobanks (where

---

(1) According to Law nº 12/93, of 22 April 1993 (with the changes introduced since then, namely, Law nº 22/2007, of 29 June 2007).

(2) According to Law nº 32/2006, of 26 July 2006 and Law nº 12/2009, 26th March, on setting standards of quality and safety for the donation, procurement, testing, processing, preservation, storage and distribution of human tissues and cells.

(3) Even though, in this context, the creation of a biological material bank was expressly prevented after the ADN profile was obtained — according to arts. 31 and f. of the Law nº 5/2008, of 12 February 2008.

there is also the indication about the existence of a collection of biological samples).

There are four biobanks created under the Law n° 12/2005, which, according to people who are working there, are legalized : the Bank of Tumors (*Banco de Tumores*) of the *Hospital de S. João*, in Oporto; the Bank of Tumors of *IPATIMUP* (Institute of Molecular Pathology and Immunology of the Oporto University), in Oporto; the Bank of Tumors of the Hospital of the University of Coimbra, in Coimbra; and the Bank of Tumors of the Almada Hospital, in Lisbon. There are four biobanks waiting for legalization : three Oncological Institutes, in Lisbon, Oporto and Coimbra, and the Institute of Molecular Medicin (*Instituto de Medicina Molecular*) of the University of Lisbon.

2. – LEGAL ASPECTS REGARDING BIOBANKS

2.1. – *General legislation*

In Portugal there is some general legislation which is applied concerning to biobanks and biomedical research.

The Law on the protection of personal data (LPPD) – Law n° 67/98, of 26 October 1998 – is a general act which transposes into the internal legal system the Directive 95/46/EC of the European Parliament and of the Council of 24 October 1995 on the protection of individuals with regard to the processing of personal data and on the free movement of such data (art. 1).

Besides this law, we have also to take into consideration the art. 35 of the Constitution of the Portuguese Republic, and the art. 195 of the Portuguese Penal Code. The art. 35 of the Constitution of the Portuguese Republic of 1976 is a provision on data protection that refers to the use of computerized data, and establishes rights and prohibitions (4). The art. 195 of the Portuguese Penal Code estab-

---

(4) Art. 35 (Use of computerized data) of the Constitution of the Portuguese Republic : «1. All citizens have the right of access to any computerized data relating to them and the right to be informed of the use for which the data is intended, under the law; they are entitled to require that the contents of the files and records be corrected and brought up to date. 2. The law shall determine what are personal data as well as the conditions applicable to automatic processing, connection, transmission and use thereof, and shall guarantee its protection by means of an independent administrative body. 3. Computerized storage shall not be used for information concerning a person's ideological or political convictions, party or trade union affiliations, religious

lish a general prohibition regarding the revelation of a secret (in certain circumstances) (5).

2.2. – *Specific legislation*

Since 2005, there is, in Portugal, a specific law concerning to biobanks and biomedical research: the Law on personal genetic information and health information (Law n° 12/2005, of 26 January 2005). This law intends to regulate the concept of information regarding health and genetic data, the circulation of information and the intervention on a human genome in the health care system, and it also states rules for the sampling of and the conservation of biological products for genetic testing or research (art. 1).

2.2.1. *The concept of health information*

The Portuguese Law on personal genetic information and health information begins by defining what may constitute health information, stating that health information is all kind of information directly or indirectly relating to health, present or future, of a (live or death) person, and to his clinical and relative history (art. 2). And the same Law establishes that health information is property of the patient (art. 3, n° 1) (6).

This express affirmation of the property of medical records by the patient has created some difficulties in Portugal. Is all the information pertaining to the records property of the patient? Or shall we make a distinction between patient information and that of the

---

beliefs, private life or ethnic origin, except where there is express consent from the data subject, authorization provided under the law with guarantees of non-discrimination or, in the case of data for statistical purposes, which does not identify individuals. 4. Access to personal data of third parties is prohibited, except in exceptional cases as prescribed by law. 5. Citizens shall not be given an all-purpose national identity number. 6. Everyone shall be guaranteed free access to public information networks and the law shall define the regulations applicable to the transborder data flows and the adequate norms of protection for personal data and for data that should be safeguarded in the national interest. 7. Personal data kept on manual files shall benefit from protection identical to that provided for in the above articles, in accordance with the law».

(5) See *infra*, point 2.8.1.

(6) The property of the information includes not only the health information (linked directly or indirectly to health, according to the notion presented in art. 2), but also the registered clinical data, the data referring to tests and other subsidiary exams, interventions and diagnostics (according to what is expressly stated in art. 3, n° 1). Note that regarding the immunological exams, according to the archival regulations of the hospitals, they were property of the patients (Directive n° 247/2000, of May 8).

physician (7), considering that the personal notes of the physician are not the property of the patient? We believe this last one is the good solution, especially because which is stated as belonging to the patient is the health information and, according to the definition given in art. 2, it will not be possible to include the personal notes of the physician.

According to art. 3, n° 1 of the Law n° 12/2005, health information can not be utilized for other purposes than those of providing care. We would also reach this conclusion upon the application of the protection of personal data regime to the processing of medical data, in accordance to art. 7, n° 4 of the LPPD (8). But this does not mean, however, that this information may not be used for health research, since the Law n° 12/2005 expressly admits this possibility (art. 3, n° 1, *in fine*) (9).

The statement of this art. 3 causes some doubts. May we accept the «free access» to the clinical process by physicians/professors/researchers at university hospitals? Could it be possible to integrate academic research or research having academic objectives in the designation «health research» used in the law (art. 3, n° 1)? And how can one reconcile this allowed «health research» (art. 3, n° 1) with the rule stated in art. 4, n° 3, of the same Law, which establishes that «health information can only be utilized by the health system under the express conditions defined in the written authorization by its owner or by whoever represents the owner»? First of all, we must say that, according to art. 7, n° 4 of the LPPD, patient's consent is not necessary for the processing of medical data. However, the LPPD is very clear when it states that the data collected for one purpose can not be used for another purpose. Art. 28, n° 1, paragraph d), of the LPPD imposes the need for an

---

(7) According with PEREIRA, André, «Dever de documentação, acesso ao processo clínico e sua propriedade. Uma perspectiva europeia», *Revista Portuguesa do Dano Corporal*, 2006 (16), p. 9 and f., and CASCÃO, Rui, «O dever de documentação do prestador de cuidados de saúde e a responsabilidade civil», *Lex Medicinæ*, n° 8 (2007), p. 27 and f.

(8) Art. 7 (The processing of sensitive data), n° 4, of the LPPD, establishes that «the processing of data relating to health and sex life, including genetic data, shall be permitted if it is necessary for the purposes of preventive medicine, medical diagnosis, the provision of care or treatment or the management of health-care services, provided those data are processed by a health professional bound by professional secrecy or by another person also subject to an equivalent obligation of secrecy and are notified to the NCDP under article 27, and where suitable safeguards are provided».

(9) Art. 3, n° 1 establishes that «health information cannot be utilized for other purposes than those of providing care, health research and other purposes allowed by the law».

authorization from the National Commission for Data Protection for the use of personal data for purposes not giving rise to their collection; and art. 7, n° 2, of the LPPD imposes the need for authorization on the part of the owner. We think that when art. 3, n° 1, of the Law n° 12/2005 allows the use of data for «health research», it seems to renounce the need for the express consent on the part of the patient. Nevertheless, according to art. 4, n° 4, «access to health information can be made available for research purposes, if in anonymous (form)» (10). Therefore, we may conclude that there will be no need for express consent since the data are in anonymous form (or did the law want to refer to another situation different from «heath research»?). If the data are not in anonymous form it will be necessary to get the authorization of NCDP and the patient's consent (arts. 7, n° 2, and 28, n° 1, paragraph a) of the LPPD).

2.3. – Reports and opinions of national institutions and other entities

In Portugal it exists the National Commission for Data Protection (NCDP) [*Comissão Nacional de Protecção de Dados – (CNPD)*], which is «the national authority endowed with the power to supervise and monitor compliance with the laws and regulations in the area of personal data protection, with strict respect for human rights and the fundamental freedoms and guarantees enshrined in the Constitution and the law» (11). Within its competence, the CNPD shall promote the dissemination and clarification on data protection rights. In this context, there is an important deliberation of the NCDP about the use of data for scientific research (Deliberation n° 227/2007) (12).

Relevant work on privacy issues is also made by *Conselho Nacional de Ética para as Ciências da Vida – CNECV* (National

---

(10) In this disposition, contrary to what occurs in art. 19, n° 7, of the Law n° 12/2005, an «irreversible» anonymity was not demanded. The Law demanded this irreversible anonymity when it referred to the use of «dry blood samples on paper, obtained in neonatal screening or others» for «genetic research.» However, nowhere does the law explain what is meant by irreversibly turned anonymous. We believe that it means the total impossibility of identification of the holder of the data, either directly or indirectly. This, in some cases of quite rare diseases may be really impossible, given the fact that, in a small country as Portugal, the physicians know exactly which families have these pathologies, therefore making the identification possible.

(11) Art. 22 of the LPPD.

(12) See *infra*, point 2.15.2.

Ethics Council for the Life Sciences). This Council is an independent body created in 1990 (13), for the purpose of «analyzing systematically the moral problems which arise out of scientific progress in the fields of biology, medicine or general health care» (14). However, the decisions taken by this Council are not binding.

2.4. – *Institutions and professionals: quality standards and accreditation processes*

In Portugal, there is no regulation for the accreditation of the centers with biological material. When these biobanks (in a broader sense than which is used by Spanish law) exist in central hospitals the access to them is often controlled by the Ethics Committees of those hospitals.

2.5. – *Ethics Committees*

In Portugal, Ethics Committees have an important role with regard to the access to the biological material for research purposes. When one can not request a new consent for the use of biological material for research purposes, Ethics Committees analyze the process and, based on the scientific meaning of the work, they will decide about the possibility to assess to the biological material or not. Often, Ethics Committees only allow the access to the material after the anonymization. One can say that not only the Ethics Committees of the central Hospitals but also the Ethics Committees of the Faculties of Medicine have an important role in the research with biological material.

2.6. – *Collection of specimens*

The Law n° 12/2005 begins by defining biobanks, calling them, initially, «bank of biological products» being «any repository of biological samples or its derivatives, with or without a limited period of storage, whether utilizing prospective collection or material previously gathered, either obtained as a component of the provision of routine health care, or by screening programs, or for research,

---

(13) The Law n° 14/90, of 9th June created it. June; now Law n° 24/2009, of 29th May, regulates CNECV.
(14) Art. 2, n° 1, paragraph a) of the Law n° 14/90, of 9 June 1990.

and that includes samples that may be identified, identifiable, turned anonymous, or anonymous» (art. 19, n° 1).

Even though the law does not define what is anonymous or turned anonymous, and noting that certain dispositions refer to an *irreversibly turned anonymous*, taking into account the various norms and which is generally understood as identified or identifiable (or «susceptible of identification» (15)) personal data, it is useful to make some distinctions. An *identified specimen* means that the specimen is stored with the complete identification of the person to whom it belongs in a direct form. An *identifiable specimen* means those cases in which the identification of the person who owns it is made indirectly (for example, through a codification of the sample in which, through a cross-examination of a code identification database, allows us to identify the person). The *anonymous samples* will be those that are collected from the very beginning without the identification of the person to whom they belong (in such a way that nothing will allow us, ever again, to know who they belonged to (16)). The *turned anonymous cases* are the cases that even though they were initially collected with the identification of the person, it is no longer possible to identify the source due to the destruction of the link, without the possibility of, without an exaggerated effort (17), «turn back». The *turned anonymous irreversibly* case is a case in which that «turning back» is completely impossible.

The collection of samples and the creation of the biobank are restricted to the purposes referred to in art. 19, n° 3 – «purpose of providing health care, including the diagnosis and prevention of illnesses, or of basic or applied research relative to health». Once again, the law uses different expressions – no longer «health research», but «basic or applied research relative to health». What does this expression mean? We believe that in this article the Law

---

(15) This is how it was defined in the Convention of the Council of Europe n° 108 in 1981 – Convention for the protection of persons in relation to the mechanized treatment of data of personal nature – and served as inspiration to Directive n° 95/46/CE, of October 24.

(16) The same cannot be said about those samples that, because they revealed some aspect of the person that is so characteristic that it allows the technical experts identify at least the family to which they belong; under these circumstances it will be quite difficult to integrate them into this category of anonymous samples.

(17) And here we remember that expression used in the Convention n° 108 of the Council of Europe that defined as personal data «any information regarding a singular person, identified or susceptible of identification («holder of the data»)» (art. 2.° paragraph a)) defining «Identifiable persons», as «a person who can be easily identified : *it does not cover identification of persons by means of very sophisticated methods.*» (*Explanatory Report*, our italics).

refers to clinical investigation, but not to genetic research (there are specific rules concerning to genetic research) (18).

Any biobank has to be constituted following authorization from the «entity accredited by the department responsible for the protection of health», *i. e.* the Ministry of Health, and if it refers to a biobank with samples that are identified, identifiable or turned anonymous not irreversibly it is also necessary the authorization of the NCDP. If, however, a biobank is created only with anonymous or irreversibly turned anonymous samples (in such a way that the previously obtained identification can never again be connected to the sample) the NCDP's authorization is no longer needed (19). Conversely, the requirements to the creation of a biobank increase when the collection of samples is significant and includes a considerable portion of the population. According to art. 19, n° 18, of the Law 12/2005, the creation of biobanks that describe a certain population demands the favourable judgement of the National Ethics Council for Life Sciences, and if it is a biobank that is «representative of the national population» it demands also the favourable judgement of the Portuguese Parliament. In all cases, one can only deposit in the biobanks samples whose request for integration was made by a physician (art. 19, n° 4).

2.7. – *Property of the specimens*

Art. 18 («Collection and conservation of the biological material»), n° 2, of the Law 12/2005 establishes that «the stored material is the property of the persons from whom it was obtained and, after his/her death, of his/her relatives». The art. 19, («DNA banks and banks of other biological products»), n° 13, states that «the stored biological material is considered property of the person from whom it was obtained or, after his/her death, or incapacity, of his/her relatives, and must be stored while there is proof of its usefulness to the present or future relatives». Therefore, the rule is: the samples are property of the patient and, after his/her death, of his/her relatives.

---

(18) About this see *infra*, points 8. and 11.2.
(19) This is understandable since the NCDP only must intervene when, at stake, is a personal information, something that, according to the LPPD means that it will be a set of information of an identified or identifiable person (according to art. 3, paragraph a)).

2.8. – Protection of privacy

2.8.1. The general duty of confidentiality of the medical staff, non-medical researchers and assistants

Art. 195 of the Portuguese Penal Code establishes a general prohibition regarding the revelation of secret in the absence of an agreement on the part of the holder of the information and if the information became known to the agent because of state, occupation, employment, profession or art. This protection is reinforced as far as personal data protection through art. 47 of the LPPD, establishing an aggravation of the penalty when the secret was revealed by public officials (n° 2, paragraph a), when the conduct was carried out with the intention of obtaining financial advantage or illicit benefit (n° 2, paragraph b), or when the revelation of the secret «jeopardizes the reputation, the honour and consideration or the intimacy of someone else's private life» (n° 2, paragraph c). Since we know that the legal assets protected by the article foreseen in the Penal Code is that of the protection of the reservation of private life and, simultaneously, the credibility of the agents of certain professions, the express mention made to privacy referred in paragraph c) of the n° 2 of art. 47 of the LPPD does not seem to offer anything new. Furthermore, it seems to be difficult to attune this norm and the legal type of the basic crime foreseen in the Penal Code, even though we may say that art. 47, n° 1 of the LPPD, when it forbids the revelation of secret, its purpose, more that the simple protection of the right to the preservation of private life, is to protect the right to informative self-determination, as a right that guarantees that other right to the preservation of private life (20).

2.8.2. Specificities regarding biobanks

Preoccupied with the threat to the preservation of the private life of the storage of biological material, the Law n° 12/2005 determines in its art. 19, n° 8, that the storage of identified material shall be avoided, and requires a clear control of the access to the biological material, namely through a limitation of the number of people

---

(20) For this attempt to reconcile diferent dispositions, see MONIZ, Helena, «A protecção de dados pessoais perante a informática (o caso especial dos dados referentes à saúde), *Revista Portuguesa de Ciência Criminal*, n° 7 (1997), p. 231 and f.

allowed to have access to it, as well as through the creation of the minimal conditions that guarantee security as far as loss, alterations or destruction. These rules necessarily implies exhaustive control of the people having access to the locations where the materials are stored, as well as the creation of infrastructures that can assure the preservation of the storage conditions such as, for example, the creation of alternative sources of energy in order to assure that refrigerators are always turned on. Furthermore, n° 9 of the same article only allows the use of samples when they are anonymous or were rendered irreversibly anonymous, with a limit on the instances when studies on identified or identifiable samples are allowed (21). In this latter case, it is imperative to carry out the codification of the samples, with the codes stored in a different location, «but always in public institutions» (art. 19, n° 11) (22). The law also forbids commercial entities to store identified or identifiable biological material. These can only work with anonymous materials or those rendered anonymous (art. 19, n° 10).

Besides this confidentiality requirement assured by law, there is another – that of the conservation of the samples and the maintenance of a certain quantity that may allow its reuse, namely for «diagnostic of family illness, in the context of genetic tests on these people and their families» (art. 19, n° 14).

2.9. – Consent

There are two agreements required at the time of the creation of the biobank: the agreement for the collection of the sample (according to art. 18, n° 1, of the Law n° 12/2005, that establishes not only the agreement for the collection of the sample when it is only destined for treatment objectives but also another agreement if the same sample is going to be used for research purposes); and the agreement for the use and integration of the sample in the biobank (art. 19). In this latter case the law expressly requires a written consent and establishes that certain information must be

---

(21) «Only anonymous or irreversibly turned anonymous samples can be used, with the identified and identifiable samples limited to studies that cannot be carried out otherwise» (art. 19, n° 9, of the Law 12/2005).

(22) Beyond this, the law also states «if the bank include identified or identifiable samples and the possibility of communication of the results of the study is foreseen, a physician specialized in genetics must be involved in this process» (art. 19, n° 12).

given at the time of its attribution: biobank purposes; who is responsible for the biobank; types of investigation to be carried out; potential risks and benefits of the research; length of storage; measures taken to assure the privacy and confidentiality of the participants; and estimate regarding the possibility of communication or not of the results obtained through this material (art. 19, n° 5).

2.10. – *Use of specimens for objectives in variance to those of the collection*

As a general rule, one may state that the samples can only be used for the purposes that led to their collection – tests relating to assistance and research purposes, with the respective authorizations given in separate (art. 18, n° 1, of the Law 12/2005).

However, there are exceptional cases in which it is permitted to use a patient's samples for prevention purposes or in order to provide assistance to another relative. Art. 18, n° 7 expressly states that «all direct line relatives and those of the second degree in the collateral line (brothers) can have access to a stored sample, if it is necessary to better know their own genetic statute, but not to know the statute of the person who owns the sample or his/her relatives.» (23)

Art. 18, n° 1 determines that the authorization for the collection of biological products for research purposes must include «the objective of the collection and the period of conservation of the samples and of the products derived from them». This means that it must be expressly stated that the purpose of the collection is research – but will it be necessary to expressly state what research it is? Or will it be sufficient to say that it is «health research» or «clinical research» or «epidemiological research»? Art. 18, n° 4 establishes that «the biological samples whose collection was destined to a different objective cannot be used in tests relating to assistance nor in research purposes, unless authorized by the person who owns them or, after his/her death or incapacity, by his/her relatives, or after irreversible anonymity». Even from reading this n° 4, we do not see

---

(23) This disposition must not be confused with art. 18, n° 6, that refers to access (by relatives) to the genetic information, contrary to n° 7 that refers to access (by relatives) to the biological material itself, note, however, that, after the holder's death, the biological material belongs to the relatives, according to art. 18, n° 3 *in fine*.

how, to collect a sample, it can be demanded an express statement about the concrete research. However, through another track, this must be demanded. If one begins by demanding an enlightened consent, this only occurs when the person had the freedom of will and the freedom of decision – therefore, there must be a minimum of precision about the concrete research. For example, a person allows that his/her sample will be used for a certain research in oncological illnesses – we think that there is not the obligation to enter into further detail about the specific type of investigation that will take place. However, this minimum of precision will already impede that the same sample will be used for research in neurological illnesses, for example. This, in truth, is understandable; otherwise the enlightenment needed for proffering that agreement will not be present, jeopardizing the validity of the consent.

One must also take into consideration the text of art. 18, n° 5, according to which the «samples collected for a specific medical or scientific purpose can only be used with the express authorization of the people involved or their legal representatives».

But all of this does not mean that one cannot use biobanks that were previously created for certain objectives and that now seems to be needed for other investigations. This seems to be possible if, from the beginning they are used retrospectively or when, and taking in consideration the «quantity of data and subjects, their age or other comparable reason», it is not possible to obtain an authorization for the use for other purposes (art. 19, n° 6, of the Law 12/2005) (24). In these cases the samples can be used for other purposes, with one limitation – these other purposes must be only circumscribed to «objectives of scientific research or acquisition of epidemiological or statistical data» (art. 19, n° 6, *in fine*). The question remains: what is «scientific research purposes» in a law which already used other expressions such as «health research», «clinical research», «genetic research», «basic research», «research applied to health», «scientific research in the field of health» ...

One must add to this the total prohibition of the use of the sample for «patent registration or any financial gain» (art. 18, n° 8).

---

(24) Different objectives from those agreed to when the sample was collected (under the terms of arts. 18, n° 1, and 19, n° 1).

2.10.1. *Excursus*: *reference to a biobank created on the basis of specimens used to carry out the PKU test («teste do pezinho») : legal recognition of the database; legal recognition of the biobank?*

Regarding the possibility of the retrospective use of biobanks under the conditions established in art. 19, n° 6, that we referred to above, one must add that in specific cases – collection of blood for the PKU test (*testes do pezinho*) – the law established a specific rule. According to art. 19, n° 7, of the Law 12/2005, «the conservation of dry blood samples on paper obtained through neonatal screening or others (...) [can] be used for (...) genetic research, if previously turned irreversibly anonymous». We do think, however, that this requirement to grant anonymity falls to the side when the premises contained in art. 19, n° 6, are carried out – the use of these samples for research, when it is not possible to obtain consent given the quantity of data and of subjects, is possible if the samples are used for scientific research purposes and if, for that, one considers that the use for «scientific research» (as the article says) also includes genetic research.

But, even if it is not so, the use of dry blood samples on paper obtained through neonatal screening does not always constitute a «case of retrospective use» (art. 19, n° 6)? In these cases one may also use the samples for purposes of scientific research under the terms of art. 19, n° 6. Therefore, that what was to be limited, limiting the investigation based on the samples collected for the «little foot» tests to genetic research and only with samples irreversibly turned anonymous, ends up being obtained without this anonymity process in the case of retrospective usage, and only with the objective of scientific research (investigation other than genetic research, since this one is indeed limited by the requirement of the irreversible anonymity process). If this were not the intended result, art. 19, n° 7 should have begun by stating «excepting the previous number, ...». It is clear that every research, in principle, must be carried out without identified samples, as established by art. 19, n° 9; the researcher has to prove if the investigation requires the identification of the sample (25).

---

(25) I believe that this justification must be presented at the time of the request for the creation of the biobank, under the terms of art. 19, n° 2.

2.11. – Specific questions concerning to local communities

Although we have large groups of immigrants especially from African countries they are not isolated communities so they do not to require specific rules.

2.12. – Length of specimen storage

Law 12/2005 does not establish any rule, even though one may conclude that the samples can be stored while they are useful to the pursuit of the objectives and ends that served as the basis for its collection (here one can draw some parallels with what happens regarding personal data bases) (26).

Regarding this problem of the length of time of storage, we believe that one must articulate it with the rule that says that the sample is the property of the donor and after his/her death or incapacity, of his/her relatives (arts. 18, n° 2 and 19, n° 13, of the Law 12/2005). Therefore, there is a need, from the very beginning, to determine the length of storage, otherwise one runs the risk of the relatives, after the death of the donor, eventually demand the sample. Such cases may happen because they may need it, for example, to carry out a study regarding a genetic illness in the family. Even though the sample cannot be used for purposes of assistance or research if it was collected for different reasons (art. 18, n° 4), it certainly can if there is a new authorization from the holder or, after his/her death (or incapacity), authorization from the relatives. Therefore, the use of the sample collected for a biobank for research purposes can, after death, be used for another objective whenever the relatives authorize it.

As stated in art. 19, n° 15, of the Law 12/2005, the researcher responsible for the biobank must always inform the person who gave the authorization about the «loss, alteration or destruction, as well as of his decision to abandon one type of investigation or of closing the bank.»

---

(26) See *infra*, point 11.3.

2.13. – National and International transfer and circulation of specimens

2.13.1. Guarantee of the custody chain

Being a considerably important matter for whoever carries out the investigation, with much of the success and credibility of the results of this research depending on it, nothing is expressly referred to the guarantee of the custody chain in the law. Even though, one can say that, regarding this subject, the *guidelines* (from the International Scientific Associations) established for this must be followed.

2.13.2. Transfer of samples or collections of biological materials to other national or foreign entities

According to the art. art. 19, n° 17, of the Law n° 12/2005, «the transfer of a large number of samples or collections of biological materials to other national or foreign entities must always respect the objectives of the creation of the bank for which the agreement was obtained and be approved by the responsible ethics committees».

If the shipment of biological material is accompanied by the shipment of personal data, one must distinguish if the information is sent to EU countries or not. When the information is sent to EU countries, the transfer is freely allowed (art. 18 LPPD). Regarding countries not in the EU, the transfer must comply with the established in arts. 19 and following of the LPPD: this transfer will only be allowed if the State where the data are being transferred to guarantees an «adequate level of protection» (art. 19 of the LPPD). This «adequate level of protection» will have to be evaluated by the NCDP, at the time of the request for authorization for the creation of the personal database, since it is a base with research purposes, which requires that authorization.

2.14. – Rights on research results

There are not special rules about research results using biological material.

2.15. – Another questions

2.15.1. Subsidiary application of the LPPD

a) *The processing of medical data*

As mentioned before, according to the LPPD (27) there was an express legal authorization for the treatment of medical data, if used for the purposes referred to in art. 7, n° 4. (28) In other words, it is not necessary to obtain an express authorization. Consent is only required when the data are used for other objectives, even though it may seem, based on the Law n° 12/2005, that the use of these data for purposes of «health research» does not presupposes that express consent, because of the express legal authorization.

Access to medical data (29), according to the general rules, may only occur through the holder (as it actually happens with access to any personal data), or through any other person duly authorized by the holder of the data. As with the LPPD, access to medical data is only admitted «through a physician» (30) (art. 3, n° 3). How-

---

(27) This law is completed by art. 35 of the Constitution of the Portuguese Republic, which refers to the fundamental right to informational self-determination.

(28) See *supra*, footnote 11.

(29) The medical data should only be inserted by the physician that assisted the person, being bound by secrecy (according to art. 5, n° 4). The insertion must be carried out according to the respective deontological norms and the consultation of the clinical file can only be made by the «physician in charge of the health care in favour of the person (...), notwithstanding the epidemiological, clinical or genetic research that may be carried out on the same» (art. 5, n° 5); excepting what is stated in art. 16 of the same law, regarding research on human genomes, in which it is established that this must follow the general rules respecting «scientific investigation in the field of health,» being subjected to the approval by the ethics committees of the hospitals, universities or research, and always requiring the informed and written consent of the person. From this point, many are the doubts that assail us : what are the general rules regarding scientific research in the field of health? Is the objective here to make a distinction between genetic information and health information, knowing that in this latter case it seems that the health research is possible without the need for consent from the holder of the data or any authorization from an ethics committee, and that regarding the genetic information that consent and this authorization are needed? I do believe it is so. Incidentally, the entire Law n° 12/2005 pretends to clearly distinguish genetic information and the remaining information about health. And, taking into account what is stated in art. 5, n° 5 in which a distinction between epidemiological, clinical, and genetic research is expressly made, we are led to conclude that health research will be the general designation that comprehends all these three types of research, with special and more restrictive rules for genetic research.

(30) What seemed to be controversial until very recently, we cannot stat now with much certainty. According to what seems to be the European evolution also now and after the Law on the Access to administrative documents that was recently modified (Law n° 46/2007, of 24 August 2007), access to the clinical file may occur without the intervention of the physician. However, this law does not apply to the cases in which the clinical file is in a private institution because it does not bind private entities.

ever, if the clinical file is in a public institution, the access does not depend on the auspices of a physician (31). This does not mean that access to the clinical file may imply access to data which do not contain health information. That is, the personal notes of the physicians do not appear to be included in the concept of «health information.» This does not also mean that this difference in treatment does not create problems of a practical nature, since there will be a need to differentiate, within a clinical file (whether on paper or on a computer) between health information owned by the patient and the notes of the physician(s)/nurse(s). Incidentally, and using the notion of clinical file used in the Law n° 12/2005 (art. 5, n° 2 – «each clinical file must contain all the available medical information that pertains to the person»), this only includes the medical information and not the information of the physician. Nonetheless, it is a fact that art. 6 of the same law ends up establishing a different regime in reference to genetic information (32).

Moreover, regarding access to medical data, one must underline the restriction imposed in art. 3, n° 2 *in fine* that expressly admits that the holder of the health information may not have access to it whenever there are» exceptional circumstances, duly justified, and in which it is unequivocally demonstrated that this (access) may be detrimental» – is the recognition of an idea of therapeutic privilege (also according to art. 156 of the Portuguese Penal Code) (33). This possibility of non-communication to the patient when the knowledge of a certain information may be detrimental to him, placing «his life in danger» or when that knowledge might be susceptible of «causing grave damage to his physical or psychic health» (art. 157 of the Portuguese Penal Code) will create an added responsibility on the physician/health professional since the respect for this requirement imposes an *effective* knowledge of the person of the patient (34).

---

(31) According to art. 7 of the Law n° 46/2007.

(32) Art. 6, n° 4 : «The genetic information that does not have immediate implications on the present state of health (...) may not be included in the clinical file, except in the case of medical genetics consultations or services, with appropriate and separate archives».

(33) About the crime of arbitrary medical-surgical interventions, see ANDRADE, Costa *Comentário Conimbricense do Código Penal*, tomo I, Coimbra : Coimbra Editora, 1999, annotation to arts. 156 and 157.

(34) It remains to be seen which would be the crime committed by the physician who, not paying attention to his/her patient gives him/her all the health information causing, with this, that the patient becomes so desperate that, in the end, decides to commit suicide. Will the phy-

b) *The processing of genetic data*

The LPPD does not distinguish between medical data and genetic dada since, based on art. 7, n° 4, it allows the treatment of medical data, including genetic data and sexual information. However, this equalization does not occur in Law n° 12/2005 that, regarding genetic data, has some special requirements. First of all, the genetic information cannot be included in the clinical file unless it might have immediate implications on the state of health (art. 6, n° 4 of the Law n° 12/2005).

Regarding the rule applicable to genetic data bases, it is the regime referred to in the LPPD as imposed by the remission in art. 7, n° 2 of the Law n° 12/2005 (35).

---

sician be accused of negligent homicide? Or of an offence to the physical integrity with endangerment of life? How can one establish the nexus of imputation between the result of death and the conduct of having informed in excess, of having carried out in its entirety the duty to inform? Is it normal and foreseeable, given the normal levels of knowledge, that A will commit suicide after being informed that he/she is carrying a fatal virus? Even if it is, what was the crime committed by the physician? Homicide? Incitement to suicide? Even if we state that with that conduct the physician created a forbidden danger of producing a result, and the result consists in the materialization of that danger (premises to the theory of the connexion of the risk) is it possible to place this situation in the context of the protection of the norm?

And even if one agrees that the non-compliance with the therapeutic privilege constitutes a violation of the *legis artis*, can we still understand that we are faced with a crime of negligent medical-surgical interventions, that art. 150, n° 2 seems to foresee, and establishes punishment for those who «carry out interventions or treatments that violate the *legis artis* and create, in this manner, a danger to the life or danger of grave offence to the body or to the health»? It is, however, a fact that the danger to health did not directly derive from the medical-surgical intervention that, in the case of suicide, due to «excessive» information, did not even took place.

(35) Specific rules on genetic tests are created – demand for an informed consent, expressed through writing, communication of results only to the party, execution only though a request made by a physician, need for genetic counselling, prohibition of genetic tests for purposes of life or health insurance, prohibition of use of genetic information by insurers based on previous tests made by a client, impossibility of insurance refusal based on family background, prohibition of basing a selection of a candidate for a job on the through the requirement of previous genetic tests, prohibition of genetic testing for adoption purposes (neither on the adoptee child, nor the prospective adopting parents) are some of the caveats imposed by this Law n° 12/2005 (according to arts. 9, 12, 13 e 14). We must also note the right indicated in art. 11, n° 3 according to which «no one can be discriminated against, under any form, namely in his/her right to medical and psycho-social treatment and to genetic counselling, for refusing to be subjected to a genetic test» – which seems to allow, therefore, the refusal of carrying out genetic tests even against the impositions by the insurer company for the signing of an insurance contract, thus benefiting from the same conditions as anyone else who did not refuse; however, this point will be the object of specific regulation, according to art. 177, n° 2 («Genetic tests or the use of genetic information is regulated under special legislation») of Decree-Law n° 72/2008, of 16 April 2008 (legal rule of the insurance contract), even though one must not forget about the rules regarding good-faith in contracts – also according to recent legislation on insurance contracts, in which there is Express reference to «without prejudice to the duties of information owed by the insured, the celebration of the contract may depend on declaration about the state of health and medical exams related to the insured person, for the purpose of risk evaluation.»

Also here in the context of genetic data, access is permitted to the holder of the data. The problem arises regarding the possibility of other relatives having access. If, on the one hand, art. 6, n° 9, expressly allows knowledge about one's own genetic information and also if a specific file or registry contain genetic information on their family («the citizens have the right to know if a clinical file contains genetic information on themselves and their family»), it does not appear to us that this, in itself, allows that he/she may have knowledge of the genetic information of the family. This knowledge can only occur if «in special circumstances (...) the information may have relevance for the treatment or prevention of the recurrence of an illness in the family» and if used in the context of genetic counselling «even if it no longer is possible to obtain the informed consent of the person to whom it belongs» (art. 18, n° 6 of the Law 12/2005).

2.15.2. *The Deliberation n° 227/2007 of the Portuguese National Commission for Data Protection*

There is an important deliberation of the NCDP about the use of data for scientific research: the Deliberation n° 227/2007 (36).

The NCDP decided that «(...) the units of the health system can only use the personal health data for purposes of scientific research under the terms alluded in the written consent by the holder. Thus, in the case of the treatment given to personal data carried out in the context of research studies in the health area, the legitimacy will have to derive from the free, specific, informed consent (paragraph h) of art. 3 of the LPPD) expressed by the holder (n° 2 of the art. 7 of the LPPD) in writing (n° 3 of the art. 4 of the Law no 12/2005)» (37).

According to NCDP «free consent means that the holder does not know of any conditioning factors or dependencies at the moment of his declaration that may affect the formation of his/her will and, also, that he/she may revoke, without penalties and with retroactive effect, the consent that he/she may have given» (38). And «specific consent means that the consent refers to a concrete factual

---

(36) NCDP, Deliberation n° 227/2007, of 28 May 2007, available at: http://www.cnpd.pt/bin/decisoes/2007/htm/del/del227-07.htm
(37) NCDP, Deliberation n° 227/2007, *cit.*, p. 5.
(38) NCDP, Deliberation n° 227/2007, *cit.*, p. 5.

contextualization, to a chronological actuality, precise and balanced, and to a specific situation. The specific consent puts aside the instances of preventive and generalized consent, given so as to cover a plurality of operations.» (39) And, «since the consent must be, obligatorily, written, for security reasons and trust in the proceedings, the holder must receive a copy of the written consent given» (40).

In the case of a retrospective study, the NCDP demands that whenever the initial consent does not include the new usage, the person responsible for the data base will have to request a new authorization, this being a condition without which the study will not be allowed to be carried out. However, the Commission understands that, given the possibility of retrospective use of specimens of biological materials for investigation, allowed by art. 19, n° 6 of the Law n° 12/2005, then the utilization of connected personal data is already authorized by this rule. However, it does limit this possibility to the use of data directly linked to the specimens. Regarding other data, health data, namely inserted in the clinical file, only exceptionally will that consent be dispensable; for this reason «it will be necessary to unequivocally demonstrate the existence and importance of the public interest of the study or research in question, public interest that must be carried on in an immediate and direct form by the results of the research (the results of the research must achieve immediately and directly the public interest in question, which must be of unquestionable importance to the community, not being enough that the research achieve the public interest in an indirect, oblique, reflexive or remote form)» (41).

The NCDP is also quite restrictive regarding the usage of health data for research for academic theses. In these cases, it is either the author of the thesis himself who creates a personal database, having always to request the consent of the holders of the data, or, if it is a research whose public interest has been attested to by the Ethics Committee of the University, accompanied by the favourable opinion of the Ethics Committee of the Hospital Unit (42).

---

(39) NCDP, Deliberation n° 227/2007, *cit.*, p. 5.
(40) NCDP, Deliberation n° 227/2007, *cit.*, p. 5.
(41) Deliberation n° 227/2007, *cit.*, p. 6.
(42) Deliberation n° 227/2007, *cit.*, p. 7-8.

According to the NCDP's deliberation «under the terms of art. 5, n° 1, paragraph e) of the LPPD, personal data, including identified or identifiable biological samples, can only be conserved during the period necessary to the achievement of the objectives inherent to the collection or of the subsequent treatment» (43). And, «after the expiration of the conservation period, the responsible entity must proceed to the destruction of the personal data, draw up an official report, and send a copy to the NCPD. This, however, does not preclude that the data might be conserved after having been turned anonymous» (44).

Since the use of medical data for purposes of research is not under the purview of art. 7, n° 4 of the LPPD, any treatment with this objective must be preceded by authorization from the NCPD, under the terms of art. 28, paragraph a) of the LPPD. Besides, we already know that the data may only be used for purposes of collection, and only with the express consent of the NCPD will they be usable for different objectives (according to art. 18, n° 1, paragraph d) of the LPPD). Now, regarding scientific research, there is a problem on how to integrate this prohibition in defence of a right to privacy with the right to the freedom of investigation, namely health research (45). Exactly because of this, the NCPD understood that «there are cases in which the legitimacy condition for treatment of personal health data – such as what happens with the retrospective studies of personal health data – for purposes of scientific research, is resolved, in the absence of a free, specific informed and express consent, with the rigid examination of the concrete and effective public interest of the research, that may lead to other conditions of legitimacy – legal basis or authorization by the NCPD» (46). However, the commission understood that, whenever the studies may be carried out without the identification of the holder of the data, this method should be followed; if it not possible, it will be necessary to use codified/anonymous data. It should

---

(43) Deliberation n° 227/2007, cit., p. 9.
(44) Deliberation n° 227/2007, cit., p. 9.
(45) Art. 73, n° 4 of the Portuguese Constitution (CRP – Constituição da República Portuguesa) exactly states a need to enhance scientific research.
(46) Deliberation n° 227/2007, cit., p. 3.

be added that the use of personal data is only allowed in cases of absolute necessity (47).

2.16. – *Conclusions*

These are the first steps towards the legalization of existing biobanks, and to others that may be formed. But we are far from existing regulations in other European countries such as Spain. What could cause some problems such as that recently I have been asked – what are the necessary procedures for the legalization of a bank of human milk? Be covered by the rules of Law n° 12/2005? Perhaps it is time to supplement the existing rules, taking into account the various international instruments that have emerged.

---

(47) Deliberation n° 227/2007, *cit.*, p. 4. Even though the text is not very clear, the NCDP begins by stating : «If it is not possible to carry out the study with anonymous data, the use of codified data must still be privileged, even if these may be, through the application of a decoding key, converted in personal data» (p. 4). Later it continues by stating that «The use of personal health data for purposes of scientific research is only admitted as a last resort, and in the face of the direst necessity. Therefore, the responsible entity, in the notification of the treatment of personal data, must justify the need to carry out the study in an identified or identifiable form» (p. 4). Now, does not that what previously was designated as «codified» fall under the notion of «identifiable»?

LEGAL AND SOCIAL IMPLICATIONS OF CREATING BANKS OF BIOLOGICAL MATERIAL IN SPAIN

BY

Carlos María ROMEO CASABONA

Pilar NICOLÁS JIMÉNEZ

AND

Sergio ROMEO MALANDA

Summary : 1. The facts : The position of biobanks and scientific research with human biological samples in Spain. 1.1. A General Overview of Biobanks in Spain (Geographical Distribution, Length of Time Established, Facilities Available, etc.). 1.2. Examples of Significant Biobank. 1.2.1. Hospital Biobanks (for example, Hospital Clinic de Barcelona Biobank). 1.2.2. Biobank Networks (For Example, the RTICC). 1.2.3. Network Biobanks (For Example, the Fundación BIO Bank). 1.2.4. National Banks (For Example, BNADN the National Cell Lines Bank). a) The National DNA Bank (BNADN) (www.bancoadn.org). b) The National Stem Cell Lines Bank. 2. Legal Framework. 2.1. General Applicable Legislation. 2.2. Specific Law. 2.2.1. Law 14/2007 of 3 July on Biomedical Research. 2.2.2. The legal framework that applies to Biobanks in the case of biomedical research. 2.3. Reports and Opinions From Different National Institutions and Other Organisations. 2.4. Institutions and Professionals : Standards of Quality and Accreditation Requirements. 2.5. Ethical Research Committees. 2.6. Collection of Samples (Invasive Intervention). 2.6.1. General Arrangements. 2.6.2. Children or People with a Disability. 2.6.3. Collection from a Cadaver. 2.6.4. Use of Gametes, Pre-embryos, Embryos, and Foetuses. a) Chapter I of Title III of the LIB (Arts. 28 and 29) cover the donation of embryos and human foetuses, and their biological structures. b) The legal regulations governing the use of gametes and pre-embryos for biomedical research in Spain are included in Law 14/2007 on Biomedical Research and Law 14/2006 regarding assisted human reproductive procedures. 2.7. Ownership of the Sample. 2.8. Protection of the Donor's Privacy (Obligation of Confidentiality and the Security of Data Files and Samples). 2.8.1. Application of the Rules Regarding the Protection of Personal Data. a) The Reasons for Applying the Rules Regarding the Protection of Personal Data. b) The right to access and cancellation. c) Security measures. 2.8.2. The Duty of Confidentiality. 2.9. The Scope of Consent (Generic or Specific). 2.10. Use of Samples Obtained for Another Purpose. 2.10.1. General

Framework. 2.10.2. Use of Samples without Expressed Consent from the Donor. 2.11. Specific Matters in Regard to Local Communities. 2.12. Maintenance: Security Standards, Duration of Storage. 2.13. Transfer and National and International Transportation. 2.13.1. General Arrangements. 2.13.2. Arrangements Applicable to Biobanks. 2.13.3. International Transportation of Biological Samples. 2.14. Donating, Transferring, and Ceding of Rights over the Research Results Free of Charge. 2.15. Other issues. 2.16. Conclusions.

1. – THE FACTS :
THE POSITION OF BIOBANKS AND SCIENTIFIC RESEARCH WITH HUMAN BIOLOGICAL SAMPLES IN SPAIN (1)

1.1. – *A general overview of Biobanks in Spain (geographical distribution, length of time established, facilities available, etc.)*

At this time it is difficult to give a general overview of the biobanks in Spain because there is no systematic catalogue of these facilities. The Biomedical Research Law foresees the creation of a National Biobanks Registry, through which the competent authorities (autonomous communities and the Ministry of Science and Innovation) will authorise biobanks, register those authorised biobanks, and register their most relevant characteristics (ownership, structure, types of collections they store).

In addition, *sensu stricto*, since the implementing regulation for the Biomedical Research Law has not gone into effect, there are no authorized biobanks as such (except the National Stem Cell Lines Bank), although there are structures that are clearly created in accordance with the requirements of the Biomedical Research Law, some of which are detailed in the examples described in sections 4-7.

The only systematic analysis conducted up to this point in Spain, in order to catalogue and audit the collections and biobanks, was carried out in 2005 by the National DNA Bank at the request of the Instituto de Salud Carlos III (ISCIII). Although the results of this study are out of date, they reveal some interesting characteristics. The geographical distribution was irregular, with nearly 70 %

---

(1) This report was written by Enrique de Alava Head, Molecular Pathology. Deputy Director, DNA National Bank. Centro de Investigación del Cáncer IBMCC (Universidad de Salamanca-CSIC).

of the facilities located in Madrid and Catalonia. The oldest biobanks were of the hospital type (see section 4) and date from 1985. However, more than 90% of the biobanks were created from 2001 onwards, at the same time as the cooperative research structures were developed. These structures, (cooperative research networks on shared themes, biomedical research centres network), were promoted by the ISCIII. For the most part they did not have space specifically designated for bank activities, or else the space available was not greater than 20 square meters in area. In a few cases they had technical personnel assigned to them. The facilities were in general safe and functional. The use of written consent forms for research was widespread. However, very few of them had a certified quality management system or computer applications specifically designed to be used in biobanks. It is, however, important to keep in mind that this information corresponds to two years before the Biomedical Research Law went into effect, after which there has been a notable effort to adapt Spanish biobanks. The following examples correspond to several biobank models described in Spain's regulatory framework.

1.2. – Examples of significant Biobanks

1.2.1. Hospital Biobanks (for example, Hospital Clinic de Barcelona Biobank)

http://www.clinicbiobanc.org/es_index.html

The Institut d'Investigaciones Biomèdiques August Pi i Sunyer (IDIBAPS) is one of the benchmark research centres in Catalonia, Spain, and Southern Europe, and has the highest production level in Spain. Three long established scientific organizations cooperate at the IDIBAPS centre: the Hospital Clinic de Barcelona (HCB), the Universitat de Barcelona (UB), and the Institut d'Investigaciones Biomèdiques de Barcelona del CSIC (IBB-CSIC), with institutional support from the Autonomous Community of Catalonia.

As a result of its role as a benchmark hospital and its commitment to research, the Hospital Clinic de Barcelona is an ideal environment for the creation of a Biobank. It has had organised collections of biological samples for research since 1985. The hospital biobank was established in 2006. Located on Calle Córsega 176, next to the Hospital Clinic de Barcelona, the biobank is located in an ideal place to respond to the growing demand for biological samples of proven quality, as a result of an increase in the multidisciplinary collaboration between different scientific fields (clinical-basic-applied).

Just like in any hospital bank, the collections/projects around which the Biobank is structured demonstrates the interest of the hospital research teams. In the case of the Hospital Clinic Biobank, according to their web page they focus on:

Metabolic Diseases

PR: Dr. Ramon Gomis

Biological samples and related information about patients who are diagnosed with the most prevalent metabolic diseases: diabetes, obesity, and dyslipaemia.

Inflammatory Bowel Disease

PR: Dr. Julià Panés

Bank of samples of proven quality for phenotypes of ulcerative colitis and Crohn's disease.

Gastrointestinal and Pancreatic Oncology

PR: Dr. Antoni Castells

A collection of biological samples from individuals affected by or at risk of gastrointestinal and pancreatic neoplasias.

Neurological Diseases

PR: Dr. Francesc Graus

Available soon

Psychiatric Disorders

PR: Dr. Rosa Catalán

The Mental Disorders Bank promotes the collection of samples from individuals affected by, or at risk of having, a severe mental disorder, as well as from healthy individuals.

Maternal-Foetal Medicine

PR: Dr. Eduard Gratacós

Biological samples from cases of complications in pregnancy, as well as from expectant mothers and low risk foetuses.

1.2.2. *Biobank networks (for example, the RTICC)*

www.rticc.org

When only tumour banks are considered, Spain holds an exceptional place in the international scientific community as far as development of cooperative models for this type of activity is concerned. It is clear that other countries have a greater number of units dedicated to this activity, primarily as the result of a tradition of public and private institutions allocating resources, as well as a tradition of broader scientific research. However, the factor that differentiates the Spanish experience is its open and cooperative character, which is serving as a model for developing other similar networks in numerous countries in Europe, America, and Asia, as well as that of international programmes.

The earliest Spanish cooperative experience was promoted by the Programa de Patología Molecular del Centro Nacional de Investigaciones Oncoloógicas (CNIO) [National Molecular Pathology and Oncology Research Centre Programme], started in September 2000. The scope of their work is national and the objective is to promote tumour banks with high standards in Spanish hospitals and their functional integration into a cooperative network. They aim to base this work on technical procedures and homogeneous ethical requirements, quality assurance techniques, and centralised coordination. However the biobanks and the actual tissues are owned by the hospital. Therefore, it is not just a single biobank but rather a cooperative network and organisation of hospital biobanks in which 28 institutions in 10 autonomous communities participate, along with four additional biobanks that are currently in the process of being set up.

Alongside this plan, new, independent, cooperative networks emerged between 2001 and 2005 in:
- Castilla and Leon (8 hospitals)
- Catalonia (11 hospitals)
- Asturias (4 hospitals) and
- Andalusia (13 hospitals)

This autonomous environment is associated with the Spanish health plan transferred to the autonomous communities. It is also not very different from the Inter-territorial Network Plan promoted by the CNIO. This centre is currently vigorously promoting territorial networks in various autonomous communities, without them losing their affiliation with the inter-territorial networks through doing so.

The co-existence of four autonomous networks and one inter-autonomous network, far from being a problem, has established a cooperation programme at a national level, as a result of their common design and particularly as a result of their firm commitment to cooperation. This has been demonstrated since 2001 when the National Tumour Bank Consortium was created. Although with slight differences in organisation and design, all these networks maintain common objectives and projects. Therefore, wherever the network is located the sample collections are stored locally, in the institution that obtained them, where they can be used for the purposes stated on the patient consent form and by the corresponding external committees.

Each network has a central coordinating office which guarantees confidentiality, reliability, quality policy, and approval from research agencies and ethics committees. These offices operate according to the principle of «honest broker,» as intermediaries between the tumour banks and researchers, while the management of the samples is local.

This collaboration was institutionalised in 2003 through the Red Temática de Investigación Cooperativa en Cáncer (RTICC) [Cooperative Cancer Research Network] financed and sponsored by the Instituto de Salud Carlos III. The network specifically includes a tumour banks programme in which 23 institutions are directly involved, almost all of them affiliated to some of the networks previously mentioned. Furthermore, the integration of these networks expands the scope of activity and coordination of the RTICC's Tumour Bank Programme to more than 40 hospital facilities.

Since 2003 the RTICC's Tumour Banks programme has maintained a structure which allows all autonomous community or inter-autonomous community networks to adopt the same technical and ethical protocols, a common system to identify and trace the samples and a common quality control programme, all of which was accepted by consensus.

During this period the RTICC network has provided more than 10,000 samples for approximately 180 projects, which have generated at the same time more than 10 articles (with an average impact of 7 points) and which cite the network biobanks as the source of their samples.

The international influence of the so called «Spanish design» for biobanks described above should be stressed. It is constantly involved in the main scientific forums, through: participants being invited to give papers at numerous sector and general conventions and meetings; active participation in international scientific societies in the sector (the International Society for Biological and Environmental Repositories – ISBER); participation in international expert groups (Marble Arch International Working Group in Biobanking), and participation in study groups focused on sponsoring international biobank programmes (TuBaFrosT, Europa contra el Cáncer, BBMRI, P3G, etc.)

1.2.3. Network Biobanks (for example, the Fundación BIO Bank)

http://www.bioef.org

The Basque Biobank for Research (O + Ehun) was provided with a network structure by the BIO Foundation. The participants in this are: the six public Basque hospitals (Cruces, Donostia, Basurto, Galdakao, Txagorritxu, and Santiago Apóstol); the Basque Centre for Transfusions and Human Tissues in Osakidetza; the Instituto Oncológico de San Sebastián private clinic, and the Policlínica Gipuzkoa private clinic. Each nodule of the Biobank collects, processes, and stores biological samples, all coordinated through a computing platform under the direction of the Fundación BIO. This acts as the coordinating nodule and carries out the management of samples, the coordination of procedures and quality criteria and cooperation with other state and foreign centres.

Two characteristics differentiate the Basque Biobank, in comparison to the old «tissue banks» and hospital sample collections for research. Firstly, the specific network structure includes practically the entire autonomous community. Secondly, resources are supplied which are primarily focused on providing support to doctors. These doctors have enough interest in science to occasionally stop their routine medical care and obtain biological samples for the research carried out by others. The Fundación BIO promotes the recognition of the supporting role of the doctor as the provider of the fundamental components of all scientific research : the medical knowledge and the biological samples.

The first part of the Basque Biobank, the DNA section, started to become a reality in 2004. Currently it has completed all the structural development of all its sections. The biobank design was preceded by, and supported for a long time by, a close relationship with the Fundación BIO and the Bioethics and Human Genome Department at the University of Deusto, by visits to different centres in autonomous communities and by the creation of biobanks in foreign countries.

The Basque Biobank has already participated in approximately 60 health service-university-company research projects, having transferred more than 8,000 biological samples to the scientific-technological community.

Finally, it is worth emphasising that the Basque Biobank for Research, in addition to serving as a tool for the world health field, contributes innovation in the country's productive sector, while also producing its own innovations.

1.2.4. *National banks (for example, BNADN the National Cell Lines Bank)*

a) *The National DNA Bank (BNADN) (www.bancoadn.org)*

is a technological support programme for biomedical research created at the beginning of 2004 by the Fundación Genoma España (the Spanish Genome Foundation), with the purpose of strengthening the development of genome research in Spain. The BNADN, structured as a central node with four nodes for diseases (cardiovascular, metabolic, neuropsychiatric, and oncological) has become a benchmark biobank in Spain for the collection, storing, and management of DNA samples.

The BNADN was officially established on March 16, 2004 when the agreement for its establishment was signed between the Fundación Genoma España, the Health Council of Castilla and Leon and the University of Salamanca. During the first phase of development the BNADN created a DNA sample collection representative of the healthy population resident in Spain, as well as relevant information related to the samples, such as the health condition and lifestyle habits of the donors. The central node of the BNADN (legally part of the University of Salamanca) is located in the Salamanca Cancer Research Centre. To carry out their work, they have signed several cooperation agreements with different regional transfusion Centres and hospital blood banks, as well as with the Fibromyalgia and Chronic Fatigue Syndrome Foundations.

In October 2006, starting with an expansion meeting sponsored by the Fundación Genoma España, the BNADN incorporated into its structure 4 new nodes which will be responsible for collecting DNA samples from patients diagnosed with the most prevalent diseases in Spain (diseases such as cardiovascular, metabolic and neuropsychiatric disease and cancer). These nodes are mainly based in hospitals.

The mission of the National DNA Bank is to receive, process, and store DNA samples, plasma, and cells from volunteer donors, as well as information related to the health and lifestyle of the donors of the samples. The DNA samples and the related information correspond to donors that represent the population resident in Spain. These are made available to the scientific community in order to facilitate, promote, and develop national and international scientific research regarding human evolution, genetic/genome diversity in relation to health and the origin of diseases and their treatments.

b) *The National Stem Cell Lines Bank*

The National Stem Cell Lines Bank is configured as a network structure with several nodes, coordinated by a central node (RD 2132/04 and SCO/393/06), the objective of which shall be to guarantee the availability of human embryo and adult stem cells for biomedical research across Spain. The Cell Lines Bank is attached to the Subdirección General de Investigación en Terapia Celular y Medicina Regenerativa (Deputy General Directorate of Cell Therapy and Regenerative Medicine Research) at the Instituto de Salud Carlos III. Currently there are three nodes, one in Barcelona, another in Valencia, and the central node is located in Granada.

2. – LEGAL FRAMEWORK

2.1. – *General applicable legislation*

On 3 July 2007 Law 14/2007 on Biomedical Research in Spain (LIB) was approved. This Law devotes its Title V to: «Genetic analysis, biological samples, and biobanks.» This title is divided in four chapters: I. General provisions, II. Genetic analysis and treatment of personal genetic information, III. Use of human biological samples with the purpose of biomedical research, and IV. Biobanks.

This specific legislation establishes that Law 41/2002 of 14 November shall be a supplementary law, a basic regulator of patient autonomy and the rights and obligations in regard to clinical information and documents, as long as it is not incompatible with the principles in this Law and Organic Law 15/1999 of 13 December, on the Protection of Personal Information (Final Provision, Article 2).

Law 41/2002 refers to the implementation of the patient's right of autonomy and regulates the requirement for prior consent for procedures in health care and in the clinical history recording system. It is important to underline that it establishes how the right to access to information related to health is to be exercised. It maintains the general duty of health professionals to maintain confidentiality, and the need to implement the measures necessary to ensure adequate preservation of documentation (with reference to the provisions in the law regarding the protection of personal information).

Law 15/1999 is the transposition of European Directive 45/46/EC. It establishes the principle of the protection of personal information and a specific, strengthened system for certain especially protected information, amongst which is information regarding health. The regulation that implements this law defines information of a personal nature related to health as «information concerning the past, present and future physical or mental health of an individual. In particular, it includes information related to the health of individuals that refers to their percentage disability or genetic information about them» (Article 5.1 g). It is worth pointing out that this regulation refers to: the need for explicit and prior consent to process information of a personal nature related to health;

the procedures through which to exercise the right to access, rectify, object to or cancel personal information, and the guarantee of the records safety, including the need to implement a series of technical measures which vary according to the information in question. In the case of information related to health (such as genetic information) these measures are more demanding.

The indications for the supplementary application of this law in matters regulated by the LIB [Biomedical Research Law] are of great importance, given that biological samples are not in themselves information but rather «information carriers.» As such, initially these were not covered by this regulation. They were explained more fully in the reference of the law to the final provision, article 2.

2.2. – Specific law

2.2.1. Law 14/2007 of 3 July on biomedical research

The LIB acknowledges that biomedical research and health sciences are key tools to improving the quality of life and life expectancy of people and increasing their well being, and that biomedical research and health sciences have substantially changed both methodologically and conceptually in the last few years.

Specifically, it emphasises that the collection, use, storage, and transfer of biological samples for diagnostic and research purposes has increased significantly, and that ethical and legal uncertainties have been created that have to be properly regulated.

The LIB has attempted to respond to the challenges that biomedical research raises in general and particularly in relation to human biological samples, and to establish an adequate framework for the exploitation of the results for the benefit of the health and well being of society. The LIB has established a regulatory framework to respond to the new scientific challenges, and at the same time guarantee the protection of the rights of individuals who could be affected. In that spirit, one of the key purposes of this law is to ensure fundamental human rights, together with other related legal rights acknowledged in Spanish Law, and particularly prominent in the Constitution of the European Council's Convention on Biomedicine, are respected and protected. Consequently, the Law declares that the health, interests and well being of any human being that participates in biomedical research prevail over the interests of society or science.

This law is fundamental in nature, which means that it will be subject to regulatory implementation by the autonomous communities within the scope of their jurisdiction, and by the central government in specific matters. In particular, among other matters, the development of regulations are expected regarding: the internal, intra-communitarian and extra-communitarian exchange of biological material of human origin for research; the basic requirements for accreditation and authorisation of the centres, services, and biomedical equipment related to the collection and use of any biological material of human origin for biomedical research, and the operation and organisation of the National Biobanks Registry for Biomedical Research (Final Provision, Article 3).

The Biomedical Research Law (LIB) defines biological samples as «any biological material of human origin that is susceptible to conservation and that may contain information about a person's genetic characteristics» (Art. 3 o)).

Whole human organs must be excluded from this definition if they are not susceptible to preservation (2) while maintaining their «structure, vascularisation, and capacity to develop physiological functions with a significant degree of autonomy,» elements which are essential to their definition as organs. If this requirement is missing, there is no obstacle to considering them as human tissue (3) and, in short, as biological samples for our purposes.

Similarly, the concept of biological sample must exclude gametes given that these do not contain an individual's complete genetic information. Human embryos and foetuses must also be excluded, since biological samples are part of the human body, differentiated and separated from the body. However, the cells and tissues that can be extracted from these are included in this concept.

---

(2) EUROPEAN GROUP ON ETHICS IN SCIENCE AND NEW TECHNOLOGIES, *Opinion on ethical aspects of human tissue banking*, 1998, section 1.5.

(3) Tissues are «all the constituent parts of the human body formed by cells». Directive 2004/23/CE (Art.3.b).

In order to analyse the legal system that applies to biological samples, their double nature must be considered (4): on the one hand, they are biological elements, on the other, they are information carriers. It is fitting to ask about their ability to be considered as biological elements separate from the human body. Regarding their condition as information carriers, it is necessary to analyse the possible application of this to the principles of protection of personal information.

2.2.2. The legal framework that applies to Biobanks in the case of biomedical research

The LIB distinguishes between collections of samples and biobanks, and acknowledges the latter as agencies qualified to provide support for research, and whose existence and development the law wants to promote.

A specific framework for these facilities is established in chapter four of Title V of this Law. In addition, the Final Provision, Article 3 of the Law provides for the implementation of the regulations, and among other matters the basic requirements for accreditation and authorisation of the centres, services, and biomedical equipment related to the collection and use of any biological material of human origin for biomedical research, and the operation and organisation of the National Biobanks Registry for Biomedical Research.

A biobank for medical research is a public or private, non-profit institution that accepts one or several biological sample collections destined for biomedical research, organised by a technical unit with quality assurance criteria, order, and purpose, regardless of whether it stores samples for other reasons.

It must have a specific organisation, internal regulation, be authorised, and be registered in the National Biobanks Registry, which will soon be created.

---

(4) NICOLÁS JIMÉNEZ, Pilar, «Los derechos del paciente sobre su muestra biológica: distintas opiniones jurisprudenciales (The Rights of patients over their biological samples: different legal opinions)», *Revista de Derecho y Genoma Humano (Journal of the Law and the Human Genome)*, nº 19 (2003), pp. 208 and 218; the same author, *La protección jurídica de los datos genéticos de carácter personal (The legal protection of personal genetic information)*, Inter-University Department of Law and the Human Genome-Comares, Bilbao-Granada, 2006, p. 337. The double nature of biological samples is also commented on by KAYE, Jane, «Do we need a uniform regulatory system for biobanks across Europe?», *European Journal of Human Genetics*, nº 14 (2006), p. 247.

Regarding organisation, the biobank must have a director, a scientific director, and file supervisor. It will be affiliated with two external committees, one scientific and the other ethical that will advise the scientific director on its functions, and will evaluate requests by the biobank to transfer samples and information relating to them.

The biobank will draft its own regulation, which will contain at a minimum the following:

a) The requirement to formalise by agreement consent to the transfer of samples or collection of samples.

b) The criteria for accepting samples at the biobank.

c) The procedure through which researchers can request samples from the biobank

d) The administrative procedure for requesting samples from the biobank.

e) The general criteria for refusing the provision of samples to researchers. Such refusal must be justified in each case.

Gaining authorisation to establish a biobank is mandatory and is the responsibility of the autonomous communities or general state administration, as appropriate. In order to grant authorisation, it will assess whether the aim of the biobank is of scientific interest, and whether the organisational conditions required are being met, as well as whether the biobank is complying with other requirements established by law. It is expected that through an initiative from the Health Ministry and as a result of general interest national biobanks will be created. The autonomous communities can take similar initiatives, in particular with the aim of providing biobanks where they are lacking, within the territorial limits of the autonomous community.

Finally, it is stipulated that the autonomous authorities or the general state administration, as appropriate, will conduct inspections and control the activities of the biobanks in order to ensure compliance with the provisions of the law. When appropriate, it may be determined that the biobank must be shut down or closed, with instructions on where the collection stored by biobank is to be rehoused.

2.3. – Reports and opinions from different national institutions and other organisations

There have been very few documents from national institutions in Spain regarding the ethical and legal implications of the use of biological samples for biomedical research. It is worth stressing that the Spanish Bioethical Committee was officially established on October 22, 2008, in compliance with the provision in Article 77 and others of the LIB, and that up to that time there was no institution in Spain in charge of issuing reports or recommendations on matters related to the ethical and social implications of biomedicine and health sciences.

The Fundación Insituto Roche [Roche Institute Foundation] for integrated public health solutions issued in 2006 the «Practical Guide for the Use of Biological Samples for Biomedical Research» (5), which was presented at the headquarters of the Health and Consumer Ministry. That document, drafted by a multidisciplinary work team, gathered together in a comprehensive manner all the legal, ethical, and technical requirements recommended for the entire procedure for using samples.

Another interesting document is the document published in 2006 (6) by the Bioethical Committee of Catalonia and endorsed by the Council for Health of the Catalan Government regarding the «ethical problems of storing and using biological samples». This publication was also the result of multidisciplinary work and contains some interesting recommendations.

In addition, some ethical research committees have published recommendations to guide researchers in their use of this material, and to draft the information sheet and consent form for the donor. It is worth mentioning the «recommendations regarding ethical aspects of the human material sample collections or banks for biomedical research» from the Ethics Committee of the Rare Disease Research Institute (CEIIER) of the Instituto de Salud Carlos III (Ministry of Science and Innovation), dated 27 February, 2007 (7).

---

(5) http://www.institutoroche.es/actividades2.php?ap=jornadas&taula=jornadas&id=48.
(6) http://www.gencat.cat/salut/depsalut/pdf/mostresbio01.pdf.
(7) http://www.isciii.es/htdocs/centros/enfermedadesraras/pdf/Muestras_rev_Esp_PS1.pdf.

The information sheet and consent form drafted by the Ethics research committee of the Basque Country is also interesting (8), as are the guidelines for evaluating requests to collect and store biological samples in order to conduct genetic studies during clinical trials involving medicine (9), by the Clinic of Navarra Ethics Research Committee.

There is no substantial difference between the criteria recommended in these documents, and as a fundamental point in all of them it is worth mentioning the importance they give to the need for informed consent by the subject, as the fundamental requirement for the use of the samples.

2.4. – *Institutions and professionals: standards of quality and accreditation requirements*

There is a provision for the regulatory implementation to establish b) «the basic requirements for accreditation and authorisation of biomedical centres, services, and equipment related to the collection and use of any biological material of human origin for biomedical research» (final provision, Article 3 b of the LIB). This regulation establishes the conditions required to store the material, as well as the professional requirements for personnel at the centres.

In addition, in the case of genetic analyses conducted in the health field, it is stipulated that the entire genetic counselling process and analyses be conducted by qualified personnel in accredited centres that meet the quality requirements that are established for that purpose by the regulation (Article 56).

2.5. – *Ethical research committees*

As stated in Article 62 of the LIB, in order to conduct a research project with human biological samples, it is essential to have approval from the Ethics research committee (CEI) of the centre that will be conducting the research.

In Spain, the proceedings of the Ethical Clinical Research Committees (ECRCs) are regulated by Royal Decree (RD 223/2004 of

---

(8) http://www.euskadi.net/r33-2732/es/contenidos/informacion/comite_etico/es_8123/adjuntos/Modelo_de_consentimiento_genérico_para_cesión_de_muestras_biológicas_para_investigación_versión_13_2_09.pdf.

(9) http://www.cfnavarra.es/salud/docencia.investigacion/textos/normas_ceic_genetica.pdf.

6 February, and by Law 29/2006 of 26 July, on guarantees and rational use of medicines and health products. In addition, the autonomous communities have developed their own regulations.

These Committees are authorised to evaluate the ethical and legal aspects of conducting a clinical trial with medicines or health products.

However, the Third Transitional Provision of Law 14/2007 establishes that «Ethical Clinical Research Committees will cease to exist starting from the moment when the Ethical Research Committees are established. Until these Committees are established, the Ethical Clinical Research Committees that are operating at centres that conduct biomedical research can assume the jurisdiction of the centres.» Currently, work is being done to prepare a law that will make reference to this adaptation process.

Article 12 of the LIB concisely establishes the requirements that ERCs must comply with, which will be developed in the corresponding regulation, and which basically coincide with the provisions for the current ECRCs in operation:

– They must be duly accredited by the competent authority in the corresponding autonomous community or, in the case of the centres controlled by the General State Administration by their competent authority, so as to ensure independence and impartiality. For accreditation, at least some of the following criteria will be considered: the independence and impartiality of their members in relation to biomedical research project promoters and researchers, as well as their interdisciplinary composition. The competent authorities will be able to decide to create research ethics committees that will carry out their activities in two or more centres that are conducting biomedical research.

– The Ethics research committee for the centre shall exercise the following functions:

a) Evaluating the qualifications of the principal researcher and the research team, as well as the feasibility of the project.

b) Considering the methodology, as well as the ethical and legal aspects of the research.

c) Assessing the balance of risks and expected benefits resulting from the study.

d) Overseeing compliance with procedures that ensure the traceability of samples of human origin, without prejudice to the provisions in the protection of personal information law.

e) Reporting, with prior assessment of the research project, all biomedical research that involves interventions in human beings or the use of biological samples of human origin, without prejudice to other reports that must be issued. It cannot authorise or develop research projects without prior approval from the ethics research committee.

f) Developing guidelines for good practice in accordance with the principles established by the Bioethics Committee of Spain, and processing the conflicts and disciplinary action that non-compliance may generate.

g) Coordinating their activities with other similar committees in other institutions.

h) Ensuring confidentiality and exercising any other functions that may be assigned by regulations developed by the LIB.

– The members of the ethics research committees must submit a statement of activities and interests, and shall abstain from taking part in deliberations and votes in which they have a direct or indirect interest in the matter under evaluation.

2.6. – *Collection of samples (invasive intervention)*

2.6.1. *General arrangements*

The invasive procedure to collect a sample and the subsequent procedures of use, as well as the consents that must be obtained are two different issues, even though both can take place at the same time and all the information is obtained through one single procedure.

An invasive procedure is understood to be «any intervention conducted for the purpose of research and which involves a physical or psychological risk for the affected subject (letter t, Article 3, of the LIB). Categorising a procedure as invasive does not depend on whether the risk is minimal or remote. Therefore, for example, taking blood must be considered as an invasive procedure.

If an invasive procedure involves a higher risk, the research cannot be performed. In effect the LIB establishes that the effects on health and the discomfort that the participating subjects can suffer during research can only be mild and temporary in nature (Article 3 u of the LIB).

In short, obtaining biological samples for research through an invasive procedure requires a risk evaluation, and in addition written consent from the subject, preceded by the information detailed in Article 50 of the LIB being given both orally and in writing, namely:

a) The purpose of the research or line of research for which consent is given.

b) Expected benefits (both for the donor and for society). Potential economic benefits for the researcher, which may result from the research or which they hope to obtain from it.

c) Potential inconveniences associated with the donation and collection of samples, including the possibility of subsequently being contacted for the purpose of obtaining new data or to get new samples.

d) The identity of the person responsible for the research.

e) The right to revoke the consent and the effects of that, including the possibility of destroying the sample or making it anonymous.

Such effects shall not be extended to the data that results from the research which has already taken place.

f) The place where analysis will be performed and the destination of the sample at the end of the research: dissociation, destruction, or other research, as the case may be, will also require compliance with all requirements stipulated in this law. In the event that these actions are not known of at that time, an agreement will be established to provide notice of them as soon as they become known.

g) The right to know the genetic information that is obtained from the analysis of the donated samples.

h) Ensuring the confidentiality of the information obtained, indicating the identity of the individuals who will have access to the donor's personal information.

i) The possibility of information being obtained regarding their health from the genetic analysis that will be conducted on the biological sample, as well as their right to choose whether or not to be given this information. The donor must also be warned of the implications for their family of the information that may be obtained and the advisability of the donor giving them this information if appropriate.

In addition, it is appropriate to also inform the donor about the following: the sample should be freely given (without prejudice to possible compensation which may be deemed appropriate); the individual does not have any economic rights should there be any financial gains resulting from the research; the source of financing for the research project (10); the individual or his/her family can use the same samples should it be necessary for health reasons (Art. 58.4 of the LIB); in the event the sample is preserved, the conditions of the preservation, objectives, future uses, transfer to third parties, and conditions to be able to withdraw it or request that it be destroyed (Art. 61.1 of the LIB).

If the biological samples are submitted to a process of anonymity then the donor, will receive only the information included in a), b), c), and d) of Article 59, referred to above. In addition, the donor must be informed that in that case it will not be possible to withdraw consent since it will not be possible to link the sample with his or her identity.

In addition, in general Spain has established that for all invasive research there is a prior obligation to insure for damages that could derive from it to the individuals on whom it is performed (Article 18.2), and compensation for damages suffered as a consequence of their participation in the research project (Article 18.1) (11).

---

(10) Cf. Art. 15.2.i) LIB.

(11) In addition, «if for any circumstance the insurance does not fully cover the damages caused, the research developer, researchers responsible for the research, and the hospital or centre where it was conducted will jointly be liable for the damages, even if not guilty, bearing the burden of proof. Neither the administrative authorisation nor approval from the Ethics research committee will exempt them from liability» (Article 18.3 LIB).

«It is assumed, unless otherwise proven, that the damages that affect the health of the individual who was the subject of the research, while it was performed, and during the year following its conclusion, have been produced as a consequence of the research. However, once the year ends, the subject of the research will be required to prove damage and the connection between the research and the damaged caused» (Article 18.4 LIB).

2.6.2. Children or people with a disability

When children or people with a disability are involved, sample collection is subject to some specific requirements:

According to Art. 58.5 of the LIB «the collection of biological samples from children and people with a disability for biomedical research shall be subject to the following conditions: a) the necessary steps will be taken to guarantee that the risk from the procedure is minimal for the donor; b) that from the research significant knowledge can be obtained about the disease or situation that is the object of the research that is of vital importance to understanding, alleviating, or treating it; c) that this knowledge cannot be obtained by any other means; and d) that the legal representative of the child or the person with the disability has given their authorisation, or if appropriate, there are guarantees regarding proper consent from the donor.»

2.6.3. Collection from a cadaver

The LIB has not regulated in a specific manner the system of obtaining samples from cadavers for biomedical research. In the regulation developed, which has not yet been approved, there is provision for an extraction system similar to that used for organs, cells, and tissues for transplant. The extraction can be conducted in the event that the subject authorised it while alive, or when the subject did not leave an explicit statement of opposition. For this purpose, the family members of the deceased, the professionals that treated the individual at the hospital, any documented previous instructions, and in all cases, the National Advance Directives Registry will all be consulted.

In the case of samples taken from cadavers, prior agreement will also be required from the biobank and the care centre where the death took place, or the relevant undertaker, institute of forensic medicine, or morgue.

2.6.4. Use of gametes, pre-embryos, embryos, and foetuses

Given that the use of gametes, pre-embryos, embryos, and foetuses is a matter that is outside the scope of the LATINBANKS Project, this subject will not be dealt with in detail in this report. However, the following points are noted:

a) *Chapter I of Title III of the LIB (Arts. 28 and 29) cover the donation of embryos and human foetuses, and their biological structures*

Human embryos that have lost their biological capacity to develop, and dead human embryos or foetuses, can be donated for biomedical research or other diagnostic, therapeutic, pharmaceutical, clinical, or surgical purposes. Foetuses that are prematurely or spontaneously expelled shall be clinically treated while they are biologically viable, with the purpose of fostering their development and independent life. Measures are established to ensure that the interruption of pregnancy will never have the donation, and subsequent use of embryos or foetuses or their biological structures as the end purpose.

The following are requirements for the donation to take place:

a) That the donor or donors of the embryos or foetuses have granted prior written and explicit consent. If the donor is a minor or a person with a disability, the legal representatives' consent will also be needed.

b) That before granting their consent, the donor or donors, or if appropriate, their legal representatives were informed in writing regarding the purpose for which the donation may be used, the consequences of the same, as well as the interventions that will be performed to extract the cells of embryological or foetal structures, the placenta or the placental lining, and the risks that may result from said interventions.

c) That the embryos or foetuses from pregnant women were either expelled spontaneously or induced, and it was not possible to maintain independent life.

d) That the donation and subsequent use should never have financial or commercial purposes.

In the event that the embryos or foetuses come from women who have died, it is necessary to ensure that there is no record of their explicit opposition to their use. If the deceased was a child or person with a disability, the donation will take place unless there is a record of explicit opposition from those who, during the life of the deceased, acted as their legal representatives.

b) *The legal regulations governing the use of gametes and pre-embryos for biomedical research in Spain are included in Law 14/2007 on Biomedical Research and Law 14/2006 regarding assisted human reproductive procedures.*

Donation for research purposes is among the different potential destinations given for surplus cryopreserved pre-embryos arising from assisted reproductive procedures, semen, ovocytes or cryopreserved ovarian tissues. (Article 11.4 of Law 14/2006).

The fertilisation of human ovules for any purpose other than human procreation is prohibited (Art. 160.2 of the Criminal Code)

Research or experimentation with surplus ovocytes or pre-embryos that come from assisted reproductive procedures must comply with the following requirements (Article 34 of the LIB):

- That there is duly authorised informed consent. In the case of pre-embryos, the consent must have been given by the woman, or in the case of a woman married to a man, also by the husband prior to the generation of pre-embryos.
- That the research respects the ethical principles of the applicable legal framework, and complies with the principles of appropriateness, feasibility and suitability. These principles should also apply to the principal researcher, the research team, and the facilities in the centre in which the research will be conducted.
- That it is based on a research project that is authorised by the state authorities or the relevant autonomous government, with a prior report of approval from the Committee for the Safeguard of the Donation and Use of Human Cells and Tissues.

2.7. – *Ownership of the sample*

The LIB does not explicitly make declarations about the ownership of biological samples and the eventual exercise of ownership rights over these. However, it does establish an indirect legal statute by regulating its treatment. From this legal framework definitive conclusions about the ownership of samples cannot be drawn.

Regarding the transfer of biological samples for research purposes, the strict regulation contained in the LIB raises serious doubts as to whether this really implies a transfer of ownership, which in all cases would be free of charge (a donation) (12). According to Art. 58.4, «if for health reasons the donor or family needs the samples, they may use them, as long as they are available and they are not anonymised.» This provision in itself is not an obstacle to understanding that donating a sample free of charge implies a transfer of the ownership of the sample. A specific legal clause revoking the donation could simply be established as happens with the donation of other biological material (13). On the contrary, the existence of this provision can lead to an understanding that in effect the donation has resulted in a transfer of property. If it were not so, it would make no sense to establish a specific revocation clause. In addition, the fact that the law uses the term «donation» at all times cannot be overlooked. However, in Art. 60.3 the LIB poses some doubts in that regards. According to this provision, «consent (to transfer biological samples) can be revoked either fully or for certain specific purposes at any time. If the withdrawal of consent refers to any use of the sample, the destruction of the sample will immediately follow.» Indeed, this provision can generate doubts regarding the transfer of the sample if it does lead to the transfer of ownership (14). In the event that the sample is the researcher's property, the will of the donor would not entail a right over it as a material object but rather only over the consequences of its use, insofar as these affect the donor (since they are sources of personal information). That is to say, the new owner (the researcher or hospital) could refuse to destroy and continue using or storing the sample after it was subjected to an anonymisation process (15). In that case the donor would only have the capacity to

---

(12) Cf. arts. 7.I, 45. c) and 58.3 LIB.

(13) Cf. Art. 5.2 of Law 14/2006 of 26 May, on assisted reproductive procedures : «The donation can only be revoked if the donor needs the donated gametes for herself, as long as on the date of revocation these are still available. After the revocation the donor will reimburse any kind of expenses incurred by the receiving centre.»

(14) For DIAZ MARTINEZ, Ana, «Harm caused during biomedical research and the performance of genetic studies : conduct and omissions that determine liability and lead to the payment of compensation», *Diario La Ley*, September 19, 2007, p. 4, under no circumstances would sample ownership go to the centre to which it was transferred. However, this argument is not based on the provision in the LIB but rather in the understanding that property rights do not apply to biological samples.

(15) Cf. ANGOITIA GOROSTIAGA, Victor, «Extracción de órganos y de tejidos de donantes vivos con fines de trasplante y prohibición de lucro y utilización de una parte del cuerpo humano (Capítulos VI y VII)», (Extraction of organs and tissues from live donors for transplant purposes and the prohibition of profit and use of a part of the human body (Chapters VI and VII) in Carlos María ROMEO CASABONA (ed.), *El Convenio de Derechos Humanos y Biomedicina : su entrada*

decide in regard to the identified use of the sample, given that other types of rights would be affected.

In accordance with the above, it could be argued that the transfer of ownership of biological samples would only be possible if it was transferred as an anonymous sample and only in that instance could one properly argue that the sample had been «abandoned». Otherwise, the sample assignee (hospital, researcher, biobank, etc) would only be a holder of the sample, with the capacity to use it according to legal provision and, where appropriate, contractual provision (in the terms expressed by the assignor when giving consent) (16).

Regardless of whether the right to ownership of the sample is acknowledged, which would allow it to be used, and regardless of whether or not the biological sample donated for biomedical research purposes implies a transfer of property to a third party, this would not resolve in and of itself all the problems, given the particular characteristics of this material. In effect, with regard to the material object, the sample is a thing that is subject to legal transactions (without prejudice to the restrictions that have been established). However, it is an information carrier of great importance, which poses certain additional questions, such as for example, whether the handing over of the sample to a third party eliminates the donor's capacity to control the sample. For that reason, it is not very productive conducting an interpretation of the provisions in the LIB in terms of ownership of the biological sample, which as we have been able to observe, leads us to a dead end. On the contrary, the legal framework governing this must be analysed from the perspective of the sample's condition as a highly sensitive carrier or source of personal information.

Furthermore, even if we could incontrovertibly establish who is the owner of the biological sample (should there be one), many of

---

en vigor en el ordenamiento jurídico español, (The Convention of Human Rights and Biomedicine: its integration into Spanish law) Cátedra de Derecho y Genoma Humano-Comares,(Department of Law and the Human Genome-Comares), Bilbao-Granada, 2002, pp and ff. 314 and; NICOLÁS JIMÉNEZ, Pilar, *La protección jurídica de los datos genéticos de carácter personal*, (The legal protection of personal genetic data) Cátedra Interuniversitaria de Derecho y Genoma Humano-Comares, (The Interuniversity Department of Law and the Human Genome-Comares), Bilbao-Granada, 2006, p. 358, note 228.

(16) That is also the position of the European Society of Human Genetics, Recommendations on data storage and DNA banking for biomedical research: *technical, social and ethical issues*, 2001, Recommendation 27, paragraphs a) and b).

the practical effects that would traditionally go along with property rights become secondary with regard to its treatment. This happens, for example, with the destruction or loss of the sample as a result of a lack of due care.

2.8. – Protection of the donor's privacy (obligation of confidentiality and the security of data files and samples)

When using biological samples for biomedical research the right to privacy and self-determination regarding information must be respected. These are fundamentally different rights even though at times they converge (17).

2.8.1. *Application of the rules regarding the protection of personal data*

a) *The reasons for applying the rules regarding the protection of personal data*

Regardless of the legal status granted to personal biological samples, where their use involves obtaining personal data, the use of these samples will in all cases be subject to Organic Law 15/1999 of 13 December, on Personal Data Protection (LOPD) (18) In addition, one must bear in mind that the information obtained from biological sample analysis is health information, that is, information that is particularly sensitive and subject to special guarantees. However, it should not be ignored that when biological samples are used in biomedical research, these will usually be accompanied by the patient's medical information (the patient's disease and the treatment provided, etc.) The greater the information that accom-

---

(17) As Articles 45 and 5.1 of the LIB warn, when biological samples for biomedical research are used, the principles related to protection of personal information must be guaranteed. The principle of the donor's right to privacy and the duty of confidentiality are summarised in chapter II, on the use of genetic information, where a system is established to be applied to the use of samples and biobanks.

(18) *See.* ROMEO CASABONA, Carlos María, «Utilización de muestras biológicas y bancos para la investigación biomédica», (The use of biological samples and biobanks for biomedical research) *IV Congreso Mundial de Bioética*. (IV World Bioethics Congress) *Ponencias y comunicaciones*, (Papers and Articles) Sociedad Internacional de Bioética, (International Bioethics Society), Gijón, 2005, pp. 85 and ff., where he states that «there are two relevant aspects of biological samples : the sample system in itself, in regard to the material element, and the personal genetic information that it carries ...»

panies the sample, the greater its usefulness and the greater the return obtained from it.

Therefore, the above is completely understandable in the sense that the treatment of personal samples must be governed by the same regulations that govern sensitive personal data (19). It must be remembered that the samples are the physical media from which sensitive personal data is obtained and it is logical that similar guarantees be demanded for the treatment of these samples.

The Organic Law on Personal Data Protection (LOPD) that implements the fundamental law for the protection of data is very clear in regard to the scope of its application. Art. 2.1 of the LOPD states that «the current Organic Law shall apply to personal information registered in physical media, which may be susceptible to treatment, and all subsequent modalities of use of that information by public and private sectors.» That is to say, the principles of data protection only apply to the data, and not to the media that contains it or from which data is or could be extracted (20).

The LIB regulates the treatment of biological samples for research (in Chapter III of Title V), subjecting them to the system established in Chapter II of Title V on the treatment of personal genetic information.

In accordance with the LIB, biological samples can be categorised into one of the following three categories (in a parallel with

---

(19) *See.* ROMEO CASABONA, Carlos María, «Utilización de muestras biológicas y bancos para la investigación biomédica», (The use of biological samples and biobanks for biomedical research) *IV Congreso Mundial de Bioética.* (IV World Bioethics Congress) *Ponencias y comunicaciones,* (Papers and Articles) Sociedad Internacional de Bioética, (International Bioethics Society), Gijón, 2005, pp. 87 and ff NICOLÁS JIMÉNEZ, Pilar, «Los derechos del paciente sobre su muestra biológica: distintas opiniones jurisprudenciales», (Patients' Rights over their biological samples: different legal opinions), *Revista de Derecho y Genoma Humano, (The Journal of Law and the Human Genome),* nº 19 (2003), p. 217 («la muestra es objeto de los principios de la protección de datos de carácter personal») (the sample is the object of the principles of personal data protection); MARTÍN URANGA, Amelia, MARTÍN-ARRIBAS, Mª Concepción, DI DONATO, Jeanne-Hélène and POSADA DE LA PAZ, Manuel, *Las cuestiones ético-jurídicas más relevantes en relación con los biobancos,* (The most relevant ethical-legal questions in relation to biobanks), Instituto de Salud Carlos III-Ministerio de Sanidad y Consumo, (Carlos III Health Institute-Ministry of Health and Consumption), Madrid, 2005, p. 21 («Los principios de protección de datos de carácter personal deben regir por analogía en la utilización y trasvase de muestras») (The principles of personal data protection must be governed through analogy with the use and transfer of samples).

(20) In that same sense, see. NICOLÁS JIMÉNEZ, Pilar, «Los derechos del paciente sobre su muestra biológica: distintas opiniones jurisprudenciales», (The rights of patients over their biological samples: different legal opinions), *Revista de Derecho y Genoma Humano,* (The Journal of Law and the Human Genome), nº 19 (2003), p. 221; DATA PROTECTION WORKING PARTY, *Opinion 4/2007 on the concept of personal data,* 20 June 2007, p. 9.

the categorisation used in relation to personal information), depending on the degree of likelihood of identifying the person from whom the sample came: a) biological samples associated with an identified person; b) biological samples associated with an identifiable person; and c) anonymous biological samples.

Samples associated with an identified person are those that are clearly and directly associated with the person from whom they were obtained.

Samples associated with an identifiable person are samples that are not directly attributed to a specific person, since they are not directly or indirectly identified. However, the connection between the sample and the person is possible through different mechanisms, which can be easily put into practice. The LIB describes *coded biological samples or reversibly dissociated samples,* which it defines as «samples that are not associated with an identified or identifiable person since the information that could identify the donor was substituted or detached using a code that allows the procedure to be reversed.» (Art. 3.r of the LIB).

Finally, *anonymous samples* are those in which the identity of the source subject is unknown and identification is not possible since such samples have been obtained anonymously, or because even though they were obtained with an identification they have subsequently been anonymised. Hence the LIB distinguishes between *non-identifiable biological samples or anonymous* and *anonymised biological samples or irreversibly dissociated samples*. The former would be one that was «collected without contact with an identified or identifiable person whose origin, consequently, is unknown and it is impossible to trace their origin» (Art. 3. q) of the LIB). An *anonymised or irreversibly dissociated biological sample* is a «sample that cannot be associated with an identified or identifiable person since the connection with the information that identifies the subject was destroyed or because this association requires an unreasonable effort» (Art. 3. p) of the LIB) (21). The requirement of reasonable effort, once again, demonstrates the connection between personal

---

(21) Art. 3. c) LIB defines anonymisation of a biological sample as the process by which it stops being possible to establish by reasonable means the connection between the sample and subject to which it refers.

biological samples and personal information (22). If the measures are *not reasonable*, the person will not be considered as identifiable and the samples will be moved to the category of anonymous samples. Measures that require a disproportionate amount of time, expense, and work shall not be considered reasonable measures (23).

b) *The right to access and cancellation*

– Article 15 of the LOPD establishes that the interested party shall have the right to request and obtain personal data that was processed, the origin of this data, and the communication conducted or expected to be conducted about this data. However, Law 41/2002 regulates this right in regard to access to data related to medical history.

More specifically, the LIB establishes that the donor «shall be informed of the personal genetic data that will be obtained from the genetic analysis,» about which the subject will be informed, as previously stated, before granting consent for the samples to be used.

Several categories of information must be differentiated in relation to the exercise of this right:

Firstly, the subject has the right to access the general results of the research (Article 27 of the LIB).

Secondly, the subject will be informed of relevant health information that is obtained from the research, under the terms provided for in the subject's consent. In effect, the option to know or not know the results will be given to the subject before using the samples.

Thirdly, when it is information that is not relevant to the subject's health, the subject can request access to this information. Data that is not scientifically validated must be excluded, given that it should not be considered as «verifiable». (Consider for exam-

---

(22) Recital 26 of Directive 95/46/CE of 24 October 1995, relating to the protection of individuals and concerning the processing of personal data and its free circulation states that «to determine whether a person is identifiable all the means that could be reasonably used by the person responsible for handling the data and by any other people to identify the person must be taken into consideration». In relation to this according to principle 1 of Recommendation no. R (97) 5, of 13 February 1997, of the Committee of Ministers of the Council of Europe to member states on the *Protection of Medical Data* states «an individual will not be considered to be identifiable if identification requires an unreasonable amount of time and resources».

(23) Cf. Art. 3.i) LIB.

ple conclusions that are not definitive or are simply posed as a hypothesis).

– In regard to the power to revoke consent previously given, this is established in the LIB 4.3, and subsequently more specifically in relation to the use of biological samples for research. Thus Art. 60.3 establishes that «consent can be revoked fully or for certain specific purposes at any time. If the withdrawal of consent refers to any use of the sample, its destruction will immediately follow, without prejudice to the preservation of the information that results from the research, which was conducted previously.»

From the above it can be inferred that there could be a full or a partial withdrawal of consent thereby permitting the use of the sample in other types of research. However, if the donor wishes to recover the samples for health reasons, Art. 58.4 of the LIB states that, «if, for health reasons the donor or the family need the samples, they may use them as long as they are available and are not anonymised.»

Therefore, if the withdrawal of consent affects only the identification of the samples, these can be anonymised and continue being used for biomedical research. If to the contrary, the withdrawal of consent refers to any use whatsoever of the samples, these shall be destroyed.

The effects of the withdrawal of consent will not extend to the information that results from the research which has already been carried out (Article 59.1e).

c) *Security measures*

As stated above, the new regulation implemented by the LOPD (Royal Decree 1720/2007 of 21 December) explicitly includes genetic information in the same category as health information, which must be subjected to a high degree of security. In effect, «in addition to the basic and medium level measures, high level measures will be applied to the following files or processing of personal data : a) Those that refer to information regarding ideology, union membership, religion, beliefs, racial origin, health, or sexual lifestyle (Art. 81.3 of the regulation).

Title VII the regulation specifies the security measures for processing personal data (24). In addition, the Spanish Agency for the Protection of Data has drafted a «Security Guide,» that is available on their web page (25), to facilitate the work of the person responsible for the file and, where applicable, the individual in charge of data processing. In effect, according to Article 9 of the LOPD, «the person in charge of the file, and where applicable, the individual in charge of data processing, must adopt the technical and organisational measures needed to guarantee the security of personal data and avoid its modification, loss, unauthorised handling or use, taking into account the state of technology, the nature of the information stored, and the risks to which these are exposed, whether they come from human action, the physical medium, or nature.»

In short, these are the measures that must be applied according to the level of each category of information and the type of file (26).

	Basic level	Medium level	High level
THE PERSON RESPONSIBLE FOR SECURITY		The person responsible for the file must designate one or more security supervisors (it is not a delegation of responsibility.) The person responsible for security is in charge of coordinating and controlling the document measures.	

---

(24) This title is divided into four chapters : I. General provisions (Articles 79-87); Chapter II. From the security document (Article 88); Chapter III. Security measures that apply to files and electronic handling (with three sections that distinguish three levels, basic-article 89 to 94 –, medium – articles 95 to 100 –, and high – articles 101 to 104); Chapter IV. Security measures that apply to non-electronic files and processing (with three sections that distinguish the three levels, basic-article 105 to 108 –, medium – articles 109 to 110 –, and high – articles 111 to 114).

(25) https ://www.agpd.es/portalweb/canaldocumentacion/publicaciones/common/pdfs/guia_se guridad_datos_2008.pdf.

(26) Pages 10 to 12 of the Security Guide developed by the Spanish Agency for Data Protection.

	Basic level	Medium level	High level
PERSONNEL	Functions and obligations of different users or the profiles of the users clearly defined and documented. Definition of control functions and authorisations delegated by the person responsible for security. Dissemination among the personnel of the regulations that affect them and the consequences of non-compliance.		
INCIDENTS	Incidents register: Type, time it was detected, person notified, effects, and corrective measures Procedure to notify and manage events.	ONLY ELECTRONIC FILES Write out procedures to recover the data, person that recovers it, information restored, and if applicable, information recorded manually. Authorisation from the person responsible for the files to recover information.	
ACCESS CONTROL	Updated list of users and access authorised. Control of permitted access for each user according to the functions assigned. Mechanisms to prevent unauthorised access to information or resources. Grant permission to access data only to authorized personnel. Same conditions for external personnel with access to data resources.	ONLY ELECTRONIC FILES Control physical access to locations where the information systems are located.	ONLY ELECTRONIC FILES Access register: User, time, file, type of access, authorised or denied. Monthly review of the register by the person responsible for security. Kept for 2 years. This register is not necessary if the person responsible for the file is an individual or the sole user ONLY NON-ELECTRONIC FILES Control authorised access. Access identification for documents accessible by multiple users.
IDENTIFICATION AND VERIFICATION	ONLY ELECTRONIC FILES Personalised identification and verification. Procedure to assign and distribute passwords. Encrypted storage of passwords. Periodic change of password (<1 year).	ONLY ELECTRONIC FILES Limited number of repeated attempts by non-authorised individuals.	

	Basic level	Medium level	High level
MEDIA MANAGEMENT	Media inventory. Identification of the type of data it contains or labelling system. Restricted access to the place of storage. Authorisation of removal of media (including email) Measures to transport and destroy media.	ONLY ELECTRONIC FILES Register of media receipt and issuing : document or media, date, issuer/recipient, number, type of information, form of delivery, individual authorised to receive/issue.	ONLY ELECTRONIC FILES Confidential labelling system. Information encryption of distributed media. Information encryption in portable devices outside the facilities (avoid the use of devices that do not have encryption, or adopt alternative measures).
BACKUP COPIES	ONLY ELECTRONIC FILES Weekly backup copies. Procedure to generate backup copies and data recovery. Weekly verification of procedures. Data reconstruction starting from the last copy. Manual recording if applicable, if there is documentation that allows it. Tests with actual data Security copy and application of the corresponding security level.		ONLY ELECTRONIC FILES Backup copy and recovery procedures in a place other than where the equipment is located.
CRITERIA FOR FILING	ONLY ELECTRONIC FILES Filing of documents must be conducted according to the criteria that enable review and location, in order to guarantee the exercise of the right to Access, Correct, Cancel, and Object (ARCO)		
STORAGE	ONLY ELECTRONIC FILES Storage devices that have mechanisms that prevent opening by unauthorised users.		ONLY ELECTRONIC FILES Cabinets, filing cabinets for documents in areas with access protected by doors with locks.
MEDIA MANAGEMENT	ONLY ELECTRONIC FILES During the review or processing of documents, the person in charge of these must exercise due diligence and safeguard them to prevent unauthorised access.		
COPYING OR REPRODUCING			ONLY ELECTRONIC FILES Can only be carried out by authorised users. Destruction of unwanted copies.

	Basic level	Medium level	High level
AUDITING		At least every two years, internal or external. Must be carried out after substantial changes in the information systems with security repercussions. Verification and monitoring of the adapted measures. Report on the detection of deficiencies and proposed rectifications. Analysis by the person responsible for security and conclusions made by the person responsible for files.	
TELECOMMUNICATIONS			ONLY ELECTRONIC FILES Data transmission through encrypted electronic networks.
DOCUMENTATION TRANSFER			ONLY ELECTRONIC FILES Measures that prevent access or handling.

2.8.2. *The duty of confidentiality*

In regard to genetic information the LIB has taken into consideration the general obligation of biomedical professionals to maintain confidentiality both in the medical care and research fields. In effect, according to Article 51, «1. Staff who has access to genetic information during the exercise of their duties will be required to keep that information confidential at all times. Personal genetic information can only be revealed to third parties with explicit written consent from the person to whom that genetic information refers. If it is not possible to publish the results of the research without identifying the donor, such results will only be able to be published with their consent (...).» And according to Article 50: «1. Healthcare professionals at the centre or the facility where the clinical history of the patient is preserved shall have access to the information contained therein, as long as it is pertinent for the care provided to the patient, without prejudice to the obligation of protection and confidentiality to which they are subject. 2. The personal genetic information can only be used for epidemiological, public health, research or teaching purposes if the relevant donor has explicitly provided consent, or when the information has been anonymised ...»

This confidentiality requirement extends to third parties, including biological family members. The rule is that given that the donor is the owner of the information, only the donor can make decisions regarding the communication of that information, including when it concerns family genetic counselling : «In the case of genetic analysis being carried out for several family members, the results will be filed and communicated to each one of them individually. In the case of people with disabilities or children, their guardians or legal representatives will be informed» (Article 50.2 of the LIB).

As a consequence, where the information is of interest to family members, it should be the donor who makes the decision as to whether this information is conveyed to those family members, and the donor must be informed of this before giving consent for the analysis. According to Article 47, which lists the points that should be conveyed to the donors before obtaining their genetic information, donors must be advised of the «implications that the information that will be obtained might have for their family members, and that if donors decide that this information is to be conveyed to family members it is the donors themselves who will do this» (section 5).

Regarding exceptions to this general rule, according to Article 50.3, «in exceptional circumstances and in the interests of public health, the competent authorities, with prior approval from the authority responsible for data protection, may authorise the use of encrypted genetic information, always ensuring that it cannot be linked to, or associated with, the donor by third parties.»

In addition, although it is not explicitly stated in the LIB, we should remember that there are provisions within the Spanish legal system that are considered as justifiable cause for the duty of secrecy to be breached such as fulfilling a duty or where it is considered to be essential.

2.9. – *The scope of consent*
(generic or specific)

It is essential to obtain consent from the donor before using the sample for research. Consent as well as the information provided prior to consent being given must be in writing (27). However, «if the research subject cannot write, consent can be given using any other medium established by law, which leaves a record of the donor's wishes» (Art. 4.1.IV of the LIB). However, this requirement does not exempt the researcher from the requirement to give a verbal, more detailed explanation of the procedure to the research participants.

The purpose of providing prior information is so that the donor can grant consent while being aware of its significance and implications. The terms established when this information is given determine the scope of the consent, given that the samples can only be used in accordance with these terms. The minimum content of the information provided, as has already been stated, is detailed in Art. 59 of the LIB:

As indicated in Article 59, donors will be informed of the purpose of the research or line of research for which they are giving consent. The consent, therefore, would have to be limited to a «line of research,» which can be wider in scope than the specific project. It is essential that all the issues listed in Article 59 are communicated to the donor as these are precisely the criteria that limit the scope of the consent given.

However, according to Article 70.2 of the LIB: «Regardless of that established in the previous paragraph (application of the provision in chapter III for biological samples in general), biological samples that are deposited in the banks can be used for any biomedical research, under the terms prescribed by Law, as long as the donor, or if appropriate, the donor's legal representative, has given their consent to that effect.»

That is to say, if a sample is to be stored in a biobank the terms of consent can be extended. The explanation for this difference is that the law has stipulated that biobanks must have a formal structure and be subject to controls that reinforce the guarantees given that the donor's rights will be respected. But there was a concern to further develop this system for storing samples so as to make it a more useful tool for research and a way of doing this is to make the requirement regarding respecting donors' rights more flexible.

---

(27) *See* Arts. 4.1.I, 45. d), 58.1 and 59 LIB.

2.10. – Use of samples obtained for another purpose

2.10.1. General framework

Once the sample has been used for the primary purposes of diagnosis and treatment, there may be surplus material left over. Frequently this material will be destroyed, or if proper medical care of the patient requires this it may be stored. However, there may also be an interest in using the sample for other purposes. In this case, in addition to the consent for diagnosis or treatment, consent for subsequent use or storage for different purposes must also be obtained.

Art. 58.2 of the LIB establishes that the «consent of the donor will always be required whenever researchers want to use biological samples for biomedical research, when these were originally obtained for a different purpose, whether or not the samples are anonymised.» However, Art. 60.1 of the LIB establishes that «consent shall be granted either at the time the sample is obtained, or subsequently for a specific research project.» This will depend on whether or not the secondary purpose of research is known at the time consent is obtained.

In addition, at the time consent is given the donor must clearly understand that refusal to give consent will in no way affect the quality of medical treatment that he or she receives. Regarding this, Art. 6 of the LIB states that «... a person cannot be discriminated against as a result of their refusal ... to donate biological materials, specifically in regard to the provision of the appropriate medical care.»

Furthermore, the use of part of the biological material for biomedical research «cannot interfere with the histopathological, cytomorphological, phenotypical or molecular diagnosis of the patient, nor with its use for other primary purposes, such as the evaluation of prognosis parameters; in other words, only material surplus to the aforementioned purposes, can be used for research purposes» (28).

---

(28) GRUPO PARA EL USO DE MUESTRAS BIOLÓGICAS PARA INVESTIGACIÓN BIOMÉDICA, Guía práctica para la utilización de muestras biológicas en investigación biomédica, (The Use of Biological Samples for Biomedical Research Group, Practical guide for using biological samples in biomedical research), Instituto Roche, Madrid, 2006, p. 25.

If the secondary destination for the sample is still unknown at the time consent is obtained, then consent related to the use of the biological sample shall be granted subsequently (when the new use is proposed), and specifically for that particular research project (Art. 60.1 of the LIB). Finally, if the material associated with an identified or identifiable person enables the researcher to know the identity of or contact the donor, then it is the researcher's responsibility to contact the donor to obtain consent to use the existing biological samples for the new purpose.

2.10.2. *Use of samples without expressed consent from the donor*

Although the general rule is that biological material may only be used if the donor has provided consent, in many cases this may not be possible.

Spanish law has recognized this possibility in the LIB, differentiating between biological samples obtained before the Law went into effect in July 5, 2007 and those obtained subsequently.

Temporary Provision, Article 2 of the LIB concerns *samples stored before the Law went into effect*. According to this provision, «biological samples obtained before the Law went into effect can be used for biomedical research when the donor has given consent or when the samples have been anonymised. Nevertheless, it can include encrypted or identified samples for biomedical research without consent from the donor if an unreasonable effort is required to obtain this consent, as indicated in paragraph i) of Article 3 of this Law, or if it is not possible to obtain consent because the source subject has died or cannot be located. In that case, a determination of approval will be requested from the appropriate Ethics research committee, which will have to take into consideration the following requirements as a minimum : a) That it is research of general interest; b) that the research would be less effective or not possible without identifiable information from the donor; c) that the donor has not expressed any objection; and d) that the confidentiality of personal information is guaranteed.»

Under this provision, the following considerations can be made in relation to samples obtained and stored before July 5, 2007 : a) whenever possible, it is most appropriate to ask for consent from the donor to use the biological samples stored before the Law went into effect; b) it is possible to use these samples without the donor's consent as long as samples are anonymised; c) under exceptional conditions, it is also possible to use identified samples without the donor's consent but in this case certain requirements must be met, which shall be evaluated by the appropriate Ethics research committee. Amongst these is the requirement for use of the identified sample to be justified; d) if anonymised samples are to be used, this does not exempt the intervention of the ethics research committee, whose mandatory report will in all cases be in accordance with Art. 62 of the LIB. However, in this case the Committee will only have to verify the date the samples were collected, and the requirement for consent from the donor for all those samples obtained before the Law went into effect will not apply; e) the samples can be used by any person or institution, regardless of who obtained them and where they are stored.

In addition, with regard to biological samples obtained after the Law went into effect, Art. 58.2 II of the LIB establishes the following : «Notwithstanding the foregoing [requirement for consent from the donor to use biological samples for biomedical research which were obtained for a different purpose], under exceptional circumstances encrypted or identified samples can be used for biomedical research without consent from the donor if it is not possible to obtain this consent or it represents an unreasonable effort in the sense established in article 3. i) of this Law. In that case, approval will be requested from the appropriate Ethics research committee, which will have to take into consideration the following requirements as a minimum : a) that it is for research of general interest; b) that the research will be conducted by the same institution that requested the consent to obtain the samples; c) that the research would be less effective or not possible without identified information from the donor; d) the donor has not expressed any objections; e) that the confidentiality of personal information is guaranteed.»

Although this provision is written in a similar manner as the one that deals with samples obtained before the law went into effect the legal requirements for each one, however, differ substantially. The Temporary Provision, Article 2 (samples obtained before the law went into effect) is based on the fact that the samples in question can be used for research purposes without the consent of the donor as long as they are anonymous, and the special rules contained in the temporary provision, Article 2 are required only if researchers want to use the samples as identified samples and without the consent of the donor. Otherwise, in the situation we are considering now (samples obtained after the law went into effect), the intent of the law is very clear in the sense that the researcher cannot *under any circumstances* use such samples without the consent of the donor by simply anonymising them as is firmly established in Art. 58.2.I of the LIB.

In all cases, whether they are biological samples obtained before the law went into effect or subsequent to that time, the general rule should be to use anonymous samples. In this regard, we should keep in mind that the impossibility of locating or contacting the donor is precisely what has led the search for an alternative solution. We should never lose sight of the fact that the right to scientific research (29), which this legal provision attempts to guarantee should always be exercised while fully respecting the rights of the individuals who are participating in the research. In this case, these rights are the rights to privacy and data protection (30), which must be done in such a manner that in those cases where the Law establishes limitations of these rights (31), this must be carried out in the least harmful manner possible. In all cases, what is not acceptable is the option of anonymising the sample to avoid obtaining consent, when there is a possibility of contacting the donor (32).

2.11. – *Specific matters in regard to local communities*

The only mention made by Spanish law about this matter, in relation to the particular characteristics of genetic studies in population groups, is reflected in Articles 3 and 58 of the LIB.

---

(29) Cf. Art. 20.1 EC.

(30) Cf. Art. 18.1 and 4 EC.

(31) Art.7.3 of the LOPD establishes that, «personal data which refers to racial origin, health and sexual lifestyle can only be solicited, processed and transferred when, for reasons of general interest a law permits it or the individual gives express consent» In short the LIB covers the requirement for legal provision demanded by the LOPD for the processing of personal data without the consent of the donor. It should be remembered that although the processing of biological samples does not fall within the scope of the LOPD if these are linked to an identified or identifiable individual the information that is obtained from them will be personal information subject to provision of the LOPD.

(32) Cf. CHALMERS, Dan, «Ethical Principles for Research Governance of Biobanks», *Journal of International Biotechnology Law*, n° 3 (2006), pp. 227 ff.

In article 3 b) the term «population genetic analysis» is defined as research «the purpose of which is to understand the nature and magnitude of the genetic variations within a population or between individuals of the same group or from different groups.»

In these studies, according to Article 58.6 «local and ethnic traditions will always be guaranteed, avoiding at all times stigmatising and discriminating practices.»

This must be noted in relation to the requirements for prior consent that is necessary for the use of samples and genetic information for biomedical research. For consent to be valid, the information that is provided before consent is given must be appropriately communicated, in a manner that guarantees understanding of the content and scope. Therefore, the communication must be conducted while keeping in mind the characteristics of each subject: age, education, intellectual capacity, and also culture.

Although it is not explicitly stipulated, it is however inferred from these requirements that it will be necessary to establish essential mechanisms to comply with that requirement. The most obvious requirement could be the need for a translation, but others should not be disregarded, such as for example, seeking a representative who knows the cultural customs of the specific ethnic group to which the research subjects belong to participate in the information process, even though the act of consent will be individual.

2.12. – Maintenance: security standards, duration of storage

According to Art. 61.1 of the LIB, «... the biological samples (not anonymous) used in biomedical research will be preserved only as long as they are necessary for the purposes that justified the collection, unless the donor has granted explicit consent for other subsequent uses.»

The duration of storage will depend on different factors, such as the purpose of the file, storage space, the type of material stored, and the processing to which it was subjected. Hence, if consent was not granted to store the sample beyond the specific research project, then material should be destroyed at the end of this project (33). However, if there is authorisation from the donor (such as for example, when there is consent to store the sample in a biobank) it appears then there is no obstacle to prolonging the duration of the file for a more extended period, always in accordance with the terms about which the donor was informed and to which the donor consented.

In a similar sense to the above, regarding biological samples obtained and stored for diagnostic purposes, from Art. 67.4 of the LIB it is understood that these cannot be preserved for more time than needed to comply with the objectives established for the samples. If there is a desire to preserve the biological samples for other purposes (usually for research) once they have been used for their original purpose, then consent must be obtained from the donor.

With regard to the security measures that apply to the information that results from the analysis or that is associated with the samples, see heading 2.8.1.C.

For professional requirements and the requirements relating to biobanks see section 2.4.

2.13. – *Transfer and national and international transportation*

2.13.1. *General arrangements*

As stated in section 2.6.1, the terms of use discussed with the donor before consent was given delimit the scope of how the sample can be used. We should keep in mind that amongst other matters the donor must be informed of the purpose of the research or line of research to which consent is being given, the identity of the person responsible for the research, and the place where the analysis will be performed. If these circumstances change, for example, when there is an intention to transfer the sample to another researcher or use it in another research project, the donor must be informed once again about these aspects so as to give the appropriate consent. In effect, as was also stated in that section, the donor should be informed of what will happen to the sample at the conclusion of the research : dissociation, destruction, or other research. In this latter

---

(33) Unless new consent is obtained or the requirements to use the samples without the donors' consent are met, in accordance with the provisions in Art. 58.2 LIB.

case, the requirements established in the LIB must be complied with, that is to say, the requirement for explicit and specific consent.

In short, as discussed for the transfer of samples, the donor's expressed consent is required. This should be given before the research takes place. This may be when the original consent is given, if it is possible, at that time, to give the donor all the necessary information required by law. This arrangement does not apply if the sample has been anonymised with the prior consent of the donor.

2.13.2. *Arrangements applicable to Biobanks*

As discussed above, consent for storage and use of samples deposited in biobanks is given in broader terms than when given for collections or for specific research projects. In effect, the purpose of creating a biobank is to make quality biological samples available to the scientific community. A commitment to public service, together with the guarantees required from these establishments justify a special system, through which consent is given in broader terms and an expressed consent is not required for the biobank to transfer samples to researchers.

It is important to indicate that the donors retain their rights over their own samples and related information, given that: firstly, the donor has the right to access all information related to the use of the sample in the research for which it has been provided; secondly, the sample can only be transferred to projects that are approved by the appropriate ethics committee; thirdly, the donor has the right to withdraw consent for the use of the sample; and fourthly, in specific cases expressed consent will be needed to use the sample, for projects that are more likely to have ethical implications.

2.13.3. *International transportation of biological samples*

The LIB deals with this issue in Art. 11, according to which, «inter-community and extra-community importing and exporting of biological samples of human origins for biomedical research covered by this Law shall be governed by the provisions that are established by law.» (34)

In regard to the export of samples, until this regulation is enacted the international circulation of personal information established by the LOPD shall apply : if the information is destined for a member country of the European Union, the system is similar to national transfer. Otherwise, the donor should be explicitly informed of the conditions in the country of destination in regard to protection of personal data before giving consent for the transfer

As far as samples that come from other countries are concerned, we should emphasise that the ethics research committee that evaluates the projects would have to make certain that, when the biological samples used come from other countries, the equivalent guarantees required by Spanish legal regulation were observed during the collection and transfer.

2.14. – Donating, transferring, and ceding of rights over the research results free of charge

In general, Article 45 c) of the LIB establishes that «the entire process for donation, transfer, storage and use of biological samples by donors as well as depositors should be not for profit. Personal genetic information cannot be used for commercial purposes.»

The donation of biological samples for biomedical research must be free of charge (article 7 of the LIB), although financial compensation can be determined for physical discomfort, expenses, and other inconveniences that may result from providing the sample (Article 58.3 of the LIB).

Any advertisement or promotion by authorised centres that encourage the donation of cells or human tissues must respect the

---

(34) Currently there is a regulation, Royal Decree 65/2006 of the 30 January, through which requirements for importing and exporting biological samples are established. It specifies conditions for the importing and exporting of samples of biological material and establishes a voluntary registration system which allows their continuous importing and exporting. However, this Royal Decree only applies, as established in its article 1 to «the importing and exporting of biological samples for human diagnosis or research. Therefore, it is not applicable to research with biological samples *in vitro*. According to this final provision, Art. 3 of the LIB, «the government is able to decide how many provisions are necessary for the development and implementation of this law, and in particular to establish : a) the regulations for internal, intra-communitarian and extra-communitarian exchange and circulation of biological material of human origin for research purposes ...».

altruistic nature of this donation, and under no circumstances encourage donation by offering compensation or financial benefits.

In addition, the transfer of samples to be used in biomedical research by a centre cannot involve financial or commercial purposes, and can only involve the expense of obtaining, preserving, handling and sending samples, and other expenses of a similar nature (Article 69.3 of the LIB).

Finally, the research results patent system, where it concerns biotechnical patents, was established by Law 10/2002 of 29 April, which amends Law 11/1986 of 20 March, so as to incorporate Directive 98/44/EC related to the legal protection of biotechnical inventions into Spanish law. As its name indicates, the origin of this reform is found in the approval of Directive 98/44/EC of 6 July 1998, concerning the legal protection of biotechnological inventions, which has a two-fold purpose: on the one hand, to coordinate European law regarding biotechnical patents, and on the other, to contribute to the development of biotechnical research in Europe so that it remains on a par with others, mainly in relation to the United States and Japanese biotechnological markets.

The requirements for patentability are included in Article 4 of this Spanish law. According to this law new inventions are patentable when: they are not accessible to the public by any means; they entail inventive activity which had not occurred even to an expert on the subject, and they have the potential for industrial application. This industrial application must be capable of being manufactured and the results must be useful in industry even if the objective is a product that is composed of or has biological material included in it, or consists of a procedure through which biological material is produced, transformed or used. Biological material that is isolated from its natural environment or produced by a technological procedure can be the object of an invention, even if it had previously existed in a natural state.

Hence, despite affirming that the human body is not patentable in the different phases of its creation and development, and that neither is the simple discovery of one of its elements, including the sequence or partial sequence of a gene, Article 4 then goes on to clarify that an isolated element of the human body or one obtained through a technical procedure, including the total or partial sequence of a gene, could be considered as a patentable invention, even where the structure of this element is identical to a natural element. In addition, it is explicitly required that the industrial application of a total or partial sequence of a gene should clearly be stated in the patent application.

In short, a human gene that has industrial application, i.e. a new use, and is isolated from the human body or was obtained by means of a technical procedure can be patented, unless its commercial exploitation is contrary to public order or social mores. In particular, the following will not be patented because it is considered contrary to public order (Article 5 of the Patents Law): procedures to clone human beings, procedures to modify the germinal genetic identity of humans, the use of human embryos for industrial or commercial purposes, or procedures to modify the genetic identity of animals and which involve suffering for the animals involved without providing any substantial medical or veterinary benefits for humans or animals, and the resulting animals from such procedures.

When donating a sample the donor waives all financial rights or any other types of rights over the results which could derive either directly or indirectly from the research conducted on the biological sample (Article 7 of the LIB). Therefore these rights will belong, in general, to those who have applied to register the results of their research with the appropriate registering authorities at the patents office (35).

2.15. – *Other issues*

Human genetic research has raised concerns from the beginning, in regard to the potential discrimination that could result from the collection of this information for the individual providing the sample. It has been suggested that the situations where this risk may have the greatest impact for the individuals concerned are related to employment and insurance contracts.

The LIB includes a general and explicit prohibition against discrimination in its Article 6, under the following terms: «No one shall be subject to any discrimination as a result of their genetic characteristics. Neither can a person be discriminated against as a

---

(35) See *Guía Práctica para la utilización de muestras biológicas en la investigación biomédica*. (Practical guide for the use of biological samples in biomedical research), *op. cit.*, p. 98.

result of their refusal to undergo genetic analysis, give their consent to participate in biomedical research, or donate biological materials, and specifically in regard to providing appropriate medical care.» In addition, as was previously stated, Article 58.3 warns of the need to avoid stigmatising and discriminatory practices in genetic diversity studies.

In addition, the mechanisms that make this prohibition effective are the limits placed on the uses and purposes of genetic analysis (36), the conditions under which it can be carried out (37) and the responsibility of professionals to keep the data they have access to confidential, which we referred to above.

Specifically, Article 4 of the employee's statute recognises the principles that guarantee privacy and non-discrimination in the work setting: «In regard to work, employees have the right to: ... c) not be discriminated against when seeking employment or after being employed ... or discriminated against for physical, psychological, or sensory reasons, as long as the employee is capable of performing the work or job in question; ... e) with respect to their privacy and with due consideration for their dignity.» Finally, not hiring an individual can only be justified if a specific situation impedes the proper performance of the work that is required and not if it is a matter of genetic predisposition or future illness (38).

With regard to the responsibility to oversee the health of employees, Article 22 of the Occupational Risk Prevention Law establishes the obligation that the employer has to provide an occupational health service to periodically monitor employees' health in relation to the inherent risks at work. This supervision can only be carried out if employees give their consent. The only exception to the voluntary nature of health checks is when workers' representatives state that it is essential to assess the effects of conditions at work on the health of the workers so as to assess whether the workers'

---

(36) «Genetic analysis will not be used to identify whether or not individuals have a disease, are carriers of a genetic variant that predisposes them to developing a specific disease or that affects their response to particular treatment» (article 46 of the LIB).

(37) «The responsable autonomous community or state authority will accredit the public or private centres that may carry out genetic analysis and that, in all cases must comply with that established in articles 46-57 of this law (article 57 of the LIB).

(38) See ROMEO CASABONA, Carlos María, Los genes y sus leyes. El derecho ante el genoma humano, (The law in relation to the human genome), Cátedra Interuniversitaria de Derecho y Genoma Humano, (The Inter University department of Law and the Human Genome), Comares, Bilbao-Granada, 2002, pp. 76 and ff.

health is being damaged by the work environment or whether an individual's state of health is a threat to other workers or other people connected with the company or when compulsory health checks are established in law in relation to specific risks and particularly dangerous activities. In all cases, the health assessments or tests chosen and performed must be those which cause the least amount of discomfort for the employees and which are proportional to the risk. The information related to the supervision of employees' health cannot be used to discriminate against or to the detriment of the employees. Access to personal medical information shall be limited to medical personnel and the health authorities that conduct employee health supervision, and cannot be provided to the employer or other individuals without the employee's expressed consent. Notwithstanding the above, the employer and the persons or entities responsible in matters related to prevention shall be informed of the results obtained from the evaluations conducted with regard to the employees' capacity to perform the job or the need to introduce or improve the protection or prevention measures, with the purpose of properly developing their functions with regard to prevention.

In reference to insurance policies, there are no specific provisions about the use of health information, except those in the general provisions of the LIB referred to above, and the regulation concerning purchase of insurance policies in Spain (Law 50/1980 of 8 October, on insurance policy) from which it can be inferred that:

1. The performance of genetic analysis to evaluate the risk for life insurance policies or diseases is against Spanish law.

2. The detection of a genetic mutation does not mean that the subject is sick. Therefore, while there are no symptoms, it does not affect the individual's actual health. Thus, giving a negative response to a question about general health, even while knowing of the pathological genetic mutation, does not imply bad faith.

3. The duty to declare when responding to a health questionnaire is limited. There is no obligation to declare genetic information that is already known, if not asked about the specific disease that it relates to.

4. There is no duty to declare genetic information that is known after the individual has been hired.

5. There is a duty to declare information about a genetic mutation already known to you, if you are specifically asked about that disease. Genetic information is treated the same as other circumstances that have an effect on the evaluation of insurable risk.

6. At this time there is no evidence that this type of questioning is being conducted in Spain as a prior condition to the purchase of an insurance policy. There is no data that confirms that the prohibition of this practice would substantially affect adverse selection by insurers. However, if the practice of carrying out analyses is extended, this would result in a disproportionate distribution of information that is contrary to the essence of this type of contract.

7. In this situation, the most advisable step would be for companies to establish a moratorium on testing, as has been done in other countries, until they are able to verify how this diagnostic system evolves and its effect on individual, social, and commercial interests (39).

2.16. – Conclusions

The regulation concerning the use of biological samples and biobanks for biomedical research in Spain acknowledges that research is a key tools to improve the quality of life and life expectancy of people. The Law has established a general regulatory framework to respond to the new scientific challenges, and at the same time guarantee the protection of the rights of individuals who could be affected. This regulation has taken into account the international principles of the UNESCO and the Council of Europe in this matter.

The Spanish regulation is based in two fundamental basis, the need of promoting the scientific research, and the respect of the subject rights. In this sense, provisions concerning privacy, confidentiality, prohibition of discrimination, need of consent, right to acces to the data, etc... have been implemented. And as the same

---

(39) *See* ROMEO CASABONA, Carlos María, *Los genes y sus leyes. El derecho ante el genoma huano*, (Genes and their laws. The law in relation to the human genome), *op. cit.*, pp. 83 and ff.; and NICOLÁS, Pilar, «Obtención y utilización de datos genéticos en la contratación de seguros. La difícil concreción de la prohibición de discriminación», *Los avances del Derecho ante los avances de la Medicina*, (Obtaining and using genetic data in insurance contracting. The difficulty of implementing the prohibition on discrimination in Advances In Law In Relation To Advances In Medicine), Universidad Pontificia de Comillas, Thomson, Madrid, 2008, pp. 865-881.

time, with adequate guarantees, some flexibility is previewed in some cases. The ethics committees have an important role in the evaluation of the particular conditions of each project.

The Law also distinguishes between collections of samples and biobanks, and acknowledges the latter as agencies qualified to provide support for research, and whose existence and development the law wants to promote. Biobanks became an institutions with some characteristics that justify a special status, as the possibility of the storage of samples for broad purposes in the framework of scientific research.

Despite of the existing regulation, that deals with the most important issues of the use of samples for research, it is previewed a legal development of particular topics, such as international transfer of samples and further details refering biobanks.

In short, the road has begun to go but work remains pending. And they are different actors involved in this task. The legislator, who must still complete the regulatory framework; the managers of research centers and hospitals, who must implement forecasts and provide the necessary infrastructure for this purpose; the researchers, who have to adapt to the regulation, which a major shift in traditional conceptions; the administration, that should support, even financially, a new framework in biomedical research with biological samples; and finally, the research subjects themselves and society in general, to be made aware of necessary role of collaborators, while the recipients of the benefits of research.

PART III.

References

NATIONAL BIOBANKS

Argentina

1. Public bank of blood from the umbilical cord (Garrahan Hospital, Buenos Aires)

It initiated its activities the 29th of April 2005. It is regulated by INCUCAI's resolution number 319, mentioned before. The obtaining of blood samples (collection of blood from the placenta) is done through the puncture of the umbilical vein, under the advice of the Ministry of Health. The informed consent obtained is based on the general principles, accepted by the universal doctrine. Rules about saving and conservation of materials are technical rules approved by the INCUCAI based on international legislation. The anonymity and confidentiality of whoever gives the samples is sufficiently protected. Until now the samples were only used for bone marrow transplant. Despite this, there is a research project about «phenotypic and functional characterization of hematopoietic progenitor cells from the human umbilical cord blood», whose main objective is:

– To characterize immunophenotypic stem cells and hematopoietic progenitor cells of blood from the umbilical cord.
– To evaluate the proliferation capacity and differences *in vitro* of cells from the blood from the umbilical cord.
– To evaluate the self-renovating capacity of cryopreserved stem and hematopoietic progenitor cells obtained from umbilical cord blood.

In this project, the bank's samples will be used, acquiring a mixed character.

2. Bank of the Multidisciplinary Cell Biology Institute in the City of La Plata (IMBICE)

This is an old research institute that works within the CONICET system and the Investigation Committee of Buenos Aires. There is a cell and tissue bank (human as well as animal). The bank does not have a specific regulation, observing analogically the principles established by the INCUCAI.

3. Bank of the Laboratory of Blood Products (University of Córdoba)

It was founded in 1963, and its work is attached to the tissue bank of the Córdoba Hospital, together since 2002 forming the «Tissue Bank of Córdoba Province». It is ruled by the INCUCAI's directives. The samples are stored in freezers at minus 80 degrees. The subject's identity is preserved. When professionals use the material they must return a stub in order to assure the traceability of the product. The obtained products are used in dental surgery, maxillofacial reconstruction, dental implants, traumatology surgery and similar. There is almost no research and the only progress obtained has been in processing methods : The ones who provide the material are voluntary donors, not for profit, from Argentina, Uruguay and Chile. From this raw material, several medicines of great strategic value are created : For the validation research the WHO recommendations and the regulations of the European Union (Committee for Proprietary Medical Products) are still being used.

4. Tissue bank of the Biotar Group (Rosario)

The tissue bank of the Biotar Group's purpose is to satisfy the increasing demand for tissue needed by medical professionals for the comprehensive treatment of their patients. Regardless of this, it has a research area that uses stock from the same biobank. This area has agreements with universities from Buenos Aires and Córdoba. The bank has a building structure, human resources, proceeding material and quality controls suitable for processing fresh, frozen or freeze-dried osteo-muscular tissues. It respects the applicable rules from the INCUCAI and is in a position to provide the community with implant tissue whose processing control is of the highest quality, assuring the exact traceability of the transplants.

5. The Favaloro Foundation's Homografting bank

It was created in 1994 thanks to the initiative of Dr. Roberto R. Favaloro in response to the development of new techniques of valve replacement, which require the use of homografting. Ever since, much experience been accumulated in the processing, cryopreservation and cardiovascular tissue implants, placing it nowadays as one of the most important banks in the world. Its authorities are studying the use of the stored material for scientific research, in which case it would become a mixed bank.

6. Bank of the Experimental Medicine and Basic Sciences Institute (ICBME – according to its initials in Spanish –) of the Italian Hospital of Buenos Aires.

This Institute works with clinical applications, especially in the repair, replacement or regulation of cells, tissues and organs, with the purpose of recovering functional damage caused by congenital defects, degenerative diseases and traumas. This technology includes the use of stem cells with non-conventional purposes, the use of trophic factors, genetic engineering, tissue engineering and advanced cell therapy. The mentioned directives of the INCUCAI regulate the bank of biological material. At present one of the projects of greatest interest is related to the establishing of DNA and RNA banks (in several pathologies), so the basic investigation will be incorporated and we will have mixed banks.

Brazil

1. Foundation for the Support of Research of the State of Rio de Janeiro *(Fundação de amparo à pesquisa do estado do Rio de Janeiro – FAPERJ)*

http://www.faperj.br/boletim_interna.phtml?obj_id = 178

2. National Institute of Cancer *(INCA – Instituto Nacional do Câncer)*

http://www.inca.gov.br/conteudo_view.asp?id = 1094

Chile

Generally, no Biobanks were found but some collections for different purposes were, which although they are not totally in line with the research, are set out below:

1. Life Bank *(Banco de Vida)*

National bank of blood from the umbilical cord, which contains stem cells fundamental to the treatment of blood diseases, available for patients who require a bone marrow transplant. Established through an agreement between the Faculty of Medicine of the Universidad Católica and its Obstetrics and Gynaecology department and the Genómika Foundation.

2. Immortalised neurons

Institute of Biomedical Sciences (Instituto de Ciencias Biomédicas – ICBM). Dr. Pablo Caviedes. Production of immortalised cellular lines for *in vitro* research.

Colombia

1. Corporation for Biologic Research *(Corporación para Investigaciones Biológicas)*

www.cib.org.co

2. Catholic University Javeriana – Human Genetics Institute *(Pontificia Universidad Javeriana, Instituto de Genética Humana)*

www.javeriana.edu.co/Genetica/

3. National Institute of Cancer *(Instituto Nacional de Cancerología – Cohorte HPN y Gástrico)*

www.incancerologia.gov.co

4. National Institute of Forensic Service and Forensic Sciences *(Instituto Nacional de Medicina Legal y Ciencias Forenses)*

www.medicinalegal.gov.co

5. NeuroBank of the Neurosciences Group of the University of Antioquia *(Neurobanco del Grupo de Neurociencias de Antioquia)*

http://neurociencias.udea.co

6. National University – School of Pharmacy *(Universidad Nacional – Facultad de Farmacia)*

Costa Rica

1. Cellular and Molecular Biology Research Center of the University of Costa Rica *(Centro de Investigación en Biología Celular y Molecular de la Universidad de Costa Rica – CIBCM)*

http://www.cibcm.ucr.ac.cr/

2. The National Center for High Technology *(Centro Nacional de Alta Tecnología -CENAT)*

www.cenat.ac.cr

3. Central American of Population Center. CRELES Project *(Centro Centroamericano de Población. Proyecto CRELES)*
http://ccp.ucr.ac.cr/creles/descripc.htm

4. Health Research Institute of the University of Costa Rica *(Instituto de Investigaciones en Salud de la Universidad de Costa Rica – INISA)*
www.inisa.ucr.ac.cr

5. Newborn Screening Program *(Programa Nacional de Tamizaje Neonatal y Alto Riesgo)*
http://www.tamizajeneonatal.com/

FRANCE

Determining how many biobanks exist is a tedious task, especially because there are different types of biobanks in France. Indeed, nowadays, it is difficult to estimate how many biobanks there are in France and no two people have the same number. For instance, in an international survey taken in 2001, some authors believed there were 67 human biobanks in France even though only 9 human biobanks are recorded on the website of the French Consultative Committee on Biological Resources. In an interview, Georges Dagher, representative of the biological collections at the National Institute of Health and Medical Research and member of the French Consultative Committee on Biological Resources, said that there are «between 40 and 50 well structured biological resource centres» which first appeared between 2001 and 2006.

It is difficult to check how many biobanks exist in France in part because France did not regulate biobanks until relatively recently. Indeed, while biobanks have existed for decades, regulations first appeared only about ten years ago. French law now requires biobanks to make a declaration or seek authorization. Since many biobanks existed previous to this law, some biobanks never fulfilled these formalities.

Germany

1. Addiction Medicine Research Association of Baden-Wuerttemberg
http://www.zi-mannheim.de/630.html
2. Blood Donor Biobank (Munich)
http://biobank.blutspendedienst.com/home.html
3. Brain-Net
http://www.bain-net.net/
4. Clinical Research Group of Molecular Neurogenetics (Munich)
http://www.nefo.med.uni-muenchen.de/Forschungshauptseite/experimentelle_nro /molekulareneurogenetik
5. Competence Network Acute and Chronic Leukaemia
http://www.kompetenznetz-leukaemie.de
6. Competence Network Chronic Ulcerative Colitis (CED)
http://www.kompetenznetz-ced.de
7. Competence Network Heart Insufficiency (Berlin)
http://www.knhi.de
8. Competence Network Hepatitis
http://www.kompetenznetz-hepatitis.de
9. Competence Network HIV/AIDS
http://www.kompetenznetz-hiv.de
10. Competence Network Malignant Lymphomas
http://www.lymphome.de
11. Competence Network Paediatric Oncology and Haematology (POH)
http://www.kompetenznetze.de/navi/de/root,did=28412.html
12. Competence Network Rheumatism
http://www.rheumanet.org
13. Competence Network Stroke
http://www.kompetenznetz-schlaganfall.de
14. CRIP: Central Research Infrastructure for Molecular Pathology
http://www.ibmt.fraunhofer.de/fhg/ibmt/biomedizintechnik/biodatenbanken_crip/

15. EPIC European Prospective Investigation into Cancer and Nutrition (Heidelberg)
http://www.dkfz.de/de/klepidemiologie/arbeitsgr/ernaerepi/ee_p01_epichd.html

16. EPIC European Prospective Investigation into Cancer and Nutrition (Potsdam)
http://www.dife.de/de/index.php?request=/de/forschung/projekte/epic.php

17. GENOMatch
http://www.tembit.de/web/de/genomatch.asp

18. GEPARD – Competence Network on Parkinson's Disease
http://www.kompetenznetz-parkinson.de

19. German Collection of Microorganisms and Cell Cultures (DSMZ)
www.dsmz.de

20. German Network of Hereditary Movement Disorders (GENMOVE)
http://www.genemove.de

21. German Research Network on Schizophrenia (Bonn and Munich)
http://www.kompetenznetz-schizophrenie.de

22. Heinz Nixdorf Recall Studie
http://www.recall-studie.uni-essen.de/recall_info.html

23. Indivumed Inc. – Center for Cancer Research at the Israelite Clinic Hamburg
http://www.indivumed.com

24. Interdisciplinary Network Heart Insufficiency
http://www.medpoli.uni-wuerzburg.de

25. KORA-gen: Cooperative Health Research in the Region of Augsburg
http://epi.gsf.de/kora-gen/

26. Laboratory for Molecular Medicine at the University of Erlangen
http://www.frauenklinik.klinikum.uni-erlangen.de/e2201/e162/index_ger.html

27. LURIC – Ludwigshafen Risk and Cardiovascular Health Study

http://www.luric.de

28. National Center for Tumor Diseases (Heidelberg)

http://www.klinikum.uni-heidelberg.de

29. Nephroblastom SIOP 2001 / GPOH (Saarbruecken)

http://www.kinderkrebsinfo.de/wilms

30. Network Muscular Dystrophy (MD-NET)

http://www.md-net.org

31. PATH – Patients Tumorbank of Hope

http://www.stiftungpath.org/

32. PopGen

http://www.popgen.de

33. Pseudoxanthoma Elasticum (PXE)

www.pxe.org/

34. Research Institute for Health Protection at Workplace (BGFA)

http://www.bgfa.ruhr-uni-bochum.de

35. SEPNET – Competence Network on Sepsis

http://www.kompetenznetz-sepsis.de

36. Study of Health in Pomerania (SHIP)

http://www.medizin.uni-greifswald.de/cm/fv/ship.html

37. The Dementia Competence Network

http://www.kompetenznetz-demenzen.de

38. Therapy Study ALL-BFM 2000

http://www.uni-kiel.de/all-studie/All_stu_l.htm

Mexico

The report considered the data given by the biobanks that voluntarily answered the surveys, and as such the following list does not include comments of their relevance in the national context. Only the National Institute of Genomic Medicine, the INMEGEN biobank, a bank devoted to demographic research and decoding

Mexicans' genomic map, could be considered as the most important biobank in the country.

National Autonomus University of Mexico, UNAM

1. School of Odontolgy
2. School of Medicine
3. Biotechnology Institute
4. Cellular Physiology Institute
5. Biomedical Research Institute

National Polytechnical Institute, IPN

6. Advanced School of Medicine
7. National Biological Sciences School
8. Center for Genomics and Biotechnology
9. Department for Physiology, Biophysics and Neurosciences

National Health Institutes

10. National Cardiology Institute «Ignacio Chávez»
11. National Medical Sciences and Nutrition Institute «Salvador Zubirán»
12. National Respiratory Diseases Institute
13. National Neurology and Neurosurgery Institute «Dr. Manuel Velasco Suárez»
14. Oncology National Institute
15. National Genomics and Medicine Institute
16. National Institute on Public Health
17. Institute for Epidemiologic Diagnosis and Reference

Public Hospitals

18. Mexico's General Hospital
19. Mexican Children's Hospital "Federico Gómez"
20. Pediatrics Hospital

Mexican Social Security Institute (IMSS) : The IMSS has several biobanks distributed in the following laboratories :

21. Neurological Diseases Medical Research Unit
22. Human Genetics Medical Research Unit
23. Medical Research in Nutrition Unit
24. Metabolic Diseases Medical Research Unit
25. Developmental Biology Medical Research Unit
26. Thrombosis, Hemostasia and Atherogenesis Medical Research Unit
27. Immunology and Infectology Medical Research Unit
28. Biomedical Research Center of the West
29. Biomedical Research Center of the Northeast
30. Biomedical Research center of the East
31. Infectious and Parasitic Diseases Medical Research Unit
32. Reproductive Medical Research Unit
33. Immunochemistry Medical Research Unit
34. Oncology Medical Research Unit.

Social Security and Services Institute for the State Workers (ISSSTE) : The ISSSTE has several biobanks distributed in the following laboratories :

35. Biochemistry Laboratory
36. Regenerative Medicine and Cellular Therapy Laboratory
37. Conjunctive Tissue Laboratory
38. Genomic Medicine Division

Portugal

1. Bank of Tumors (Banco de Tumores) of the Hospital de S. João
2. Bank of Tumors of IPATIMUP (Institute of Molecular Pathology and Immunology of the University of Porto), in Oport
3. Bank of Tumors of the Hospital of the University of Coimbra, in Coimbra
4. Bank of Tumors of the Almada Hospital, in Lisbon.

Spain

1. Hospital Biobanks

http://www.clinicbiobanc.org/es_index.html

The Institut d'Investigaciones Biomèdiques August Pi i Sunyer (IDIBAPS) is one of the benchmark research centres in Catalonia, Spain, and Southern Europe, and has the highest production level in Spain. Three long-established scientific organizations collaborate at the IDIBAPS centre: the Hospital Clinic de Barcelona (HCB), the Universitat de Barcelona (UB), and the Institut d'Investigaciones Biomédiques de Barcelona del CSIC (IBB-CSIC), with institutional support from the Autonomous Community of Catalonia.

As a result of its role as a benchmark hospital and its commitment to research, the Hospital Clinic de Barcelona is an ideal environment for the creation of a Biobank. It has had organised collections of biological samples for research since 1985. The hospital biobank was established in 2006. Located on Calle Córsega 176, next to the Hospital Clinic de Barcelona, the biobank is located in an ideal place to respond to the growing demand for biological samples of proven quality, as a result of an increase in the multidisciplinary collaboration between different scientific fields (clinical-basic-applied).

2. Biobank Networks

www.rticc.org

The earliest Spanish cooperative experience was promoted by the Programa de Patología Molecular del Centro Nacional de Investigaciones Oncoloógicas (CNIO) [National Molecular Pathology and Oncology Research Centre Programme], started in September 2000. The scope of their work is national and the objective is to promote tumour banks with high standards in Spanish hospitals and their functional integration into a cooperative network. They aim to base this work on technical procedures and homogeneous ethical requirements, quality assurance techniques, and centralised coordination. However the biobanks and the actual tissues are owned by the hospital. Therefore, it is not just a single biobank but rather a cooperative network and organisation of hospital biobanks in which 28 institutions in 10 autonomous communities participate, along with four additional biobanks that are currently in the process of being set up.

Alongside this plan, new, independent, cooperative networks emerged between 2001 and 2005 in : Castilla and Leon (8 hospitals); Catalonia (11 hospitals); Asturias (4 hospitals) and Andalusia (13 hospitals).

This autonomous environment is associated with the Spanish health plan transferred to the autonomous communities. It is also not very different from the Inter-territorial Network Plan promoted by the CNIO. This centre is currently vigorously promoting territorial networks in various autonomous communities, without them losing their affiliation with the inter-territorial networks through doing so.

The co-existence of four autonomous networks and one interautonomous network, far from being a problem, has established a cooperation program at a national level, as a result of their common design and particularly as a result of their firm commitment to cooperation. This has been demonstrated since 2001 when the National Tumour Bank Consortium was created. Although with slight differences in organization and design, all these networks maintain common objectives and projects. Therefore, wherever the network is located the sample collections are stored locally, in the institution that obtained them, where they can be used for the purposes stated on the patient consent form and by the corresponding external committees.

3. Network Biobanks

http://www.bioef.org

The Basque Biobank for Research (O + Ehun) was provided with a network structure by the BIO Foundation. The participants in this are : the six public Basque hospitals (Cruces, Donostia, Basurto, Galdakao, Txagorritxu, and Santiago Apóstol); the Basque Centre for Transfusions and Human Tissues in Osakidetza; the Instituto Oncológico de San Sebastián private clinic, and the Policlínica Gipuzkoa private clinic. Each nodule of the Biobank collects, processes, and stores biological samples, all coordinated through a computing platform under the direction of the Fundación BIO. This acts as the coordinating nodule and carries out the management of samples, the coordination of procedures and quality criteria and cooperation with other state and foreign centres.

4. National Banks

4.1. *The National DNA Bank (BNADN)*

(www.bancoadn.org)

Is a technological support programme for biomedical research created at the beginning of 2004 by the Fundación Genoma España (the Spanish Genome Foundation), with the purpose of strengthening the development of genome research in Spain.

4.2. *The National Stem Cell Lines Bank*

The National Stem Cell Lines Bank is configured as a network structure with several nodes, coordinated by a central node (RD 2132/04 and SCO/393/06), the objective of which shall be to guarantee the availability of human embryo and adult stem cells for biomedical research across Spain.

NATIONAL INSTITUTIONS

Argentina

1. Unique Central National Institute for the Coordination of Ablations and Implantations *(Instituto Nacional Central Único Coordinador de Ablación e Implante – INCUCAI)*

www.incucai.gov.ar

2. National Ministry of Health *(Ministerio de Salud de la Nación)*

www.msal.gov.ar

3. Federal Council of Health *(Consejo Federal de Salud – COFESA)*

www.msal.gov.ar/htm/site/cofesa-index.asp

4. National Ethics Committee in Science and Technology *(Comité Nacional de Ética en la Ciencia y la Tecnología)*

www.cecte.gov.ar

5. Permanent Education in Bioethics Program *(Programa de Educación Permanente en Bioética)*

www.redbioetica-edu.com.ar

Brazil

1. National Council of Health *(Conselho Nacional de Saúde – CNS)*

http://conselho.saude.gov.br/

2. Ministry of Health *(Ministério da Saúde)*

http://portal.saude.gov.br/portal/saude/Gestor/area.cfm?id_area=938

3. National Council of Local Health Secretaries *(Conselho Nacional de Secretarias Municipais de Saúde – CONASEMS)*

www.conasems.org.br

4. National Council of Health Secretaries *(Conselho Nacional de Secretarios de Saúde)*
www.conass.org.br

5. Oswaldo Cruz Foundation *(Fundação Oswaldo Cruz – Fiocruz)*
www.fiocruz.br

6. National Institute of Cancer *(Instituto Nacional de Câncer – INCA)*
www2.inca.gov.br

7. Francisco Mauro Salzano. Researcher
http://dgp.cnpq.br/buscaoperacional/detalhepesq.jsp?pesq=1820725602041611

8. Foundation for the Support of Research of the State of Rio de Janeiro *(Fundação de Amparo à Pesquisa do Estado do Rio de Janeiro – FAPERJ)*
http://www.faperj.br/boletim_interna.phtml?obj_id=178

Chile

1. Ministry of Health *(Ministerio de Salud)*
http://www.minsal.cl

2. National Commission for Scientific and Technological Research *(Comisión Nacional Científica y Tecnológica)*
http://www.conicyt.cl

3. Forensic Service *(Servicio médico legal)*
http://www.sml.cl

Colombia

1. Intersectorial National Bioethics Commission *(Comisión Intersectorial de Bioética – CIB)*
www.cib.org.co

2. Education Committee of Human Resources for Science and Technology *(Comité de Formación de Recursos Humanos para la Ciencia y la Tecnología – COLCIENCIAS)*
www.colciencias.gov.co

3. Administrative Department of Science, Technology and Innovation *(Departamento Administrativo de Ciencia, Tecnología e Innovación - Colciencias)*

www.colciencias.gov.co

4. National Council of Human Talent in Healthcare *(Consejo Nacional de Talento Humano en Salud)*

5. Corporation for Biological Research *(Corporación para Investigaciones Biológicas)*

www.cib.org.co

6. Attorney General *(Fiscalía General de la Nación)*

www.fiscalia.gov.co

7. Colombian Institute of Immunology *(Fundación Instituto de Inmunología de Colombia)*

www.fidic.org.co

8. Health Sciences University Foundation *(Fundación Universitaria de Ciencias de la Salud)*

www.fucsalud.edu.co

9. University Hospital of the Samaritan *(Hospital Universitario de la Samaritana)*

www.hus.org.co

10. National Institute of Cancer E.S.E. *(Instituto Nacional de Cancerología E.S.E.)*

www.incancerologia.gov.co

11. National Institute of Dermatology (*Instituto Nacional de Dermatología*)

www.dermatología.gov.co

12. National Institute of Legal Medicine and Forensic Sciences (*Instituto Nacional de Medicina Legal y Ciencias Forenses*)

www.medicinalegal.gov.co

13. National Institute of Health (*Instituto Nacional de Salud*)

www.ins.gov.co

14. National Institute of Food and Drug Monitoring *(Instituto Nacional de Vigilancia de Medicamentos y Alimentos - INVIMA)*

www.invima.gov.co

15. Ministry of Social Protection *(Ministerio de la Protección Social)* www.minproteccionsocial.gov.co

16. Catholic University Javeriana – Human Genetics Institute *(Pontificia Universidad Javeriana, Instituto de Genética Humana)*

www.javeriana.edu.co/Genetica/

17. National Superintendence of Health *(Superintendencia Nacional de Salud – SUPERSALUD)*

www.supersalud.gov.co

18. University of Antioquia – School of Medicine *(Universidad de Antioquia – Facultad de Medicina)*

http://www.udea.edu.co/portal/page/portal/portal/A.Informacion-Institucional/H.UnidadesAcademicas/A.Facultades/Medicina

19. Neurosciences Group of the University of Antioquia *(Grupo de Neurociencias de la Universidad de Antioquia)*

http://neurociencias.udea.co

20. University of La Sabana *(Universidad de La Sabana)*

www.unisabana.edu.co

21. University of Los Andes *(Universidad de Los Andes)*

www.uniandes.edu.co

22. Externado University of Colombia *(Universidad Externado de Colombia)*

www.uexternado.edu.co

23. Pedagogical and Technological University of Colombia *(Universidad Pedagógica y Tecnológica de Colombia)*

www.uptc.edu.co

24. Popular Catholic University of Risaralda *(Universidad Católica Popular del Risaralda)*

www.ucpr.edu.co

25. National University of Colombia *(Universidad Nacional de Colombia)*

www.unal.edu.co

26. University Libre Seccional Cali *(Universidad Libre Seccional Cali)*

www.unilibrecali.edu.co

27. University of Cartagena *(Universidad de Cartagena)*

www.unicartagena.edu.co

Costa Rica

1. Costa Rican Department of Social Security. Centre for Strategic Development and Information on Health and Social Security Social *(Caja Costarricense de Seguro Social. Centro de Desarrollo Estratégico e Información en Salud y Seguridad Social – CENDEISSS)*

www.cendeisss.sa.cr/etica/01-PRESENaa.html

2. Ministry of Health – National Council of Health Research *(ministerio de Salud – Consejo Nacional de Investigación en Salud)*

www.ministeriodesalud.go.cr

3. University of Costa Rica *(Universidad de Costa Rica)*

www.ucr.ac.cr

4. Institute for Health Research of the University of Costa Rica *(Instituto de Investigaciones en Salud de la Universidad de Costa Rica – INISA)*

www.inisa.ucr.ac.cr

France

1. French Consulting Committee on Biological Resources

This Committee is formed by representatives from research organisations as well as French ministries and public administrations involved in life sciences. Its purpose is to promote centres which can offer access to high quality biological resources.

www2.enseignementsup-recherche.gouv.fr/comite/ccrb.htm

2. National Institute of Health and Medical Research (In French «INSERM»)

INSERM is the only French public organization entirely dedicated to biological, medical and public health research. Its researchers are committed to studying all human illnesses, whether common or rare.

www.inserm.fr/en/home.html

3. National Ethics Advisory Committee for life science and health

The Committee's primary mission is to produce opinions and reports on issues referred to it. Its freedom and independence lend legitimacy to its recommendations. Its purpose is to provide the referring authority an in-depth perspective allowing everyone to build their own opinion.

www.ccne-ethique.fr/theccne.php

4. French Agency of Sanitary Security of the Health Products (in French «AFSSAPS»)

AFSSAPS guaranteed effectiveness, quality and good use of medications and health products intended for humans.

www.afssaps.fr

5. The Biomedicine Agency

The Biomedicine Agency is in charge of the sector of transplants, procreation, embryology and genetics. The Agency evaluates and controls these activities, gives authorization.

www.agence-biomedecine.fr

6. National Commission for Data Protection and Liberties

Founded by the law of January 6, 1978, the CNIL is an independent administrative authority protecting privacy and personal data.

www.cnil.fr

7. The High Authority of Health (before the National Agency of Accreditation and Valuation of Health)

The High Authority of Health was set up by the French government in August 2004 in order to bring together under a single roof a number of activities designed to improve the quality of patient care and to guarantee equality within the healthcare system. HAH activities are diverse. They range from assessment of drugs, medical devices, and procedures to publication of guidelines to accreditation of healthcare organisations and certification of doctors. All are based on rigorously acquired scientific expertise. Training in quality issues and information provision are also key components of its work programme.

www.has-sante.fr/portail/jcms/j_5/accueil

8. National Academy of Medicine

The National Academy of Medicine works in close cooperation with all other Academies, especially the Institute of France Academy of Sciences, the Academy of Pharmacy and the Academy of Agriculture. The Academy has a delegate in all main institutions of health.

www.academie-medecine.fr

9\. National Cancer Institute

The National Cancer Institute was created by the Public Health Act of 9 August 2004, under the Cancer Plan, to enable a long-lasting, coordinated national policy against cancer. Placed under the tutelage of the Ministries of Health and Research, it brings together all of the players involved in the fight against cancer in France.

www.e-cancer.fr

10\. Interregional Delegation for Clinic Research in France *(Délégation interrégionale à la Reserche Clinique d'Ile de France)*

www.drrc.ap-hop-paris.fr

Germany

1\. German National Ethics Council *(Deutscher Ethikrat)*

www.ethikrat.org

2\. Enquête-Commission

http://www.bundestag.de/bundestag/ausschuesse17/gremien/enquete/index.jsp

3\. Central Ethics Commission *(Zentrale Ethik-*Kommission*)*

www.zentrale-ethikkommission.de

4\. Telematic Platform for Medical Networks *(TMF)*

www.tmf-ev.de

5\. Office of Technology Assessment at the German Parliament *(Büro für Technikfolgen-Abschätzung beim Deutschen Bundestag – TAB)*

www.tab-beim-bundestag.de

6\. University of Greifswald

www.uni-greifswald.de

7\. University of Erlangen

www.uni-erlangen.org

8\. University of Wuerzburg

www.uni-wuerzburg.de

9\. University of Kiel

www.uni-kiel.de

10. University of Freiburg
www.uni-freiburg.de
11. University of Ulm
www.uni-ulm.de
12. University of Heidelberg
www.uni-heidelberg.de
13. University of Potsdam
www.uni-potsdam.de

MEXICO

1. Federal Control Commission for Sanitary Risks (COFEPRIS)
A branch of the Mexican Health Agency, it is in charge of regulating, controlling and promoting sanitary facilities and procedures established in the General Health Legislation. This Commission is in charge of formulating and issuing the official norms regarding any activities, services and establishments performed by biobanks given that they work with human samples for research.
www.cofepris.gob.mx

2. National Council for Science and Technology (CONACYT)
It is in charge of promoting the structure and function of a national network of groups and research centers. This network's main objective is to define the strategies, joint programs and actions, the efficient use of human and financial resources and the enhancement of infrastructure in relevant areas of national development. Among its most relevant responsibilities, this network has to design the study programs that will allow professionalizing research and by doing so, strengthening and multiplying research groups and their interaction. It also has to promote the creation of new groups and centers, and to create networks in strategic areas of knowledge. Private or public groups and research centers related to the use of human samples for research, either independent or belonging to institutions of higher education, may voluntarily ascribe to this network.
www.conacyt.mx

3. National Autonomous University of Mexico *(Universidad Nacional Autónoma de México – UNAM)*

www.unam.mx/

4. Legal Research Institute (IIJ)

www.juridicas.unam.mx/

5. Health Agency

http://www.e-salud.gob.mx/wb2/eMex/eMex_SSA_

6. National Health Institutes

http://www.salud.gob.mx/unidades/cgins/institutos.html

7. Public Hospitals

http://www.e-salud.gob.mx/wb2/eMex/eMex_SSA_

8. Federal Commission for Protection against Sanitary Risks (COFEPRIS)

www.cofepris.gob.mx/

9. Bioethics National Commission (CNB)

www.cnb-mexico.salud.gob.mx/

10. National Institute of Genomic Medicine (INMEGEN)

www.inmegen.gob.mx/

11. Federal Institute of Access to Information (IFAI)

www.ifai.org.mx/

12. National Polytechnical Institute (IPN)

www.ipn.mx/

13. Mexican Social Security Institute (IMSS)

www.imss.gob.mx/

14. Social Security and Services Institute for the State Workers (ISSSTE)

www.issste.gob.mx/

Portugal

1. National Commission for Data Protection *(Comissão Nacional de Protecção de Dados)*

www.cnpd.pt

2. Administrative Documents Acces Commission *(Comissão de Acesso aos Documentos Administrativos)*

www.cada.pt

3. National Council for Life Sciences *(Conselho Nacional de Ética para as Ciências da Vida)*
www.cnecv.gov.pt/cnecv/pt/

4. Bioethics Association of Portugal *(Associação Portuguesa de Bioética)*
www.apbioetica.org/?lingua = pt

Spain

1. Spanish Bioethics Committee *(Comité de Bioética de España)*
Created through Law 14/2007 of July 3rd on Biomedical Research (BOE July 4th) as a «collegiate, independent and consultative professional body, which will develop its responsibilities, with full transparency, on materials related to the social and ethical implications of Biomedicine and Health Sciences». The Committee was established on October 22nd 2008 and forms part of the Ministry of Science & Innovation.

Its mission is to issue reports, proposals and recommendations for public authorities at state and regional level on matters related to the ethical and social implications of Biomedicine and Health Sciences. Equally, it is responsible for establishing the general principles for the production of codes of good practice in scientific research and for representing Spain in supranational and international forums and bodies involved in bioethics.

www.comitedebioetica.es

2. Carlos III Health Institute *(Instituto de Salud Carlos III)*
It is appointed by the Ministry of Science and Innovation. It promotes, manages and evaluates research on health sciences; it coordinates research activities into health sciences, with regard to the National Plan for Scientific Research, Development and Technological Innovation and European Union framework research and development programmes.

www.isciii.es

3. Coordinating Centre for Clinical Research Ethics Committees *(Centro Coordinador de los Comités Éticos de Investigación Clínica* [directory of all accredited Clinical Research Ethics Committees (CEIC's) in Spain])

It is a unit appointed by the Ministry of Health and Consumer Affairs whose objective is to assist the Clinical Research Ethics Committees in sharing suitable and homogeneous evaluation quality and criteria standards and to promote flexibility in the process of obtaining a single opinion. Equally, it should promote common evaluation criteria in the Clinical Research Ethical Committees. A directory with all the accredited Clinical Research Ethics Committees in Spain can be found on its Website.

www.msc.es/profesionales/farmacia/ceic/home.htm

4. Inter-University Chair, Provincial Government of Biscay, in Law and the Human Genome, Deusto University, University of the Basque Country *(Cátedra Interuniversitaria Diputación Foral de Bizkaia de Derecho y Genoma Humano, Universidad de Deusto, Universidad del País Vasco)*

www.catedraderechoygenomahumano.es

5. Health Sciences Foundation *(Fundación de Ciencias de la Salud)*

www.fcs.es

6. Víctor Grifols i Lucas Foundation *(Fundación Víctor Grifols i Lucas)*

www.fundaciogrifols.org

7. Institute Borja of Bioethics *(Instituto Borja de Bioética)*

www.ibbioetica.org

8. Bioethics and Law Observatory *(Observatorio de Bioética y Derecho)*

www.pcb.ub.es/bioeticaidret/

9. International Society of Bioethics *(Sociedad Internacional de Bioética)*

www.sibi.org

NATIONAL LEGISLATION

Argentina

1. National Decree 512/95: Regulation of the Act 24.139 of Organ Transplantation and Anatomic Human Material

http://www.hcdn.gov.ar/

2. Resolution 260/99: Rules for the habilitation of Tissue Banks of skeletal muscle and the osteoarticular system, and the authorization of the Bank's professionals.

http://www.incucai.gov.ar/docs/resoluciones/resolucion_incucai_260_99.pdf

3. Resolution 148/01 related to the habilitation of establishments and professional teams for skin implants.

http://www.incucai.gov.ar/docs/resoluciones/resolucion_incucai_148_01.pdf

4. Resolution 188/97: Rules for the habilitation of eye tissue banks and professional authorizations.

http://www.incucai.gov.ar/docs/resoluciones/resolucion_incucai_188_97.pdf

5. Resolution 29/97: related to the habilitation of homograft valve banks and professionals' authorizations.

http://www.incucai.gov.ar/docs/resoluciones/resolucion_incucai_029_97.pdf

6. Resolution 149/01 about technical and operational rules for the obtaining, processing, cryopreservation and liberation of amniotic tissue.

http://www.hcdn.gov.ar/

7. Resolution 314/04 states rules for the habilitation of hematopoietic progenitor cell banks (B-CPH) obtained from umbilical vein blood and the placenta, destined for allogeneic transplants.

http://www.hcdn.gov.ar/

Brazil

1. Federative Republic Constitution of Brazil, 1988.

http://www.planalto.gov.br/ccivil_03/Constituicao/Constituiçao.htm

2. Draft Law n° 3078, 2000. It talks about the collection of organic materials for individual identification through DNA isolation, without offending or violating the exempted dispositions in article 5th of the Federal Constitution, which disciplines procedures for ADN tests and provides other dispositions.

http://ghente.org/doc_juridicos/pl3078.htm

3. Provisional Measure 2.186-16/2001. Regulates number II of the §1° and §4° of the art. 225 of the Constitution; arts. 1°, 8° (line «j»), 10° (line «c»), 15° and 16 (lines 3 and 4) of the Biologic Diversity Convention. Regulates the access to genetic resources, the protection and access to associated traditional knowledge, sharing of benefits and access to technology and technology transfer for its conservation and use, and other matters.

https://www.planalto.gov.br/ccivil_03/MPV/2186-16.htm

4. Biosecurity Law. Law n° 11.105 (24/March/2005). This act regulates numbers II, IV and V of the §1° of art. 225 of the Constitution; it establishes safety standards and mechanisms for monitoring activities related to Genetically Modified Organisms (GMO) and their derivatives; this act also established the National Council of Biosecurity (CNBS); restructures the National Commission of Biosecurity (CTNBio); states the National Biosecurity Policy (PNB); repeals Act 8.974 (5/January/1995), and the Provisional Measure 2.191-9 (23/August/2001), and the arts. 5°, 6°, 7°, 8°, 9°, 10° and 16° of the Act 10.814 (15/December/2003), and establishes other matters.

http://www.planalto.gov.br/ccivil_03/_Ato2004-2006/2005/Lei/L11105.htm

5. Indian statute. Law 6.001 (19/December/1973).

http://www.planalto.gov.br/ccivil_03/Leis/L6001.htm

6. Civil Code 1916. Law 3.071 (1/January/1916).

http://www.planalto.gov.br/ccivil_03/LEIS/L3071.htm

7. Civil Code 2002. Law 10.406 (10/January/2002).

http://www.planalto.gov.br/ccivil_03/LEIS/2002/L10406.htm

8. National Council of Health, Resolution n. 196 (10/October/ 1996). Directives and regulations for rules of research involving human beings.

http://conselho.saude.gov.br/resolucoes/reso_96.htm

9. National Council of Health, Resolution n. 304 (9/August/2000). Directives and regulating rules of research involving human beings – Indigenous peoples' areas.

http://conselho.saude.gov.br/resolucoes/2000/Reso304.doc

10. National Council of Health, Resolution n. 340 (8/July/2004). Directives for the Ethical Analysis and Procedure of Human Genetics Special Thematic Area Research Projects.

http://conselho.saude.gov.br/resolucoes/2004/Reso340.doc

11. National Council of Health Resolution n. 347 (13/January/ 2005). Directives for the Ethical Analysis of research projects which involve the storage of materials or use of stored materials in previous researches.

http://conselho.saude.gov.br/resolucoes/2005/Reso347.doc

CHILE

1. Political Constitution of the Republic of Chile (Articles 5, 19 No. 4 and 19 No. 12).

http://www.leychile.cl/Navegar?idNorma=242302

2. Law 20.120, on Scientific Research on Human Beings

http://www.fondecyt.cl/578/articles-27523_recurso_1.pdf

3. Law 19.628 on the Protection of Privacy

http://www.leychile.cl/
Navegar?idNorma=141599&idParte=0&idVersion=

4. Exempt Resolution 134, of 1994, approves general technical standard N°2 on Ethics Committees in health services and repeals Technical DPI No. 10, modified by Exempt Resolution No. 1856 of 1999, from the Ministry of Health

http://salunet.minsal.gov.cl/pls/portal/docs/PAGE/TRANSPARENCIA/G_SEREMI/SEREMI15_NORMAS/MARCO_NORMATIVO_RESOL.134-1994.PDF

5. Technical Standard No. 57 : Regulation of the execution of clinical trials which use pharmaceuticals in human beings, Ministry of Health, Chile, 2001

http://www.ispch.cl/formularios/norma_tec/norm_tec_n_57.pdf

COLOMBIA

1. Colombia Constitution (Articles 1, 13, 15, 16, 27, 69, 70, 86, 152, 330)

www.banrep.gov.co/regimen/resoluciones/cp91.pdf

www.cna.gov.co/cont/documentos/legislacion/constitucion.pdf

2. Law 9, 1979. By which sanitary actions are established.

www.alcaldiabogota.gov.co/sisjur/normas/Normal.jsp?i = 1177

www.cdmb.gov.co/normas/ley91979.htm

3. Law 23, 1981. Code of Medical Ethics.

http://juriscol.banrep.gov.co:8080/basisjurid_docs/legislacion/normas_buscar_cont.html

4. Law 29, 1990, on the promotion of scientific research and technological development.

www.ins.gov.co/?idcategoria = 1290&download = Y

5. Law 21, 1991. By which Convention 169 of the Indigenous people of independent countries, 1989 is approved.

http://juriscol.banrep.gov.co:8080/basisjurid_docs/legislacion/normas_buscar_cont.html

6. Law 919, 2004, that forbids the commercialization of human anatomical components for transplants.

www.secretariasenado.gov.co/senado/basedoc/ley/2004/ley_0919_2004.html

7. Law 938, 2004. By which the Organic Statute of the General Attorney is issued.

www.secretariasenado.gov.co/senado/basedoc/ley/2004/ley_0938_2004.html

8. Law 1164, 2007. By which rules concerning Human Talent in Health are announced.

www.secretariasenado.gov.co/senado/basedoc/ley/2007/ley_1164_2007.html

9. Law 1266, 2008, with special dispositions regarding the rights of data protection, and that regulates the management of personal data in data files, especially financial, commercial, regarding services and data coming from other countries.

www.secretariasenado.gov.co/senado/basedoc/ley/2008/ley_1266_2008.html

http://www.icbf.gov.co/transparencia/derechobienestar/ley/2008/ley_1266_2008.html

10. Law 1286, 2009. By which Law Nº 29 of 1990 is modified and converts COLCIENCIAS in Administrative Department, strengthens the National System of Science, Tecnology and Innovation in Colombia, and announces other resolutions.

http://web.presidencia.gov.co/leyes/2009/enero/ley12862301 2009.pdf

http://www.icbf.gov.co/transparencia/derechobienestar/ley/2009/ley_1286_2009.html

11. Decree 3380, 1981. By which Law Nº 23 of 1981 (Code of Medical Ethics) is regulated.

www.mineducacion.gov.co/1621/articles-103328_archivo_pdf.pdf

12. Decree 786, 1990. By which Title IX of the Law Nº 9 of 1979, concerning the clinic autopsy and forensic practices, as well as the viscerotomys is partially regulated, and other resolutions are announced.

http://www.presidencia.gov.co/prensa_new/decretoslinea/1990/abril/16/dec786161990.pdf

13. Decree 1571, 1993. By which Title IX of the Law Nº 9 of 1979, concerning the operation of Institutions for extraction, processing, preservation and transport of human blood or their derivatives is partially regulated; the National Network of Blood Biobanks and the National Council of Blood Biobanks is set up; and other resolutions are announced.

http://www.alcaldiabogota.gov.co/sisjur/normas/Normal.jsp?i=14527

14. Decree 1546, 1998. By which Laws 9^a of 1979 and 73^a of 1988, concerning the obtaining, donation, preservation, storage, transport and use of anatomical human components, and the proc-

ess for the transplantation of these components in human beings are partially regulated.

http://www.presidencia.gov.co/prensa_new/decretoslinea/1998/agosto/04/dec1546041998.pdf

http://www.alcaldiabogota.gov.co/sisjur/normas/Normal.jsp?i=14522

15. Decree 1177, 1999. Restructures the National Institute of Cancer.

http://www.minproteccionsocial.gov.co/VBeContent/library/documents/DocNewsNo11089DocumentNo7760.pdf

16. Decree 1101, 2001. The Intersectorial Bioethics Commission is set up.

http://www.presidencia.gov.co/prensa_new/decretoslinea/2001/junio/07/dec1101072001.pdf

http://www.minproteccionsocial.gov.co/VBeContent/library/documents/DocNewsNo9192DocumentNo7825.pdf

17. Decree 2112, 2003. By which the accreditation and certification of public and private laboratories engaged parenthood testing with genetic markers of DNA and other provisions is regulated.

www.alcaldiabogota.gov.co/sisjur/normas/Normal.jsp?i=9563

18. Decree 2493, 2004. By which Law 9 of 1979 and 73 of 1988, in relation to the anatomical components, is partially regulated.

http://www.alcaldiabogota.gov.co/sisjur/normas/Normal.jsp?i=14525

19. Decree 2323, 2006. By which Law 9 of 1979 in connection with the National Network of Laboratories and other purposes is partially regulated.

http://www.ins.gov.co/index.php?idcategoria=5813#

20. Resolution 13437, 1991. By which a format for collecting information on the institutions providing health services is adopted.

www.minproteccionsocial.gov.co/VBeContent/library/documents/DocNewsNo352211.pdf

21. Resolution N° 008430, 1993. By which the standards, technical and administrative in health research are established.

http://www.ins.gov.co/?idcategoria=1395

22. Resolution 1995, 1999. By which the standards for the management of health records are established.

http://www.alcaldiabogota.gov.co/sisjur/normas/Normal.jsp?i=16737#0

23. Resolution 485, 2002. By which the procedure for the delivery of cadavers and anatomical components obtained from the same, for purposes of teaching and research, is regulated.

http://www.alcaldiabogota.gov.co/sisjur/normas/Normal.jsp?i=5970

24. Resolution 002640, 2005. By which articles 3, 4, 6 (paragraph 2), 7 (number 10), 25 and 46 of the Decree 2493 of 2004 and other provisions are regulated.

http://www.alcaldiabogota.gov.co/sisjur/normas/Normal.jsp?i=17328

http://www.ins.gov.co/?idcategoria=1382

25. Resolution 005108 de 2005. By which the Manual of Good Practice for Tissue Banks and Bone Marrow and enacting other provisions is established.

http://web.invima.gov.co:8080/Invima///normatividad/docs_sangre/resolucion_5108_2005.htm

26. Resolution 2378, 2008. By which Good Clinical Practice for institutions conducting medical research in humans is adopted.

http://www.minproteccionsocial.gov.co/VBeContent/library/documents/DocNewsNo17655DocumentNo7224.PDF

27. Decision 391, 1996. Common Regime on Access to Genetic Resources.

www.comunidadandina.org/normativa/dec/D391.htm

28. Decision 486, 2000?. Common Provisions on Industrial Property.

http://www.comunidadandina.org/normativa/dec/D486.htm

Costa Rica

1. General Health Act N° 5395 of October 30, 1973.
http://www.netsalud.sa.cr/leyes/libro3.htm

2. General Regulations for the Operation of Health Establishments and Related Establishments, issued by means of Executive Decree N⁰ 30571-S of June 25, 2002, published in *La Gaceta* N⁰ 138 of July 18, 2002.

http://www.disaster-info.net/PED-Sudamerica/leyes/leyes/centroamerica/costarica/salud/Reglamento_30571.pdf

3. Costa Rican Association of Microbiologists and Clinical Chemists Act and its Regulation No. 771 of October 25, 1949.

http://www.colegiomicrobiologoscr.org/descargas/LeyOrg%ElnicadelColegiodeMicrobi%F3logos-ley771.doc

4. Act No. 5462 Statute of Microbiology and Clinical Chemistry Services.

http://www.colegiomicrobiologoscr.org/descargas/EstatutoServiciosMicrobiolog%EDayQu%EDmicaCl%EDnica-ley5462.doc

5. Code of Ethics of Microbiologists and Clinical Chemists.

http://www.colegiomicrobiologoscr.org/descargas/Codigodeetica.doc

6. Executive Decree N⁰ 12 of September 30, 1957. Rules of the College of Microbiologists.

http://www.colegiomicrobiologoscr.org/descargas/ReglamentoInternoCMQCDE12.doc

7. Norms for the authorization of Immunohematology Departments and Blood Bank. N° 30697-S of September 23, 2002.

http://www.ministeriodesalud.go.cr/normas/0506norma%20inmunohematologia%20y%20bancos%20de%20sangre.pdf

8. Regulations for Biomedical Research in assistance activities of the Costa Rican Social Security Fund of November 17, 2005.

http://www.cendeisss.sa.cr/etica/reglamentobiomedica.pdf

9. Investigator Brochure. Guide to procedures for research with human beings in the University of Costa Rica. 2006.

http://www.ts.ucr.ac.cr/formulas/secinv-manual-investigador.doc

10. Ministry of Health. Executive Decree No. 31078-S (2003). Rules for research involving human beings.

http://www.ministeriodesalud.go.cr/reglamentos/31078-s.pdf

NATIONAL LEGISLATION

FRANCE

1. Law 94-654 (29/July/1994), governing the donation and use of elements and products of the human body, medically assisted reproduction, and prenatal diagnosis
http://www.sante.gouv.fr/pdf/94-654.pdf

2. Law 2004-800 (6/August/2004) on bioethics.
http://www.legifrance.gouv.fr/affichTexte.do?cidTexte=JORFTEXT000000441469

3. Decree No. 95-682 (9/May/1995) for the application of Chapter V of the 1978 Act
http://www.legifrance.gouv.fr/affichTexteArticle.do;jsessionid=4ACDFDC3FF5919AF73A7FC5AEDF349D1.tpdjo14v_2?cidTexte=JORFTEXT000000354742&idArticle=LEGIARTI000006541545&dateTexte=19950511&categorieLien=id#LEGIARTI000006541545

4. Decree 2007-1220 (10/August/2007), on gathering, conservation, and preparation of human samples for scientific use.
http://www.legifrance.gouv.fr/affichTexte.do?cidTexte=JORFTEXT000000829163&dateTexte=

5. Order of 29 December 1998 approving the rules of good practice in conservation, processing and transportation of human tissues used for therapeutic purposes.
http://www.legifrance.gouv.fr/jopdf/common/jo_pdf.jsp?numJO=0&dateJO=19990108&numTexte=00389&pageDebut=00389&pageFin=

6. Order of 16 August 2007 laying down the model file including the protocol on samples for scientific purposes of human organs, tissues or cells.
http://www.legifrance.gouv.fr/affichTexte.do?cidTexte=JORFTEXT000000274627&dateTexte=

GERMANY

1. Basic Law for the Federal Republic of Germany (Grundgesetz für die Bundesrepublik Deutschland)
https://www.btg-bestellservice.de/pdf/80201000.pdf

http://www.gesetze-im-internet.de/bundesrecht/gg/gesamt.pdf

2. German Civil Code (Bürgerliches Gesetzbuch – BGB)

http://www.gesetze-im-internet.de/englisch_bgb/

http://bundesrecht.juris.de/bgb/index.html

3. German Criminal Code (Strafgesetzbuch – StGB)

http://www.gesetze-im-internet.de/englisch_stgb/index.html

http://www.gesetze-im-internet.de/stgb/

4. Federal Data Protection Law, 2002 (Bundesdatenschutzgesetz – BDSG)

http://www.bdd.de/Download/bdsg_eng.pdf

5. German Medicines Act (Arzneimittelgesetz - AMG)

http://www.bfarm.de/nn_424934/EN/BfArM/BfArMService/AMG__en/amg-node-en.html__nnn=true

6. Gene Diagnostic Law (Gendiagnostikgesetz – GenDG)

http://www.buzer.de/gesetz/8967/index.htm

http://dip21.bundestag.de/dip21/btd/16/105/1610532.pdf

7. Tissue Law (Gewebegesetz – GewebeG)

http://www.buzer.de/gesetz/7833/index.htm

http://bundesrecht.juris.de/gewebeg/index.html

8. Cancer Registry Law (Krebsregistergesetz – KRG)

http://www.tumorzentrum-suhl.de/krg.pdf

9. Hessian Data Protection Law (Hessisches Datenschutzgesetz – HDSG)

http://www.datenschutz.hessen.de/hdsg99.htm

10. Copyright Law (Urheberrechtsgesetz – UrhG)

http://www.iuscomp.org/gla/statutes/UrhG.htm

http://bundesrecht.juris.de/bundesrecht/urhg/gesamt.pdf

http://bundesrecht.juris.de/urhg/index.html

11. Patent Law (Patentgesetz – PatG)

http://bundesrecht.juris.de/patg/index.html

http://bundesrecht.juris.de/bundesrecht/patg/gesamt.pdf

12. Stem Cell Law (Stammzellgesetz – StZG)

http://www.bmj.de/files/-/1146/Stammzellgesetz%20englisch.pdf

http://bundesrecht.juris.de/stzg/index.html

http://bundesrecht.juris.de/bundesrecht/stzg/gesamt.pdf
13. Embryo Protection Law (Embryonenschutzgesetz – ESchG)
http://www.bmj.de/files/-/1147/ESchG%20englisch.pdf
http://bundesrecht.juris.de/eschg/index.html
http://bundesrecht.juris.de/bundesrecht/eschg/gesamt.pdf

Mexico

1. Political Constitution of the United Mexican States
http://www.scjn.gob.mx/PortalSCJN/RecJur/Legislacion/ConstitucionPolitica/ConstitucionPolitica.htm
2. Federal Law of Transparency and Access to Government Public Information
http://www.diputados.gob.mx/LeyesBiblio/index.htm
3. Guidelines for the Protection of Personal Data
http://www.sre.gob.mx/acerca/marco_normativo/doc/lin_protdatospers.pdf
4. General Law on Health
http://www.diputados.gob.mx/LeyesBiblio/index.htm
5. Health Rules on matters of Health Research
http://www.salud.gob.mx/unidades/cdi/nom/compi/rlgsmis.html
6. Mexican Official Regulation of biological infectious and dangerous residues
http://www.salud.gob.mx/unidades/cdi/nom/087ecolssa.html
7. The Law of Science and Technology
http://www.diputados.gob.mx/LeyesBiblio/index.htm
8. Federal Law of Administrative Responsibilities of Civil Servants
http://info4.juridicas.unam.mx/ijure/fed/134/default.htm?s=
9. Protection of Personal Data Law for the Federal District
http://www.asambleadf.gob.mx/index2.php?pagina=14
10. Penal Code for the Federal District
http://www.asambleadf.gob.mx/index2.php?pagina=191

Portugal

1. Law on personal genetic information and health information (Law 67/98, of 26 October 1998)
  http://dre.pt/pdf1sdip/1998/10/247A00/55365546.pdf
2. Law on personal genetic information and health information (Law 12/2005, of 26 January 2005)
  http://dre.pt/pdf1sdip/2005/01/018A00/06060611.pdf
3. Art. 35 of the Constitution of the Portuguese Republic
  http://www.portugal.gov.pt/Portal/PT/Portugal/Sistema_Politico/Constituicao/
4. Art. 195 of the Portuguese Penal Code
  http://dre.pt/pdf1sdip/2007/09/17000/0618106258.pdf

Spain

1. Law 14/2007, 3 July, on Biomedical Research.
  http://www.boe.es/aeboe/consultas/bases_datos/doc.php?coleccion=iberlex&id=2007/12945
2. Law 41/2002, 14 November, that regulates the autonomy of the patient and rights and duties related to clinical information and documentation.
  http://www.boe.es/aeboe/consultas/bases_datos/doc.php?coleccion=iberlex&id=2002/22188
3. Organic Law 15/1999, 13 December, on the protection of Personal Data.
  http://www.boe.es/aeboe/consultas/bases_datos/doc.php?coleccion=iberlex&id=1999/23750
4. Royal Decree 1720/2007, 21 December, that approves the regulation that develops Organic Law 15/1999, 13 December, on the protection of Personal Data
  http://www.boe.es/aeboe/consultas/bases_datos/doc.php?coleccion=iberlex&id=2008/00979

BIBLIOGRAPHY

AA.VV., *Guía Práctica para la utilización de muestras biológicas en investigación biomédica*, Instituto Roche, Madrid, 2006.

ABEL, Francesc and CUSÍ, Victoria, «Bancos de información genética. Problemas éticos y jurídicos», *El juez civil ante la investigación biomédica, Cuadernos de Derecho Judicial*, X, Consejo General del Poder Judicial, Madrid, 2004.

AGENCE DE LA BIOMÉDICINE, *Banque de sang placentaire autologue*, nov. 2007.

AGENCE DE LA BIOMÉDICINE, *Délibération*, n° 2007-CO-41, 9 nov. 2007.

AGENCE DE LA BIOMÉDICINE, *Rapport annuel – Bilan des activités*, 2006, pp. 178-179.

AGENCE FRANÇAISE DE SÉCURITÉ SANITAIRE POUR LES PRODUITS DE SANTÉ, *Contribution aux Etats Généraux de la Bioéthique*, février 2009.

AGENCE NATIONAL POUR L'ACCRÉDITATION ET L'ÉVALUATION DE LA SANTÉ, *Recommandations pour la cryopreservation de cellules et tissus tumoraux dans le but de realiser des analyses des analyses biomoleculaires*, 2000.

AGENCIA ESPAÑOLA DE PROTECCIÓN DE DATOS, *Guía de seguridad de datos*, Madrid, 2008.

ALKORTA IDIAKEZ, Itziar, «Human Tissue and Cells Regulation in Spain : looking at Europe to solve inner contradictions?», *Revista de Derecho y Genoma Humano / Law and the Human Genome Review*, nr. 29, 2008.

ANDRADE, Costa, «Consentimento em Direito Penal Médico – o consentimento presumido», *Revista Portuguesa de Ciência Criminal*, 14, 2004.

ANDRADE, Costa, *Comentário Conimbricense do Código Penal I, articles 156 and 157*, Ed. Coimbra, Coimbra, 1999.

ANDRADE, Costa, *Consentimento e Acordo em Direito Penal (Contributo para a Fundamentação de um Paradigma Dualista)*, Ed. Coimbra, Coimbra, 2004.

ARCHILA PEÑALOSA, Emilio José, «Radiografía de patentamiento del genoma humano», *La propiedad inmaterial*, n° 1, 2001, pp. 81-101.

ASSISTANCE PUBLIQUE DES HÔPITAUX DE PARIS, «Vademecum juridique», 30 mars 2008, http://www.drrc.ap-hop-paris.fr/ressources_biologiques/document_types_rb.php.

BELLIER, L., *Devenir des biothèques transfusionnelles «donneurs» en France : quel devoir de garde. Pour quelle durée? Quelles conséquences pour le donneur?*, Université Paris Descartes-Paris V, Mémoire DEA sous la dir. G. Moutel et J.J. Cabaud.

BELLIVER, F. and NOIVILLE, C., *Les biobanques*, Paris, PUF, Coll. Que-sais-je?, 2009.

BELLIVIER, F., NOIVILLE, C. and LABRUSSE-RIOU, C., *Contrats et vivan : le droit de la circulation des ressources biologiques*, France, L.G.D.J., Traité des contrats, 2006.

BERNAL VILLEGAS, Jaime, «Genética y cultura», www.universia.net.co.

Bossi, J., «European Directive of October 24, 1995 and Protection of Medical Data: The Consequences of the French Law Governing Data Processing and Freedoms», *European Journal of Health Law*, 9, 2002, pp. 201-206.

Botá Arque, Alexandre, Contribution of CIOMS Guidelines 2002 to Biotechnological Development. Assumption of Responsibility by Scientists. On-line at http://www.scielo.cl/pdf/bres/v36n2/art05.pdf [downloaded on 05.11.2007].

Bourel, M. and Ardaillou, R., *Les centres de ressources biologiques dans les établissements de soins*, Académie nationale de Médecine, 2002.

Breyer, Patrick, «Offene Rechtsfragen bei der Gründung Medizinischer Versorgungszentren», *Medizinrecht (MedR)*, 2004, p. 660.

Callies, I., Montgolfier, S de, Moutel, G. and Hervé, C., «Enjeux éthiques des collections d'échantillons humains dans le cadre de la recherché : le point sur les avancées et les incohérences du projet de loi relative à la bioéthique», *Droit, déontologie et soin*, vol. 4, n° 2, 2004, pp. 148-164.

Cambon-Thomsen, A., Ducournau, P., Gourraud, P.A. and Pontille, D., «Biobanks for genomics and genomics for biobanks», *Comparative and functional genomics*, vol. 4, 2003, pp. 628-634.

Cambon-Thomsen, A. and Rial-Sebbag, E., «Collections d'échantillons biologiques : aspects éthiques et réglementaires», *Revue d'épidémiologie et de santé publique*, n° 51, 2003, pp. 96-126.

Cantosperber, M., *Ethiques d'aujourd'hui*, Séminaire 1, Ecole normale supérieure Ier semester 2003, PUF, 2004.

Cardozo de Martinez, Carmen Alicia, *Ética en investigación : una responsabilidad social*, Pontificia Universidad Javeriana y Universidad nacional de Colombia, Bogotá, 2008.

Cares Lay, Víctor Ignacio, Prospective study of the benefits of the implementation of an automated system of microbiological analysis in the University of Chile Hospital Clinic, in 2005, on-line at http://www.cybertesis.cl/tesis/uchile/2005/cares_v/sources/cares_v.pdf. [downloaded on 05.11.2007].

Casado da Rocha, Antonio and Etxeberria Agiriano, Arantza, «El consentimiento informado ante los biobancos y la investigación genética», *Arbor*, Vol. CLXXXIV, núm. 730, 2008.

Casado da Rocha, Antonio and Seoane, José Antonio, «Alternative consent models for biobanks : the new spanish law on biomedical research», *Bioethics*, vol. 22, number 8, 2008.

Casas Zamora, Juan Antonio, «The challenges of bioethics in Latin-America: Equity, health and human rights», in *Bioethics, Health Care, Equity, Quality, Rights*, Fernando Lolas Stepke (editor), Series of Publications – 2000, Regional Bioethics Programme. Division of Health and Human Development, Pan-American Health Organisation. World Health Organisation, LOM Editions, Santiago, December 2000.

Cascão, Rui, «O dever de documentação do prestador de cuidados de saúde e a responsabilidade civil», *Lex Medicinae*, 8, 2007.

Caze de Montgolfier, S., *Collecte, stockage et utilisation des produits du corps humain dans le cadre des recherches en génétique : état des lieux historique, éthique et juridique; analyse des pratiques au sein des biothèques*, Thèse de doctorat, Université Paris Descartes-V, 2002.

CLAYES, A., *Rapport fait au nom de la Commission spéciale sur le projet de loi relatif à la bioéthique*, Assemblée nationale, 2002.

COMITÉ CONSULTATIF NATIONAL D'ÉTHIQUE POUR LES SCIENCES DE LA VIE ET DE LA SANTÉ, *Éthique et recherche biomédicale : rapport 2003*, Documentation française, France, 2006.

COMITÉ CONSULTATIF NATIONAL D'ÉTHIQUE POUR LES SCIENCES DE LA VIE ET DE LA SANTÉ, *Commercialisation des cellules souches humaines et autres lignées cellulaires*, Avis n° 93.

COMITÉ CONSULTATIF NATIONAL D'ÉTHIQUE POUR LES SCIENCES DE LA VIE ET DE LA SANTÉ, *Problèmes éthiques posés par les collections de matériel biologique et les données d'information associées : «biobanques», «biothèques»*, Avis n° 77, 20 mars 2005.

COMITÉ CONSULTATIF NATIONAL D'ÉTHIQUE POUR LES SCIENCES DE LA VIE ET DE LA SANTÉ, *Les banques de sang de cordon ombilical en vue d'une utilisation autologue ou en recherche*, Avis n° 74.

COMITÉ CONSULTATIF NATIONAL D'ÉTHIQUE POUR LES SCIENCES DE LA VIE ET DE LA SANTÉ, *Réexamen des lois de bioéthiques*, Avis n° 60.

COMITÉ CONSULTATIF NATIONAL D'ÉTHIQUE POUR LES SCIENCES DE LA VIE ET DE LA SANTÉ, *La non-commercialisation du génome humain. Rapport. Réflexions générales sur les problèmes éthiques posés par les recherches sur le génome humain*, Avis n° 27.

COMITÉ CONSULTATIF NATIONAL D'ÉTHIQUE POUR LES SCIENCES DE LA VIE ET DE LA SANTÉ, *L'application des tests génétiques aux études individuelles, études familiales et études de population. (Problèmes des «banques» de l'ADN, des «banques» de cellules et de l'informatisation des données)*, Avis n° 25.

COMITÉ CONSULTATIF NATIONAL D'ÉTHIQUE POUR LES SCIENCES DE LA VIE ET DE LA SANTÉ, *La non-commercialisation du corps humain*, Avis n° 21.

COMITÉ CONSULTATIF NATIONAL D'ÉTHIQUE POUR LES SCIENCES DE LA VIE ET DE LA SANTÉ, *Les problèmes posés par le développement des méthodes d'utilisation de cellules humaines et de leurs dérivés*, Avis n° 9.

COMITÉ CONSULTATIF NATIONAL D'ÉTHIQUE POUR LES SCIENCES DE LA VIE ET DE LA SANTÉ, *Les registres médicaux pour études épidémiologiques et de prévention*, Avis n° 4.

COMITÉ DE ÉTICA DEL INSTITUTO DE INVESTIGACIÓN DE ENFERMEDADES RARAS, INSTITUTO DE SALUD CARLOS TERCERO, «Recomendaciones sobre los aspectos éticos de las colecciones de muestras y bancos de materiales humanos con fines de investigación biomédica», *Revista Española de Salud Pública*, número 2, 2007.

COMITÉ INTERNATIONAL DE BIOÉTHIQUE DE L'UNESCO (CIB), *Journée d'auditions publiques sur els données génétiques*, Unesco, 2003.

DAGHER, G. interview réalisé par Cabut S., «Biobanquier un métier d'avenir», *Libération*, 25 novembre 2006.

DELFOSSE, M. and BERT, C., *Bioéthique, droits de l'homme et biodroit : recueil de textes annotés internationaux, régionaux, belges et français*, Larcier, Belgique, 2005.

Der Hessische Datenschutzbeauftragte, *30. Tätigkeitsbericht*, Wiesbaden, 2001.

Der Hessische Datenschutzbeauftragte, *33. Tätigkeitsbericht*, Wiesbaden, 2004.

Deutsch, Erwin and Spickhoff, Andreas, *Medizinrecht*, 5. ed., Berlin, Heidelberg, New York et al, 2003.

Díaz Martínez, Ana, «Daños causados en la investigación biomédica y la realización de estudios genéticos : conductas y omisiones determinantes de responsabilidad y resarcimiento», *Diario La Ley*, 19 de septiembre de 2007.

Ducournau, P., Cobbaut JP. and Bouvet, A., «Le consentement à la recherche en épidémiologie génétique : le «rituel de confiance» en question : de la confiance à la réflexivité : commentaire», *Sciences sociales et santé*, vol. 23, n° 1, 2005, pp. 5-42.

Duguet, A.M., Bévière, B., Boucly, G., Rial, E. and Cambon-Thomsen, A., «Les droits des patients et les Bio sources – L'utilisation des éléments du corps humain», *Journal de Médecine Légale Droit Médical*, vol. 50, n° 1-2, 2007, pp. 55-62.

Duguet, A.M., Fecteau, C., Biga, J., Moutel, G. and Hervé, C., «Les informations génétiques, droits des patients et confidentialité depuis la loi du 4 mars 2002», *Médecine et droit*, 2004, n° 65, pp. 35-41.

Enquete-Commission, *Law and Ethics of the Modern Medicine, Final* Report, Bundestagsdrucksache 14/9020, Berlin, 2003.

Fagniez, Pl. and Giraud, F., *Rapport fait au nom de la Commission mixte paritaire chargée de proposer un texte sur les dispositions restant en discussion du projet de loi relatif à la bioéthique*, Commission mixte paritaire assemblée nationale/Sénat, 2004.

Faria, Adriano Lopes de, «Cancer». http://www.ufv.br/dbg/BIO240/AC%20050.htm.

Fica C., Alberto, Ruiz, Gloria and Ali, Yunes. *Hospital Waste Management Regulations*. Draft or review date : October, 2000. Date approved by Intra-hospital Infection Committee (IIH) : October, 2000. In the same way, the Joint Position of the Chilean Society for the Control of infections and hospital epidemiology and the Chilean Society for infectious diseases, available in electronic format at http://www.cepis.ops-oms.org/cursoreas/e/fulltext/desechos.pdf.

Fidalgo, Sónia, «Determinação do perfil genético como meio de prova em processo penal», *Revista Portuguesa de Ciência Criminal*, 1, 2006.

Figueroa, G., *Genetic information and the right to personal identity*. Paper presented to the Second Latin-American Meeting on Bioethics and the Human Genome, Buenos Aires, Argentina, November 1998.

Freund, Georg and Weiss, Natalie, «Zur Zulässigkeit der Verwendung menschlichen Körpermaterials», *Medizinrecht (MedR)*, 2004, p. 346 ff.

García Amez, Javier, «La cesión interna de datos genéticos en el derecho español. Un problema aún por legislar», *Revista de Derecho Informático*, núm. 092, 2006.

Garcia, Javier, «La protección de los datos sanitarios y genéticos en España. Un análisis desde los principios generales de protección de datos de carácter personal», *Revista de Derecho y Genoma Humano / Law and the Human Genome Review*, núm. 24, 2006.

GOMEZ G., Alberto, «El Banco Biológico Humano», *Revista Javeriana*, Tomo 118, julio, 1992.

GONZÁLEZ DE CANCINO, Emilssen, «Patentes sobre genes humanos», *Derecho y Vida*, n° XXXVIII, 2004.

GRAND, E., HERVÉ, C. and MOUTEL, G., *Les éléments du corps humain, la personne et la médecine*, L'Harmattan, France, 2005.

GROUPE EUROPÉEN D'ÉTHIQUE (GEE), *Les aspects éthiques des banques de sang de cordon ombilical*, avis n° 19, 2004.

HALÀSZ, Christian, *Das Recht auf biomaterielle Selbstbestimmung*, Berlin, 2004.

HERVÉ, C., KNOPPERS, B.M. and MOLINARI, Pa., «Les pratiques de recherche biomédicale visitées par la bioéthique», *Premières journées scientifiques de l'Institut international d'éthique biomédicale (IIREB)*, Paris, Décembre 2001, Dalloz, 2003.

HIRTZLIN, I., DUBREUIL, C. and CAMBON-THOMSEN, A. et al., Eurogenbank Consortium, «An empirical survey on biobanking of human genetic material and data in six EU countries», *European journal of human genetics*, vol. 11, 2003, pp. 475-488.

INSTITUT NATIONAL DE LA SANTÉ ET DE LA RECHERCHE MÉDICALE (INSERM), *Tests génétiques*, Inserm, Repères, France, 2003.

INSTITUT NATIONAL DU CANCER, *Les tumorothèques hospitalières*, novembre 2006.

JANSEN, Roberta, «Brasil will have centers for ADN tests», *Science Journal(SBPC)*, http://www.jornaldaciencia.org.br/Detalhe.jsp?id=14577.

JONES, DG., GEAR, R. and GALVIN, K.A., «Stored human tissue : an ethical perspective on the fate of anonymous, archival material», *Journal of medical ethics*, vol. 29, n° 6, 2003, pp. 343-347.

KATZ-BENICHOU, G., «Le cordon et l'embryon : analyse économique et bioéthique», *Revue générale de droit médical*, n° 24, 2007, pp. 13-22.

KATZ-BENICHOU, G., «Umbelical cord blood banking : economic and therapeutic challenges», *International journal of healthcare technology and management*, vol. 8, n° 5, 2007, pp. 464-477.

KNOPPERS, BM. and HERVÉ, C., «Matériel biologique et informatisation : beaucoup de bruit pour rien?», *Symposium de l'Institut International de Recherche en Éthique Biomédicale (IREB)*, Études hospitalières, France, 2006.

KOTOV. Miguel, (Editor), *Bioethics and research on humans and animals*. Papers presented to the workshop of the same name organised by Conicyt, 2006, Santiago, Chile.

KOUMBA MANFOUMBI, Diane, *Les biobanques et la propriété industrielle*, Master 2 – Droit de la bioéthique – 2008-2009.

KREFFT, Alexander R., *Patente auf human-genomische Erfindungen. Rechtslage in Deutschland, Europa und den USA*, Schriftenreihe zum gewerblichen Rechtsschutz, München, 2003.

KUITENBROUWER, F., HOOGHIELSTRA, T. and ENGELSCHION, S. et al., «The protection of individuals with regards to the processing of personal data with special regard to medical data», *European journal of health law*, vol. 9, n° 3, 2002, pp. 173-227.

LAUFS, Adolf, *Arztrecht*, 5 ed., München, 1993.

LG KÖLN, *Neue Juristische Wochenschrift (NJW)*, 1995.

LG RAVENSBURG, *Neue Juristische Wochenschrift (NJW)*, 1987.

LIPPERT, Hans-Dieter, «Forschung an und mit Körpersubstanzen – Wann ist die Einwilligung des ehemaligen Trägers erforderlich», *Medizinrecht (MedR)*, 2001, p. 406 ff.

LOLAS, Fernando and others (Editors), Health Research. Ethical Dimension. On-line at http://www.uchile.cl/bioetica/doc/manual_bioetica%20.pdf [downloaded on 05.11.2007].

LORENZI, J., «Le nouveau régime juridique des tissus du corps humain», *Bulletin de l'Ordre*, déc. 2000, pp. 545-554.

MANAOUIL, C., DECOURCELLE, M. and GIGNON, M. et al., «Retour sur 'l'affaire' de la chambre mortuaire de l'Hôpital Saint-Vincent de Paul à Paris», *Journal de médecine légale – Droit médical*, n° 4, vol. 50, 2007-07, pp. 231-237.

MARTÍN URANGA, Amelia, MARTÍN ARRIBAS, Concepción, DI DONATO, Jeanne-Hélène and POSADA DE LA PAZ, Manuel, *Las cuestiones ético-jurídicas más relevantes en relación con los biobancos*, Instituto de Salud Carlos III-Ministerio de Sanidad y Consumo, Madrid, 2005.

MARTRILLE, L., DUGUET, AM., ZERILLI, A., SALIERO, G. and BACCINO, E., «Constitution de collections en anthropologie; intérêt scientifique et aspects éthiques», *Journal de médecine légale – Droit médical*, n° 1, vol. 47, 2004, pp. 31-37.

MATHEY, N., «L'encadrement de l'entrée dans le commerce juridique des cellules souches», *Revuegénérale de droit médical*, n° 24, 2007, pp. 53-70.

MCNALLY, E. and CAMBON-THOMSEN, A., European Commission, Science et Société, *Ethical, legal and social aspects of genetic testing : research, development and clinical applications / Recommandations sur els implications éthiques, juridiques et sociales*, 2004.

MENASCHE, P., CHNEIWEISS, H., LASSALE, C., LE DEAUT, J.Y., POULETY, P. and QUESTIAUX, N., «Libres propos sur 'lavis n° 93 du CCNE : commercialisation des cellules souches humaines et autres lignées cellulaires», *Cahiers du Comité consultatif national d'éthique pour els sciences de la vie et de la santé*, n° 49, 2006, pp. 36-53.

MONIZ, Helena, «Notas sobre a protecção de dados pessoais perante a informática (o caso especial dos dados pessoais relativos à saúde)», *Revista Portuguesa de Ciência Criminal*, 7, 1997.

MONIZ, Helena, «Notas sobre biobancos com finalidades de investigação biomédica», *Lex Medicinae*, ano V, Maio, 2009, n° 10, p. 51 e ss.

MONIZ, Helena, «Os problemas jurídico-penais da criação de uma base de dados genéticos para fins criminais», *Revista Portuguesa de Ciência Criminal*, 12, 2002.

Moniz, Helena, «Privacy and intra-family communication of genetic information», *Revista de Derecho y Genoma Humano / Law and the Human Genome Review*, núm. 21, Julio-Diciembre, 2004.

Moniz, Helena, «Segredo Médico», *Revista Portuguesa de Ciência Criminal*, 10, 2000.

Morvan, S., *Les flux transfrontières de produits biologiques d'origine humaine : un aspect nouveau du droit du commerce international*, Thèse de doctorat, Université de Bourgogne, Editions hospitalières, 2002.

Moutel, G. and Hervé, C., *Le consentement dans les pratiuqes de soins et de recherche en médecine : entre idéalismes et réalités cliniques*, L'Harmattan, France, 2003.

Moutel, G., Montgolfier, S. De, Duchange, N., François, I and Hervé, C., «Evaluation éthique des lois de bioéthique à partir de deux exemples : les banques d'ADN et le devenir des embryons», *Journal de médecine légale – Droit médical*, n° 6, vol. 46, 2003, pp. 438-448.

Moutel, G., Plu, I., Callies, I., Duchange, N., Grand-Foret, E., Mamzer, M.F., Kreis, H. and Hervé, C., «Collecte et stockage de produits et éléments du corps humain en vue de la recherche biomédicale : quels enjeux et quelles régulations ?», *Journal de Médecine Légale Droit Médical*, N° 6-7, Vol. 50, 2007, pp. 343-352.

Nationaler Ethikrat, «Biobanken für die Forschung. Stellungnahme», 2004, www.ethikrat.org.

Nicolás, Pilar, «Los derechos del paciente sobre su muestra biológica : distintas opiniones jurisprudenciales», *Revista de Derecho y Genoma Humano / Law and the Human Genome Review*, Nr. 19, 2003.

Nicolás, Pilar, *La protección jurídica de los datos genéticos de carácter personal*, Cátedra Interuniversitaria de Derecho y Genoma Humano, Comares, Bilbao, Granada, 2006.

Nys, Herman and Fobelets, Geraldine, «The regulation on biobanks in Spain», *Revista de Derecho y Genoma Humano / Law and the Human Genome Review*, Nr. 29, 2008.

Office parlementaire d'évaluation des choix scientifiques et technologiques (OPECST), *La biométrie : compte rendu de l'audition publique du jeudi 4 mai 2006*, OPECST, France, 2006.

Ohly, Ansgar, «Die Einwilligung des Spenders von Körpersubstanzen und ihre Bedeutung für die Patentierung biotechnologischer Erfindungen», *Materielles Patentrecht, Festschrift für Reimar König, Köln et al.*, 2003, p. 417 ff.

Oliveira, Guilherme de, «Estrutura jurídica do acto médico, consentimento informado e responsabilidade médica», *Temas de Direito da Medicina*, Publicações do Centro de Direito Biomédico, 1, 2.ª ed., Ed. Coimbra, Coimbra, 2005.

Oliveira, Guilherme de, «O fim da «arte silenciosa» (o dever de informação dos médicos)», *Temas de Direito da Medicina*, Publicações do Centro de Direito Biomédico, 1, 2.ª ed., Ed. Coimbra, Coimbra, 2005.

Organisation de coopération et de développment économiques, *Biological Resource Centres : underpinning the future of life sciences and biotechnology*, 2001.

Palandt and Heinrichs et al., *BGB-Kommentar*, 64. ed., München, 2005.

PEI, S., «Banques de cellules ES: vers une capitalization», *Biofutur*, n° 267, 2006, pp. 35-39.

PEREIRA, André «Dever de documentação, acesso ao processo clínico e sua propriedade. Uma perspectiva europeia», *Revista Portuguesa do Dano Corporal*, 16, 2006.

PEREIRA, André Dias, *O consentimento informado na relação médico-paciente – Estudo de direito civil*, Publicações do Centro de Direito Biomédico, 9, Ed. Coimbra, Coimbra, 2004.

PONTIFICIA UNIVERSIDAD JAVERIANA, Instituto de Genética Humana, «Reglamento para las colaboraciones investigativas nacionales e internacionales con material biológico y DNA humano colombiano», *Revista Semillas*, N.10, junio de 1997.

RENGIFO GARCÍA, Ernesto, *Propiedad intelectual. El moderno derecho de autor*, 2ª ed., Ed. Universidad Externado de Colombia, Bogotá, 1997.

ROBIENSKI, Jürgen, *Die Auswirkungen von Gewebegesetz und Gendiagnostikgesetz auf die biomedicinische Forschung. Biobanken, Körpermaterialien, Gendiagnostik und Gendoping*, Verlag Dr. Kovac, Hamburg, 2010.

ROMEO CASABONA, Carlos María, *Utilización de muestras biológicas y bancos para la investigación biomédica*, Instituto de Investigaciones Jurídicas, Universidad Nacional Autónoma de México, México, 2005.

ROMEO CASABONA, Carlos María, *Utilización de muestras biológicas humanas con fines de investigación biomédica y regulación de biobancos*, en Sánchez-Caro/Abellán (Coords.), «Investigación biomédica en España: aspectos bioéticos, jurídicos y científicos», Comares, Granada, 2007.

ROMEO CASABONA, Carlos María, «Genetics, Tissue and Databases», *European Journal of Health Law*, Vol. 11, 2004, 57-75.

ROMEO CASABONA, Carlos María, «Protección Jurídica del Genoma Humano en el Derecho Internacional: El Convenio Europeo sobre Derechos Humanos y Biomedicina», *Genética y derecho*, Madrid: Consejo General del Poder Judicial, 2001, v. 36, pp. 295-328.

ROMEO MALANDA, Sergio and NICOL, Dianne, «Protection of Genetic Data in Medical Genetics: A Legal Analysis in the European Context», *Revista de Derecho y Genoma Humano / Law and the Human Genome Review*, núm. 27, Julio-Diciembre 2007.

SALAS IBARRA, Sofía, Ethical aspects of biomedical research. Current challenges to research in developing countries [downloaded on 05.11.2007].

SÁNCHEZ CARO, Javier and ABELLÁN, Fernando, *Datos de Salud y Datos Genéticos. Su protección en la Unión Europea y en España*, Derecho Sanitario Asesores, Granada, 2004.

SANTOS, Manuel J. «bioethics and Fondecyt». On-line at http://www.fondecyt.cl/comite_bioetica/libro_bioetica/art1.pdf [downloaded on 05.11.2007].

SCHUENEMANN, Hermann, *Die Rechte am menschlichen Körper*, Frankfurt a.M. et al, 1985.

SCHULTE IN DEN BÄUMEN, Tobias, PACI, Daniele and IBARRETA, Dolores, «Data Protection in Biobanks – A European challenge for the long-term sustainability of

Biobanking», *Revista de Derecho y Genoma Humano / Law and the Human Genome Review*, Nr 31, 2009.

SEOANE RODRÍGUEZ, José Antonio, «De la intimidad genética al derecho a la protección de datos genéticos. La protección iusfundamental de los datos genéticos en el Derecho español (a propósito de las SSTC 290/2000 y 292/2000, de 30 de noviembre) (Parte I y II)», *Revista de Derecho y Genoma Humano / Law and the Human Genome Review*, Nr. 16 y 17, 2002.

SIMON, Jürgen, «La dignidad del hombre como principio regulador en la Bioética», *Revista de Derecho y Genoma Humano / Law and the Human Genome Review*, Nr. 13, 2000.

SIMON, Jürgen W., PASLACK, Rainer and ROBIENSKI Jürgen et al., *Biomaterialbanken - Rechtliche Rahmenbedingungen*, Medizinisch Wissenschaftliche Verlagsgesellschaft, Berlin, 2006.

SOLA RECHE, Esteban, «La protección penal de los datos personales genéticos en Derecho Español», *Genética y Derecho Penal. Previsiones en el Código Penal Español de 1995*, Cátedra Interuniversitaria de Derecho y Genoma Humano, Ed. Comares, Bilbao, Granada, 2000.

SPRANGER, Tade Matthias, «Die Rechte des Patienten bei der Entnahme und Nutzung von Körpersubstanzen», *Neue Juristische Wochenschrift (NJW)*, 2005, p. 1084 ff.

STUHRMANN-SPANGENBERG, Manfred and SCHMIDTKE, Jörg, «Erster Massen-Gentest in Deutschland», *Forschung & Lehre*, 2005, p. 128 f.

SUÁREZ ESPINO, Mª Lidia, *El Derecho a la intimidad genética*, Marcial Pons, Madrid, 2008.

TAB – OFFICE OF TECHNOLOGY ASSESSMENT AT THE GERMAN PARLIAMENT, *Biobanks for the human medicine Research and Application*, Workreport No. 112, Berlin, 2006.

TAUPITZ, Jochen, «Wem gebührt der Schutz im menschlichen Körper?», *Archiv für civilistische Praxis (AcP)*, 191, 1991, p. 201 ff.

THOUVENIN, D., «Les banques de tissus et d'organes : les mots pour les dire, les règles pour les organiser», *Petites Affiches*, n°35, 18 fév. 2005, pp. 31-42.

VACAREZZA Y., Ricardo, Scientific Ethical Evaluation Committees. http://www.fondecyt.cl/comite_bioetica/libro_bioetica/art9.pdf [downloaded on 05.11.2007].

VALENCIA ZEA, Arturo, *Derecho civil : Parte general y persona*, T. I., 15ª ed, Bogotá, 2002.

VALLEJOS A., Carlos. Ethical aspects of clinical research. http://www.med.ufro.cl/Recursos/GISIII/linkeddocuments/apunte_eticainv1.pdf. [downloaded on 05.11.2007].

VON FREIER, Friedrich, «Körperteile in der Forschung zwischen leiblicher Selbstverfügung und Gemeinbesitz», *Medizinrecht (MedR)*, 2005, p. 321 ff.

WELLBROCK, Rita, «Datenschutzrechtliche Aspekte des Aufbaus von Biobanken», *Medizinrecht (MedR)*, 2003, p. 78 ff.

WIERZBICK, I. J., «'Non' aux banques privées de sang placentaire», *Biofutur*, n° 237, 2003, pp. 6-7.

Wolf Le, Lo B., «Untapped potential : IRB guidance for ethical research use stored biological materials», *IRB : ethics and human research*, n° 5, vol. 26, 2004, pp. 1-8.

Zentrale Ethikkommission, «Die (Weiter-)Verwendung von menschlichem Körpermaterial für Zwecke medizinischer Forschung», Berlin, 2003, http://www.zentrale-ethikkommission.de/cgi-bin/printVersion.cgi.

Annex

I. – LIST OF FREQUENTLY ASKED QUESTIONS

I. – FOUNDATION AND ORGANIZATION OF BIOBANKS

1. – *What are the legal requirements for establishing a biobank?*

ARGENTINA (ARG): There is no legal regulation on this matter. The resolution 319/04 from INCUCAI (Unique Central National Institute for the Coordination of Ablations and Implantations) regarding the approval of hematopoietic stem cells banks from the umbilical vein.

Annex I to this resolution bears the title «rules for the approval of hematopoietic stem cell banks».

It is stipulated therein that the following documentation must be provided:

– Identification and approval.

– Director's details.

A plan indicating the location of the hematopoietic stem cell and umbilical cord blood bank and the different sections of which they are comprised.

BRAZIL (BR): Research involving human beings in Brazil, as well as being subject to areas of the law arising from the 1988 Constitution, is governed by the pre-established rules set by the resolutions of the National Council of Health. For the purpose of biobanks, the following are relevant: Resolution no. 196, dated October 10th, 1996 c/c Resolution no. 347, dated January 13th, 2005.

CHILE (CH): The regulation of biobanks is under preparation in Chile, as a development of law 20.120, on scientific research involving human beings.

COLOMBIA (COL): The general requirements applicable, pursuant to civil and administrative legislation, for the establishment of legal entities. Law 9 of 1979 demands, as a requirement for the installation and operation of all establishments, that a health licence be obtained from the Ministry for Social Protection or from the entity to which this power is delegated. Although there is no specific regulation for biobanks, Resolution 8430 of 1993 issued by the then Ministry of Health (Now Social Security) states that all institutions which intend to carry out research on human beings are bound to draft an internal procedures manual to support compliance with the regulations contained in the Resolution (Article 3).

Biobanks have a specific owner to whom all rights and obligations correspond, which means that they may have legal status themselves as they are registered to a legal entity (university, hospital, etc.). If the biobank is linked to a legal entity which is deemed to be a health service provider in accordance with Decree 1011 of 2006, Article 1, the regulations which establish and regulate the Obligatory System of Health Quality Guarantee for the General Social Security System in terms of the

Unified Registration System, the Authority for the improvement of the quality of healthcare service, the Unified accreditation system and the Quality information system.

Equally, with regard to data protection, there will be an administrator who will be responsible for the database.

COSTA RICA (CR): The General Health Act stipulates the requirements necessary to operate health laboratories and the restrictions such activities are subject to. Article 83 defines microbiology and clinical chemistry laboratories, which comprise, among others, blood banks. These are defined as an entire establishment where human blood and blood derivatives are obtained, stored, manipulated and supplied.

This law outlines the requirements necessary to operate blood banks as well as the restrictions such activities are subject to. For example, paragraph 90 sets states that any individual or legal entity wishing to install and operate a blood bank needs, to be authorized by the Association of Microbiologists and Clinical Chemists, before being registered with the Ministry.

Article 91 provides that in order to establish and operate blood banks, the interested parties must state, when registering with the Ministry, the nature and techniques involved in the processes they intend to carry out. They must submit background information certified by the Association of Microbiologists and Clinical Chemists, certifying that the establishment meets the regulatory conditions required for its due operation. This must include: informationregarding the person who will be technically responsible for its operation; confirmation that it has adequate facilities and equipment for the collection, manipulation, classification and storage of blood and its derivatives, as well as systems for establishing the identification, health status and blood donor register. The Association of Microbiologists and Clinical Chemists will be responsible for supervising these establishments, notwithstanding the Ministry's control and surveillance capacities.

FRANCE (FR): a) To be able to justify a scientific or therapeutic interest.

b) To have a scientific representative who has a diploma in medicine or pharmaceutical studies or a PHD in the area of life and health sciences.

GERMANY (GER): There are no requirements for establishing a biobank, if the material is only used for research purposes (not for medical use on humans). There are only requirements for establishing blood- and organ banks in §20 b and c AMG (see IV. 1.).

MEXICO (MX) (1): The General Law on Health establishes, in article 315, that organ, tissue and cell banks require authorization from the health authorities. The Federal Commission for Protection against Health Risks (COFEPRIS), a branch of Mexico's Health Agency, regulates, controls, promotes and exercises authority in relation to health regulation,.This is stated in the General Law on Health. Given that biobanks handle human samples for research they fall under the supervision of COFEPRIS.

---

(1) Before we answer it is important to clarify that this questionnaire was created reflecting on countries that already have specific legislation on biobanks. In Mexico, as in most Latin American countries, there is no specific legislation and therefore we cannot provide detailed answers.

PORTUGAL (PT): a) Having prior authorization from the government department responsible for health issues.

b) Having prior authorization from the National Commission for Data Protection

Biobanks can only be constructed for the purposes of providing health care,basic research or applied health research.

We are waiting for a new law that will define the rules for licensing biobanks and for the promotion of safeguards forbiobanks.

SPAIN (SP): a) To be able to justify a scientific interest in the objectives of the biobank.

b) To establish the organization required by law : an identified owner a director, a person who is responsible for the database, and that the biobank is answerable to a designated external ethics and scientific committee.

2. – Is official permission required?

ARG: Yes, pursuant to the established terms.

BR: Only the approval of an Ethics Committee, registered with the National Commission for Ethics in Research.

CH: Not specifically, but in general the health authorities must be informed before establishing a laboratory in Chile. To be able to carry out DNA data processing accreditation from the Ministry of Health is required.

COL: Yes and it depends on the way in which it is set up.

CR: Yes, from the Health Ministry

FR: If the samples of the biobank are stored for therapeutic purposes or with the aim of using them for scientific purposes authorization is required.

If the samples are stored for scientific purposes a simple declaration will be sufficient.

GER: No.

MX: Health authority authorization is required by the health institutions dedicated to the harvesting, analysis, conservation, preparation and provision of organs, tissues and cells and organ, tissue and cell banks. Therefore, it is our opinion that biobanks require authorization from COFEPRIS as we explained in question 1.

PT: See previous answer.

SP: Authorisation from a public authority is required.

3. – Is there an official registry for biobanks?
Is there an obligation to register biobanks?

ARG: They should be registered with INCUCAI, which is the applicable authority.

BR: Yes. With CONEP, but the registry has not yet been created.

CH: No.

COL: There is no special official register in our country for biobanks. In the event that a biobank was linked to a health service entity, that entity would be required to register as a special approved health service entity as established in Art. 10, Decree 1011 of 2006.

CR: Yes, biobanks must be registered with the Health Ministry and must obtain authorization from that body to be established and operate.

FR: The law establishes an obligation of declaration or authorization but there is no obligation to register a biobank and there is no official registry.

GER: No.

MX: No.

PT: No, there is no official registry for biobanks, but every database with personal data must be registered with the National Commission for Data Protection.

SP: There is an obligation to register biobanks. The registry has not been created.

II. - THE LEGAL FORMS OF BIOBANKS

1. - Which legal forms (2) are possible for biobanks?

ARG: There are no regulations regarding the legal status under which they should operate (public agencies, autarchic entities, associations, corporations, etc.).

BR: There is no regulation for this.

CH: Any institution, public or private, can create collections in Chile.

COL: In general they are linked to higher education establishments, such as universities or hospitals. Both university and hospital institutions may be public or private. Some belong to foundations or corporations which may be categorised as universities or hospitals.

CR: Any institution, public or private can create a biobank.

FR: Any institution or association, public or private can create a biobank.

GER: Any legal form that is allowed under German company law.

MX: Due to a lack of legislation we cannot answer this question.

PT: Any institution, public or private can create a biobank.

SP: Any institution, public or private can create a biobank.

2. - What are the advantages and disadvantages of these legal forms for biobanks?

ARG: Since there is no regulation no advantages or disadvantages can be established.

BR: There is no regulation for this.

CH: The disadvantage is that there is uncertainty in respect of the powers the biobank operators at the time of collecting human specimens for research. Addition-

---

(2) Private or public, foundation or other association.

ally, they do not adequately guarantee the rights of holders of the samples, or whether they can control the use made of them by researchers

COL: Those biobanks linked to or belonging to a university are immersed in a more favourable environment for permanent technical and research updating. Those linked to or belonging to public hospitals may have a better wealth and diversity of samples. Seemingly, all have the advantage of being non-profit organisations. It is very difficult to know if the financial and quality control systems are operating in the best possible way in the public or the private sector.

CR: There is no information in this regard.

FR: The advantages are firstly that the creation of biobanks is simple and that it encourages biomedical research. The disadvantage is the lack of clarity, the authorities have no oversight and no proper control over biobanks.

GER: There are no special advantages or disadvantages for biobanks. The question of which legal form is the best depends on the usual» questions about taxes, liability, etc.

MX: The law does not consider this question.

PT: Only authorized biobanks can collect samples, keep them and use them. Those samples collected without consent being given to retain them in a biobank may only be usedfor the purposes set out during the process of collecting the sample. The consent needed for samples to be retained in biobanks is broader than the consent needed for the collection of biological material for research purposes.

SP: The advantages are firstly that, according to legal requirements, the samples are obtained, stored and transferred with strict quality guarantees; and secondly that the subject's consent can be given in broader terms than those for a non authorized biobank (collection).

3. – Do legal requirements exist concerning the sustainability and the safeguarding of a biobank's inventory (3)

ARG: There are no specific provisions.

BR: There is no regulation for this.

CH: No.

COL: There are related regulations with protective measures which guarantee the physical integrity of premises or equipment, but we are unaware of any regulation directly related to the guarantee of the safeguarding if biological material stored in a biobank.

CR: There are no specific regulations for this.

FR: There are requirements concerning the technical conditions of storage but nothing to ensure the durability of the institution which is in charge of this storage.

GER: No, only the rules in general, like the data protection law.

MX: Although there is no mention in the law concerning the sustainability of the inventory, there are general rules regarding the safeguarding of the inventory. All

---

(3) Inventory means the collections of samples in the biobank.

establishments founded according to the General Law on Health must have a person in charge liable before the Mexican Health Agency. All data in the possession of a public entity is protected by the Protection of Personal Data Law of the Federal District as well as at a federal level by the Federal Law of Transparency and Access to Government Public Information.

PT: No.

SP: The biobank must draw up a working plan which includes the economic resources needed for carrying out the activity.

4. – Which regulations and requirements exist in case of the insolvency of a biobank?

ARG: See previous answer.

BR: There is no regulation for this.

CH: This matter is not regulated.

COL: In Colombia, law 1116 of 2006 which establishes the business insolvency regime in the Republic of Colombia and issues other provisions, it is residual in nature; therefore all legal entities without a special insolvency regime are governed by this law.

Article 3 lists those entities expressly excluded from its application; among which the following are mentioned: Health Promoting Entities, Administrators of the Subsidised Health System for the General System of Social Security in Health and Health Service Providers as well as organisations governed by public law, regional and decentralised organisations. Biobanks will be within the scope of application of this law so long as they are not set up as or as part of the aforementioned organisations.

With regard to competency, since law 1116 is applicable if they are set up, as they generally are, as not-for-profit organisations, in the process event of insolvency the Civil Judge of the Circuit in which they are domiciled shall be informed, as indicated in Art. 6 of the law.

CR: There are no specific regulations for this.

FR: French legislation does not consider this.

GER: There are no special regulations in the event of insolvency of a biobank in Germany.

MX: The law does notconsider this situation.

PT: There are no regulations.

SP: In the event of a biobank closing the final destination of the samples will be specified.

5. – Which rights exist concerning the utilization of a liquidated or abandoned biobank? Who is the assignee of a BMB?

ARG: There are no specific provisions and general rules are applied.

BR: There is no regulation for this.

CH: This matter is not regulated.

COL: The fact that human biological material is generally characterised as non-proprietary assets makes it difficult to answer this question. Article 649 of the Civil Code stipulates that in the event of the dissolution of a corporation, it will determine the properties in the manner in which they were prescribed in the Articles of Association and if this case was not prescribed, it will belong to the State, with the obligation to use them for similar purposes as those of the institution.

During the liquidation period, the laws provide that a liquidator should be appointed.

CR: There are no specific regulations for this.

FR: (See answer II.4).

GER: There are no special rules. The data protection law is very important. Body material that is not anonymised and personal data can not be sold. (§§36 InsO, 811 ZPO).

In the event of liquidation, biobanks that do not carry out research but simply store and distribute material of human origin will generally be obliged to delete personal data (§30 Abs. 3 BDSG) if it is forbidden to save it. Permission to save data is governed by §14 and §28 of the BDSG. Whether the samples can be saved or not depends on the purpose for which it was obtained. In the event of th closure of the biobank the purpose for which it was established also ceases For this reason deletion of personal data is obligatory.

But there is still the option of transferring the whole database to another institution, such as another biobank if the people concerned have been informed about the transfer or universal succession. The people concerned have the right to protest and forbid any further use of the personal data.

MX: We cannot answer this question with our existing regulations.

PT: See previous answer.

SP: (See answer II.4).

III. – THE LEGAL STATUS OF BODY MATERIALS

1. – *What legal regulations exist concerning the legal status of body materials?*

ARG: There are no legal regulations regarding the care, conservation and transport of bodily material, except the provisions of resolution 319/04 with regard umbilical cord cell banks.

BR: Constitution, Law of Biossegurança and CONEP's Resolutions.

CH: Different regulations exist concerning the legal status of body materials in several frameworks: transplant, human reproduction or *in vitro* research, processing of DNA samples for purposes of criminal interest, processing of DNA samples for the purpose of establishing paternity.

COL: There are special regulations on specific matters such as transplants, reproductive biomedicine units, blood banks, tissues and bone marrow banks for example.

CR: Different regulations exist concerning the legal status of body materials in several frameworks: transplant, human reproduction or *in vitro* research.

FR: There are general regulations for the protection of the human body. In addition, several regulations exist concerning the legal status of body materials in specific situations such as transplantation or human reproduction.

GER: There are a lot of different legal regulations concerning the legal status of body materials.

Special regulations can be found in the law on transplantation (TPG) concerning organs, tissue, skin, bones etc., the law on transfusion (TFG) concerning blood and parts of the blood, and the law on drugs (AMG) concerning tissue and body material that is used for drugs.

In the law on gene diagnosis (GenDG) there are rules about using tissue for genetic examinations.

And there are also some rules about human tissue in the laws of the different German states concerning funerals (BestattG) and in the law concerning trash (KrW-/AbfG).

MX: There is no regulation that specifically addresses the legal status of body materials, though the Property Right Law states that it is not permitted to take out patents on human material, the human body or any of its components.

PT: Biological material in the biobank belongs to the person from whom it was obtained and in their absence (death or incapacity) to their relatives. But there are specific rules for biological material collected for transplantations and human reproduction.

SP: Different regulations exist concerning the legal status of body materials in several frameworks: transplant, human reproduction or *in vitro* research.

1.1. *Is body material viewed as an object?*

ARG: In reality, since there are no regulations on body material, it must be considered as an object, which should naturally be treated as material of human origin with regard to the ethical principals to be applied.

BR: Not explicitly. It's possible to donate body material (as an object) but, at the same time, some rights must be respected in relation to samples, such as privacy and informed self determination.

CH: Not explicitly. It seems that body material is an object (it is possible to donate this material and the body of a dead person is considered property owned by the heirs) but at the same time there are rights of publicity that are exercised in relation to the samples (privacy and informed self determination).

COL: Biological material separated from the body may be considered as objects but not commercial. In the case of tissue and organs, for example, Law 919 of 2004 states that it is an offence to traffic human body parts (4).

---

(4) Law 919 of 2004 which states that it is an offence to traffic human body parts. Article 2: Those who traffic in, sell or market human body parts, will be receive a prison term of three (3) to six (6) years. Paragraph: The same sentence will apply to those who extract body parts from a corpse or from a person without the corresponding authorisation, those who participate as an

CR : No, it is viewed as a part of a human being.

FR : There is no definition of the legal status of the human body or body material. Body material could be likened to an object since it can be donated. However, there are several forms of protection which are usual in relation to people and some of these were set up to protect genetic data.

GER : ody material that is separated from the body is viewed as an object, by analogy with that established in §953 BGB concerning cadavers.

MX : We cannot answer this question with our existing regulations.

PT : No. It seems that body material is an object – the law speaks about property, and requires the conservation of it while it could be useful. There are also rights, such as privacy rights related to the information obtained from the analyses of the biological material.

SP : Not explicitly. It seems that body material is an object (it is possible to donate this material) but at the same time there are rights of publicity that are exercised in relation to the samples (privacy and informed self determination).

1.2. Can body material be handled as property?

ARG : Given that body material is not deemed as commercial, pursuant to Article 954 of the Civil Code, since any related transactions are contrary to public policy, the concept of «property» does not correspond in this case.

BR : It is possible if we think that the person can have the sample back, for health reasons, for example.

CH : A property right is not explicitly recognized, but rather a right to determine use; and the subject has the right to have the sample back if he/she needs it for health reasons.

COL : Not exactly. In any case, the property would not be regulated by commercial regulations. The dispute we are aware of was resolved on the basis of fundamental rights other than property rights (5). Furthermore, legal transactions regulated by our legal system with regard to biological material such as gametes or tissue for reproduction and organs for transplants must be free.

CR : Yes, according to the Regulations for Biomedical Research in health activities of the Costa Rican Social Security Fund of November 17th, 2005.

FR : There is no explicit property right over body material. The property right applies only to a possible modification of samples.

GER : Yes, body material can be handled as property. But in addition there are also personal rights related to body material. The person from whose body the tissue was taken is not allowed to sell it. All commercialization of body tissue is forbidden.

MX : There isn't any specific regulation that resolves this matter; however the subject has the right to have the sample returned.

---

intermediary in the purchase, sale or marketing of body parts or those who advertise the need for available organs or tissue, offering or seeking any type of payment or remuneration.

(5) We do not believe that the issue alludes to intellectual property rights to information contained in the human biological material.

PT: It is recognised as a property right by law, but there is huge controversy about the true nature of this right. The subject or his/her relatives has the right to access information obtained from the sample.

SP: It is not explicitly recognized as a property right, but a right to determine use; and the subject has the right to have the sample back if he/she needs it for health reasons.

1.3. Who is the owner after the body material has been separated from the person?

ARG: Based on point 1.2, it is not applicable to speak of owner with regard to the title holder. It would be more appropriate to speak of who has the specific legal capacity with regard to the material. In this case if the material is provided in accordance with the rules and regulations, it is up to the person furnishing the material to determine its subsequent use. In the case of anonymous samples, this power does not exist.

BR: It is not explicitly indicated but, in principle, the subject.

CH: It is not explicitly indicated.

COL: The word «owner» may not be used as a synonym for title holder with traditional powers recognised in the Civil Code. The source subject, unless they declare otherwise, reserves the powers that may be exercised over the biological sample whilst this is not irrevocably made anonymous.

CR: In the context of the Costa Rican Social Security Fund (CCSS), the sample belongs to this Institution.

In the case of the UCR, (University of Costa Rica) in theory, the ownership rights apply to it, but in practice, the senior researcher has control. Nevertheless, this does not seem to be very clear, because it has also been established that when the subject withdraws his/her consent, the ownership is his/hers but the UCR keeps custody of the sample. In the case of samples sent to the National Institute of Health's repository, this is a resource of the federal government for all researchers.

In Costa Rica, some researchers believe that the subject has ownership rights over the sample.

FR: It is not explicitly indicated.

GER: In the first instance the owner of the material is the person from whom the material was taken. But when the person leaves the material in a hospital or at the doctor's surgery, it has no owner and the doctor or the hospital can become the owner.

MX: Since there is no specific regulation, in Mexico every biobank has resolved this issue differently. Some biobanks consider that the owner of the sample is the donor, others state that the research centre is the owner while others consider the researcher the owner of the sample. Finally some believe no one is the owner and that only when the research is completed, can the researcher become the rightful owner.

PT: See answer to the question 3.1.

SP: It is not explicitly indicated.

2. – *Which other rights (personal rights) exist concerning body material?*

ARG: Other than that indicated in the above point there are no other rights.

BR: If connected with the donor, all personal rights remain.

CH: Rights over the information that can be obtained from the analysis of the material: privacy and informated self determination.

COL: Constitutionally speaking, almost all fundamental rights. In the scope of which may take place involving private law, if we bear in mind that legal transactions involving body material must be free, it would appear that it is not possible to speak of real rights or personal rights to such material.

CR: Those according to the Civil Code, such as the protection of confidentiality and privacy.

FR: Rights of information and privacy.

GER: Personal rights, such as the right of informed self determination.

MX: No other rights.

PT: Rights over the information that can be obtained from the analysis of the material: privacy and informed self determination.

SP: Rights over the information that can be obtained from the analysis of the material: privacy and informed self determination.

3. – *Is it possible to delegate the rights of body material?*

ARG: If the material is registered, the person providing the sample may delegate his powers within the limits indicated.

BR: It depends. If connected with the donor, yes – those rights related to genetic identity.

CH: No.

COL: We can only answer this question through analogy; with things as they are, we recall that Article 1.2 of Resolution 13437 of 1991 from the then Ministry of Health (Now Social Protection), stated that it is the patient's right «that he/she, their relatives or representatives, in the event of unconsciousness or being underage, consent to or reject these proceedings, expressly stating their decision and hopefully in writing». Therefore, we can deduce that the source subject may delegate the decision on the use of the sample to another person, in the event that it is in accordance with the conditions set out in the regulation, at the time consent is to be obtained.

CR: Yes, the University of Costa Rica, upon request of the Scientific Ethics Committee, requires all the institutions researchers, for various reasons, when transferring human biological material from one unit to another, within the institution or to any other institution outside the University, national or international, to obtain the document *Biological Material Transfer Agreement (MTA)*. This document must be signed by the researcher who receives the samples and the one who provides them and by the legal advisors of both institutions.

FR: No.

GER : Yes, but not personal rights.

MX : If no rights are recognized over body material itis impossible to delegate them.

PT : No.

SP : No.

4. – Who is the owner of body material which is stored in a biobank?

ARG : Body material stored in a biobank belongs in principal to the biobank, without prejudice to the personal rights of the donor to which I referred in the above points.

BR : In principle, the donor.

CH : It is not explicitly indicated.

COL : There is no explicit legal indication. It depends on the legal status of the samples. If these have been subjected to an irrevocable anonymization process, the biobank may use these within the limitations set out in the law by virtue of the non-commercial nature of the human biological material. If, on the other hand, these remain linked to a determined or determinable person, the powers of use must be examined in accordance with the content of the informed consent.

CR : In the context of the Costa Rican Social Security Fund (CCSS), the sample belongs to this Institution.

In the case of the UCR, in theory, ownership rights apply to it, but in practice, the senior researcher has control. Nevertheless, this does not seem to be very clear, because it has also been established that when the subject withdraws his/her consent, the ownership is his/hers but the UCR keeps custody of the sample. In the case of samples sent to the National Institutes of Health's repository, this is a resource of the federal government for all researchers.

In Costa Rica, some researchers believe that the subject has ownership rights over the sample.

FR : It is not explicitly specified in French legislation.

GER : It depends on who has stored the material in the biobank. In most cases the material belongs to the biobank,a hospital or doctor. In the case of cryoconservation it belongs to the person from whom it has been separated.

MX : This is not specified.

PT : See answer to the question 3.1.

SP : It is not explicitly indicated.

5. – Under which circumstances is the test subject allowed to demand the return or the destruction of his sample?

ARG : The test subject reserves the power over the use of the material at all times if the material is identified.

BR : In event that he/she revokes his/her free and clear consent.

CH : It is not explicitly indicated.

COL : We do not have a regulation in this regard. Consent on these matters is considered essentially revocable; this statement may be corroborated by the regulations on donation of gametes and to organs and tissues for transplants. On the other hand, we are only aware of one actual case in which the parents of a baby requested the delivery of biological samples of a baby; in this case the Constitutional Court ordered the delivery to ensure the fundamental rights of the parents.

CR : Test subjects may demand the return of samples or their destruction when identification of the sample is feasible, according to what was agreed at the time of giving informed consent.

FR : The subject can withdraw his / her consent at any time when analyses include research on genetic data. In other cases, the rights of return and destruction are not automatic but the consent or non opposition form can make provisions for this situation.

GER : The test subject is normally allowed to demand the return and destruction of his or her samples without any reason. The return of the material is only allowed if it is not trash. Then it can be forbidden because of the laws on trash (KrW-/AbfG). It must be destroyed instead.

MX : Some research centre allow the donor to revoke his consent and claim the sample before the sample has been disassociated while other do not consider this option. Since there is no regulation to clarify this it is up to the research centre to decide.

PT : According to general rules, the subject can withdraw his/her consent at any time and justification is not required. But there is nothing expressly provided in the Act about this.

SP : The subject can withdraw his/her consent at any time and justification is not required. The consequences will be expained in the information provided prior to consent. The exception is the case when the sample has been anonymised.

5.1. *What role does anonymisation play in the rights of return and destruction?*

ARG : If the sample is anonymous or has become anonymous, there is no person who has the power to exercise the right to it.

BR : If the anonymous donor is identified, the donation ceases to be anonymous, and the subject source will retain all rights.

CH : The law provides for the encryption of the human genome data to allow identification of a person both for storage and transmission.

COL : See previous answer, specially, number 4.

CR : Anonymisation protects confidentiality and privacy.

FR : If the anonymisation is total and it is not possible to trace the donor, the rights of return and destruction cannot apply.

GER : If the material is anonymised, it will not be possible to destroy it or give it back, because the donor cannot be found.

MX : If the sample is in a public institution and the sample has not been disassociated the donor may claim his/her sample.

PT: If there is irreversible anonymisation it is impossible to re-obtain any information should the subject request it. According to the law any destruction imposes on the researcher an obligation to inform the subject – but if the sample has been irreversibly anonymised this is impossible.

SP: (See previous answer).

5.2. Do property and rescission rights depend on whether the sample has been gained for treatment or research purposes?

ARG: The use of the sample has no relevance to the aforementioned rights.

BR: There is no regulation.

CH: No.

COL: We start with the fact that, in principal, a person may not pass from being a patient to a research subject without their consent. We must also bear in mind that in the case of ongoing therapeutic treatment samples may not be made anonymous for legal reasons. The anonymization of samples would be an important point in deducing the rights and powers of the source subject.

CR: There is no legislation regarding this or any kind of information with which to answer this question.

FR: No.

GER: No, not at all, especially not property rights. In some cases the rights of rescission depends on whether the sample has been obtained for treatment or research purposes, because in some laws (TPG, TFG, GenDG) there are special rules about rights of rescission.

MX: No, the law makes no distinction.

PT: No, they are the same. Differences only exist when considering the possible retrospective use of samples.

SP: No.

5.3. What consequences relate to already existing data and research results?

BR: The withdrawal of consent by the donor does not affect the data obtained as the result of research.

CH: The withdrawal of consent by the donordoes not affect the data obtained as the result of research.

COL: None, provided that the donor's fundamental rights are respected, such as informed self-determination and privacy.

CR: The withdrawal of consent by the donor does not affect the data obtained as the result of research.

FR: It is not explicitly stated. It could be specified in the consent or non opposition form.

GER: Anonymisation and in some cases possibly the destruction of the material.

MX: Since the law does not consider this the researcher may keep the information taken from the sample.

PT: There are not specific rules about this. The law prefers research using anonymised samples, but there is nothing relating to the destruction of anonymous samples, or the elimination of information from them.

SP: The withdrawal does not affect the data obtained as the result of research.

6. – Under which circumstances is it permitted to transfer anonymised samples to third parties?

ARG: This would depend on the legal system the bank is subject to.

BR: When the subject source consents to it.

CH: It is not explicitly indicated.

COL: We do not have an explicit regulation which prohibits the circulation of samples; if anonymization is revocable, the source subject's consent would be required and, among other things, the entity which is to receive the sample should be informed.

CR: There is no specific regulation regarding this. In the case of the Universidad de Costa Rica, the Biological Material Transfer Agreement (MTA) that was mentioned before is the instrument that allows any kind of transfer of samples.

FR: It is not explicitly indicated.

GER: If the material is anonymised it is not forbidden by law to transfer the material to third parties. But it can be forbidden because of the contract with the test subject. It will not be possible to control any transfer if the sample is anonymised.

MX: As long as the patient or donor was informed when giving informed consent, the researcher may transfer the sample to third parties.

PT: In the consent form authorization for the transfer of the sample must be sought. Any transfer of samples to other entities should always respect the consent given at the time of collection and be approved by the ethics committees.

SP: Consent for anonymisation is required, and samples must be transferred to third parties only for projects that have been positively evaluated by an Ethics Committee.

6.1. What property rights exist regarding the transfer of samples to third parties?

ARG: No property rights are recognized.

BR: If the right to disposition is understood as the right to property, then the law on property rights covers all aspects of the right to disposition.

CH: It is not explicitly indicated, but consent may be acquired by application of general property law.

COL: It is not a matter of property. The transfer of non-anonymous samples does not modify the powers of the source subject. On the other hand, if the assignee is foreign, the recipient biobank must ensure that, in the country in which the former operates, the same, or better, guarantees of protection are provided to the country of origin.

CR : As mentioned in question 4, in the context of the Costa Rican Social Security Fund (CCSS), the sample belongs to this Institution.

In the case of the UCR, in theory, the ownership rights belong to the university, but in practice the senior researcher has control. Nevertheless, this does not seem to be very clear, because it has also been established that when the subject withdraws his/her consent, the ownership is his/hers but the UCR retains custody of the sample. In the case of samples sent to the repository of the National Institutes of Health, this is a resource of the federal government for all researchers.

In Costa Rica, some researchers believe that the subject has ownership rights over the sample.

FR : No property rights are recognized.

GER : The third party can / will become the owner of the material.

MX : Neither this nor the following questions can be answered since there in no regulation.

PT : The law does not mention this. It confines itself to stating that the samples are the property of those who provided them.

SP : No property rights are recognized.

6.2. Under which circumstances does transfer to third parties require the consent of the test subject/patient?

ARG : Transfer of registered samples to third parties shall require the consent of the donor subject.

BR : All, but if is impossible, consent will be given by the Ethics Committee.

CH : It is not explicitly indicated.

COL : When the samples remain linked to the test subject as a determined or determinable person.

CR : In most cases, when the issue is addressed in the informed consent form, which is usually the case. But it is also possible when samples are anonymised, they may be transferred to third parties when approved by an Ethics Committee according to the rules of the University of Costa Rica.

FR : When it is specified in the consent form or non opposition form.

GER : If the material is not anonymised.

MX : Due to a lack of legislation we cannot answer this question.

PT : Always.

SP : Always and in a specific manner. In the case that the samples are in an authorized biobank, consent could be given in a broader way.

6.3. What are the liability rights concerning transfer of samples to third parties?

ARG : The liabilities vary according to the breach of a contractual relationship or the generic common legislative relationships, if the sample is anonymous.

BR : There is no regulation.

CH : It is not explicitly regulated.

COL: In case of the assignee it seems clear that they would be liable if the samples linked to a specific or determinable person were sent without their consent. In the case of the assignee we only have one regulation regarding the admission of body parts for transplant; Article 39 of Decree 2493 of 2004, which in section 4 provides that as a requisite for authorising the entry into a country of body parts a report form the institution providing the part is required, which records the conditions under which it was obtained; in such a way this institution would be liable in the event that this information is false or inaccurate.

CR: There is no legislation regarding this, or any kind of information with which to answer this question.

FR: There are technical conditions concerning the transfer. The sender and recipient must comply with the legal requirements (declaration, authorization) and the donors' consent. However there are no specific provisions concerning the liability rights in relation to the transfer of samples to third parties.

GER: There are no special rules in Germany.

MX: The law does not consider this situation.

PT: The law does not consider this.

SP: According with the Law on Biomedical Research (article 74) «(...) Aside from the provisions in the General Health Law, the Law on the Protection of Personal Data, the Law on Assisted Human Reproduction Techniques, Basic Law on the Autonomy of the Patient and of the Rights and Obligations in Matters of Clinical Documentation and on other regulations passed by the autonomous communities in accordance with this Law, the following breaches shall be considered as 'minor', 'serious' and 'very serious':

A) 'Minor' breaches are:

Those that entail the non-compliance with any obligation or the violation of any prohibition that is provided in this Law, when, in accordance with the criteria provided in this Section, such breaches cannot be classified as 'serious' or 'very serious' breaches.

B) 'Serious' breaches are:

a) Non-observance of the prescriptions, conditions, requirements or previous authorisations that are provided in this Law for the functioning of the registries provided in this Law.

b) The omission of data, consent and references required by this Law.

c) The non-providing of data to the appropriate health authority responsible for the functioning of registries provided in this Law.

d) The breach of the conditions of confidentiality of donors' data established in this Law.

e) The non-fulfilment of the requirement not to profit from the donation of pre-embryos, embryos and foetuses in the terms provided in this Law.

f) The non-fulfilment of the norms and guarantees established for the transfer between countries of cells and tissues of human embryonic origin.

(...).

The sanctions previewed are (Article 75 of the Law on Biomedical Research)

1. 'Minor' infractions, as provided in this Law, shall be sanctioned with a fine of up to 600 Euros; 'serious' infractions, with a fine from 601 Euros to 10,000 Euros; and 'very serious' breaches with a fine from 10,001 to 1,000,000 Euros.

(...)

6. Notwithstanding the sanctions provided in this Article, 'serious' or 'very serious' breaches shall entail revocation of the authorisation granted for that research or activity.

Likewise, in especially serious cases, the exclusion of the authorisation of any of the activities regulated in this Law may be accorded for a period of one to five years. Where this measure may be imposed, the following shall be taken into account: the generated risk, the social repercussion of the infraction, the benefit obtained by the offender of the sanctioned behaviour and the previous commission of one or more breaches of this Law».

6.4. Do the regulations for the transfer of samples depend on whether the samples were obtained in the context of treatment or for research purposes?

ARG: The purpose for which the sample is taken bears no relevance.
BR: No.
CH: No.
COL: See answer 5.2.
CR: There is no difference.
FR: No.
GER: No, not by law. Only if there are special rules in a contract between the donor and the researcher.
MX: The law does not consider this question.
PT: No.
SP: No.

6.5. Is it necessary to specify the specific aim of the research that is going to be carried out in the event of the sample being transferred?

ARG: Yes, if it is possible to identify the subjects.
BR: Yes.
CH: Yes, if it is possible to identify its owner.
COL: If the possibility of transferring the samples is known when they are received —as it is the case with biobanks- the source subject should be advised of the biobank policy with regard to this matter; although, in order to establish this policy, the biobank must respect the rights and guarantees of the source subjects and, in this sense, the extent and content of the informed consent will specify the powers of the biobank with regard to the non-anonymous samples.
CR: Yes, it must be addressed in the informed consent.
FR: French law does not require this specification.

GER: Not by law. Only if there are special rules in a contract between the donor and the researcher.

MX: We cannot answer this question with our existing regulations.

PT: Yes. The transfer must always respect the purpose of the creation of biobanks for which the consent was obtained.

SP: Yes, but in the case of biobanks, the consent could be given in a broader way.

6.6. What are the consequences of claiming a possible right of return or destruction for samples already transferred?

ARG: It would have to be investigated if they are registered samples and the patient rights are unknown, or if they are anonymous samples.

BR: None. The right to withdraw consent must be always be respected.

CH: The right to withdraw consent must always be respected. The information provided prior to consent must specify the effects of withdrawal.

COL: There is no explicit regulation regarding the request for the return of samples. Consent may be withdrawn at any time «without prejudice» to the source subject. (Resolution 8430 of 1993, Article 15. G).

CR: There are no legal provisions regarding this, but the subject might sue the researcher.

FR: The right to withdraw consent concerning samples analyzed for genetic data must be always respected. However, there are no specific provisions concerning a claim to a sample that has already been transferred. The consent or non opposition form and the contract for transfer could make provision for this situation.

GER: The sample has to be destroyed, or the sample and data have to be anonymised.

MX: The law does not consider this situation.

PT: The right to withdraw consent must be always respected. The information provided prior to consent could specify the effects of withdrawal. But there is nothing about this in the law.

SP: The right to withdraw consent must always be respected. In the information provided prior to consent the effects of withdrawal must be specified.

7. – What effect will the death of a donor have regarding the storageand use of the sample?

ARG: If the subject had any right over the sample, these rights are transferred to their legal heirs.

BR: In principle none. However, the use of the material for another subordinate purpose must have the approval of the Ethics Committee.

CH: It is not explicitly regulated.

COL: By analogy with the transplant regulations, we can state that the death of the donor makes the donation irrevocable.

CR : There are no legal provisions regarding this, but according to the Civil Code the inheritor may claim some rights.

FR : When the donor dies and when the sample is made of germinal tissues or cells, the intended purpose of the sample cannot be changed.

GER : None, if the researcher, doctor or hospital has become the owner of the material.

MX : The law does not consider this situation.

PT : The relatives have the property right to the sample.

SP : The family members could ask for the anonymisation of the sample.

8. – *Do property rights have a bearing on possible rights of the biobank to use the sample or the results of the research?*

ARG : I reiterate that there are no property rights regarding this. The rights of the subjects involved will depend on the whether or not the samples are registered or whether these were freely stipulated to the donor.

BR : There is no regulation.

CH : It is not explicitly regulated.

COL : See the previous answers. In the field of intellectual property, research findings may be subject to protection through patents for example.

CR : There is no legislation regarding this or any kind of information to answer this question.

FR : No.

GER : No.

MX : We cannot answer this question with our existing regulations.

PT : No.

SP : No.

IV. – ACCESS TO BODY MATERIALS

1. – *What legal regulations exist concerning the extraction, storage, processing, and transporting of body materials?*

ARG : The practical guides to clinical research on humans (resolution 1490/2007) of the Ministry of Health contain general regulations on the issue.

BR : CONEP's Resolution 196 and 347.

CH : The Health Code, the Act concerning scientific research on human beings, regulations and resolutions exempt laboratories in relation to the destruction of samples.

COL : We do not have special regulations for biobanks. We refer to the special regulations on informed consent and research on humans.

CR : The establishments must meet the following requirements : physical plant, human resources, material resources, equipment and organization.

FR : Law n° 94-654 of July 29th 1994 relating to the donation and use of elements and products from the human body, for assisted reproduction and prenatal diagnosis and Law n° 2004-800 of August 6th 2004 relating to bioethics.

GER : There is a difference between the regulation concerning the collecting, storage, processing and transporting of body materials to be used for research and the regulation of body material that is to be used for therapeutic purposes such as transplantation. If the material is to be used for research, there is no special regulation regarding the collecting, storage, processing and transporting of the material. The institution, that collects tissue for use on humans or carries out laboratory examinations needs permission according to §20 b AMG. Institutions which store or process tissue need permission according to §20 c AMG. The licence has very strict conditions. The institution will be continuously supervised.

Tissue banks

Tissue banks are tissue institutions as defined in §1a Nr. 8 TPG. Tissue institutions are all institutions that harvest, examine, process, store and distribute tissue as defined in §1 a Nr. 4 TPG. These are all kinds of tissue which are not organs as defined in §1 a Nr. 1 TPG. Tissue banks include cornea banks, bone marker banks and sperm banks. In this case harvesting means also extracorporal harvesting in the case of sections- and material resulting from operations such as placentas for the purpose of processing. These institutions need also permission according to §§20 oder 20 c AMG.

Permission has to be given, if the institution fulfils the personnel (qualified staff) and organisational conditions in §8d and order 8 f TPG and according to §20 b I S. 3 AMG there is no reason for not giving permission.

Harvesting must be carried out by a physician (doctor) with the necessary knowledge and skills. The physician must not be the headof the institution.

All other institutions as defined in §20 b AMG only need qualified staff with the necessary experience.

According to §20 b II AMG permission is not necessary if the institution only obtains the material and has a contract with a manufacturer or processor who has permission in accordance with §20 c AMG.

According to §20 c AMG an institution that processes, stores or distributes tissue needs permission if the tissue is not processed in an industrial way or the processing procedure is well known (Herzklappen, Augenhornhäute, etc.). The institution has to fulfil the necessary conditions established in §8d TPG and there shall be no reason for permission not to be given according to §20 c II AMG. The institution must have good qualified staff, suitable rooms and facilities. According to §20 c III AMG the institution must also have a person with qualifications and experience who is responsible for ensuring that tissue and tissue products will be processed, stored and distributed in accordance with these laws. This person must have suitable academic qualifications in human medicine, biology, biochemistry or any other comparable area and at least 2 years experience of processing tissue. In the case of industrial processing the institution needs permission as specified in §§13, 21 AMG.

If the institution wants to harvest and store tissue it must have permission in accordance with both §20 b and §20 c AMG. The institutions also have to be registered in accordance with §8 f TPG. This registry is public.

Blood banks

A blood bank must have permission in accordance with §13 AMG. Bloodbanks have to fulfil the conditions established in §4 TFG (qualified staff, suitable rooms and facilities). The leader of the institution must be a physician, with the necessary qualifications in medical science. Blood banks in hospitals need special permission as established in §11 TFG.

Organ banks

According to §10 I 1 TPG the harvesting and storage of organs has to be carried out in a transplantation centre. A transplantation centre is a hospital with special permission to carry out these procedures. The transplantation and harvesting has to be carried out by a physician. Distribution has to be carried out by special institutions for organ distribution as established in §12 TPG.

There are only a few special rules in the different state's *Bestattungsgesetze (funeral laws)*, about the question of whether the use of the material for research purposes is allowed. There is a very special rule in §18 Abs. 6 Sächs. BestattG. This allows the use of body material that has been collected for medical research or from adiagnostic procedure, without the consent of the patient for the purpose of research.

MX: The regulation of this question is divided between different regulations from the Mexican Health Agency.

The Commission for Protection against Health Risks is the agency in charge of preparing and issuing the official Mexican regulations regarding products, activities, services and establishments under its authority, issuing official certificates certifying the satisfactory condition of processes, products, methods, facilities, services or activities related to the matters under its authority; exercising controlling and monitoring the regulations concerning human organs, tissues, cells and their components, their importing and exporting, and the establishments and health institutions assigned to processing these products.

Nevertheless there is a separate bylaw; the General Law on Health Regulation concerning the control of the availability of human organs, tissues and corpses., Article 90 states that all vehicles transporting any body material need a licence from the health authorities. Article 93 specifies that all organ and tissue banks must comply with the bylaw with regard to the following services: obtaining, preparing, safeguarding, preserving, supplying and keeping information relating to material of human origin, and providing adequate facilities for carrying out these activities.

Finally, concerning the harvesting of samples, there is a Mexican Official Regulation (NOM 003-SSA2-1993) concerning the collection of human blood.

PT: There is a different law on setting quality and safety standards for the donation, procurement, testing, processing, preservation, storage and distribution of human tissues and cells (Law no. 12/2009, 26th March). This law is applicable to tissues and cells of human origin intended to be used in humans. It is not applicable when they are going to be used in research involving animals or *in vitro*). It is not applicable to biological material stored in biobanks.

SP: In the framework of *in vitro* research there is a specific regulation in Section V of Law 14/2007 concerning biomedical research.

2. – *Who is permitted to perform the particular operations?*

ARG: In the case of clinical research, the person for whom the pertinent research protocol was approved

BR: No regulation.

CH: An accredited professional.

COL: *Extraction*: Specialist doctors.

Processing: A qualified professional; for example, a biologist or doctor specialised in pathology.

Storage: The organisation which has obtained the corresponding health licence. We do not have an explicit regulation which establishes quality standards; we believe that this is determined in accordance with corresponding medical and technical protocols, for example the good practice guides. Decree 1571 of 1993 from the Ministry of Health (Now Social Security) establishes the storage conditions for human blood samples and parts or blood products.

On the other hand, blood banks, professional practice groups with no physical infrastructure for the provision of health services, Reproductive Biomedical Units and all other body part banks are excluded from the application of the quality guarantee system regulations of Decree 1011 of 2006 of the Ministry of Social Protection, which defines the Obligatory System of Health Quality Guarantee of the General System of Social Security in Health, in paragraph one of Article one, as they do not deal with health service providers – according to the definition from the Article.

Transport: There are specific regulations for the transport of biological materials registered as dangerous; if regarding ground transport the regulations are in Decree 1609 of 2002 by the Ministry of Transport.

There are specialist transport companies, even internationally, for human biological samples; according to the information they provide the following regulations apply: IATA, CNS and the WHO.

CR: The researcher or someone he designates.

FR: A person who has a diploma in medicine or pharmaceutical studies or a PHD in the area of life and health sciences.

GER: Regarding the question of extraction, the rules of medical law in general are relevant. In general only a physician is allowed to perform the particular operations. In some cases the physician can delegate the extraction to qualified medical staff (e.g. collecting blood).

MX: According to article 100 of the General Law on Health only health professionals may perform any activity related to human research. All health professionals must comply with the regulation issued by the health authorities.

PT: The researcher responsible for the biobank.

SP: An accredited professional.

3. – Which operational sequences require the participation of physicians medical cooperation?

ARG: There is no specific regulation.

BR: No regulation.

CH: All professionals involved in the handling of the samples are regulated by means of their professional qualifications, but only in the final analysis do they require the participation of physicians.

COL: The extraction, processing, storage and transport stages require the intervention of a medical professional; however, we could say that with regard to the extraction and processing their participation is direct, since it is the doctor who personally carries out these operations, whilst in terms of storage and transport, the doctor monitors these activities but does not necessarily carry them out as this is carried out by auxiliaries or specialist companies hired for this purpose.

CR: Obtaining the sample and evaluating the patient's health status.

FR: A doctor is required for the harvesting of some samples. There is no specific provision on the requirement for the participation of physicians for the other operations.

GER: All research involving the patient's body requires the participation of physicians and informed consent.

MX: This is not specified.

PT: Physicians must harvest all samples stored in biobanks.

SP: There is no legal provision, but the researchers' or biobanks' protocols should establish an appropriate way to guarantee the quality of the sample, so the participation of a physician will be needed after the intervention on the patient in order to transport and maintain the sample in the best condition.

4. – Does the patient have to be informed prior to the biopsy being carried out?

ARG: Informed consent is an essential requirement for al medical acts (section IV of resolution 1490/07).

BR: Yes, in principle. However, in practice there is nothing to prevent them from being informed later.

CH: The person must be informed of the essential aspects of research, including its purpose, benefits, risks and alternative procedures or treatments. Adequate information in this respect must be given. Also, special mention should be made of the right to refuse to authorize the research or to revoke their consent at any time by any means, without any liability, penalty or their treatment being affected in anyway (L. 20120).

COL: Yes; it is considered a patient's right according to the law and jurisprudence.

CR: Yes, in every case.

FR: The patient does not have to be informed before the biopsy about the use of the sample for research purposes. Indeed, the biopsy can be carried out for a therapeutic purpose and then used for research. Thus, the information about the use of the sample for research purposes can be given to the patient before or after the biopsy.

In both cases, the patient will have information about the intervention and its physical risks before the biopsy is carried out.

GER: Yes.

MX: Informed consent is only necessary if the sample will be used for research purposes.

PT: The patient must be informed before the *use* of the sample for research purposes, because he/she must give his/her consent.

If the aim of biopsy is therapeutic then when a researcher wants to carry out research using a sample obtained for therapeutic purposes, it is necessary to ask the donor for consent.

SP: The patient must be informed before the *use* of the sample for research purposes. If this is the case tthe information provided has to include, amongst other things, details of the physical risk of the intervention.

If the biopsy is performed for therapeutic purposes, it is not necessary to inform the patient before the intervention about the potential use of the sample in research, but when a researcher wants to carry out research with a sample obtained for therapeutic purposes it is necessary to ask for consent (in this case it is not necessary to refer to physical risk).

5. – *Does the patient have to consent to the biopsy?*

ARG: Yes, as explained in the previous answer.

BR: Yes, he does. The patient has to give express consent beforean intervention can be carried out on a patient for therapeutic purposes.

CH: The patient has to give express consent before an intervention for therapeutic purposes can be performed when there is a risk; and this consent is always required if the purpose is biomedical research.

COL: Yes; it is considered a patient's right according to the law and jurisprudence.

CR: Yes, in every case.

FR: The patient always has to give express consent before theintervention is performed.

GER: Yes.

MX: Answered in question four.

PT: The patient always has to give express consent before an intervention for therapeutic purposes is performed on the patient, regardless of the degree of risk. This consent is mandatory if the purpose is biomedical research.

SP: The patient has to give express consent before an intervention for therapeutic purposes is carried out when there is a risk. This consent is always required if the purpose is biomedical research.

6. – Is there a duty to provide genetic counselling?

ARG: There is no legal regulation.

BR: No.

CH: Yes.

COL: There is a specific regulation regarding the duty to provide pertinent medical counselling in the case of those infected with HIV and sexually transmitted diseases. Article 11 of Law 23 of 1981 or the Medical Ethics Act, which establish the duty for doctors to provide continuous support to their patients, the duty to provide genetic counselling may be derived from this. We would think that, in general, the institutions which practice genetic analysis offer appropriate counselling.

CR: No, according to the legislation.

FR: Yes.

GER: Yes. In the case of genetic examinations, GenDG.

MX: No.

PT: Yes.

SP: Yes.

7. – Is there an obligation to consult an ethics committee?

ARG: Chapter III of Resolution 1490/07 of the Ministry of Health contemplates the existence of a research ethics committee which has the power to approve, reject, monitor, request modifications or suspend a clinical trial.

BR: Yes.

CH: Yes.

COL: If it is regarding samples for research, Resolution 8430 of 1993 of the then Ministry of Health, on research on humans, Article 6 G, prescribes the approval of the Research Ethics Committee for the research project; Article 16, subparagraph b, establishes that the committee should review the consent of the passive subject of the research; paragraph three of the same Article establishes the need for the committee's intervention when necessary to determine an individual's mental capacity to grant consent.

Resolution 2378 of 2008 of the Ministry of Social Protection which establishes the Good clinical practices for institutions which conduct research using drugs on humans, establishes in Article seven, paragraph one, that the it is the function of the ethics committee at such institutions to evaluate the informed consent form; equally, in the Technical Annex number 1, it is established that the ethics committee must safeguard the rights of participants in the research.

CR: Yes, in every case of biomedical research using human samples.

FR: Yes but only for samples which are prepared and stored for a scientific purpose.

GER: In some cases, if research on humans is concerned, consulting anethics committee is obligatory. But not if the tissue has been extracted before during medical treatment or diagnosis.

MX: Concerning research using human samples, article 98 of the General Law on Health states that a research commission and an ethics committee must be formed.

PT: No, there is not an obligation to consult an ethics committee before genetic counselling.

SP: Yes.

8. – Does the patient have to be informed about the use of body materials for research purposes?

ARG: Yes. This is part of the informed consent. Resolution 319/04 of INCUCAI contains an informed consent form as an annex.

BR: Yes.

CH: Yes.

COL: Yes. This is what Resolution 8430 of 1993 of the Ministry of Health (now Social Protection) establishes especially in Article 14.

CR: Yes, in allbiomedical research using human samples.

FR: Yes.

GER: No, not if the material was obtained for research. Only in some cases, if the material was obtained for the purpose of genetic examination, transfusion or transplantation.

MX: Yes, according to article 100 of the General Law on Health written, informed consent form is obligatory. The donor must also be informed of the research objectives as well as of the positive or negative impact of the research on his/her health.

PT: Yes.

SP: Yes.

9. – Does the patient have to consent to the further use of body materials for research purposes?

ARG: Yes, where the body material is individualised. In the case where the material is not individualised, no right exists.

BR: Yes.

CH: Yes.

COL: Yes, this is what we deduce from the sentences from the Columbian Constitutional Court, for example, unified judgement 337 of 1999.

CR: Yes, in all biomedical research using human samples.

FR : The patient has to consent when the research involves the analysis of genetic data. In all other cases, the patient has to be informed and his/her non- opposition must be established.

GER : No. See No. 8 above.

MX : Answered in question eight.

PT : Yes.

SP : Yes.

10. – *What legal particularities exist in the case of the harvesting and use of samples from test subjects/patients who are not able to give their consent (children, teenagers, demented persons, traumatized persons, and the deceased)?*

ARG : Resolution 1490/07 contains directives regarding informed consent with children. Those over 7 years of age must provide their consent, notwithstanding that granted by their parents (Art. 4.5.3). All other disabled individuals are included in Art. 4.3.18.

BR : When it is not possible to obtain the consent of the donor, authorization can be given by the Ethics Committee.

CH : For people who are not able to give their consent, their representatives must give consent. In the case of indigenous communities whose world view requires that the community agrees, individual patient consent is not enough.

COL : It is necessary to have the consent of the parents or legal representatives; however, jurisprudence establishes the duty to take account of and tend to serve the will of the patient or research subject, according to their age and degree of comprehension. Chapter three of the aforementioned Resolution 8430 of 1993 is dedicated to the regulation of research on under-age or physically or mentally disabled individuals.

In the case of corpses, the provisions on transplants apply, which are contained in Decree 2493 of 2004, Ministry of Social Protection, which establish the presumption of donation when a person dies without having exercised their right to decide if their organs and tissue are not to be used for transplants. If it is not possible to prove that they decided against this while alive, the presumption of donation is applied, but relatives have a minimum fixed legal period of six hours from brain death to contest this presumption.

CR : The donor's legal representative must provide authorization.

FR : The donor's legal representative must provideauthorization.

GER : In order to take samples from minors, who are capable of giving consent, it is necessarr to obtain consent fromboth the minor and his/her parents. If there is no advantage in the procedurefor the minor, a court acting as the minor's guardian always has to provide consent.

In case of persons who are not capable of giving consent, a court acting as the person's guardian is responsible for this decision.

Medical research on minors is generally not permitted.

MX: In accordance with article 100 of the General Law on Health the parents or guardians must grant consent,. In the case of the deceased a relative must give consent.

PT: The donor's legal representative has to provide consent.

SP: The donor's legal representative has to provide consent.

11. – Who is responsible for ensuring compliance with these regulations?

ARG: The person responsible for breach of the regulations regarding informed consent from minors or disabled individuals is the person who directs the research.

BR: The institution is responsible for the research.

CH: The centre in which the sample is obtained.

COL: It depends on the case. By way of example, in the case of research, the primary researcher is liable for compliance with various obligations such as obtaining informed consent. The Institute of Medical, Legal and Forensic Science is liable in the case of obtaining materials from corpses for use in research. In the framework of a clinical relationship, the doctor must obtain informed consent.

CR: The researcher and the research organization as well.

FR: The centre in which the sample is obtained and the doctor who takes the samples.

GER: First of all, the doctor who is responsible for the harvesting or the diagnostic procedure. But the hospital or biobank itself is also responsible.

MX: All health professionals are responsible under the General Law on Health and will be sanctioned according to article 100 and 101 of the General Law on Health.

PT: The person responsible for the research.

SP: The centre in which the sample is obtained.

V. – DATA PROTECTION

1. – Which legal regulations exist for the protection of a patient's data?

ARG: The country has a data protection law (25.326). On the basis that the human body material sample carries genetic information (sensitive information), all legal provisions regarding the saving, conservation, modification of information and sanctions for non-observance of the legal principles apply.

BR: The Constitution and CONEP's Resolution 196 and 347.

CH: Chile has a law on the protection of personal data, L.19628, August 22nd, 1999, «Protection of Privacy and Data Protection».

COL: Article 15 of the Political Constitution of Columbia provides as follows: «Everyone has the right to personal and family privacy and good name, and the State must respect and enforce respect of these. Equally, they have the right to know, update and amend information held on them in data banks and in archives of public and private organisations.

The freedom and other guarantees contained in the Constitution shall be respected in the collection, handling and circulation of data.

Correspondence and other forms of private communication are tamper-proof. They may only be intercepted or registered by judicial order, in the cases and under the formal legal requirements.

For tax or legal purposes and for cases of inspection, monitoring and intervention by the State the presentation of accounts and other private documents may be requested under the terms of the law».

Article 14 of Resolution 13437 of 1991 of the Ministry of Health (now Social Protection) states that: «It is the patient's right that all clinical records are treated as confidential and secret and that may only be revealed with their authorisation».

Article 8 of Resolution 8430 of 1993 of the Ministry of Health (now Social Protection) states as follows: «In research on humans, the privacy of the individual subject to research will be protected and the individual shall only be identified when the results require this and this has been authorised by the individual».

Article 1 of Resolution 1995 of 1999 of the Ministry of Health (Now Social Protection) defines clinical records as a private, compulsory and confidential document which chronologically records the patient's health condition, the medical action and other procedures taken by the health team taking care of the patient. This document may only be revealed to third parties subject to authorisation by the patient or in those situations provided by the law.

Furthermore, various Constitutional Court judgements uphold the confidentiality of such data.

CR: a) The General Law on Rights and Obligations of Patients in Public and Private Institutions (Act N° 8239 of 19-04-02)

b) The General Decree on Social Security. January 1, 2007.

FR: a) In general, for personal data: Law n° 78-17 of January 6th 1978 on data processing and freedom

b) Regarding clinical documentation: Law n° 2002-303 of March 4th 2002 on patients' rights and the quality of the health system.

c) Regarding genetic data: Law n° 94/653 of July 29th 1994 on respect for the human body.

GER: The main rules are in the data protection law (Datenschutzgesetz).

Personal data stored for the purpose of research are protected by the data protection law. The rules in §§14, 28, 30 and §40 BDSG are very important.

According to §40 Abs. 1 BDSG personal data collected and stored for the purpose of research are only allowed to be used for purposes of scientific research. Personal data must be anonymised as soon as possible. In case of liquidation of the biobank/research institution personal datahas to be anonymised, if further research is to be carried out by another research institution.

According to §40 Abs. 2 BDSG it is possible to transfer personal data in this case. The transfer of personal data to other public institutions is only allowed if this institution commits itself not to use or process the data for other purposes and to anonymise the data as soon as possible.

There are also important rules in the MBO-Ä (§9) and the penal code (§203 StGB) regarding medical staff's Schweigepflicht (duty of confidentiality).

Personal data collected together with tissue must be stored in a very safe way in accordance with §10 MBO-Ä. According to 10 Abs. 3 MBO-Ä this data has to be stored for 10 years. According to §10 Abs. 4 MBO-Ä the physician has to take care of the patients' personal data. The data storage must be very secure. Without the consent of the patient nobody is allowed to see or to use this data and it is forbidden to transfer the data.

Then there are some special rules about data protection in TFG (§§6, 11, 14 and 19 TFG), TPG (§§7, 13. f and 14 TPG), AMG and GenDG (§§7, 8, 13 GEnDG).

MX: The Political Constitution of the United Mexican States in its sixth article sets the framework for the protection of personal information stating that "The information concerning the private life and personal data shall be protected in the terms and with the exceptions provided by the law. On a federal level, the Federal Law of Transparency and Access to Government Public Information «guarantees the protection of personal data in the possession of legally bound subjects». The Guidelines for the Protection of Personal Data establish the minimum conditions and requirements to be followed for the correct handling and safekeeping of data systems. They also give a set of principles to be considered in relation to the protection of personal data, and some of them are applicable to the data contained in samples and information stored in a biobank. Finally on a regional level, the Protection of Personal Data Law for the Federal District defines personal data as «information concerning an identified or identifiable individual, and information regarding his/her ethnic origin, physical characteristics, state of health, and DNA».

PT: a) In general, for data protection: Law n.º 67/98, 26th October.

b) Regarding clinical documentation, health information, genetic information and biobanks: Law 12/2005, 26th January.

SP: a) In general, for personal data: Organic Law 15/1999, 13th December on the protection of Personal Data, and its regulatory development.

b) Regarding clinical documentation: Law 41/2002, 14th November, which regulates the autonomy of the patient and rights and duties related to clinical information and documentation

c) Regarding genetic data: Law 14/2007, 3rd July, on biomedical research.

2. – Which legal regulations exist for the protection of information gained from genetic tests?

ARG: The rules mentioned in the previous answer are applicable.

BR: The CONEP Resolutions.

CH: a) Law 20120, Sept. 22nd 2006 on scientific research involving human beings.

b) Law L.19.970, Sept. 10th, 2004 on the creation of national DNA records.

COL: Law 1266, 2008, which prescribes the general provisions of habeas data and regulates the handling of personal data contained in databases, especially financial, credit, commercial, service and data from third party countries and prescribes other provisions which contain some general provisions which are already traditional in doctrine, among which includes confidentiality and security; however, the Constitutional Court in judgement C-1011 of 2008, decided that this Law partially regulates habeas data inasmuch as it only regulates the administration data of a financial nature.

Protection has been established through jurisprudence for several years.

CR: There is no specific regulation regarding this. The General Law on the Rights and Obligations of Patients in Public and Private Institutions may be suitable for such cases.

FR: Law n° 94/653 of July 29th 1994 on respect for human body.

GER: Since 2009 there have been special rules in the GenDG. According to §13 GenDG a genetic sample is only allowed to be used for the purpose of the medical genetic examination for which it has been obtained. If the sample is not needed any longer for this purpose the sample has to be destroyed immediately by the responsible physician or the person or institution that has carried out the examination (§7 Abs. 2 GenDG). According to §13 Abs.2 GenDG the genetic sample can only be used for other purposes if this is allowed by other legal regulations (for example §18 SächsBestattG) or in the case of informed consent by the person from whom the sample has been obtained. The consent has to be written. According to §8 Abs. 2 GenDG the patient has the right to revoke consent without any reason and at any time. In the case of revocation, according to §13 I S. 2 GenDG, the sample has to be destroyed immediately.

Again the data protection law is involved.

MX: We do not have any special protection for the information gained from genetic testing.

PT: Law 12/2005 cited above.

SP: Law 14/2007, 3rd July, on biomedical research. Section V, Chapter II.

3. – *Do the donors have the right to obtain information from the BMB about the data stored on them?*

ARG: Based on law 25.326 the donor would have the right to obtain information from the bank only where the samples are identifiable.

BR: Yes.

CH: Yes.

COL: The answer is clearly affirmative when the samples remain associated with a specific or determinable person.

CR: Yes, they always have the right to information.

FR: Yes.

GER: Yes.

MX: Since most biobanks in Mexico belong to a public institution information is able to be obtained. Article 16 of the Constitution protects all personal data. However, if the information is in a private institution this might prove very difficult.

PT: Yes.
SP: Yes.

4. – Are the samples and data stored and protected separately within the biobank (e.g. different codes)?

ARG: This depends on the regulation of each bank. If there are individualised samples it is obvious that they should be duly identified.

BR: No regulation.

CH: No.

COL: In general, it appears so if separate codes and independent chains of custody are assigned.

CR: It depends on the research organization, institutional regulation or the characteristics of the research.

FR: It depends on the characteristics of the biobanks.

GER: No.

MX: Although there is no Mexican regulation that regulates this subject, all biobanks contacted in our report store all data separately from samples and keep them under different security systems. Most biobanks disassociate the sample from the donor, store it and assign a numeric code. The register which links the sample with the name of the donor is kept either in a computer under a code or in locked physical archives. Access to these registers is restricted and controlled.

PT: Yes.

SP: It depends on the characteristics of the biobanks. The donor has to be informed about the circumstances in which the samples are going to be stored, and measures to guarantee confidentiality must be undertaken.

5. – To whom is the biobank allowed to forward samples or (personal) data for research purposes- only to research scientists in public research institutions, or also to commercial enterprises (commercialization)?

ARG: This depends on the internal regulation of the bank. With regard to public banks, given that their establishment aims to protect general interests, may not provide samples to private companies.

BR: In principle, only the scientists involved with the research.

CH: Both, public or private institutions, subject to the general regulationson scientific research involving human beings. In all cases, the transfer of the sample should be free.

COL: This sort of distinction is not made, but one must remember that the circulation of personal data is restricted and the non-anonymous samples may not be circulated without the consent of the source subject.

CR: It depends on the research organization, institutional regulation or the characteristics of the research. See Costa Rican report on national and international transfer and circulation of samples.

FR : Both to public and private institutions. But the donor has to be informed regarding the recipient of these samples and data.

GER : If it is allowed at all, samples and personal data (but only with the consent of the patient) can be forwarded to scientists in public research institutions and also to commercial enterprises.

MX : There is no specific legislation concerning this particular question so the exchange of samples depends on the institution, many of the biobanks consulted have sample exchange agreements mostly with hospitals and universities.

PT : Both to public and private institutions, only for research purposes. The storage for commercial purposes by organisations of samples that have not been anonymised is not allowed.

SP : Both to public and private institutions. The criteria for transfer are the same. But in all cases, the whole process of donation, assignment, storage and use of biological samples must be devoid of financial gain or profit, both for the donors as well as for those who receive the sample. Personal genetic data must not be used for commercial purposes.

6. – *Is there an international exchange of samples and data for research purposes?*

ARG : The only bank which has a specific regulation is the Garraham hospital hematopoietic stem cell bank, which allows for the possibility of the exchange of material, criteria which has already been used.

BR : Yes.

CH : Yes.

COL : Two of the institutions which answered our survey said that they have sent samples out of the country under research agreements with other research institutes, some of which are educational institutions and others industrial, commercial or pharmaceutical businesses, but they have not received samples from abroad.

CR : Yes.

FR : Yes.

GER : Yes.

MX : From all the biobanks consulted only one has an exchange programme with a university abroad.

PT : There is no official information about this.

SP : Yes.

7. – *Is there a regulation concerning the international exchange of samples and data for research purposes?*

ARG : No, except that mentioned in the point above.

BR : Resolution 340/2004 states that the exchange of information is possible and, when international, the opportunities for the transfer of technology provided by the project must be stated. (IV.1, m).Resolution n. 347/2005 allows the samples to be exchanged. In thecase of exchange within the country, agreement between institutions is necessary, where the methods of operation and use of the stored material is described. Regarding the international transfer of material, both the agreement between the institutions involved and the legislation relation to the exporting of material must be respected. The procedures must be reported to the ethics committee so that the project may be evaluated, in accordance with that established in item 5.2.

CH: No.

COL: Only in relation to tissue for transplantation and blood.

CR: No, see answer number 6.

FR: There are some provisions in Law n° 78-17 of January 6th 1978 on data processing and freedom.

GER: No.

MX: The Federal Commission for the Protection Against Health Risks (COFEPRIS), is the agency responsible for: preparing and issuing the official Mexican regulations regarding products, activities, services and establishments under its authority; issuing official certificates certifying the satisfactory condition of the processes, products, methods, facilities, services or activities related to the matters under its authority; g inspecting and monitoring the regulation on the use of human organs, tissues and cells and their components, their import and export, the establishments themselves, and health institutions designated forthe processing of these products.

PT: No.

SP: It is under preparation (May 2009).

8. – Are the data safe from confiscation by the police or prosecutors?

ARG: They are in principle, apart from the legal exceptions (national defence, public security), (Art. 23.1 of Law 25.326).

BR: In principle, no.

CH: The processing of information obtained from the analysis of samples is subject to judicial review. Notwithstanding this, the police have powers to take samples when conducting specific research without prior permission.

COL: No, in our opinion.

CR: There is no specific regulation regarding this.

FR: According to French law only a penal judge is allowed to seizemedical records. This provision could be extended to samples and data for research purposes.

GER: They may be confiscated, but very demanding requirements have to be satisfied before this can done.

MX: Accordingly to article 22 of the Federal Law on Transparency and Access to Government Public Information, data may be confiscated by judicial order.

PT: Yes. According to the Data protection Act, using it for different purposes is impossible.

SP: Only a judge is allowed to ask for the data if they are needed in a trial.

9. – *Are the research findings classified (6)?*

ARG: This depends on the internal regulation of each bank.

BR: Yes.

CH: Not directly, but there is differentiation regulatory framework involving the treatment of genetic information.

COL: Yes, as confidential personal data. We believe it is important to clarify the situation regarding genetic data obtained in the course of criminal investigation, inasmuch as the above refers to the confiscation of data by the police.

The data obtained during the course of a criminal investigation, these remain confidential until the trial. Data which is in the competent authorities' archives are also confidential in general and may only be revealed by order of the legal authority.

CR: No.

FR: A Human Protection Committee has to assess the protection of personal data within the framework of biomedical research.

GER: No.

MX: No.

PT: There is a duty of secrecy in relation to personal genetic data (obtained as a result of research or health care).

SP: There is a duty of secrecy in relation to genetic data (obtained as a result of research or health care).

---

(6) Is there a special "duty of secrecy" in relation to research findings?

II. – GUIDELINES FOR DRAFTING A MODEL INFORMATION SHEET AND CONSENT DOCUMENT

I. – THE REQUIREMENT FOR CONSENT

– The first step will be to check, is whether consent is necessary for the use of biological samples for research purposes where these samples are originally taken for diagnostic purposes and are anonymised, taking into account each country's legal system.

– A check must be made to clarify whether there are any exceptional or special circumstances, allowed for in the national legislation, that justify the use of a sample without consent.

II. – INFORMATION PRIOR TO CONSENT: CHARACTERISTICS

– Information must be provided in writing and donors must also be given a verbal explanation.

– The explanation must be given in a way that is appropriate to the cultural characteristics and age of the donor. Special attention must be given to people in vulnerable situations (the sick, prisoners, etc) to ensure their consent is freely given and that the legal requirements of each country are taken into consideration.

– Potential donors must be given the opportunity to ask questions.

– A reasonable period of time must lapse between communicating the information and the signing of the consent form.

III. – CONTENT OF THE INFORMATION

1. – *Identifying the purpose for which the sample will be used*

– Option A. Research project
Identity of the researcher
The research team
The participating centres
The purpose of the project
Financing
Duration

– Option B. Storage in a biobank for future research projects.
Description of the purpose of the biobank
Owner
Address and website
Financing
Storage period (a determined period of time or reference to particular purposes)

2. – *The project has been approved by an independent ethics committee*

3. – *Free and voluntary donation*

The donor will not receive payment for the donation. However, it will be possible to pay the donor any costs incurred (e.g. travel).

Participation is voluntary. Refusal to participate in the research will not affect the provision of any medical care that may be required.

4. – *Benefits expected from the use/storage of the sample*

Specify that the results will not be of any direct benefit to the donor, but that the research will benefit society in general through advances in medical knowledge.

The sample cannot be used directly to make profits. However, the information generated from the studies carried out on the sample could be a source of commercial profit. The donor renounces any direct participation in these profits.

5. – *Obtaining the sample*

Where samples are obtained for research purposes, a description of the procedure to be used when taking the sample and the possible risks. A description of the type of sample that is going to be taken. The need to obtain liability insurance will be assessed.

Where samples are surplus to requirements after diagnostic testing: assess whether consent is required. If it is: the original diagnostic purpose that led to the sample being taken will be respected. Only surplus material from this procedure will be used.

6. – *What happens to the sample after the research has been carried out*

Option A: If consent is given for a specific project:
– Anonymisation
– Destruction
– Where it is wanted to use the sample for a project other than that which was originally described, the donor will receive relevant information and the donor's consent will be sought again.

Option B: If the sample has been donated to a biobank it will only be used in future research projects related to the purpose of the biobank, when this research has been favourably assessed by a research ethics committee duly approved by the health authority. These projects must comply with the universally accepted legal requirements and ethical principles.

The sample will be available should the donor require it for health reasons, provided that it has not been anonymised.

Restrictions may be placed in relation to the transfer of the sample by the biobank to others.

7. – Access to the information

The right to know the clinically relevant genetic information that is obtained as a result of the analysis of the samples donated, provided that they have not been anonymised.

As a consequence of the research, information concerning health may be obtained from the genetic analysis carried out on the biological sample. The donor will decide whether he or she wishes to receive this information or whether he or she wishes to renounce this right.

The information obtained may also be relevant for relatives. The donor will decide whether this information should be communicated to his or her relatives. If the donor decides that relatives should be informed, s/he can provide those in charge of the study with the details of these relatives so that they can be found and contacted.

When the sample is put into a biobank the donors will be given all the information about the use of their samples in research projects. In some cases it will be essential to send information to donors individually, when the sample is going to be used in projects the characteristics of which could have personal ethical implications.

8. – Data protection and confidentiality

Together with the sample, personal data will be collected such as age, sex or life style, as well as health details directly related to the pathology for which the sample is being collected.

The data will be stored using an encryption and encoding process. Only (the doctor responsible for their medical care / the person responsible for the biobank file) may connect this data to the particular donor.

The researcher and/or the development company, as applicable, will use this data when carrying out the research. The researcher and/or the development company may also use the data to support the results of the research before responsible authorities or in any public presentations they may make.

The results of the study may be communicated in scientific meetings, medical congresses or scientific publications. Strict confidentiality will always be maintained regarding the identity of the donor.

Both the researcher and, where applicable, the development company are responsible for handling the data from the study in accordance with that established in the current legislation on the protection of personal data.

9. – *The right to revoke*

Donors have the right to revoke their consent at any time. If a donor exercises this right then the sample will be anonymised / destroyed. The effects of the revocation will not extend to the data resulting from research that has already been carried out.

10. – *Exercising rights*

The identity and address of the person in charge through whom the right of access, correction, opposition and cancelation may be exercised.

11. – *Minors*

In the case of samples from minors, the requirements of the national legislation must be taken into account when justifying the research. Their legal representatives will give the necessary consent, but an assessment will be made as to whether the minor may be involved in the information and consent process.

When the donors of the sample reach the age of consent, they will be provided with information relating to the storage and use of their samples and they will have the right of access, opposition and cancellation.

12. – *People with learning disabilities*

In the case of samples from people with learning disabilities, the requirements of the national legislation must be taken into account when justifying the research. Their legal representatives will give the necessary consent, but an assessment will be made as to whether the person with learning difficulties may be involved in the information and consent process.

13. – *The deceased*

– The wishes of the donor when alive must be ascertained if possible. If stated, they must be respected.

– The need to inform the families or obtain authorisation from them must be assessed.

14. – *Jurisdiction*

Arrangements regarding the competent jurisdiction in the event of litigation must be indicated.

IV. – CONSENT SIGNATURE

– The identification details of the donor and, where applicable, the donor's legal representatives, must be included.

– The details of the professional who was in charge of communicating the information must be included.

– The need for witnesses' signatures will be assessed.

– Options for decisions regarding the communication of information and the destination of the sample after the research has been completed must be given.

III. – UNESCO. INTERNATIONAL DECLARATION ON HUMAN GENETIC DATA

16 October 2003

The General Conference,

Recalling the Universal Declaration of Human Rights of 10 December 1948, the two United Nations International Covenants on Economic, Social and Cultural Rights and on Civil and Political Rights of 16 December 1966, the United Nations International Convention on the Elimination of All Forms of Racial Discrimination of 21 December 1965, the United Nations Convention on the Elimination of All Forms of Discrimination against Women of 18 December 1979, the United Nations Convention on the Rights of the Child of 20 November 1989, the United Nations Economic and Social Council resolutions 2001/39 on Genetic Privacy and Non-Discrimination of 26 July 2001 and 2003/232 on Genetic Privacy and Non-Discrimination of 22 July 2003, the ILO Convention (No. 111) concerning Discrimination in Respect of Employment and Occupation of 25 June 1958, the UNESCO Universal Declaration on Cultural Diversity of 2 November 2001, the Trade Related Aspects of Intellectual Property Rights Agreement (TRIPS) annexed to the Agreement establishing the World Trade Organization, which entered into force on 1 January 1995, the Doha Declaration on the TRIPS Agreement and Public Health of 14 November 2001 and the other international human rights instruments adopted by the United Nations and the specialized agencies of the United Nations system,

Recalling more particularly the Universal Declaration on the Human Genome and Human Rights which it adopted, unanimously and by acclamation, on 11 November 1997 and which was endorsed by the United Nations General Assembly on 9 December 1998 and the Guidelines for the implementation of the Universal Declaration on the Human Genome and Human Rights which it endorsed on 16 November 1999 by 30 C/Resolution 23,

Welcoming the broad public interest worldwide in the Universal Declaration on the Human Genome and Human Rights, the firm support it has received from the international community and its impact in Member States drawing upon it for their legislation, regulations, norms and standards, and ethical codes of conduct and guidelines,

Bearing in mind the international and regional instruments, national laws, regulations and ethical texts relating to the protection of human rights and fundamental freedoms and to respect for human dignity as regards the collection, processing, use and storage of scientific data, as well as of medical data and personal data,

Recognizing that genetic information is part of the overall spectrum of medical data and that the information content of any medical data, including genetic data and proteomic data, is highly contextual and dependent on the particular circumstances,

Also recognizing that human genetic data have a special status on account of their sensitive nature since they can be predictive of genetic predispositions concerning individuals and that the power of predictability can be stronger than assessed at the time of deriving the data; they may have a significant impact on the family, including offspring, extending over generations, and in some instances on the whole group; they may contain information the significance of which is not necessarily known at the time of the collection of biological samples; and they may have cultural significance for persons or groups,

Emphasizing that all medical data, including genetic data and proteomic data, regardless of their apparent information content, should be treated with the same high standards of confidentiality,

Noting the increasing importance of human genetic data for economic and commercial purposes,

Having regard to the special needs and vulnerabilities of developing countries and the need to reinforce international cooperation in the field of human genetics,

Considering that the collection, processing, use and storage of human genetic data are of paramount importance for the progress of life sciences and medicine, for their applications and for the use of such data for non-medical purposes,

Also considering that the growing amount of personal data collected makes genuine irretrievability increasingly difficult,

Aware that the collection, processing, use and storage of human genetic data have potential risks for the exercise and observance of human rights and fundamental freedoms and respect for human dignity,

Noting that the interests and welfare of the individual should have priority over the rights and interests of society and research,

Reaffirming the principles established in the Universal Declaration on the Human Genome and Human Rights and the principles of equality, justice, solidarity and responsibility as well as respect for human dignity, human rights and fundamental freedoms, particularly freedom of thought and expression, including freedom of research, and privacy and security of the person, which must underlie the collection, processing, use and storage of human genetic data,

Proclaims the principles that follow and **adopts** the present Declaration.

A. – GENERAL PROVISIONS

Article 1 – Aims and scope

(a) The aims of this Declaration are: to ensure the respect of human dignity and protection of human rights and fundamental freedoms in the collection, processing, use and storage of human genetic data, human proteomic data and of the biological samples from which they are derived, referred to hereinafter as «biological samples», in keeping with the requirements of equality, justice and solidarity, while giving due consideration to freedom of thought and expression, including freedom of research;

to set out the principles which should guide States in the formulation of their legislation and their policies on these issues; and to form the basis for guidelines of good practices in these areas for the institutions and individuals concerned.

(b) Any collection, processing, use and storage of human genetic data, human proteomic data and biological samples shall be consistent with the international law of human rights.

(c) The provisions of this Declaration apply to the collection, processing, use and storage of human genetic data, human proteomic data and biological samples, except in the investigation, detection and prosecution of criminal offences and in parentage testing that are subject to domestic law that is consistent with the international law of human rights.

Article 2 – Use of terms

For the purposes of this Declaration, the terms used have the following meanings :

(i) Human genetic data : Information about heritable characteristics of individuals obtained by analysis of nucleic acids or by other scientific analysis;

(ii) Human proteomic data : Information pertaining to an individual's proteins including their expression, modification and interaction;

(iii) Consent : Any freely given specific, informed and express agreement of an individual to his or her genetic data being collected, processed, used and stored;

(iv) Biological samples : Any sample of biological material (for example blood, skin and bone cells or blood plasma) in which nucleic acids are present and which contains the characteristic genetic make-up of an individual;

(v) Population-based genetic study : A study which aims at understanding the nature and extent of genetic variation among a population or individuals within a group or between individuals across different groups;

(vi) Behavioural genetic study : A study that aims at establishing possible connections between genetic characteristics and behaviour;

(vii) Invasive procedure : Biological sampling using a method involving intrusion into the human body, such as obtaining a blood sample by using a needle and syringe;

(viii) Non-invasive procedure : Biological sampling using a method which does not involve intrusion into the human body, such as oral smears;

(ix) Data linked to an identifiable person : Data that contain information, such as name, birth date and address, by which the person from whom the data were derived can be identified;

(x) Data unlinked to an identifiable person : Data that are not linked to an identifiable person, through the replacement of, or separation from, all identifying information about that person by use of a code;

(xi) Data irretrievably unlinked to an identifiable person : Data that cannot be linked to an identifiable person, through destruction of the link to any identifying information about the person who provided the sample

(xii) Genetic testing : A procedure to detect the presence or absence of, or change in, a particular gene or chromosome, including an indirect test for a gene product or other specific metabolite that is primarily indicative of a specific genetic change;

(xiii) Genetic screening : Large-scale systematic genetic testing offered in a programme to a population or subsection thereof intended to detect genetic characteristics in asymptomatic people;

(xiv) Genetic counselling : A procedure to explain the possible implications of the findings of genetic testing or screening, its advantages and risks and where applicable to assist the individual in the long-term handling of the consequences; It takes place before and after genetic testing and screening;

(xv) Cross-matching : Matching of information about an individual or a group contained in various data files set up for different purposes.

Article 3 – Person's identity

Each individual has a characteristic genetic make-up. Nevertheless, a person's identity should not be reduced to genetic characteristics, since it involves complex educational, environmental and personal factors and emotional, social, spiritual and cultural bonds with others and implies a dimension of freedom.

Article 4 – Special status

(a) Human genetic data have a special status because :

(i) they can be predictive of genetic predispositions concerning individuals;

(ii) they may have a significant impact on the family, including offspring, extending over generations, and in some instances on the whole group to which the person concerned belongs;

(iii) they may contain information the significance of which is not necessarily known at the time of the collection of the biological samples;

(iv) they may have cultural significance for persons or groups.

(b) Due consideration should be given to the sensitivity of human genetic data and an appropriate level of protection for these data and biological samples should be established.

Article 5 – Purposes

Human genetic data and human proteomic data may be collected, processed, used and stored only for the purposes of :

(i) diagnosis and health care, including screening and predictive testing;

(ii) medical and other scientific research, including epidemiological, especially population-based genetic studies, as well as anthropological or archaeological studies, collectively referred to hereinafter as «medical and scientific research»;

(iii) forensic medicine and civil, criminal and other legal proceedings, taking into account the provisions of Article 1(c);

(iv) or any other purpose consistent with the Universal Declaration on the Human Genome and Human Rights and the international law of human rights.

Article 6 – Procedures

(a) It is ethically imperative that human genetic data and human proteomic data be collected, processed, used and stored on the basis of transparent and ethically acceptable procedures. States should endeavour to involve society at large in the decision-making process concerning broad policies for the collection, processing, use and storage of human genetic data and human proteomic data and the evaluation of their management, in particular in the case of population-based genetic studies. This decision-making process, which may benefit from international experience, should ensure the free expression of various viewpoints.

(b) Independent, multidisciplinary and pluralist ethics committees should be promoted and established at national, regional, local or institutional levels, in accordance with the provisions of Article 16 of the Universal Declaration on the Human Genome and Human Rights. Where appropriate, ethics committees at national level should be consulted with regard to the establishment of standards, regulations and guidelines for the collection, processing, use and storage of human genetic data, human proteomic data and biological samples. They should also be consulted concerning matters where there is no domestic law. Ethics committees at institutional or local levels should be consulted with regard to their application to specific research projects.

(c) When the collection, processing, use and storage of human genetic data, human proteomic data or biological samples are carried out in two or more States, the ethics committees in the States concerned, where appropriate, should be consulted and the review of these questions at the appropriate level should be based on the principles set out in this Declaration and on the ethical and legal standards adopted by the States concerned.

(d) It is ethically imperative that clear, balanced, adequate and appropriate information shall be provided to the person whose prior, free, informed and express consent is sought. Such information shall, alongside with providing other necessary details, specify the purpose for which human genetic data and human proteomic data are being derived from biological samples, and are used and stored. This information should indicate, if necessary, risks and consequences. This information should also indicate that the person concerned can withdraw his or her consent, without coercion, and this should entail neither a disadvantage nor a penalty for the person concerned.

Article 7 – Non-discrimination and non-stigmatization

(a) Every effort should be made to ensure that human genetic data and human proteomic data are not used for purposes that discriminate in a way that is intended to infringe, or has the effect of infringing human rights, fundamental freedoms or human dignity of an individual or for purposes that lead to the stigmatization of an individual, a family, a group or communities.

(b) In this regard, appropriate attention should be paid to the findings of population-based genetic studies and behavioural genetic studies and their interpretations.

B. – COLLECTION

Article 8 – Consent

(a) Prior, free, informed and express consent, without inducement by financial or other personal gain, should be obtained for the collection of human genetic data, human proteomic data or biological samples, whether through invasive or non-invasive procedures, and for their subsequent processing, use and storage, whether carried out by public or private institutions. Limitations on this principle of consent should only be prescribed for compelling reasons by domestic law consistent with the international law of human rights.

(b) When, in accordance with domestic law, a person is incapable of giving informed consent, authorization should be obtained from the legal representative, in accordance with domestic law. The legal representative should have regard to the best interest of the person concerned.

(c) An adult not able to consent should as far as possible take part in the authorization procedure. The opinion of a minor should be taken into consideration as an increasingly determining factor in proportion to age and degree of maturity.

(d) In diagnosis and health care, genetic screening and testing of minors and adults not able to consent will normally only be ethically acceptable when they have important implications for the health of the person and have regard to his or her best interest.

Article 9 – Withdrawal of consent

(a) When human genetic data, human proteomic data or biological samples are collected for medical and scientific research purposes, consent may be withdrawn by the person concerned unless such data are irretrievably unlinked to an identifiable person. In accordance with the provisions of Article 6(d), withdrawal of consent should entail neither a disadvantage nor a penalty for the person concerned.

(b) When a person withdraws consent, the person's genetic data, proteomic data and biological samples should no longer be used unless they are irretrievably unlinked to the person concerned.

(c) If not irretrievably unlinked, the data and biological samples should be dealt with in accordance with the wishes of the person. If the person's wishes cannot be determined or are not feasible or are unsafe, the data and biological samples should either be irretrievably unlinked or destroyed.

Article 10 – The right to decide whether or not to be informed about research results

When human genetic data, human proteomic data or biological samples are collected for medical and scientific research purposes, the information provided at the time of consent should indicate that the person concerned has the right to decide whether or not to be informed of the results. This does not apply to research on data irretrievably unlinked to identifiable persons or to data that do not lead to individual findings concerning the persons who have participated in such a research. Where appropriate, the right not to be informed should be extended to identified relatives who may be affected by the results.

Article 11 – Genetic counselling

It is ethically imperative that when genetic testing that may have significant implications for a person's health is being considered, genetic counselling should be made available in an appropriate manner. Genetic counselling should be non-directive, culturally adapted and consistent with the best interest of the person concerned.

Article 12 – Collection of biological samples for forensic medicine or in civil, criminal and other legal proceedings

When human genetic data or human proteomic data are collected for the purposes of forensic medicine or in civil, criminal and other legal proceedings, including parentage testing, the collection of biological samples, *in vivo* or post-mortem, should be made only in accordance with domestic law consistent with the international law of human rights.

C. – PROCESSING

Article 13 – Access

No one should be denied access to his or her own genetic data or proteomic data unless such data are irretrievably unlinked to that person as the identifiable source or unless domestic law limits such access in the interest of public health, public order or national security.

Article 14 – Privacy and confidentiality

(a) States should endeavour to protect the privacy of individuals and the confidentiality of human genetic data linked to an identifiable person, family or, where appropriate, group, in accordance with domestic law consistent with the international law of human rights.

(b) Human genetic data, human proteomic data and biological samples linked to an identifiable person should not be disclosed or made accessible to third parties, in particular, employers, insurance companies, educational institutions and the family, except for an important public interest reason in cases restrictively provided for by domestic law consistent with the international law of human rights or where the prior, free, informed and express consent of the person concerned has been obtained provided that such consent is in accordance with domestic law and the international law of human rights. The privacy of an individual participating in a study using human genetic data, human proteomic data or biological samples should be protected and the data should be treated as confidential.

(c) Human genetic data, human proteomic data and biological samples collected for the purposes of scientific research should not normally be linked to an identifiable person. Even when such data or biological samples are unlinked to an identifiable person, the necessary precautions should be taken to ensure the security of the data or biological samples.

(d) Human genetic data, human proteomic data and biological samples collected for medical and scientific research purposes can remain linked to an identifiable person, only if necessary to carry out the research and provided that the privacy of the individual and the confidentiality of the data or biological samples concerned are protected in accordance with domestic law.

(e) Human genetic data and human proteomic data should not be kept in a form which allows the data subject to be identified for any longer than is necessary for achieving the purposes for which they were collected or subsequently processed.

Article 15 – Accuracy, reliability, quality and security

The persons and entities responsible for the processing of human genetic data, human proteomic data and biological samples should take the necessary measures to ensure the accuracy, reliability, quality and security of these data and the processing of biological samples. They should exercise rigour, caution, honesty and integrity in the processing and interpretation of human genetic data, human proteomic data or biological samples, in view of their ethical, legal and social implications.

D. – USE

Article 16 – Change of purpose

(a) Human genetic data, human proteomic data and the biological samples collected for one of the purposes set out in Article 5 should not be used for a different purpose that is incompatible with the original consent, unless the prior, free, informed and express consent of the person concerned is obtained according to the provisions of Article 8(a) or unless the proposed use, decided by domestic law, corresponds to an important public interest reason and is consistent with the international law of human rights. If the person concerned lacks the capacity to consent, the provisions of Article 8(b) and (c) should apply mutatis mutandis.

(b) When prior, free, informed and express consent cannot be obtained or in the case of data irretrievably unlinked to an identifiable person, human genetic data may be used in accordance with domestic law or following the consultation procedures set out in Article 6(b).

Article 17 – Stored biological samples

(a) Stored biological samples collected for purposes other than set out in Article 5 may be used to produce human genetic data or human proteomic data with the prior, free, informed and express consent of the person concerned. However, domestic law may provide that if such data have significance for medical and scientific research purposes e.g. epidemiological studies, or public health purposes, they may be used for those purposes, following the consultation procedures set out in Article 6(b).

(b) The provisions of Article 12 should apply mutatis mutandis to stored biological samples used to produce human genetic data for forensic medicine.

Article 18 – Circulation and international cooperation

(a) States should regulate, in accordance with their domestic law and international agreements, the cross-border flow of human genetic data, human proteomic data and biological samples so as to foster international medical and scientific cooperation and ensure fair access to these data. Such a system should seek to ensure that the receiving party provides adequate protection in accordance with the principles set out in this Declaration.

(b) States should make every effort, with due and appropriate regard for the principles set out in this Declaration, to continue fostering the international dissemination of scientific knowledge concerning human genetic data and human proteomic data and, in that regard, to foster scientific and cultural cooperation, particularly between industrialized and developing countries.

(c) Researchers should endeavour to establish cooperative relationships, based on mutual respect with regard to scientific and ethical matters and, subject to the provisions of Article 14, should encourage the free circulation of human genetic data and human proteomic data in order to foster the sharing of scientific knowledge, provided that the principles set out in this Declaration are observed by the parties concerned. To this end, they should also endeavour to publish in due course the results of their research.

Article 19 – Sharing of benefits

(a) In accordance with domestic law or policy and international agreements, benefits resulting from the use of human genetic data, human proteomic data or biological samples collected for medical and scientific research should be shared with the society as a whole and the international community. In giving effect to this principle, benefits may take any of the following forms:

(i) special assistance to the persons and groups that have taken part in the research;

(ii) access to medical care;

(iii) provision of new diagnostics, facilities for new treatments or drugs stemming from the research;

(iv) support for health services;

(v) capacity-building facilities for research purposes;

(vi) development and strengthening of the capacity of developing countries to collect and process human genetic data, taking into consideration their specific problems;

(vii) any other form consistent with the principles set out in this Declaration.

(b) Limitations in this respect could be provided by domestic law and international agreements.

E. – STORAGE

Article 20 – Monitoring and management framework

States may consider establishing a framework for the monitoring and management of human genetic data, human proteomic data and biological samples based on the principles of independence, multidisciplinarity, pluralism and transparency as well as the principles set out in this Declaration. This framework could also deal with the nature and purposes of the storage of these data

Article 21 – Destruction

(a) The provisions of Article 9 apply mutatis mutandis in the case of stored human genetic data, human proteomic data and biological samples.

(b) Human genetic data, human proteomic data and the biological samples collected from a suspect in the course of a criminal investigation should be destroyed when they are no longer necessary, unless otherwise provided for by domestic law consistent with the international law of human rights.

(c) Human genetic data, human proteomic data and biological samples should be available for forensic purposes and civil proceedings only for as long as they are necessary for those proceedings, unless otherwise provided for by domestic law consistent with the international law of human rights.

Article 22 – Cross-matching

Consent should be essential for the cross-matching of human genetic data, human proteomic data or biological samples stored for diagnostic and health care purposes and for medical and other scientific research purposes, unless otherwise provided for by domestic law for compelling reasons and consistent with the international law of human rights.

F. – PROMOTION AND IMPLEMENTATION

Article 23 – Implementation

(a) States should take all appropriate measures, whether of a legislative, administrative or other character, to give effect to the principles set out in this Declaration, in accordance with the international law of human rights. Such measures should be supported by action in the sphere of education, training and public information.

(b) In the framework of international cooperation, States should endeavour to enter into bilateral and multilateral agreements enabling developing countries to build up their capacity to participate in generating and sharing scientific knowledge concerning human genetic data and the related know-how.

*Article 24 – Ethics education, training
and information*

In order to promote the principles set out in this Declaration, States should endeavour to foster all forms of ethics education and training at all levels as well as to encourage information and knowledge dissemination programmes about human genetic data. These measures should aim at specific audiences, in particular researchers and members of ethics committees, or be addressed to the public at large. In this regard, States should encourage the participation of international and regional intergovernmental organizations and international, regional and national non-governmental organizations in this endeavour.

*Article 25 – Roles of the International Bioethics Committee (IBC)
and the Intergovernmental Bioethics Committee (IGBC)*

The International Bioethics Committee (IBC) and the Intergovernmental Bioethics Committee (IGBC) shall contribute to the implementation of this Declaration and the dissemination of the principles set out therein. On a collaborative basis, the two Committees should be responsible for its monitoring and for the evaluation of its implementation, inter alia, on the basis of reports provided by States. The two Committees should be responsible in particular for the formulation of any opinion or proposal likely to further the effectiveness of this Declaration. They should make recommendations in accordance with UNESCO's statutory procedures, addressed to the General Conference.

Article 26 – Follow-up action by UNESCO

UNESCO shall take appropriate action to follow up this Declaration so as to foster progress of the life sciences and their applications through technologies, based on respect for human dignity and the exercise and observance of human rights and fundamental freedoms.

*Article 27 – Denial of acts contrary to human rights,
fundamental freedoms and human dignity*

Nothing in this Declaration may be interpreted as implying for any State, group or person any claim to engage in any activity or to perform any act contrary to human rights, fundamental freedoms and human dignity, including, in particular, the principles set out in this Declaration.

LIST OF AUTHORS

ALARD, Laurène
Researcher of the Paris 12 Val de Marne University, Paris – France.

BERGEL, Salvador Darío
Professor of Commercial Law at the Faculty of Law, University of Buenos Aires and Director of the UNESCO Chair in Bioethics at the University of Buenos Aires, Buenos Aires – Argentina.

BLUMBERG-MOKRI, Myriam
Doctor of Laws.
Lawyer at the Court of Appeal, Paris – France.

BRENA SESMA, Ingrid
Coordinator of the Centre for Legal Studies concerning Health, Institute for Legal Research of the National Autonomous University of Mexico, Mexico City – Mexico.

DONOSO ABARCA, Lorena
Assistant Professor of Ciberlaw, Faculty of Law, University of Chile; Professor of Public Law at the Central University of Chile; Senior Researcher of the Fucatel Foundation and member of the Institute of Law and Technology of Chile.

FIDALGO, Sónia
Researcher of the Biomedical Law Centre; Assistant Professor at the Faculty of Law, University of Coimbra, Portugal.

FIGUEREDO CARRILLO, Carolina
Coordinator of the Specialization Course in Law and New Life Technologies, University Externado of Colombia, Bogotá – Colombia.

FREIRE DE SÁ, María Fátima
Coordinator of the Specialization Course in Civil Law and Professor of Civil Law and Biolaw at the Pontifical Catholic University of Minas Gerais, Belo Horizonte – Brazil.

GONZÁLEZ DE CANCINO, Emilssen
Director of the Centre for Genetics and Legal Research, Faculty of Law, University Externado of Colombia, Bogotá – Colombia.

HERRERA MORENO, Jorge Iván
Researcher of the Centre for Genetics and Legal Research, Faculty of Law, University Externado of Colombia, Bogotá – Colombia.

MONIZ, Helena
Researcher of the Biomedical Law Centre, Professor of Criminal Law and Criminal Procedure, Faculty of Law, University of Coimbra, Portugal.

MORALES NEIRA, Mónica Lizet
Coordinator of the Specialization Course in Medical Law, University of Externado of Colombia, Bogotá – Colombia.

NICOLÁS JIMÉNEZ, Pilar
Project's Coordinator and Senior Researcher of the Inter-University Chair Provincial Government of Biscay in Law and the Human Genome (University of Deusto and University of the Basque Country), Bilbao – Spain.

PASLACK, Rainer
Research Director of the Department of Technology Assessment at the Corporation for Innovation and Technology Transfer in Biomedicine, Bad Oeynhausen – Germany.

ROMEO CASABONA, Carlos María
Professor of Criminal Law at the Faculty of Law, University of the Basque Country and Chair Director of the Inter-University Chair Provincial Government of Biscay in Law and the Human Genome (University of Deusto and University of the Basque Country), Bilbao – Spain.

ROMEO MALANDA, Sergio
Senior Researcher of the Inter-University Chair Provincial Government of Biscay in Law and the Human Genome (University of Deusto and University of the Basque Country) and Assistant Professor of Criminal Law at the Faculty of Law, University of Las Palmas de Gran Canaria, Las Palmas de Gran Canaria – Spain.

SIMON, Jürgen W.
Professor of Economic Law, Medical and Environmental Law, Leuphana University, Lüneburg – Germany.

VALERIO MONGE, Carlos
Director of the Costa Rican Association of Medical Law, San José – Costa Rica.

TABLE OF CONTENTS

	PAGES
Preface	V

PART I.

Biobanking : A chance for scientific research and a challenge for intellectual property rights and privacy, by Carlos María ROMEO CASABONA and Jürgen W. SIMON 3

PART II.
NATIONAL REPORTS

Legal and social implications of creating banks of biological material in Argentina, by Salvador DARÍO BERGEL 19

Legal and social implications of creating banks of biological material in Brazil, by María Fátima FREIRE DE SÁ 29

Legal and social implications of creating banks of biological material in Chile, by Lorena DONOSO ABARCA 57

Legal and social implications of creating banks of biological material in Colombia, by Emilssen GONZÁLEZ DE CANCINO, Jorge Iván HERRERA MORENO, Carolina FIGUEREDO CARRILLO and Mónica Lizet MORALES NEIRA 87

Legal and social implications of creating banks of biological material in Costa Rica, by Carlos VALERIO 153

Legal and social implications of creating banks of biological material in France, by Myriam BLUMBERG-MOKRI and Laurène ALARD 169

Legal and social implications of creating banks of biological material in Germany, by Jürgen W. SIMON and Rainer PASLACK 209

Legal and social implications of creating banks of biological material in Mexico, by Ingrid BRENA SESMA 259

Legal and social implications of creating banks of biological material in Portugal, by Helena MONIZ and Sónia FIDALGO 287

	Pages
Legal and social implications of creating banks of biological material in Spain, by Carlos María ROMEO CASABONA, Pilar NICOLÁS JIMÉNEZ and Sergio ROMEO MALANDA	311

PART III.
REFERENCES

National biobanks	363
National institutions	377
National legislation	389
Bibliography	401

ANNEX

I. – *List of frequently asked questions*	413
II. – *Guidelines for drafting a model information sheet and consent document*	449
III. – *UNESCO. International Declaration on Human Genetic Data*	455
List of authors	467
Table of contents	469

L'accès le plus direct à toute l'information juridique
www.stradalex.com

Je ne suis pas encore abonné à Strada lex et je désire connaître les conditions qui me permettront de consulter en ligne les monographies Bruylant que j'aurai acquises

☐ Je demande à recevoir le passage d'un délégué de votre maison d'édition de préférence à l'une des dates suivantes :
_____
_____

✓ Lors de son passage, le délégué me fera une démonstration des fonctionnalités de Strada lex
✓ Lors de son passage, le délégué me communiquera le prix et les conditions générales de l'abonnement à Strada lex

Je, soussigné(e),
Nom _____ Prénom _____
Société _____
N° TVA _____
Profession _____
Rue _____ N° _____
CP _____ Localité _____
Adresse e-mail _____

Signature   Date

Nous vous remercions de compléter le formulaire ci-dessus et de nous le retourner par courrier, fax ou courriel à l'adresse ou au numéro ci-dessous :

Groupe De Boeck s.a.
rue des Minimes, 39 • 1000 Bruxelles
Tél. +32 (0)2 548 07 20 • Fax +32 (0)2 548 07 22 • info@stradalex.com
www.stradalex.com • www.bruylant.be

L'enregistrement de ces données par le Groupe De Boeck s.a., 39 rue des Minimes, 1000 Bruxelles est effectué dans un but exclusivement commercial et administratif. Conformément à la loi du 8/12/1992 relative à la protection de la vie privée, vous disposez à tout moment du droit d'accès et de rectification de ces données ainsi que du droit de vous opposer au traitement de ces données à des fins de marketing direct. Tout renseignement concernant leur traitement peut être obtenu à la Commission de la protection de la vie privée, 139, rue Haute - 1000 Bruxelles.